The Manager
as Negotiator

The Manager as Negotiator

Bargaining for Cooperation and Competitive Gain

DAVID A. LAX
JAMES K. SEBENIUS

THE FREE PRESS
A Division of Macmillan, Inc.
NEW YORK

Collier Macmillan Publishers
LONDON

The Free Press
A Division of Macmillan, Inc.
866 Third Avenue, New York, N.Y. 10022

Collier Macmillan Canada, Inc.

Printed in the United States of America

printing number

1 2 3 4 5 6 7 8 9 10

Library of Congress Cataloging-in-Publication Data

Lax, David A.
    The manager as negotiator.

    Bibliography: p.
    1. Negotiation in business.   2. Management.
I. Sebenius, James K.   II. Title.
HD58.6.L39 1986   658.4   86–18420
ISBN 0–02–918770–2

To Howard Raiffa

Whose clarity of thought and expression inspire us,
Whose support as advisor and mentor made this book possible, and
Whose warmth and sincerity as a human being are a joy.

Contents

Preface

THIS BOOK EVOLVED from our weekly discussions with members of the Negotiation Roundtable, a working seminar of Harvard faculty and graduate students dedicated to learning more about negotiation and its role in management. In this quest we analyzed the negotiations in hundreds of cases involving private and public managers. As time passed, the subtleties of these *managerial* negotiations pointed up the inadequacies of our *overall* approach to negotiation, leading us to rework it heavily. A major part of this book presents these reworked principles and methods, which apply to situations faced by investment bankers, lawyers, politicians, diplomats, entrepreneurs, psychologists, social workers, engineers, and others—as well as managers. The book is written for both people who engage in such negotiations and for those who study them.

As we delved more deeply into managerial situations—into dealings with subordinates, peers, superiors, and those outside the chain of command—we constantly saw conflicting interests, potential gains from cooperation, discretion on all sides, and possibilities for opportunistic behavior. Yet these are among the key ingredients of negotiation. The more we saw these characteristics throughout organizations, the more we felt the need for a new way to look at the job of manager that took them squarely into account. Another major part of this book offers such an approach to management, again aimed both at those who manage and those who study management and organizations.

We wrestled for a long time with whether to write one book on negotiation in general and another on its managerial applications or to combine these topics in a single volume. Recounting why we chose the combined approach helps explain the book's organization. The reader will quickly see that we have a fairly broad view—some think overly so—of what can usefully be thought of as negotiation. The way we approach its analysis and practice contains elements that some find quite unfamiliar at first. Yet this conception of negotiation is woven into our discussion of key aspects of management. Making sense of a separate book on the manager would virtually require understanding our general treatment of negotiation. Given this, along with the strong mutual influence of the two subjects, we opted for a combined treatment. Hence, this book contains a development of negotiation analysis and an approach to the manager's job, two separate streams that end up flowing into each other.

We hope that the result contains insights useful to those who negotiate as well as to those who analyze the process. In order to reach a more diverse audience, we decided early on to write informally, sometimes colloquially, and to use nothing more mathematical than simple graphs. Yet our approach owes much to the formal traditions of decision analysis, game theory, economics, and statistics. Though we originally developed many of our ideas using these more specialized languages, we often felt our understanding deepen when we forced ourselves to express the underlying logic in a nontechnical manner. Some of our more technically inclined readers may find themselves translating our points back into more formal terms. We hope that this is not too high a price to pay for the content.

A word is also in order about the examples and cases that pepper the chapters. Our aim is to illustrate points about negotiation and management, not to recount history. Though virtually all the examples and cases are directly inspired by real events, we have not hesitated to simplify, to alter details, or to disguise names and settings when doing so would be more instructive.

Finally, it is our great pleasure that virtually every concept and sentence in this book is a joint product. We analyzed the various topics from points of view that frequently diverged. Reconciliation called for extended and often spirited discussion. Yet to each of us, the final product represents a pure joint gain over our individual starting points. As readers become familiar with our approach, test it against their own insights, and reconcile the differences, we hope they will find, as we did in the writing, that the result is greater than the sum of its original parts.

Acknowledgments

IN 1982, WE JOINED Howard Raiffa in founding the Negotiation Roundtable, a working seminar of Harvard faculty and graduate students interested in negotiation and in the connections between negotiation and management. The other early members of the group, including Arthur Applbaum, George Baker, Carliss Baldwin, Dennis Encarnation, Mark Moore, Malcolm Salter, Tom Weeks, and Lou Wells, also influenced our thinking, critiqued drafts of this book, and enthusiastically supported our efforts along the way. We are very grateful.

Others, including John Kotter, Frank Aguilar, Philip Heymann, Richard Neustadt, and Robert Reich, came as guests of the Roundtable and helped us to appreciate the complexities of managerial situations. Frank Aguilar's excellent cases, including the case examined in Chapter Eight, served as the basis for much stimulating thought. Robert Weber's discussion of a case from David Kreps led to the Les Winston story in Chapter One.

Larry Bacow, Max Bazerman, Walter Broadnax, Evelyn Brodkin, John Dunlop, John Hammond, Mike Porter, Don Straus, Ray Vernon, and Mike Wheeler gave us helpful comments on the manuscript.

Roger Fisher, Larry Susskind, Jeff Rubin, and our other colleagues from the Harvard Faculty Seminar on Negotiation were the sources of numerous ideas and examples that found their way into the book. We are especially grateful for the constant encouragement of Dick Neustadt, Graham Allison, and Mark Moore and for their thoughtful suggestions and criticisms. Bill Ury and Dennis Encarnation not only critiqued our work but have been terrific as colleagues and friends. Many insights into negotiation arose from Jim's work with Peter Peterson; in addition, we appreciate his cooperation during the last stages of this project.

We see ourselves as the beneficiaries of two strands of distinguished thought. The first is "non-equilibrium game theory" pioneered by Thomas Schelling and Howard Raiffa, and elaborated on in an industrial relations context by Richard Walton and Robert McKersie. In this book, we have tried to extend and tie together some of these ideas and begin to merge them with a second strand on management and the politics of organizations, as developed by Richard Neustadt, Graham Allison, Joseph Bower, and Mark Moore. To members of both groups we owe much, personally and intellectually.

It is hard to know where to start thanking Howard Raiffa. His intellectual influence pervades this book. Beyond his ideas, his support within and outside Harvard have made our joint work possible. His encouragement and praise have meant much to us. As advisor, mentor, and person, he is a gem.

We, and especially David, thank Ilana Manolson for her understanding and encouragement of our joint work, even if it meant late night phone calls or two-week trips to secluded writing spots. Her support has meant a great deal. Likewise, Jim, in particular, thanks Nancy Lewis for editorial suggestions, persistent reminders of the potential value to negotiators of a psychodynamic perspective, and all the ways she found to support this project. For the secluded writing spots, we thank the Sebenius, Kimble, and Manolson families for lending us their vacation houses.

Linda Lane's capable handling of the Negotiation Roundtable and other important administrative activities freed us to write with the confidence that everything would be taken care of, properly, the first time. Our agent, Maxine Groffsky, handled the publishing world with aplomb. The Division of Research of Harvard Business School provided generous funding that made this book and the Roundtable possible. We thank its head, Raymond Corey, and the School's Dean, John McArthur, for their support from the beginning. Likewise, the Sloan Foundation Program of Research in Public Management and the Kennedy School of Government furnished important financial support for which we are grateful.

CHAPTER ONE

The Manager as Negotiator

NEGOTIATING IS A WAY OF LIFE for managers, whether renting office space, coaxing a scarce part from another division, building support for a new marketing plan, or working out next year's budget. In these situations and thousands like them, some interests conflict. People disagree. And they negotiate to find a form of joint action that seems better to each than the alternatives.

Despite its importance, the negotiation process is often misunderstood and badly carried out. Inferior agreements result, if not endless bickering, needless deadlock, or spiraling conflict. In this book, we diagnose the causes of these problems, show how they infect negotiations, and point the way to superior outcomes.

Virtually everyone accepts the importance of bargaining to sell a building, resolve a toxic waste dispute, acquire a small exploration company, or handle like situations. Yet negotiation goes well beyond such encounters and their most familiar images: smoke-filled rooms, firm proposals, urgent calls to headquarters, midnight deadlines, and binding contracts. Though far less recognized, much the same process is involved when managers deal with their superiors, boards of directors, even legislators. Managers negotiate with those whom they cannot command but whose cooperation is vital, including peers and others outside the chain of command or beyond the organization itself. Managers even negotiate with subordinates who often have their own interests, understandings, sources of support, and areas of discretion.

In a static world, agreements once made generally endure. Yet change calls on organizations to adapt. And rapid changes call for new arrangements to be envisioned, negotiated, and renegotiated among those who know the situation best and will have to work with the results.

Certainly negotiation is a useful skill for important occasions, but it also lies at the core of the manager's job. Managers negotiate not only to win contracts, but also to guide enterprises in the face of change. Our task in this book is to show why this is so and how it can be done better.

Thus we develop a special logic for negotiators, useful inside the organization and out. It is an ambitious agenda, one that we now introduce by describing a manager's continuing efforts to settle a lawsuit. Once we discuss the dilemma that trapped Les Winston in his negotiation with an "outside" party, we focus back "inside" the organization. There, the negotiations that occupy managers' lives run up against versions of the same dilemma.

Les Winston's Dilemma

Metallurgist Les Winston was sharing a drink with his old friend Tom, a noted analyst of negotiations. Les described his ongoing ordeal trying to settle a suit brought against him by the Ammetal Corp., his former employer. If Ammetal won in court, Les's two-year-old company would be forced down from its high-flying course into bankruptcy. And their latest settlement demand—for *half* of his firm's revenues during the next ten years—seemed ruinous. Concerned, Tom pressed for details.

Les had joined Ammetal just after graduate school and had happily worked in their labs and testing facilities for the next nine years. Happily, that is, until he had a strong hunch that a new process might reduce production costs for an important specialty alloy, whose market Ammetal now dominated. While his boss had not forbidden him to work on this process, he had given Les no resources for it and had loaded him down with other tasks. Still, Les had devoted all his spare time to following up his hunch at home. Soon he was convinced that he had solved the problem and excitedly showed his results to his boss—who again seemed unimpressed, dismissing Les's work as "inconclusive." In fact he urged Les to forget the whole thing since, in his judgment, the only improvement worth making required a radically different process that no one, including Les, thought had better than a one-in-thirty chance of ever working.

That did it. Though Les really liked his colleagues and most of his job at Ammetal, especially the research, he quit to start his own firm, scraping together capital from relatives and borrowing heavily from one large backer. Eighteen months later, the modest plant that he had adapted for his process had more orders than it could handle. Best of all, Les was absolutely certain that he had just cracked the secret of the radically different process, which could, with several months of development, slash current production costs by more than half. Though he currently enjoyed about a 20 percent cost advantage over Ammetal, this new knowledge should eventually permit him to push his former employer completely out of the market.

So he was stunned to read an announcement one morning that Ammetal planned to build a large plant that obviously would use the process currently in place in his plant. (It was nearly impossible to protect such processes by patent; secrecy was the only hope.) Les was further dismayed that same day to learn that Ammetal had filed suit to enjoin *him* from further using his process. They alleged that he had violated his employment contract with them, improperly using results from his work in the Ammetal labs. When his lawyer examined his old contract and gave him only a fifty-fifty chance of a successful defense, Les's spirits sagged. It did not cheer him at all that his lawyer argued—and had also heard informally from an old partner who worked in Ammetal's legal department—that the other side could expect no more than even odds of winning a case like this.

Five months into this discouraging episode, Les had decided that some form of negotiated settlement could protect him against the chance of losing the case, avoid further legal costs, lessen his anxiety, and free him to spend his time helping his business to grow. He had initially offered Ammetal a 3 percent royalty for the next three years, and had gradually raised his offer to 15 percent during the next five years. (This was about equal to the highest royalty rate in the industry for an analogous, but friendly, licensing agreement.) But Ammetal was miles away, insisting at first on 60 percent indefinitely, and now, on a "rock-bottom final" demand of 50% for the next decade. There they had deadlocked, with the trial only a week hence.

With an air of resignation, Les finished his recitation and said to Tom, "So, that is how we stand, and all I can see is doing my damndest to increase the odds of winning that suit. Otherwise, . . . "his voice trailed off as he rolled his eyes back and sliced across his neck with his forefinger. "Except, of course, that I'll eventually recover, pick up the pieces, put together a new organization, and blow them out of the water when I get the new process going. It might even be fun, watching them write off their big new plant, which will suddenly become obsolete. But what a price for revenge!"

Tom registered all this, then leaned forward and asked Les to describe what he would *really* like to come out of it. A bit taken aback, Les thought and replied, slowly, "Well, I would really like to be left alone to continue with the current process, until the new one is perfected. That, however, will take some months and I'd need to raise a lot of money. Actually, Tom," he continued meditatively, "it may sound a little strange after all Ammetal has done, but I would most enjoy working on this new process with my good friends in the lab there—and not have to worry about all the financing and logistics and administrative headaches of running my own show. Ammetal's manufacturing and distribution networks are first class once they've got a good product. Of course, I don't want to give up the money, quite a fortune really, that would come from doing it myself. Also, freedom feels very good, especially after dealings with that jerk of a boss."

"So why not propose a joint venture?" Tom queried.

"In fact," Les replied, "I suggested just that to Albert Laxel [a social acquaintance and senior VP at Ammetal]. I ran across him playing tennis last weekend and told him how sick I was of this whole miserable thing, how I wished they would just drop the suit and forget their new plant, which they'd end up regretting anyway., I finished by tossing out the idea of jointly commercializing my new process—on the right terms, of course. He seemed sympathetic, especially about my old R&D boss, who's been on everyone's nerves for a while, who championed their newly announced alloy venture—and who undoubtedly instigated the suit against me.

"Still, Albert dismissed my idea out of hand, saying something about how this episode must be taking a real toll on me. Otherwise, why would I make such an obvious bluff about discovering the new process—which no one could take seriously, especially given my current fix, and how remote everyone, including me, had judged the odds of its working.

"The only way to convince Ammetal, would be to actually show them the new work—which there's a snowball's chance in hell of my doing now, just so they could steal it, too. The irony of all this," Les continued, "is that we would both be better off if they didn't sink a ton of money into a useless plant and if I could do only what I want with the new process—with no extraneous business stuff—and yet still profit handsomely from it."

Tom thought for a moment, and then intoned professorially, "Well, Les, maybe it wouldn't be so hard to persuade them that you have the new process and that they should think again." With Les's full attention now, Tom continued, "Why not drop your current position and better their demand for 50% of your revenues? Why not just offer them a 60% royalty on your current operation? Or really shock them by offering even more?"

Les slowly put down his drink, figuring that Tom could not possibly have been listening. "Tom, that's crazy. It wouldn't convince them of anything about my new discovery—low or high, a royalty settlement has nothing to do with it. And why on earth would I give up my only card, the even chance I have of winning the suit? If I win, they *know* I'll stay in the industry, and that they can't go ahead with their plans. Even if I only had my current process, two plants would lead to an oversupply situation. It's a very lucrative market, but the volume is not that great. That's why they've got to knock me out through the courts. I've heard of *demanding* unconditional surrender but never *offering* it."

"Les, I understand. But that's the whole point. The 60% royalty would indeed burn your bridges with your current operation. But the only way you could possibly make such an offer is to be *sure* that the new process worked. Unless you were suicidally inclined or nuts, you would not set up a situation in which the only route left for you—commercializing the new process—was a dead end. So, with a little thought, Ammetal's got to realize you're telling the truth and that they shouldn't plan to build a new plant. Of course, as you enter the final round of negotiations, you should bring in an agreement to that effect for them to sign, *but* that agreement should *also* commit them to a joint venture, where you get a very big piece of the action, once," Tom looked sly, "once they offer you your old boss's job. After all, he's been the bad guy in this from the start."

* * *

Les Winston had been caught in a simple version of a central dilemma of bargaining. Devising a joint venture to benefit both parties depended on his actually having the new process. Yet directly sharing this information would open him to gross exploitation. If Les did not really have the process and yet bluffed that he did, Ammetal would be deterred from going ahead with their plans—if they believed him. Knowing this, they would suspect any such statement from him. Les had to find a way to make his assertion credible without becoming vulnerable in doing so.

Tom's analysis suggested the means safely to untangle a self-serving bluff from a truthful signal: a seeming concession that committed Les to an action that would make sense only if he actually had the process. And this illustrates one small piece of a much broader problem with which we will grapple throughout this book: negotiators must manage the inescapable tension between cooperative moves to create value for all and competitive moves to claim value for each.

Again and again, we will find this central tension, whether in this relatively simply negotiation "outside" Les's firm or in more complex and subtle negotiations "inside" organizations—in which building trust and relationships as well as repeated dealings figure much more prominently than they did in the end game between Les and Ammetal.

Key Elements of Negotiation

Virtually everyone would concur that Les "bargained" or "negotiated" to settle the suit. (We use these two terms interchangeably.[1]) Shortly after he had rejoined Ammetal as head of the new venture, Les said, understandably, that he was relieved to have "negotiation" behind him so he "could get on with his job." By "his job", he meant working out with the CEO next year's capital budget and just how many employees would be assigned to his new project. Les meant getting the engineering and production people committed to completing the design rapidly and convincing the sales force to pro-

[1]Some authors treat "negotiation" as including the full range of interaction among the parties and consider "bargaining" to be a narrower process, taking place in the frame of negotiation. Others adopt the reverse usage. For a sample discussion of who calls which what, see Gulliver (1979:69–73). As will become clear in the ensuing chapters, however, distinctions between "wider" and "narrower" tend to blur badly, until one rigorously defines a negotiation's "configuration" and classifies actions with respect to it—at which point any bargaining-negotiation distinction is a minor implication rather than a helpful category. (See Chapter Nine.) Given this, plus the wide variation in usage, we see no special advantage in distinguishing the terms.

mote the now-cheaper alloy aggressively, even though it was only one of many products they handled. He meant talking to the accounting department to reduce some of the overhead they were allocating to his project and to modify a transfer price they had proposed for semifinished metal he would need from another division. Not to mention working out the allocation of tasks among his project team or new arrangements with his slightly edgy former peers at the R&D lab, whose boss he had replaced. To us, these aspects of his job centrally involve negotiation.

Like Les, many people have much too limited a view of the negotiation process, thinking mainly of explicit, well-acknowledged examples such as merger contests or collective bargaining. Yet its key elements occur far more widely in and out of management. Consider interdependence, some perceived conflict, opportunistic potential, and the possibility of agreement—four of the most important such elements of negotiation:

Interdependence   When Joseph depends on Laura, he cannot achieve the results he wants as cheaply, as well, or at all without her help (if only by her not interfering). Usually, dependence among people in organizations is mutual. While the reasons for a subordinate's reliance on a boss are often obvious, superiors generally depend on subordinates as well. Reasons for this include valuable, hard-to-replace skills, specialized information, or relationships with other critical players. Think, for example, of the many ways that the chief executive depends on her long-time personal secretary. Or how the shop floor supervisor relies on the one technician who can fix a key, cranky machine. Or how a sales manager needs the field knowledge of his sales force. (In turn, of course, the sales people depend on his support at headquarters and with the production and delivery people.)

Mutual dependence implies limits to how much one party can do alone, or at what cost, or how desirably. Joint action may be preferable for everyone. This possibility makes interdependence a key element that defines negotiating situations.

Obviously, those who run public organizations must cope with complex interdependencies, often by negotiation. Think of a public manager's dealings with political superiors, other governmental units, media contacts, interest groups, legislative overseers and staffs, not to mention the civil servants and others who can help or impede the agency's work. While people in private firms have always depended on one another, however, many factors have combined in recent years to increase their interdependencies. It is worth touching on a few reasons for this.[2]

Ten or twenty years ago, it was quite common for a manager to deal with a single product or service in a specific geographic area, and for the firm to concentrate mainly on that line of business. But the processes of making and distributing products or performing services are often more complex than they used to be, from the science and engineering involved to the logistics and new information technologies. These factors increase reliance on those with specialized skills.

Further, firms are often much larger than before, more diversified in products and markets, and increasingly international. More and more parts interrelate, depend on each other, and need to be harmonized. Businesses have traditionally had two-way dependencies with other parties such as customers, suppliers, banks, and unions. Yet an increased number of such parties have strong interests in the behavior of business and can greatly affect its success. Significant examples include organized consumer, community, and environmental groups and government regulators, along with the popular and business media.

Interdependence, therefore, is a fact of life for managers. And when dependent, the "powerful" and "weak" alike must take others into account when considering possible actions. The ability of one person to further his or her objectives depends, at least in part, on the choices or decisions that the others will make. The reliance of the parties—superiors and subordinates alike—on each other for the possibility of realizing joint gain, preserving working relationships, or minimally, avoiding interference, leads to some margin of liberty or irreducible discretion for each.[3] And negotiation can influence how this discretion is exercised.

Some Perceived Conflict   If neither of two parties can make a pie alone, their dependence by itself need not imply bargaining; there must be potential conflict over dividing the pie, or at least, different preferences over how to make it. A manufacturer's determination of how many small service vehicles to turn out in the fall illustrates a standard kind of conflict that produces negotiations inside the firm:

[2]For a concise discussion of how these and other factors are changing private managerial life, see Kotter (1985:16–30) and also Kochan and Bazerman (1986).

[3]Elmore (1978); Lipsky (1980); Crozier and Friedberg (1980).

the production department wants long, predictable runs of uniform models; sales wants fast turnaround, custom design, quick delivery, and deep parts inventories; the financial types want advance planning and minimal stocks.

Or consider the three-year-old firm that can now afford to hire one more senior scientist for its R&D unit. Should this person's field be advanced materials, where two key board members and the CEO—also a respected scientist—think the best new opportunity lies, or numerical controls, where the remarkably successful R&D head believes they need more depth? This process can involve much more than working out the "objectively best" choice; apart from their genuinely different beliefs about the right field, suppose that the CEO had his way on the last scientist they hired—who worked out splendidly. Yet the R&D chief is weighing an offer at a competitor's firm and is known to want more autonomy for his unit. With reasons, preferences, and stakes in apparent conflict, some negotiation between these mutually dependent executives is virtually certain.[4]

That this process could end with the CEO making a forceful "final" decision in no way takes away from the observation that they are negotiating. In fact, the CEO's command is equivalent to a take-it-or-leave-it offer in more familiar kinds of bargaining—and it could be taken or left. If the CEO were in a "strong" position, the odds are that his order would stick. If not, the process might continue. Incidentally, an ultimatum from the R&D chief could also be understood as a similar "move" in his negotiation with the CEO.

Increased interdependence of diverse people virtually guarantees the potential for conflict. The interests and perceptions of people in different organizational units—associated with different products, services, markets, programs, and functions—naturally become identified with their units. And this is even more true for third parties and those in other organizations entirely. In the words of the old saying, "Where you stand depends on where you sit."[5]

With an increasingly heterogeneous workforce, especially in terms of sex, ethnic background and age, perspectives will further diverge. More educated and professional workers come to expect and value their autonomy. All these factors exacerbate the potential con-

[4]If, here or elsewhere, the parties have *no* conflict—interests and beliefs are identical—their search for the best joint action might more aptly be called pure "problem solving."

[5]See March and Simon (1958) on subgoal identification.

flicts that have always been present in organizations. The widely noted decline in people's acceptance of formal authority often leads them to express such conflicts more openly than before. And the general slowdown in world growth has intensified resource conflicts both for public and private organizations.

Some people resist the fact that conflict pervades organizations, judging it to be unhealthy or threatening.[6] Recognizing conflicting interests can seem to legitimate differences in interest when a myth of pure shared interests might be more congenial to smooth management. Real conflicts will sometimes be diagnosed as "failures to communicate" or "personality problems." When similar problems repeatedly surface as different people pass through the same position, the diagnoses of "personality" or "communications" difficulties should be suspect. Uncomfortable as it may be to some, conflict is a fact of life in organizations. (Destructively handling it, however, need not be.)

Opportunistic Interaction[7]   Beyond dependence and conflict, the potential for each side to engage in opportunistic interaction— less than fully open motives and methods, self-interested maneuvers—is associated with bargaining situations. When two or more people try to influence each others' decisions through negotiation, they usually guard some information, move to stake out favorable positions, seek to mold perceptions and aspirations, and the like. This need not take the form of overt "gamemanship"; the facade may be highly cooperative or submissive to authority. All that is re-

[6]It is important to distinguish between situations in which different parties have interests or perceptions that conflict and a common use of the term "conflict," which connotes a dysfunctional expression of conflicting interests. See March and Simon (1958) for an example of this usage. We argue that managers in an organization will more than likely have interests or perceptions that conflict but that this need not be expressed in a destructive manner. We will generally use the term "conflict" to imply that interests or perceptions conflict—more technically, that the Pareto frontier in subjective expected utilities has more than one point—and not only that the interaction is being poorly handled. It is interesting to note that March and Simon's discussion of problem-solving, persuasion, bargaining, and politics in organizations is contained in a chapter on conflict, by which they refer only to unproductive behaviors that differ from the "normal" functioning of the firm. Our focus is on bargaining as a pervasive part of a firm's normal functioning.

[7]Rather than "opportunistic" we would prefer to use the term "strategic" in the game-theoretic sense, meaning that each party seeks advantage by taking the other's actions and plans into account in deciding what to do, expecting the other to do likewise. Yet the many other uses of "strategic" continually produced confusion among readers of early drafts. Thus, we settled on the less satisfactory "opportunistic," with its connotations of self-interested, self-conscious maneuver.

quired is that people care about their own interests, *some* of which conflict with others', and pursue them by seeking to influence decisions, not cooperating fully, turning situations to their advantage, or even resisting outright.

Without any strategic maneuvering of this sort, with no subtle or blatant jockeying for advantage, the interaction might best be called pure "problem solving." Without interaction, merely clashes of interest, "war" may be a better description than "negotiation."[8]

The Possibility of Agreement   When interdependence, conflict, and the potential for opportunism are present, people can negotiate to arrive at a joint decision that is better than their unilateral alternatives. Their goal is to find out whether an *agreement* is advantageous. Agreements can take many forms, most familiarly, a contract, a treaty, a memo confirming the choice. But agreements can be much more subtle: a nod, a word of affirmation, silent adjustment to the terms informally worked out, or other forms of tacit accord. And quite often, agreements do not formally bind the parties, or not for long. Revision of contracts and understandings is almost as common as the negotiation that led to them in the first place.

* * *

Inspecting a management situation and finding these four elements should strongly suggest the possibility of negotiation. More precisely, we characterize negotiation as *a process of potentially opportunistic interaction by which two or more parties, with some apparent conflict, seek to do better through jointly decided action than they could otherwise.* The special logic we develop in later chapters is tailored to this kind of process, which is widespread in and around organizations.[9]

[8]If the objects of certain managerial actions are located farther and farther away, the amount of opportunistic interaction among the parties may decrease. Face-to-face encounters shade into analogous but more unilateral attempts to influence the decisions of others who do not reciprocate. Nevertheless, some of the same considerations prevalent in direct, personal negotiations may be of considerable utility when a manager is engaged in such related processes of "decision influence."

[9]Later we will discuss some of the implications of this view of negotiation. But several things are worth brief note: (1) the process is *not* limited to "trades" but can aim to realize a shared interest—whether a tangible outcome that all parties want or an identical vision; (2) the elements of negotiation need *not* be fixed, that is, the parties, issues, interests, alternatives to agreement, beliefs, rules, and so on may change; (3) managers engage in a number of closely related processes (mediation, arbitration, persuasion, influencing decisions at some distance, etc.) that can be approached using much the same logic as we will develop for more "pure" negotiation.

Negotiation Is Central to the Manager's Job

Familiar negotiations readily display interdependence, conflict, and opportunistic interaction. So do many other management activities where some form of "agreement" is sought. In this section, we pick apart common dealings with subordinates, superiors, and those outside of the chain of command to see where these telltale factors are present—and thus, where negotiation analysis can be profitable.

DEALING OUTSIDE THE CHAIN OF COMMAND:
INDIRECT MANAGEMENT

Managers often find that their formal authority falls far short of their responsibilities and their success is dependent on the actions of others outside the chain of command. Though people in this predicament may yearn for more control, there is often no practical way to follow the textbook advance to match authority with responsibility. "Indirect management" is the name we give to this increasingly important phenomenon of concentrated responsibility but shared authority and resources. It calls for a very different approach from traditional line management.

Consider the job of a typical product manager in a firm such as General Foods.[10] To ensure that nothing falls between the cracks and that all efforts are productively coordinated, this person has direct profit responsibility for a particular product line. However, she must depend on many others over whom she has little or no formal authority. The product may be manufactured in an entirely separate firm; advertising is carried out in a different division; the sales force is in another chain of command; and the distributors are likewise independent. To make matters worse, these other people deal with *many* individual products and lines.

So, without being a nuisance, how can the product manager ensure that a promotional campaign comes off as planned, that manufacturing overhead is fairly allocated to her line, that snags in one part of the chain do not paralyze efforts down the line? Handling these kinds of lateral relationships requires ongoing and often subtle forms of negotiation, with emphasis on building relationships, trust, and a sense of mutual obligation among the parties. This manager needs to work out and constantly renegotiate a chain of "agreements" that ultimately result in better sales.

Public managers have traditionally confronted indirect manage-

[10]This description draws heavily on Kotter (1985: 71).

ment situations. Take the case of Tom Sullivan, a regional official of the Department of Health, Education and Welfare (HEW). One day Sullivan received a directive from then-HEW Secretary Caspar Weinberger in Washington. In effect, Sullivan was ordered to expedite the inspections for fire safety of nursing homes in Massachusetts, where many of these homes were old, many-storied, made of wood, and scandalously underinspected. Federal funds supported many of these homes and could have been withdrawn absent inspection and fire-code compliance. But this would have "thrown many old people on the streets," given the acute shortage of any such facilities. Though several state agencies had to coordinate and actually carry out the inspections, Sullivan had no formal power over any of them. Further, the Massachusetts legislature was reluctant to approve money for additional inspectors required to meet the deadlines.

Sullivan was facing a classic indirect management situation. Long experience had taught him that a "hard approach," adverse publicity and withholding funds, would almost surely boomerang, with the feds taking intense press and congressional heat for being highhanded and insensitive. So he would have to arrange a "deal" across government boundaries that would cause these inspections to be carried out. For example, he might secure compliance in return for modifying federal standards to apply more directly to Massachusetts's situation as well as offering federal personnel and money. Such aid might, incidentally, further state goals apart from the inspections. Sullivan could also appeal to shared interests in protecting old people from fire while holding the (undesirable and non-too-credible) shutdown option as an alternative. If successful, he would have crafted a series of understandings to get the inspections underway, arrived at through an overt and covert process of persuasion, inducement, and threat.

Indirect management is common when a firm procures an item or when a government official seeks to produce or procure a good or service through the actions of regional, state, local, or even private entities. More generally, it occurs with respect to those outside the chain of command—peers, parallel organizational units, or other organizations—whose cooperation is needed.[11] In all such cases, the

[11]For discussions of indirect management in a public context, see, e.g., Mosher (1980); Salomon (1981); Moore (1982); or Sebenius (1982). Kotter's (1985) treatment of lateral relationships has much the same flavor. Also see the literature on policy implementation, e.g., Pressman and Wildavsky (1973); Derthick (1975); Hargrove (1975); Van Meter and Van Horn (1975); Elmore and Williams (1976); Bardach (1977); Ingram (1977); Weinberg (1977); Rein and Rabinovitz (1978); Lipsky (1980); Sabatier and Mazmanian (1980).

"usual" internal management tools and control systems are mainly out of reach. Nevertheless, the manager who has to produce indirectly is often strictly accountable for the results. With shared authority and resources but concentrated responsibility, in short, in an age of indirect management, effective negotiation with the other sharers is often the key to success.

DEALING WITH SUBORDINATES

Though less noticed than they deserve, indirect management situations represent the "easy" case for showing the importance of negotiation to the job of a manager. Once these situations are recognized, negotiation seems as inevitable as it is in collective bargaining or out-of-court settlements. The "hard" case, though, would seem to involve subordinates and others over whom one has direct authority.

For example, when a colleague of ours once wrote about the manager's "external" functions, his choice of words clearly suggested the importance of negotiation ("*dealing* with external units," "*dealing* with independent organizations," "*dealing* with the press and public"[12] [emphasis supplied throughout]). Yet, when describing the management of "internal" operations, his language revealingly implied a much more unilateral function, where command, control, and systems hold sway ("organizing and staffing" in which "the manager *establishes* structure," "*directing* personnel and the personnel system," and "*controlling* performance"). So isn't it true that the possibilities of command and control inside the organization relegate negotiation to a peripheral role?

Commands   Though many managers instinctively recognize the extent to which they negotiate with subordinates, others subscribe to a powerful belief in the omnipotence of authority—what might be called the "British sea captain" view: "Do it or be flogged! Refuse again and be keel hauled!" If barking out orders were the essence of management, why bother discussing negotiation at all?

A good reason is the frequent ineffectiveness of command, even at the highest levels. Richard Neustadt, former White House aide and student of the American Presidency, published a widely influential analysis of presidential power. The most important ingredient, he argued, is *not* the President's ability to command, but instead his skill,

[12]Allison (1979).

will, and tenacity as a bargainer within and outside the Executive branch. In a famous passage on the limits of presidential orders, Neustadt referred to his former boss, Harry Truman:

> In the early summer of 1952, before the heat of the campaign, President Truman used to contemplate the problems of the General-become-President should Eisenhower win the forthcoming election. "He'll sit here" Truman would remark (tapping his desk for emphasis), "and he'll say, 'Do this! Do that' and *nothing will happen*. . . . Poor Ike" . . . Eisenhower evidently found it so.[13]

While a manager's unquestioned right to fire a subordinate plays a role in negotiations, it may not yield desired results. Consider the example of Felix, the young protégé of Allen, the managing partner of a financial consulting firm. Over the last year, Felix violated normal procedures, including using employees from competing projects under dubious pretenses, to generate considerable business in a new area. The executive committee decided that the firm should not pursue this area any further and after brutal discussions with Allen, Felix resigned from the firm for "personal reasons." What was the role of negotiation here?

Allen feared that Felix, if fired, would take much business and many of the firm's brightest young people with him; in turn, Felix liked the security and camaraderie of the firm. To avoid this undesirable outcome, the pair negotiated intensely but unsuccessfully to find a mutually acceptable path for Felix back to the firm's traditional areas. If such a mutually acceptable path *did* in fact exist, executing the "else" of Allen's "do this or else" ultimatum represented a *failure* of negotiation. Of course, agreement is by no means always preferable to what is possible by going separate ways.

In short, even where formal authority for the final say is clearly lodged, much direct managerial action still involves negotiation. Initial proposals to do this or that elicit contrary preferences, arguments for reformulation, and mutual adjustment, but often also convergence to final agreed action. Think of organizing a sales campaign, working out who will have which responsibilities for an upcoming client meeting or interagency session, or the deliberations over a new facility's timing and location.

Interdependence, conflict, the existence of an irreducible degree of discretion and autonomy throughout organizations, the difficul-

---

[13]Neustadt (1980:9).

ties and costs of monitoring and enforcing orders, as well as the decentralized and far-flung presence of information needed even to
formulate many commands have all led many organizational analysts
to rank command as but one—albeit important—among numerous
means for influencing others.[14]

We do not mean to imply that sensible superiors do not tell workers what to do, or that command is generally an inefficient management tool. The real question is *not* "negotiation versus authority." A
subordinate often goes along with an order because doing so is part
of a larger bargain with the superior. For example, in return for other
considerations, Joe may give Janet the right to direct him within the
limits of an overarching agreement. Yet both the content of the commands and the limits themselves are often subject to tacit renegotiation.

More importantly, a serious direct order functions exactly the
same as a take-it-or-leave-it offer in conventional negotiation: one
party stakes a great deal of credibility on a "final" proposal, intending the other to accept it or forget any agreement. Of course, the final offer, just like a command, may succeed *or* fail. It is more likely
to work (1) the more appealing it is in substance to the person on the
receiving end; (2) the worse that person's other alternatives to going
along, (3) the less it is taken as an affront, and (4) the more credible its
"finality." Thus our later analysis of final offers in conventional negotiation will strongly bear on the effective use of command and authority in management.[15]

In sum, three main reasons lead us to look at negotiation even
where commands are a possible way of dealing with subordinates.
First, management by edict can be ineffective, especially where interdependence is high. Second, even where useful, commands make up
only a fraction of the manager's world. And, third, the formal exercise of authority itself is part and parcel of a larger negotiation.

Management Systems   Beyond personal interactions with subordinates, managers devote much attention to an array of traditional
administrative tools. These usually include systems to affect budgets,
information, compensation, personnel, and the organization's structure.

[14]Dahl and Lindblom (1963); McGregor (1960).

[15]In Chapter Fourteen, we will look more closely at the intimate relations among
negotiation, command, and authority.

Early managerial theories sought strategies to design and structure organizations for efficiency with respect to particular goals. Such early views and their later descendants conceived of organizations as rationally seeking to maximize specified values. In these conceptions, management consists of detailing a set of objectives, assigning responsibilities and performance standards, appropriately arranging incentives and sanctions, monitoring performance, and making internal adjustments to enhance the attainment of goals.[16] The first such theories saw organizations almost as physical mechanisms; subsequent versions saw more complicated "systems" to be controlled.[17] But central to such systems views is the potent, if inadequate, image of management as equivalent to "command and control," which we discussed in the last section.

Direct management systems try to set the rules for organizational interaction. Typically, however, they do not even pretend to eliminate the discretion that inevitably flows from the interdependence of the people in the organization. And considerable bargaining accompanies their design, implementation, and use.

Consider a situation that we will analyze in detail in Chapter Eight. A few years ago, a major chemical corporation, like many other companies and units of government, adopted a "zero-base" budgeting system. In our example, Chris Hubbard, the manager of one of the larger divisions, has just emerged from an unprecedented stormy meeting of his department heads who have been trying to arrive at overall budget rankings. Hubbard wants the final rankings to reflect his overall divisional strategy, but also to strengthen this new budget process and to enhance a sense of cooperation and teamwork. He would prefer the department heads to agree on a budget allocation rather than to impose one on them. But, however the result is reached, it will constitute the division head's opening "position" at

[16]For a summary of this view, see Elmore (1978:191).

[17]Landau and Stout (1979:148) observe how commonly and intensely held is this systems view that "to manage is to control." With respect to the "management control system (MCS)," they note that it has so pervaded the discipline of applied management science as to

have become its central preoccupation. In its literature, now vast in proportion, the term itself (MCS) has been used to cover and to commend a variety of formulas—PPB, PERT, CPM, MBO, Command and Control, and all manner of information systems. That these have not as a group produced striking successes, that many of them show a sustained record of failure, has not served to diminish either the expected utility or the normative appeal of the concept. Enthusiasm remains high, efforts to secure foolproof management control systems continue unabated, promising to perpetuate what must now appear as an unending cycle of vaunted introduction and veiled discard.

the corporate budget meeting that will decide on overall allocation of financial resources.

How close does Hubbard come to managing by pure "system engineering?" Not very. In effect, he is negotiating for a preferred outcome—on the budget, on how the new process is used, and on teamwork. As he seeks closure, Hubbard has many bargaining tools at his disposal: possibilities of exchange, options to alter material and psychological incentives, potential to link or separate other issues, techniques of persuasion, occasions to make shared interests salient, and potential to influence the very terms of discussion. In fact Hubbard's role as a negotiator closely resembles that of a mediator, but one with a strong interest in the content of any "agreement." It also comes close to that of an arbitrator who has the means of shaping or even imposing a settlement if the participants cannot.

With skill, Hubbard may be able to convert a situation that his subordinates perceive as "zero-sum"—where one's budget seems to come only at the expense of another's—into a more cooperative quest for the best divisional strategy for all. He is also engaged in tacit negotiation with his subordinates over the precedent of how seriously and constructively they will take this new budget process. But the interdependence, conflict, and possibilities for opportunism make a wide range of outcomes entirely possible.

More generally, studies of the actual workings of information, policy development, and budgeting systems reveal something far from the antiseptic, efficient image of internal command and control. After detailed observation, Joseph Bower concluded:

> Perhaps the most striking process of resource allocation as described in this study, is the extent to which it is more complex than managers seem to believe. . . . The systems created to control the process sometimes seemed irrelevant to the task. They were based on the fallacious premise that top management made important choices in the finance committee when it approved capital investment proposals. In contrast, we have found capital investment to be a process of study, bargaining, persuasion, and choice spread over many levels of the organization and over long periods of time.[18]

[18]Bower (1970:320–1). Similarly, instead of finding a rational maximizing process as postulated by economic explanations, Wildavsky (1984) described an essentially political process over budget formulation in the public sector. Recent work on both public and private processes of strategy and policy formation reveals analogous situations (Porter, 1980; Bourgeois and Brodwin, 1982).

In sum, conflict, dependence, and possibilities of opportunistic maneuvering again reveal bargaining to be an important part of the manager's inside job. Of course, to emphasize the bargaining is not to reduce the organization to a bucket crawling with crabs, each seeking to clamber onto the back of others. Rather, organizational structure and systems often strongly affect internal negotiations. By the same token, however, these systems are themselves the subject and results of negotiation.

The Cooperative Approach   Many people instinctively reject the idea of the manager as commander or systems engineer and look toward a more cooperative view.[19] During the 1930s, this orientation produced the human relations movement.[20] From the 1950s through the early 1970s, this approach produced studies of leadership[21] and participative management,[22] along with methods of organizational development and change that stressed building interpersonal trust, openness, communications, and other strategies that assumed a natural congruence between the goals of individuals and organizations.[23] The most recent version of this school takes cues from Japanese management and centers around the concept of "organizational culture"[24] and efforts to change behavior in a manner that is consistent with the values and philosophies of the top executives in the organization.

In evaluating this tradition, it is crucial to realize that all these approaches rest on the assumption that, at bottom, "organizations are homogeneous units."[25] Even though common values are important, these conceptions are incomplete since they tend to ignore or downplay widespread clashes of interest and perception in and around organizations. Along with varying degrees of autonomy and abilities to

[19]This discussion follows Thomas Kochan and Anil Verma (1983:15–17) extremely closely.

[20]Mayo (1933).

[21]Fleischman et al. (1955).

[22]Likert (1961, 1967).

[23]Argyris (1964); Schein (1969); and Beckhard (1969).

[24]Ouchi (1981).

[25]Kochan and Verma (1983:16). They continue that all these approaches assume "that strategies for changing or controlling behavior in a way that is consistent with a single value system are functional for individuals, organizations, and society as a whole." Kochan and Verma (1983:16–17).

resist orders, recognition of conflict leads straight back to the key role of bargaining.[26]

Beyond Pure Command, Systems, and Cooperation   If reliance on command ignores interdependence and discretion and if a pure cooperative approach is blind to conflict, what view takes account of these important aspects of management?[27]

Along with many others,[28] we find it useful to look at organizations as arenas in which people with some different interests negotiate for status, effect on decisions, and relative advantage in the allocation of scarce resources. Thus a boss's formal position in the hierarchy is important but only one of many factors that affect the outcomes of this continuing contest. Others include specialized knowledge, a reputation for expertise, control of resources or information, alternatives available to the parties, and the ability to mobilize external support. Thus, how things turn out may only weakly relate to the preferences of who is "in command."

People converge to decisions by visible and hidden bargaining. This process does not require that the parties agree on common goals, not does it necessarily require that everyone concur in the outcome. It only requires that they adjust their behavior mutually if they

[26]March and Simon (1958) noted that the usual economic theory of the private firm simply assumes away differences in goals and perceptions within organizations. Dissatisfied with this premise and conventional theories of organization, Cyert and March (1963) elaborated a theory of the business firm as a collection of bargaining coalitions. They argued that the nominal goals of the organization are vague and unhelpful as guides to overall decision making. Instead, constant conflict among subunits based on their particular organizational interests offers a far more accurate image of decision making. See also Strauss (1978); Bacharach and Lawler (1981); Pfeffer (1981); Huntington (1961); Snyder, Buck, and Sapin (1962).

[27]The following two paragraphs closely follow Elmore's very nice synthesis of this line of argument (1978:217–218).

[28]Footnote 26 cites a few of the many studies that have documented the widespread presence of bargaining, especially in private settings. In arguing for the utility of a similar interpretation in the public sector, Allison (1971) noted that "the decisions and actions of governments are . . . political resultants . . . in the sense that what happens is not chosen as a solution to a problem, but rather results from compromises, conflict, and confusion of officials with diverse interests and unequal influence." In his review of well over one hundred detailed case studies, Herbert Kaufman (1958:55) wrote ". . . the case studies . . . point up the intricate process of negotiation, mutual accommodation, and reconciliation of competing values from which policy decisions emerge and reveal administration as process and as politics. . . . These same elements appear in *virtually every case* regardless of the level of government, the substantive programs, the administrative echelons, and the periods described." (Emphasis supplied.)

have an interest in preserving a working relationship as a means of allocating resources and making joint decisions. By implication, management consists of influencing—by a host of means not limited to direct orders, systems manipulation, or appeals to common goals—a complex series of bargained decisions that reflect the preferences, interpretations, and resources of subordinates.[29]

To some, the very idea of negotiation signals weakness. Indeed, the manager who negotiates allows others' interests to affect the outcome. As we see it, though, this is not "weak"; negotiation makes sense only when agreement promises *joint* improvement—for superior as well as subordinate—over what is possible by unilaterally imposed penalities, brute force, or other noncooperative options. And the boss's "final offer" (command) can certainly be very tough. We would not replace the visionary leader with the indecisive manager who cajoles and pleads. In our view, strong negotiation buoys leadership and vice versa.

DEALING WITH SUPERIORS

If our premise is right, that superiors inevitably negotiate with subordinates, then the reverse must also be true. Of course, a boss depends on those who work for him to perform needed tasks as well as for knowledge and expertise. And subordinates whose perceptions and interests may differ depend on their boss for resources, information, and backing. Hence, the ingredients for negotiation "up." (Of course, "subordinates" themselves are often middle managers.) Even entrepreneurs, who may have little apparent need for any dealings with "superiors," must often negotiate with potential financial backers over amounts of resources, sharing of rewards and risk, and the control others will exercise.

The importance of this kind of negotiation is especially obvious in public settings. Consider the case of attorney Irene Malik, recently

[29]Obviously, management is more than negotiation. When a manager employs an analytic process to, say, conceptualize a strategy for the firm or agency, or figure out what consumers or clients really want, we do not consider negotiation to be taking place. Similarly, accounting for resources, designing and installing new technologies, fulfilling certain legal requirements, acting in a figurehead or symbolic capacity, engaging in certain public relations or advertising campaigns, gathering competitor intelligence in a library or from some outside sources, or going through the mechanics of hiring and firing need not be understood as negotiation. Likewise, it is not normally helpful to classify actions completely decided by voting, adjudication, or dictatorship as bargaining. Of course, negotiation may go on "in the shadow" of and be heavily affected by these other activities.

appointed head of the Toxic Waste Division (TWD) of her state's Environmental Protection Department. The legislature created the TWD to oversee a new toxic waste cleanup law. Now Malik must chart a course through ill-defined legal and political terrain. Though the law provides formal authority, its wording allows a broad range of interpretations. For guidance, support, and resources, Malik must rely on her superiors in the Environmental Protection Department, the budget office, the governor, as well as the state legislature's finance and environmental committees. Little is more important to her mission than obtaining what she needs from these entities, yet each of them seems to tug in a different direction. In turn, of course, these "superior" bodies look to her for producing various results. Malik must carefully tend to these ongoing, linked negotiations if she is to succeed.

Even setting the strategy for a firm like General Motors or Volkswagen—an activity normally thought to be the sole prerogative of the firm—requires that top management negotiate with a variety of parties, including the board members who can grant necessary authority. In a provocative paper, Malcolm Salter argued that firms in politically salient industries like automobiles implicitly negotiate their strategies with state and federal political leaders, environmental, health, and safety officials, and in some instances with unions, key institutional shareholders, and other "stakeholders."[30] And, when top management fears a takeover, the opinions of large shareholders and influential directors about the firm's direction typically have greater sway.

Managers at all levels have goals. Perhaps these come from personal visions, long experience, the workings of sophisticated analytic processes, readings of legislative intent, or consideration of historical precedent. But to go forward, the manager typically must deal with direct superiors and, perhaps, a variety of other "superior" bodies. Beyond formal authority, these groups can help with financial capital, personnel allocations, charters, licenses, information, positive publicity, quiet or visible backing, or, at least, agreements not to attack. Of course, each of these groups wants *its* purposes furthered. The manager offers the potential for this to happen. Hence their interdependence.

Yet the match of goals between the manager and these other entities is often imperfect. The necessary authority and resources are contested; the manager wants more with fewer strings while superi-

[30]Salter (1984).

ors prefer to give less with more strings. Also to be worked out—tacitly or explicitly—are a set of expectations, a measurement system, an unspoken set of "good conduct" provisions, as well as the eventualities under which the various understandings may be revised or revoked.

Generally, there is a considerable range of accommodation within which all sides would prefer to continue the relationship rather than pursue their ends elsewhere. In short, their mutual dependence implies a zone of possible agreement. Within this zone, there is conflict and maneuvering. The joint desirability of convergence to some point induces negotiation. Though critical, this kind of negotiation with superiors has traditionally received scant attention from students of management.

* * *

The picture that emerges from this discussion is of a manager constantly at the nexus of two evolving networks of agreement, constantly building, maintaining, and modifying them. One set of agreements concerns goals, authority, resources, and expectations; the other involves actual production. At a minimum, these two should be consistent; ideally, they will strongly reinforce each other.

Resistance to the Role of Negotiation

The last section illustrated the key role of negotiation in dealings outside the chain of command ("indirect management"), as well as with subordinates and superiors. Indeed, negotiation—even over *whether* to negotiate explicity—is inescapable in most managers' jobs. Though this seems evident to many, some people remains skeptical. Impressions that "real" management is mainly the exercise of unilateral control and authority seem as resistant as cockroaches.

Such resistance can come from too narrow a conception of negotiation: it is simply incongruous to imagine IBM's sleek headquarters as a bazaar teeming with white-collared hagglers. As this chapter has illustrated, we use "negotiation" much more expansively. It may be acknowledged and explicit or unacknowledged and tacit. The basis for agreement may be a conventional quid pro quo or it may include actions that further identical interests but that do not involve a material or psychic exchange. Along with more "standard" gambits are actions intended to persuade; to alter the issues, parties, alternatives to agreement, and evoked interests; as well as to learn and to transform perceptions of the situation. An agreement, if one results, may range in form from a legal document to an implicit understanding. Such a result may effectively and permanently bind the parties or it may be fragile and renegotiable. Public and private managers find themselves in all kinds of situations that require this process and closely related activities that are amenable to similar analysis (mediation, arbitration, changing the game, influencing decisions at some remove). The "manager as negotiator" is a shorthand reference to this complex of roles,[31] not a claim that managers must constantly sit across tables from subordinates and others patiently trading proposals.

Some people unconsciously resist the idea of managerial negotiation since overt recognition of the widespread bargaining in organizations can strain systems of status and hierarchy.[32] It can also legitimate the actual differences in the participants' goals. Thus, problems that really involve bargaining will often be organizationally defined as problems whose solution can be found technically or through more careful analysis in terms that mask the actual conflict.

Moreover, some standard images of good management leave little room for "inside" bargaining. To recognize its existence is inevitably to recognize some indeterminancy of outcomes as well as mutual dependence and conflict. Certainly, some tough managers will argue, effective command, control, or careful manipulation of subordinate routines should drive out these pathologies. And, the successful shaper of organizational culture achieves consensus on values, norms, and purposes; not conflict, opportunistically employed discretion, and unpredictability. Because the existence of bargaining seems to imply a failure of management when viewed through such common lenses, some may miss the existence and even virtues of manager-negotiators.

"Negotiation Abounds." Manager to Academic: "So What?"

At this point, one might be tempted to say "Yes, Virginia, there is important negotiation in organizations." Since many studies seem to

---

[31]We might have chosen what some analysts would have seen as more accurate terms that were less evocative and less clearly tied to the kind of prescription that we develop for negotiators. But somehow, the leading rivals—"manager as interactive decision maker," "manager as participant in mixed-motive, mutual influence processes," or "manager as partisan mutual adjuster"—made our choice easy.

[32]March and Simon (1958:119–121) incisively make this argument.

stop at the triumphant discovery that this indeed is the case,[33] one might next be tempted to say, not impolitely, "so what?"[34]

This skeptical reaction has merit. Most academic studies tend toward careful, analytic description. And though bargaining has been widely studied outside organizations, with a few exceptions,[35] systematic prescriptive approaches have remained underdeveloped.

Unfortunately, most popular negotiation handbooks are little better, falling mainly into two categories. First are those promising to show "How to get yours and most of theirs too" (e.g., arrive *only* by stretch limousine or helicopter; make your chair slightly higher than theirs; have them face a painfully bright light; start dealing with the real issues at midnight when they have a dawn plane). Other handbooks seek converts to the "win-win" religion and seem to assume that "meaningful communication" can unfailingly convert implacable enemies into one big happy family. And everywhere are the negotiation fortune cookies, containing solemn messages that tend to be obvious, useless, or wrong: "Timing is of the essence. It's all psychology. Be creative. Always keep communication lines open. Seek power. Use it shrewdly. Get the real facts."

A deeper and more useful approach to negotiation is needed. It must encompass more than parties formally exchanging offers to fashion a quid pro quo. It must allow for the subtlety of interests in shared purposes and intense concern with process as well as more tangible stakes. It must incorporate a shifting mix of cooperative and competitive elements. It must admit moves to change the "game" itself. It should be systematic and adapted to managerial considerations.

We approach this task in the spirit of decision analysis, highlighting negotiation characteristics capable of generalization across varied

[33]See, e.g., Bacharach and Lawler (1980); Bazerman and Lewicki (1983); or, the flood of manuscripts that arrives when one starts a new journal on negotiation.

[34]Or more precisely and politely, as Kochan and Verma say (1983:15–16):

Yet, much of this conceptual discussion has been heard before. The framework for studying organizations as political systems, and the discussion of conflict, power, and negotiations, is insightful and refreshing, but all of these works are still focused at the level of paradigm development and articulation. None of them take us far down the conceptual ladder to suggest strategies for organizational design and principles for guiding organizational activity that can be used by individuals interested in influencing or changing organizations or the behavior of individuals within them.

[35]Most notably, Raiffa (1982). We do not intend to dismiss the considerable value of descriptive work. But, along with Kochan and Verma's (1983) remark in footnote 34, we hope to avoid the continued rediscovery that there *is* negotiation in organizations; instead, we especially welcome descriptive work in areas that will aid prescription. See Raiffa's (1982) discussion of "asymmetrically prescriptive/descriptive research."

managerial situations. We seek to develop advice for a particular person without assuming strict rationality of all participants.[36] The principles we set forth in the next several chapters apply most directly to negotiations aimed at reaching contracts or formal understandings. As we proceed, we will hint at more subtle applications that we treat directly later.

Our task, then, is to develop a special logic of negotiation, helpful both to practitioners and students of the process. We have designed this logic to be hospitable, not closed. Lessons from other approaches and from experience should only enhance its value.[37]

[36]In Howard Raiffa's terminology, we take an "asymmetrically prescriptive" approach.

[37]Other approaches are quite valuable. Notable studies have been insightfully done in particular disciplines such as collective bargaining (e.g., Walton and McKersie, 1965; Kochan, 1980) and diplomacy (Iklé, 1964; Zartman and Berman, 1982) or for special positions like the presidency (Neustadt, 1980) or bureaucratic decision making (Allison, 1971). Historians describe many past diplomatic encounters; the memoirs of such figures as Talleyrand, Bismarck, and Kissinger provide a great deal of insight. Anthropologists analyze negotiation and conflict resolution in terms of culture, myth, ritual, symbol, kinship relations, and the like (Nader and Todd, 1978; Gulliver, 1979). Social psychologists conduct laboratory experiments to establish behavioral propositions (Rubin and Brown, 1975; Pruitt, 1981). Game theorists and mathematical economists impose strict conceptions of rationality and investigate the behavior of fully rational individual actors in well-structured, circumscribed situations (Luce and Raiffa, 1957; Roth, 1979). And others have blazed brilliant paths taking game theory as a starting point but without its self-imposed, exceedingly restrictive assumptions (Schelling, 1960, 1966; Raiffa, 1982).

PART I

NEGOTIATION ANALYSIS

CHAPTER TWO

The Negotiator's Dilemma: Creating and Claiming Value

THIS CHAPTER INVESTIGATES the essence of the negotiation process. We assume that each negotiator strives to advance his interests, whether they are narrowly conceived or include such concerns as improving the relationship, acting in accord with conceptions of equity, or furthering the welfare of others. Negotiators must learn, in part from each other, what is jointly possible and desirable. To do so requires some degree of cooperation. But, at the same time, they seek to advance their individual interests. This involves some degree of competition.

That negotiation includes cooperation and competition, common and conflicting interests, is nothing new. In fact, it is typically understood that these elements are both present and can be disentangled. Deep down, however, some people believe that the elements of conflict are illusory, that meaningful communication will erase any such unfortunate misperceptions. Others see mainly competition and take the cooperative pieces to be minimal. Some overtly acknowledge the reality of each aspect but direct all their attention to one of them and wish, pretend, or act as if the other does not exist. Still others hold to a more balanced view that accepts both elements as significant but seeks to treat them separately. In this chapter, we argue that *all* these approaches are flawed.

A deeper analysis shows that the competitive and cooperative elements are inextricably entwined. In practice, they cannot be separated. This bonding is fundamentally important to the analysis, structuring, and conduct of negotiation. There is a central, inescapable tension between cooperative moves to create value jointly and competitive moves to gain individual advantage. This tension affects virtually all tactical and strategic choice. Analysts must come to grips with it; negotiators must manage it. Neither denial nor discomfort will make it disappear.

Warring Conceptions of Negotiation

Negotiators and analysts tend to fall into two groups that are guided by warring conceptions of the bargaining process. In the left-hand corner are the "value creators" and in the right-hand corner are the "value claimers."

VALUE CREATORS

Value creators tend to believe that, above all, successful negotiators must be inventive and cooperative enough to devise an agreement that yields considerable gain to each party, relative to no-agreement possibilities. Some speak about the need for replacing the "win-lose" image of negotiation with "win-win" negotiation, from which all parties presumably derive great value. For example, suppose that the mayor of a southern city learns when negotiating with the city's police union that, compared to the union, she places relatively greater weight on wage reductions than on the composition of a civilian review board. She may find that offering changes in the composition of the board for previously unattainable wage reductions may create benefit for both parties compared to the otherwise likely agreement with higher wages and with the current civilian review board composition.

Communication and sharing information can help negotiators to create value jointly. Consider the case of a singer negotiating with the owner of an auditorium over payment for a proposed concert. They reached impasse over the size of the fee with the performer's demands exceeding the owner's highest offer. In fact, when the amount of the fixed payment was the issue, no possibility of agreement may have existed at all. The singer, however, based his demand on the expectation that the house would certainly be filled with fans while the owner projected only a half-capacity crowd. Ironically, this difference in their beliefs about attendance provided a way out. They reached a mutually acceptable arrangement in which the performer received a modest fixed fee plus a set percentage of the ticket receipts. The singer, given his beliefs, thus expected an adequate to fairly large payment; the concert-hall owner was happy with the agreement because he only expected to pay a moderate fee. This "contingent" arrangement, of the sort discussed in Chapter Five, permitted the concert to occur, leaving both parties feeling better off and fully willing to live with the outcome.

In addition to information sharing and honest communication, the drive to create value by discovering joint gains can require ingenuity and may benefit from a variety of techniques and attitudes. The parties can treat the negotiation as solving a joint problem; they can organize brainstorming sessions to invent creative solutions to their problems. They may succeed by putting familiar pieces of the problem together in ways that people had not previously seen, as well as by wholesale reformulations of the problem.

Roger Fisher and Bill Ury give an example that concerns the difficult Egyptian-Israeli negotiations over where to draw a boundary in the Sinai.[1] This appeared to be an absolutely classic example of zero-sum bargaining, in which each square mile lost to one party was the other side's gain. For years the negotiations proceeded inconclusively with proposed boundary lines drawn and redrawn on innumerable maps. On probing the real interests of the two sides, however, Egypt was found to care a great deal about sovereignty over the Sinai while Israel was heavily concerned with its security. As such, a creative solution could be devised to "unbundle" these different interests and give to each what it valued most. In the Sinai, this involved creating a demilitarized zone under the Egyptian flag. This had the effect of giving Egypt "sovereignty" and Israel "security." This situation exemplifies extremely common tendencies to assume that negotiators' interests are in direct opposition, a conviction that can sometimes be corrected by communicating, sharing information, and inventing solutions.

Value creators advocate exploring and cultivating shared interests in substance, in maintaining a working relationship, in having a

[1]Fisher and Ury (1981).

pleasant nonstrident negotiation process, in mutually held norms or principles, and even in reaching agreement at all. The Marshall Plan for economic rehabilitation of postwar Europe arose in part from the common interests in a revitalized Europe seen by Truman, Marshall, many in Congress, as well as numerous key Europeans. The Marshall Plan thus created great value for many.

We create value by finding *joint gains* for all negotiating parties. A joint gain represents an improvement from each party's point of view; one's gain need not be another's loss. An extremely simple example makes the point. Say that two young boys each have three pieces of fruit. Willy, who hates bananas and loves pears, has a banana and two oranges. Sam, who hates pears and loves bananas, has a pear and two apples. The first move is easy: they trade banana for pear and are both happier. But after making this deal, they realize that they can do still better. Though each has a taste both for apples and oranges, a second piece of the same fruit is less desirable than the first. So they also swap an apple for an orange. The banana-pear exchange represents an improvement over the no-trade alternative; the apple-orange transaction that leaves each with three different kinds of fruit improves the original agreement—is a joint gain—for both boys.

The economist's analogy is simple: creativity has expanded the size of the pie under negotiation. Value creators see the essence of negotiating as expanding the pie, as pursuing joint gains. This is aided by openness, clear communication, sharing information, creativity, an attitude of joint problem solving, and cultivating common interests.

VALUE CLAIMERS

Value claimers, on the other hand, tend to see this drive for joint gain as naive and weak-minded. For them, negotiation is hard, tough bargaining. The object of negotiation is to convince the other guy that he wants what you have to offer much more than you want what he has; moreover, you have all the time in the world while he is up against pressing deadlines. To "win" at negotiating—and thus make the other fellow "lose"—one must start high, concede slowly, exaggerate the value of concessions, minimize the benefits of the other's concessions, conceal information, argue forcefully on behalf of principles that imply favorable settlements, make commitments to accept only highly favorable agreements, and be willing to outwait the other fellow.

The hardest of bargainers will threaten to walk away or to retaliate harshly if their one-sided demands are not met; they may ridicule, attack, and intimidate their *adversaries*. For example, Lewis Glucksman, once the volatile head of trading activities at Lehman Brothers, the large investment banking firm, employed the hardest sort of bargaining tactics in his bid to wrest control of Lehman from then-Chairman Peter G. Peterson after being elevated to co-CEO status with Peterson. As co-CEO, Glucksman abruptly demanded full control of the firm, making a thinly veiled threat that unless his demands were met, he would provoke civil war at Lehman and take the entire profitable trading department elsewhere. When Peterson and others desperately sought less damaging accommodation, Glucksman conveyed the impression that "his feet were set in cement," even if that meant the destruction of the firm. (Ultimately, Peterson left with a substantial money settlement and Glucksman presided briefly over a shaken Lehman that was soon sold at a bargain price to American Express.)

At the heart of this adversarial approach is an image of a negotiation with a winner and a loser: "We are dividing a pie of fixed size and every slice I give to you is a slice I do not get; thus, I need to *claim* as much of the value as possible by giving you as little as possible."

A Fundamental Tension of Negotiation

Both of these images of negotiation are incomplete and inadequate. Value creating and value claiming are linked parts of negotiation. Both processes are present. No matter how much creative problem solving enlarges the pie, it must still be divided; value that has been created must be claimed. And, if the pie is not enlarged, there will be less to divide; there is more value to be claimed if one has helped create it first. An essential tension in negotiation exists between cooperative moves to create value and competitive moves to claim it.

While creating value by exchanging civilian review board provisions for wage reductions, the southern city mayor may be able to squeeze out large wage reductions for minor changes in the composition of the civilian review board. Or, the concert hall owner may offer the singer a percentage of the gate combined with a fixed fee that is just barely high enough to induce the singer to sign the contract. Even when the parties to a potential agreement share strong common interests, one side may claim the lion's share of the value an agreement creates. To achieve agreement on plans to rebuild Europe Truman was forced to forego much of its value to him by not incorporating it into his election campaign and by explicitly giving credit to others—the *Marshall* Plan sounds quite different from what he would have preferred to call the *Truman* Plan.

The Tension at the Tactical Level

The tension between cooperative moves to create value and competitive moves to claim it is greatly exacerbated by the interaction of the tactics used either to create or claim value.

First, tactics for claiming value (which we will call "claiming tactics") can impede its creation. Exaggerating the value of concessions and minimizing the benefit of others' concessions presents a distorted picture of one's relative preferences; thus, mutually beneficial trades may not be discovered. Making threats or commitments to highly favorable outcomes surely impedes hearing and understanding others' interests. Concealing information may also cause one to leave joint gains on the table. In fact, excessive use of tactics for claiming value may well sour the parties' relationship and reduce the trust between them. Such tactics may also evoke a variety of unhelpful interests. Conflict may escalate and make joint prospects less appealing and settlement less likely.

Second, approaches to creating value are vulnerable to tactics for claiming value. Revealing information about one's relative preferences is risky. If the mayor states that she gives relatively greater weight to wage reductions than to civilian review board composition, the union representative may respond by saying that the union members also feel more strongly about wage reductions, but would be willing to give in a little on wage reductions if the mayor will compensate them handsomely by completely changing the board. The information that a negotiator would accept position A in return for a favorable resolution on a second issue can be exploited: "So, you'll accept A. Good, Now, let's move on to discuss the merits of the second issue." The willingness to make a new, creative offer can often be taken as a sign that its proposer is able and willing to make further concessions. Thus, such offers sometimes remain undisclosed. Even purely shared interests can be held hostage in exchange for concessions on other issues. Though a divorcing husband and wife may both prefer giving the wife custody of the child, the husband may "suddenly" develop strong parental instincts to extract concessions on alimony in return for giving the wife custody.

In tactical choices, each negotiator thus has reasons not be open and cooperative. Each also has apparent incentives to try to claim value. Moves to claim value thus tend to drive out moves to create it. Yet, if both choose to claim value, by being dishonest or less than forthcoming about preferences, beliefs, or minimum requirements, they may miss mutually beneficial terms for agreement.

Indeed, the structure of many bargaining situations suggests that negotiators will tend to leave joint gains on the table or even reach impasses when mutually acceptable agreements are available. We will use an extended, simplified example of a cable television operator negotiating with a town over the terms of the cable franchise to explore the tactical dilemmas that often lead to suboptimal outcomes.

Stone versus Ward

Mr. Stone, representing MicroCable Inc., and Mayor Ward, representing the town council of a town we will call Clayton, are negotiating three issues: the price the town residents would have to pay for their subscriptions, the date by which the system would be fully operational (the completion date), and the number of cable channels to be offered.

The Mayor places greatest weight on a speedy completion date, in part because of his upcoming reelection campaign. Within the range of feasible prices and numbers of channels, he cares approximately the same about the price, which he would like to minimize, and the number of channels, which he would like to maximize. The cable company gives greatest weight to price and the least weight to the number of channels. MicroCable would of course like the highest price and the slowest completion, but perhaps surprisingly, Stone estimates that, though providing more channels involves additional costs, it would ultimately pay off handsomely because he will be able to sell more pay TV subscriptions. Neither party is certain about the other's beliefs and preferences. If both were to reveal their preferences to a third party and to ask her to construct a jointly desirable agreement, the agreement might well specify the maximum number of channels, a high price, and a relatively fast completion.

In preparing for the negotiation, Mayor Ward recalls the experience of a colleague who had negotiated with a different cable firm.

His colleague had publicly expressed a strong interest in a quick completion time—which he ultimately obtained but only after being unmercifully squeezed on price. Mayor Ward fears that Stone would respond opportunistically to a similar announcement, insisting that fast completion would be very costly for him but that perhaps he could arrange it only in return for very high prices and few channels. Such an agreement would be barely acceptable to the Mayor and the town, but would, the Mayor guesses, be quite desirable for Stone. In other words, Mayor Ward fears that if he attempts to jointly create value by sharing information about his preferences, Stone will attempt to claim the value by being misleading about his preferences. Thus, the Mayor elects to be a bit cagey and plans to downplay his interests in completion and the number of channels. He also plans to exaggerate his interest in a low price, with the hope of ultimately making a seemingly big concession on that issue in return for a big gain on completion and channels.

Stone has similar inclinations. If he lets the Mayor know that he is much more concerned with price than with speed of completion and that he actually wants more channels, he reasons, he will have given up all his bargaining chips. Mayor Ward would, he guesses, initially offer a moderately high price but only in return for an unbearably early completion date. And, he fears that the Mayor would use the town's political process to make it difficult to be dislodged from his offer. Thus, Stone is also afraid that if he attempts to create value by sharing information about his preferences, the Mayor will attempt to claim that value by being opportunistic about his and may also try to make a binding commitment to his preferred position. So, Stone also chooses to be cagey, but plans to let the Mayor and the town know, early on, that a moderate completion time and a moderate number of channels are barely possible and are very costly to him. He has an assistant prepare slides detailing the costs, but not the revenue forecasts, of additional channels. The assistant also prepares financial analyses that are intended to show that he will need high prices to recoup the cost of even such moderate concessions. Ultimately, he hopes to concede a little on the completion date for a modest price increase, and to appear magnanimous in making a final concession of the maximum number of channels for a last major price increase.

The negotiation begins in the conference room at Clayton City Hall. The Mayor welcomes Stone and his associates. He talks at some length about the value that his town's citizens place on cable television and about the fine reputation of Stone's firm. He then expresses his strong hope and belief that Clayton and MicroCable will come to a mutually beneficial agreement as the first step in a working relationship. Stone thanks the Mayor for his warm welcome. He feels that it is important to draw attention to their common ground: both the town and MicroCable want to see a fine cable system in Clayton. In this negotiation, they are thus looking out for each other's interests.

As the formal negotiation starts, Mayor Ward and Stone begin to thrust and parry. The Mayor stresses the importance the city places on keeping the price down. He also mentions that speedy completion and a large number of channels would be preferred by Clayton's residents. Stone responds sympathetically but explains the high cost of even normal completion times and of the number of channels in a basic system. Adding channels to the system and accelerating construction of the system faster than its "normal rate" are sufficiently costly that a cable franchise would be virtually unprofitable. He presents financial analyses showing the costs both of more channels and of "accelerated" completion dates.

Unable to counter directly, Mayor Ward alludes to (not yet formally received) strong offers by other cable operators. Stone parries by mentioning another town that eagerly seeks the superior MicroCable system, but says that he would of course rather do business in Clayton. They move beyond this minor impasse by concentrating on the price, in which both sides have expressed strong interest. They bargain hard. The Mayor claims that neither the town council nor the citizenry could approve a franchise with anything more than a moderate price, unless the services were extraordinary. Stone then cites still more of his financial analyses. Each searches for a favorable wedge. After arguing about different definitions of "fair and reasonable profit" and "fair return on investment," they compromise by agreeing on the price reached in a negotiation between a neighboring town and one of MicroCable's competitors. The Mayor never realizes that Stone could be more flexible on completion dates and does not arrange as early a date as he might have gotten for the price. And, ironically, Stone's careful financial presentation about the costs of adding channels makes it difficult for him to offer the town the maximum number of channels without losing face. The bargaining is tense, but they ultimately settle at a compromise on each issue: a moderate price, a moderate completion date, and about half the maximum number of channels.

Both men leave feeling good about the outcome. As Stone says to his assistant, "We didn't get everything we wanted but we gave as good as we got." Before the town council's vote on the franchise agreement, the Mayor describes the negotiation as a success: "If both sides complain a bit about the agreement, then you know it must be a good deal." The town council approves the proposal unanimously.

In the negotiations, each of the parties was afraid that his attempt to create value by sharing information would be exploited by the other's claiming tactics. Each chose to attempt to mislead or claim a bit, in self-protection. And, relative to what was possible, they ended up with an inferior solution. They left joint gains on the table. Both would have preferred the maximum number of channels and both would have preferred a higher price in return for earlier completion. A pity, but not uncommon.

The Negotiator's Dilemma

Let us abstract from this example. Consider two negotiators (for continuity named Ward and Stone) each of whom can choose between two negotiating styles: creating value (being open, sharing information about preferences and beliefs, not being misleading about minimum requirements, and so forth) and claiming value (being cagey and misleading about preferences, beliefs, and minimum requirements; making commitments and threats, and so forth). Each has the same two options for any tactical choice. If both choose to create value, they each receive a good outcome, which we will call GOOD for each. If Ward chooses to create value and Stone chooses to claim value, then Stone does even better than if he had chosen to create value—rank this outcome GREAT for Stone—but Ward does much worse—rank this outcome TERRIBLE for him. Similarly, if Stone is the creative one and Ward is the claimer, then Ward does well—rank this outcome for him as GREAT—while Stone's outcome is TERRIBLE. If both claim, they fail to find joint gains and come up with a mediocre outcome, which we call MEDIOCRE for both. Figure 2.1 summarizes the outcomes for each choice. In each box, Ward's payoff is in the lower left corner and Stone's is in the upper right. Thus, when Ward claims and Stone creates, Ward's outcome is GREAT while Stone's is TERRIBLE.

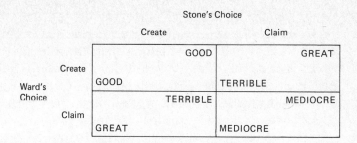

FIGURE 2.1:   The Negotiator's Dilemma

The lower left entry in each cell is Ward's outcome; the second entry is Stone's.

Now, if Ward were going to create, Stone would prefer the GREAT outcome obtained by claiming to the GOOD outcome he could have obtained by creating; so, Stone should claim. If, on the other hand, Ward were going to claim, Stone would prefer the ME-DIOCRE outcome from claiming to the TERRIBLE outcome he would receive from creating. In fact, no matter what Ward does, it seems that Stone would be better off trying to claim value!

Similarly, Ward should also prefer to claim. By symmetric reasoning, if Stone chooses to create, Ward prefers the GREAT outcome he gets by claiming to the the GOOD outcome he gets from creating. If Stone claims, Ward prefers the MEDIOCRE outcome he gets from claiming to the TERRIBLE outcome he gets from creating.

Both negotiators choose to claim. They land in the lower-right-hand box and receive MEDIOCRE outcomes. They leave joint gains on the table, since both would prefer the GOOD outcomes they could have received had they both chosen to create value and ended up in the upper-left-hand box.

This is the crux of the Negotiator's Dilemma.[2] Individually rational decisions to emphasize claiming tactics by being cagey and misleading lead to a mutually undesirable outcome. As described,

[2]Several authors have discussed versions of similar negotiation dilemmas. See for example Zartman (1976) and Pruitt (1981). In our judgment, the best such discussion, usefully developed in a different direction, can be found in Walton and McKersie (1965, 1966). An abstract version of a similar dilemma is currently being investigated by game theorists studying bargaining with incomplete information. One major result, due to Myerson (1979), is that in highly simplified situations that are analogous to the ones we discuss, fully honest revelation of private information by individual bargainers and Pareto efficiency cannot simultaneously be achieved. This is a starkly abstracted analogue of the result we describe that tends to result from the tension between cooperative moves to create value and competitive moves to claim it individually.

this situation has the structure of the famous "Prisoner's Dilemma."[3] In such situations, the motivation to protect oneself and employ tactics for claiming value is compelling. Because tactics for claiming value impede creation, we expect negotiators in many settings to leave joint gains on the table. And, over time, the inexorable pull towards claiming tactics is insidious: negotiators will "learn" to become value claimers. A negotiator inclined towards sharing information and constructive creative, mutually desirable agreements, after being skewered in several encounters with experienced value-claimers, may bitterly come to alter his strategy to a more self-protective, value-claiming stance. Williams' description of new attorneys learning to negotiate out-of-court settlements is consistent with this analysis:

> During the first few months of practice, they encounter some attorneys who hammer them into the ground, exploiting and taking advantage of them at every turn, and others who are trying to teach them how to be good lawyers. The experience is not calculated to engender trust in fellow officers of the court. Rather, the tendency in young lawyers is to develop a mild paranoia and to distrust everyone. This is unfortunate, because some opponents are providing valuable information, albeit in subtle ways.[4]

Because both sides in our negotiation would prefer to end up with a GOOD-GOOD (create-create) outcome rather than a MEDIOCRE-MEDIOCRE (claim-claim) one, experience may "teach" negotiation

[3]In addition to the payoff structure, the classic Prisoner's Dilemma involves rules of interaction: no communication and the inability of the parties to make prior, communicated, binding commitments to one choice or the other. Under these rules, the equilibrium in a single play of the Prisoner's Dilemma is for both players to defect (claim). (For a perceptive discussion of the Prisoner's Dilemma, see Luce and Raiffa, 1957). In negotiations, of course, communication is possible, and credible irreversible commitments to cooperate are difficult but not always impossible to make. Thus, we suggest that the structure of the Negotiator's Dilemma implies a tendency for both parties to choose to claim value, but not that this is an irrevocable equilibrium. Moreover, we shall argue below that a negotiation in fact contains a sequence of choices with much the same structure, though again the rules of interaction differ. The economic equilibrium for playing a finite number of repetitions of the Prisoner's Dilemma is to defect (claim) in every play. But experimental results suggest that people playing the finitely repeated Prisoner's Dilemma often do better than the "rational" players of game theory and are sometimes able to cooperate for substantial mutual gain. Thus, we do not take the analogy to the repeated Prisoner's Dilemma to imply that people will use game-theoretic equilibrium strategies, but to suggest a powerful tendency toward such behavior.

[4]Williams (1983:29).

lessons that both sides, like Williams's young attorneys, would be better off not having "learned."

Taking the Negotiator's Dilemma Metaphor Seriously but Not Literally

The Negotiator's Dilemma characterizes the whole of a negotiation. Yet the Dilemma is a simplification, a metaphor. As presented, it appears to condemn each negotiator to a once-and-for-all choice as a creator or claimer; clearly there are many choices along the way.

The dilemma is also meant to apply to each tactical choice. Even here, the line between "creating" and "claiming" need not be clear-cut. A negotiator can reveal information early, late, throughout, or not at all; she can mislead by omission, commission, or be straight. She may discover a new option for mutual benefit, a joint gain, but present it in such a way that it emphasizes only agreements highly favorable to her. She may offer a creative proposal or hold back because it conveys sensitive information about tradeoffs or minimal requirements. Yet at a basic enough level, tactical choices embody the creating-claiming tension, even if they contain elements of both.

Thus, we take the Negotiator's Dilemma seriously, even though we do not take the matrix representation literally. The tension it reflects between cooperative impulses to create value and competitive impulses to claim it is inherent in the large and in the small. The essence of effective negotiation involves managing this tension, creating while claiming value.

This chapter presents a broad-brush portrait. To understand what is involved in managing this central tension, we must return with finer brushes to several parts of the canvas:

1. What precisely does it mean to create value? Where do joint gains really come from? What tactics are required to realize them?
2. What do we mean by claiming value? What tactics are appropriate.
3. If negotiation involves an inescapable tension between competitive and cooperative impulses, how can one manage it effectively?

4. Can't we manage this tension by separating the creating from the claiming? Why not do all the creating first and then just divide the cleverly created joint gains? Or, why not get the hard claiming out of the way and then try to find all the available joint gains? What other choices do we have?

A Roadmap in Pictures

The quest for answers to these and related questions animates Part I of this book. The remainder of this chapter lays out the elements of negotiation we will examine and explains the relations among them. As we go along, we also introduce a graphical metaphor that will help organize the ideas we develop.

The point of negotiation is for each negotiator to do better by jointly decided action than he could do otherwise, better than his "no-agreement alternatives." For example, recall the humble example of Willy and Sam whose trade of bananas, pears, and apples we discussed earlier. If they had been unable to reach agreement, there would be no trade at all. The no-agreement alternative for each boy was to keep whatever fruit he had. Chapter Three somewhat ironically begins our tour through negotiation analysis by looking outside the negotiation itself and focusing attention on the crucial and often neglected role of no-agreement alternatives.

Once a negotiator establishes his no-agreement alternative, he seeks to improve on it by jointly decided action. Thus, he needs a deep understanding of his interests. Chapter Four discusses interests and provides a logic and method for making the sometimes painful tradeoffs among them.

Negotiators jointly create value by harmonizing their interests, much as Willy and Sam did in finding mutually beneficial trades. In Chapter Five, we ask where joint gains really come from and set forth the different ways that interests can be converted into joint gains.

Figure 2.2 graphically illustrates one such joint gain. The horizontal axis shows the value of an agreement to Willy. Thus, points farther to the right represent agreements that better serve Willy's interests. Similarly, the vertical axis shows the value of an agreement to Sam. The more Sam values an agreement, the higher it is on the graph. The point labeled 0, at the origin, represents Sam and Willy's no-agreement alternative, no trade at all. Their first trade, where Willy gives Sam a pear in exchange for a banana, makes both happier

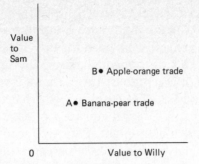

FIGURE 2.2: **Joint Gains From Trade**

because each prefers what he received to what he gave up. This new agreement is represented by point A; the fact that it is northeast of the no-agreement point reflects the fact that both Sam and Willy prefer the trade. This trade "created value" and thus represents a joint gain with respect to no agreement. Similarly, their next trade of an apple for an orange, represented by point B, makes each of them still happier. Because point B represents a joint gain compared to point A, B is to the northeast of A. Chapter Five goes well beyond such simple trades in showing ways for joint action to create value.

But value is both created and claimed. Figure 2.3 shows a third agreement, point C, that is also a joint gain compared to Willy and Sam's original agreement, point A. Willy prefers point C to point B and Sam prefers the reverse. By clever tactics to claim value, Willy may induce Sam to accept point C. Thus, Willy would have claimed most of the jointly created value. Of course, Sam may be employing similar tactics to reach point B so *he* can claim the lion's share of the jointly created value. Chapter Six explores how value is claimed.

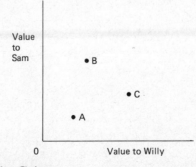

FIGURE 2.3: **Joint Gains**

Willy and Sam prefer agreements B and C to agreement A. Willy prefers C to B and Sam prefers B to C.

Indeed, if Sam had discovered agreement C, he might never mention it to Will. Instead, he might seek to make agreement B salient, emphasize its desirability, and then push for early closure hoping that Willy never discovers that agreement C exists. Or, Sam might vigorously assert that C is not acceptable to him, that it is simply worse for him than agreement A. In either case, the way that the value is created affects the way it is divided; the process of creating value is *entwined* with the process of claiming it. Effective negotiation requires managing the tension between the need to create value and the need to claim it. How this is and can be done is the subject of Chapter Seven.

By being clever, Willy and Sam may find agreements that both prefer to point B and others that both prefer to C. But the effects of their cleverness are necessarily limited. Eventually, they will find that they cannot improve on certain agreements for one boy except at the other's expense. In more complex bargains, there are a large number of such agreements, as illustrated in Figure 2.4. The set of such agreements is known as the "possibilities frontier" or the "Pareto frontier." From any point on the frontier, Willy cannot find another agreement that makes him better off without making Sam worse off. This frontier is an abstraction, an heuristic, that is usually not known to the negotiators. It represents what is ultimately possible by joint action after the negotiators have shared all information about themselves and exhausted all creativity and ingenuity. Because the parties know different things, each will have his own perceptions of what is jointly possible (where the possibilities frontier lies). Throughout this book, we will again and again refer to this image of a possibilities frontier as perceived by the parties.

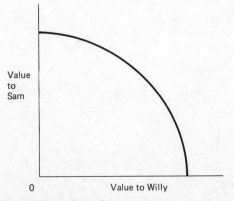

FIGURE 2.4:   **The Possibilities Frontier**

So far, we have assumed that a fixed set of negotiators with well-defined interests and fixed no-agreement alternatives meets to discuss a given set of issues. But a negotiator can also create and claim value by adding a new issue or excluding one, bringing in a new party or leaving one out, improving her no-agreement alternatives or making another's alternatives worse, and so on. Every element of the negotiation can itself be subject to tactical manipulation. In Chapter Nine, we enumerate many ways to change the game and provide means to decide whether such changes are likely to help. Thus, we complete our framework by incorporating ways that a negotiation's structure evolves over time.

In short, this logic of negotiation guides the logic of the chapters that follow and the approach we espouse. Any feasible joint action must do better for the parties than their alternatives to agreement; Chapter Three studies this minimum requirement. But "doing better" is only measured by one's interests, which are the subject of Chapter Four. Fashioning the means of doing better—jointly creating value—follows in Chapter Five. Chapter Six explores how individuals claim value and some of the ethical issues raised in the process. The ways that negotiators and third parties can or might manage the tension between the conflicting needs to create and claim value are examined in Chapter Seven. Chapter Eight explores the themes developed thus far by dissecting the case of a complex budget determination. Proceeding further with the basic argument, Chapter Nine adds an "evolutionary" dimension, analyzing how negotiators also create and claim value by bringing in a new issue, excluding a party, and more generally, by changing the game itself. Chapter Ten summarizes our approach as a whole and takes a look at the often misunderstood concept of negotiating "power."

The subjects we have chosen to examine bear on each part of a model of possible joint action. In this sense, our analysis and prescriptions form a whole to which a myriad of richer contextual aspects may be related.

CHAPTER THREE

Alternatives to Agreement: The Limits of Negotiation

PEOPLE FACED WITH upcoming negotiations often seek advice. Invariably, many if not most of their questions have a tactical slant: Should I make the first contact? By phone, in person, by mail, or through a third party? Wear a dark suit and meet in an expensive restaurant near my office? Order them strong drinks and keep them up late before getting down to serious discussion? Make the first offer? Press them to begin? Start high and concede slowly? Settle the easy issues first? Act conciliatory, tough, threatening, or as a joint problem solver? Arrange for a "hardhearted" partner? Find "fair" sounding principles to back up my position?

By focusing on such tactical choices, negotiators may miss a more fundamental point. The current negotiation is typically but a *means* to an end: One seeks by negotiation to satisfy one's interests better through jointly decided action than one could otherwise.[1] Each par-

---

[1]In some cases, of course, the negotiation process can be an end in itself or be directed at something other than reaching an agreement. Sometimes "negotiation" is a good pretext for getting people to talk and listen to each other. One or more of the participants may simply want to confront another or vent emotion. Someone may genuinely enjoy verbal conflict without any desire for accord on substance. Beyond seeking agreement, nations often use formal negotiations to spread propa-

ty's best alternative without agreement implies the lower limit of value that any acceptable agreement must provide. For each side, the basic test of any proposed joint agreement is whether it offers higher subjective worth than that side's best course of action absent agreement. When preparing for a negotiation, it is critical to analyze one's own no-agreement alternatives and to assess how the other parties will perceive and value theirs. This focus on negotiation as but one of several means for advancing one's interests helps determine whether to negotiate at all, whether to continue the process, whether to accept a proposal, and whether an agreement, once reached, will be secure.

In certain negotiations such as collective bargaining or the purchase of expensive items, alternatives to agreement—strikes, lockouts, other price quotes—are obvious, well-defined, and tactically prominent. For example, the threat to strike if concessions are not made may loom large in some negotiations. Yet in some cases, bargainers systematically overestimate the attractiveness of their no-agreement alternatives. In other situations, no-agreement alternatives are less salient. Especially in complex negotiations, it is a common error for bargainers to ignore their alternatives to agreement and instead to focus mainly on tactics and the bargaining process itself. In such situations, no-agreement alternatives may function more as last resorts or afterthoughts than as primary influences.

Moves "away from the table" that shape the parties' alternatives to agreement can strongly affect negotiated outcomes. Indeed, searching for a better price or another supplier, cultivating a friendly merger partner in response to hostile takeover negotiations, or preparing an invasion should talks fail to yield a preferable outcome may have greater influence on the negotiated outcome than sophisticated tactics employed "at the table."

Like commitments, threats, and promises, moves to alter no-agreement alternatives can fundamentally affect the bargaining process. As Chapter Ten discusses, because changes in no-agreement alternatives can affect the set of possible bargained outcomes, the ability to change alternatives is often associated with notions of bargaining "power."

---

ganda, gather intelligence, influence third parties or other audiences, maintain contact, divert their couterparts' attention from something else, or communicate on other matters entirely. See Iklé (1964). It is quite common for a tacit or indirect "negotiation" to address the issue of whether the parties should even negotiate explicitly. (One thinks of the negotiation involved in "getting parties to the bargaining table" in some industrial disputes. Or agreement to negotiate formally may settle a long-standing de facto negotiation over status, e.g., Israel and the PLO.)

Alternatives Limit the Bargaining Range

A simple case illustrates how no-agreement alternatives limit the set of possible negotiated outcomes. With modest profits over the last two years the IRMAN Printing Co. feels financially shaky. Last year, it shifted from fine arts printing to more remunerative areas but still has in its shop a rare, high-quality European fine art press that is no longer used, though its condition is nearly perfect. A well-to-do local amateur is planning to open a shop to do exactly this kind of fine arts printing, inquires about where such equipment might be found and soon offers $1000 for the press. IRMAN shop manager Deb Berman's first impulse is to sell for whatever she can get; otherwise it would continue to gather dust. As she thinks about it, though, she calls a junk dealer and asks how much he would give her to cart off the device as scrap; he asks its weight and offers "about $500." Given that, the $1000 possibility seems appealing. The press is exotic and was, at its original cost of $10,000, expensive as presses go; thus, other buyers seem pretty unlikely. Yet Deb realizes that this press is almost certainly the only one of its general type in the region and that a new one now costs $12,000.

Pursuing this line further, Deb calls a local university art department about the possibility of donating the press. Given their response, she estimates the value of the tax deduction from such a charitable donation to be approximately $2500. After a small negotiation dance, she and the prospective buyer agree on a price of $3500.

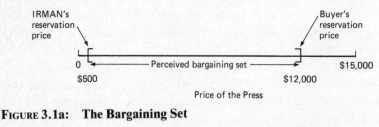

FIGURE 3.1a: The Bargaining Set

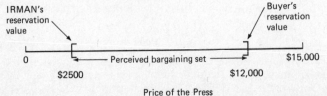

FIGURE 3.1b: The Bargaining Set Changed by a New Alternative

By getting another no-agreement alternative, IRMAN's manager raised her reservation value from $500 to $2500 and thus shifted the perceived bargaining set.

Thus, as Figure 3.1a depicts, the initially perceived *bargaining set* (or *bargaining range* or *zone of possible agreement*) ran between Deb's $500 alternative (junk the press) and the $12,000 valuation of the other party's no-agreement alternative (buy a new one). When Deb found out about the tax deduction option, the bottom end of the bargaining set shifted from $500 to $2500 (Figure 3.1b). At this point Deb should not have accepted anything below $2500 in the bargaining. (In Chapter Six, we will evaluate tactics useful in situations such as Deb's more carefully. For now, though, we cannot help asking why—given IRMAN Printing's precarious finances, knowing the buyer's need and his best no-agreement alternative of $12,000—she did not commit stubbornly to a price much nearer the top of the bargaining set.)

In a situation as simple as this one it is obvious that the no-agreement alternatives imply the limits of the bargaining set. Changes in them may alter the outcome. But at all stages of the process, it is *perceptions* of the alternatives that are critical to behavior. Thus, as discussed in Chapter Six, moves to change such perceptions figure prominently among tactics for claiming value. In general, *bargainers do not know whether an agreement is even possible*. As such much activity centers on the parties trying to discover whether a bargaining set exists at all (in Figure 3.2a, no bargaining range exists), whether the perceived bargaining set is highly favorable to the seller (see Figure 3.2b) or whether it favors the buyer (Figure 3.2c).

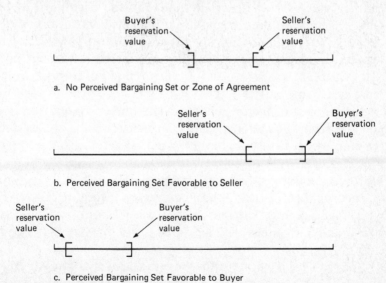

FIGURE 3.2:   **Possible Bargaining Sets**

But, what is clear in situations as simple as IRMAN's may become much less so when no-agreement alternatives are more complex. Yet the same basic points hold.

Alternatives May Take Varied and Subtle Forms

Alternatives can be as varied as the negotiating situations they circumscribe. They may be certain and have a single attribute: an iron-clad competing price quote for an identical new car. They may be contingent and multiattributed: going to court rather than accepting a negotiated settlement can involve uncertainties, trial anxieties, legal fees, time costs, and precedents that contrast with the certain, solely monetary nature of a pretrial accord. Alternatives may change over time with new information, interpretations, competitive moves, or opportunities. In case of no agreement, the *status quo ante* may be superseded by something much worse for one side: a now-neutral island nation may intend to lease its naval base to one superpower if current negotiations fall through with the other. In multiparty and organizational negotiations, one side's alternatives may be the set of agreements that could be reached by potential opposing coalitions. Outright threats by one party to change the no-agreement alternatives of another are commonly made: the Godfather's "offer you can't refuse." Or, the best alternative to the negotiated agreement may be simply to keep negotiating: in arms control, organizational deliberations, or minor marital disputes, failure to agree may involve worse relations, foregone benefit, and altered settlement possibilities, but in any case the necessity may remain of continued dealings among the same parties.

Common managerial moves to change alternatives involve unilaterally seeking to alter penalties, organizational systems, and even the employment relation itself (firing). Where others perceive such unilateral potential to be higher, the manager's ability to negotiate his preferred outcomes correspondingly rises. Where the possibilities of such actions are less, the manager-as-negotiator may feel in a weaker bargaining position. (Later, we will look at the sometimes strong and sometimes tenuous agreements that are the basis of authority relations.)

In all these disparate situations, the central analytical feature of alternatives flows from the bargainer's evaluation of no agreement compared with that of agreement. There is a strategic commonality regardless of whether the alternatives are certain or uncertain, have one, many, or different attributes, are static or dynamic, or depend or do not depend on other bargaining parties.

A variety of well-developed techniques exist to help understand and evaluate many of these types of alternatives to negotiated agreement.[2] The subjective expected utility of the no-agreement alternative provides a strict lower bound for the minimum worth required of any acceptable settlement; one's *reservation value* or *reservation price* (also sometimes called bottom line, threat, or "resistance point") is any settlement that gives exactly this minimum expected utility. Thus, Deb's reservation value in the preceding example was $500 and then increased to $2500 when she discovered a superior no-agreement alternative.

Evaluating No-Agreement Alternatives

To avoid accepting offers substantially less desirable than their no-agreement alternatives and to assess the potential gains to be had, negotiators clearly should *evaluate* what the alternative actions are likely to be for all sides. Sometimes it is appropriate for this evaluation to make use of sophisticated technical tools[3] but often careful thought will suffice.

---

[2]When alternatives are uncertain or change over time, as when the no-agreement alternative involves going to court, decision analysis can provide a systematic guide to action (Raiffa, 1968, 1982). Multiattribute value and utility theory can clarify comparisons of outcomes and no-agreement alternatives when they have many attributes, even when the features of the alternatives differ from those of the agreements (Keeney and Raiffa, 1976; Barclay and Peterson, 1976). In certain cases, there are many possible alternatives to negotiation, for example, many possible buyers for a house, each with associated uncertainties and costs of discovery. In such cases, optimal search theory can provide strategies for searching efficiently among the alternatives and valuing the expected findings from such a search (Lax, 1985). Where the parties' alternatives to agreement are interdependent, concepts from game theory—including the dynamics of threats and counterthreats as well as the many variants of coalition analysis—can help bargainers understand their alternatives and, in so doing, better understand the rationale for bargaining (Luce and Raiffa, 1957; Raiffa, 1982).

[3]See footnote 2 for a list of some of these technical tools.

An intergovernmental example illustrates the importance of evaluating no-agreement alternatives that change in interesting ways over time. Over a number of years, several states spent large amounts of money on certain types of social services, partially in the expectation of federal reimbursement. The circumstances were murky, the amounts of money ran into the billions, and it was not clear whether this was good public policy or merely a loophole in laws and regulations. For a number of years, however, these state claims against the federal government had been a considerable thorn in the side of federal-state relations. When the Carter administration came into office, it placed improved intergovernmental relations high on its priority list. Still, finances were tight and budgets were under intense scrutiny. Thus, both the federal government and the states cared about money and the relationship. Relative to its fiscal interests, however, the federal government—and especially the Department of Health, Education and Welfare (HEW), which would be responsible for the disbursement—appeared to value relationship improvements more heavily than did most of the states.

Early in the new administration's tenure, negotiations over these social services claims resumed in earnest. HEW Undersecretary Hale Champion, the federal official in charge of these talks, thought very hard about tactics and approaches within the negotiations themselves but he also focused a great deal of attention on the parties' alternatives to a negotiated agreement.

If the parties did not reach agreement voluntarily, they would let the courts decide. In previous suits over these claims, the two sides had already taken steps down this path. The federal government had demonstrated its commitment to a legal battle by appealing earlier adverse court decisions on rather narrow grounds. Yet for all sides, the prospect of continued legal battles was unappealing: the outcomes were uncertain, many resources would be expended, and the opportunity for an improved relationship could be lost in the ensuing adversarial process. In fact, the hoped-for value of voluntary agreement impelled both sides toward a solution. If they settled this longstanding problem by themselves, it could set an excellent procedural precedent and have benefits in many other areas.

Yet, in preparing to negotiate, the federal official thought hard about the role of time and realized that in at least five distinctive ways it worked strongly against the states' alternatives to a negotiated agreement with the federal government.

First, inflation was eating away at any possible settlement. The administration could credibly threaten to tie up the claims in court for many more years.

Second, beyond this economic cost to the states from a failure to agree, important political factors rendered a settlement much less valuable to the states if delayed beyond gubernatorial elections. The money allocated for social sevices had been spent years ago—for the states it was a sunk cost. Any state administration receiving reimbursement in effect would get a windfall which could be crucial toward, say, balancing a current state budget or funding a favorite program. State governors' terms were all shorter than or equal to the tenure of the new federal administration. The credible federal threat to drag out the legal process could thus deny the governors great political credit.

A third factor working against certain states was the frequent turnover in their personnel who could back up their cases in court. In effect, as their ability to substantiate their legal claims eroded, the quality of those states' best alternatives declined over time relative to that of the federal government.

Fourth, Champion portrayed administration eagerness to settle this issue as a sort of "fading opportunity" for the states. This divisive issue briefly held HEW Secretary Joseph Califano's attention. Yet Califano's alternative to any sort of agreement on claim settlement was simply to ignore the dispute. The claims would move off his priority list and would be handled at the same low bureaucratic echelons where they had been inconclusively mired for years before.

Finally, there was a complex sequence of administrative and legislative steps required to pay any settled claims during the current budget cycle. Unless the process began very soon, actual payment would be delayed until the next cycle. To get the necessary bureaucratic wheels turning required a prompt settlement.

Thus, the worsening of their alternatives over time seemed to push the states toward early settlement for a variety of reasons. Each of these factors, of course, had exactly the opposite effect on the federal government's monetary alternatives to a negotiated agreement. Any claims settled and paid in the future would be paid with cheaper dollars and, critically, as a budget liability to a later—not the current—administration. Relative to many states, the federal ability to uphold its legal case would not erode. Moreover, Califano's alternative to spending time trying to settle this issue was to occupy himself with a host of other pressing questions. Balancing these apparently time-related federal advantages on monetary interests, however, was the deeply felt loss of the opportunity to better relations with the states. The value of a voluntary agreement would be lost if the new administration decided to take its best alternative to agreement and face the states in court.

These factors heavily influenced state and federal perceptions of the zone of possible agreement. In particular, the states seemed to feel pressed by the threatened erosion of a settlement's monetary value. By carefully evaluating the states' no-agreement alternatives, the federal negotiators were able to estimate the states' reservation price. The federal negotiators then made a take-it-or-leave-it offer that they felt exceeded the states' minimum requirements but was far short of the states' loudly proclaimed demands. The sides did reach an agreement far below the states' original claims but one that was realistic given their alternatives. The result did, however, have the strong benefit of improving intergovernmental relations across a variety of issues.

Because negotiation is a *means* of doing better by joint action than would be possible otherwise, it should not be surprising that nonnegotiation courses of action will sometimes prove to be the superior means. Recall how Allen, the mentor of a very ambitious young man in a financial consulting firm found himself trying to renegotiate the terms of the young man's association with the firm. Felix, the young man, had made a great deal of money for the firm but had done so in a direction contrary to the strategy agreed to by the firm's principals. Moreover, Felix had gone far "outside normal procedures" in furthering his aims. Allen, his mentor and the managing partner, could envision many possible joint arrangements that would be good from the firm's point of view. But, ultimately, any set of terms that Allen proposed as being acceptable to the firm seemed worse to Felix than separation (and vice versa). Carefully focusing both sides' attention on their unilateral alternatives—firing Felix or his leaving—clarified the ultimate resolution. Though his choice to leave might be regarded as a failed negotiation, it was probably a superior outcome for both sides.

In a more strident vein, President Ronald Reagan's early dealings with professional air traffic controllers over their contract was resolved when the President fired them all and activated a contingency plan to run the nation's air traffic control system. From Reagan's perspective, decisive, noncooperative action not only settled the air traffic situation but sent strong signals for moderation to other public employee unions and enhanced the President's reputation for toughness. Again, this case suggests a "failure" of negotiation that for at least one participant offered a superior alternative to any negotiable agreement.

Even in these more complex situations, negotiation is still but a means to an end. As such, effective practice requires evaluating alternatives to agreement and comparing them to possible agreements. When the alternatives are superior, the negotiator should take them. There seems to be a widespread popular belief in the potency of various tactical ploys. A simple focus on alternatives to agreement limits the range in which *any* slick tactic should work. Consider the would-be buyer of a trucking company who psychoanalyzes the seller, brainstorms, details the businesses's flaws, creates a friendly ambiance at a meeting site that nonetheless drips with trappings of his importance, and ends up artfully making an offer. He is simply wasting his time if the seller cares mostly about money and has elicited a better offer elsewhere.

Moves to Change No-Agreement Alternatives

To change the bargaining range favorably, negotiators may seek to improve their no-agreement alternatives. Similarly, they may try to worsen the other sides' alternatives or simultaneously to alter both ends of the bargaining range. Thus, firms that seek other, higher offers responding to hostile takeover bids sometimes seek to merge with new firms offering a higher price than the initial bid. But the original bidder often increases its bid and purchases the firm instead.

When preparing for a future negotiation, one side may seek a favorable agreement for itself by worsening the other side's alternatives to it. For example, in the early 1960s, Chilean expropriation of Kennecott Copper's El Teniente mine seemed increasingly likely.[4] In preparing to negotiate the terms of expropriation, such as the timing, compensation, and any continued management involvement with the mine, Kennecott sought early on to involve a variety of other parties to change the nature of Chile's alternatives to agreement on Kennecott's preferred terms. Somewhat surprisingly, the company offered to sell a majority interest in the mine to Chile. Kennecott planned to use the proceeds of this sale of equity along with money from the U.S. Export-Import Bank to finance the expansion of the mine. The

[4]Smith and Wells (1975).

Chilean government guaranteed this loan and made it subject to New York law. The company then insured as much as possible of its assets under a U.S. guarantee against expropriation. The mine's output was to be sold under long-term contracts with Asian and European customers and the collection rights for these contracts were sold to a consortium of European banks and Japanese institutions.

The result of all this maneuvering was that customers, governments, and creditors shared Kennecott's concern about future changes in Chile. Moreover, the guarantees and insurance improved Kennecott's alternatives if no deal could be worked out with the host country. When no agreement could be reached and Chile acted to expropriate the operation, Kennecott was able to call this host of parties in on its side. Though the mine was ultimately nationalized, Chile's worsened unilateral alternatives to Kennecott's preferred outcome seemed to give the firm a better position in the dealing than those of similar companies such as Anaconda that did not take such actions.

When no-agreement alternatives are interdependent, one can simultaneously improve one's alternatives while worsening another side's. The 1971 Maltese-British negotiations over renewed base rights provide an instructive example.[5] Britain had enjoyed the use of a Maltese naval base and had extended its use to other NATO countries. Nevertheless advances in ship design and warfare methods had rendered the Maltese bases of considerably less importance than they were, say, during World War II, when Malta had played a crucial role for the Allies. To obtain much improved base rental terms, however, the Maltese made highly visible overtures to the Soviet Union about locating one of their bases in Malta. They also approached Libya and other Arab states for large assistance payments in return for Malta's neutrality.

At a simple level, this increased the attractiveness of Malta's alternatives to negotiated agreement with the British. But the same moves made Britain's alternatives to agreement with Malta considerably worse. As the *Times* of London noted, "What is important . . . is not that [the facilities] are badly needed in an age of nuclear war but that they should not on the other hand be possessed by Russia." Not only did these actions put pressure directly on Britain, but NATO anxiety, which the Maltese carefully cultivated, served indirectly to increase the pressure on Britain. Beyond quadrupling their base

[5]Wriggens (1976).

rental payments from the British, other NATO members ultimately agreed to provide supplemental aid to Malta. Without passing judgment on the tactics employed, it is worth highlighting the fact that the Maltese actions to improve their own alternatives and worsen those of others did appear to shift both sides' perceptions of the bargaining range in a way that favored Malta. This appeared to result in a substantially better agreement for Malta.

While one should consider improving one's no-agreement alternatives, shoring up vulnerable ones, or generating new ones, such actions typically involve expending resources such as effort, time, and money. In general, resources should go toward affecting alternatives until the expected improvement in the value of the outcome from expending additional resources just equals the cost of doing so.[6] (Naturally, this involves subjective calculation.) Worsening others' alternatives may create additional costs. When such behavior is seen as out of bounds, it may induce retaliation and conflict escalation as well as set unfortunate precedents for future behavior. Whether moves to change another party's no-agreement alternatives are seen as legitimate and appropriate depends, of course, on the parties' prior understandings and accepted norms of behavior.

Inflated Perceptions of Alternatives Are Common

A negotiator's evaluation of alternatives depends on perceptions. As Chapter Six discusses in detail, many tactics for claiming value involve attempts advantageously to shape others' perceptions of the bargaining range. Moreover, it is well to keep in mind that different people perceive the same outcomes differently. In some settings, negotiators fail to analyze their no-agreement alternatives and implicitly undervalue them. In others, where alternatives tend to be well-defined, negotiators systematically make the opposite mistake.

---

[6]More precisely, taking simultaneous account of other tactical possibilites, one should expend resources to enhance alternatives or generate new ones if the subjective probability distribution of negotiated outcomes thereby improves sufficiently to offset the expenditure. Optimal search theory shows that, to set a reservation price for the negotiation, one need not actually expend resources to search when the distribution of possible negotiated outcomes would not thereby be changed. In such a case, one merely needs to take such prospects into account when calculating the reservation price. When the search for alternatives can change the distribution of negotiated outcomes, one may well search less promising distributions of alternatives if actually finding a better alternative would sufficiently improve the outcome distribution. Lax (1985) discusses these issues in more detail.

In an experiment at Harvard, the findings of which have been
replicated in many contexts with students and executives, players
were given detailed information about the history of an out-of-court
negotiation over insurance claims arising from a personal injury
case.[7] They were not told whether the negotiators settled or if the case
went to court. Each player was assigned the role either of the insurance company representative or the plaintiff. After reading the case
file, the players were privately asked to give their true probability estimates that the plaintiff would win the case and, given a win, the expected amount of the ultimate judgment. Systematically, those assigned the role of the plaintiff estimated the chances of winning and
the expected amount of winning as much higher than those assigned
the role of the insurance company-defendant. Players who were not
assigned a role prior to reading the case gave private estimates that
generally fell between those of the advocates for each position.

Similar results have been found in cases involving the worth of a
company that is up for sale. Even given identical business information, balance sheets, income statements, and the like, those assigned
to buy the company typically rate its true value as low, while those assigned to sell it give much higher best estimates. Neutral observers
tend to rank the potential someplace in between.

These results, in combination with many other negotiation experiences,[8] suggest that in certain classes of situations, advocates tend
to overestimate the attractiveness of their alternatives to negotiated
agreement. If each side has an inflated expectation of its alternatives,
no zone of possible agreement for negotiation may exist. Awareness
of this common bias dictates a conscious attempt to be more realistic
about one's own case, not to "believe one's own line" too much, and
to be aware of and seek to alter counterparts' estimates of their alternatives.

A number of tactics can help deflate unrealistic perceptions. At a
minimum one may seek advice from uninvolved parties whose estimates are not colored by their roles. So-called mini-trials can bring
executives of opposing sides together to hear the others' arguments
presented in a mock courtroom setting.[9] Firsthand exposure to the
other side's point of view may alter executives' estimates of the court
alternative which may have been derived from overly optimistic cor-

[7]See Raiffa (1982). Similar experiments were performed by Bazerman and Neale
(1983).

[8]See also Bazerman (1983).

[9]See Goldberg, Green, and Sander (1985).

porate counsel. Roger Fisher even suggests establishing *settlement* divisions of law firms or general counsels' offices (whose lawyers would not be involved in the court "alternative"), separate from *litigation* departments whose lawyers would prepare cases for trial. Of course, the optimistic biases of the litigators might even make them more effective advocates if no settlement could be achieved.[10]

One often hears that a particular dispute is not "ripe" or "mature" for negotiation or resolution. This state of affairs often arises when the sides have incompatibly optimistic estimates of their non-cooperative alternatives. For example, a consortium of midwestern power companies proposed to build a significant dam to bring electricity at lower rates to the area's customers. Environmentalists opposed this plan, claiming that it would damage the downstream habitat of the endangered whooping crane. Farm groups lined up against the project, fearing that the dam would reduce water flow in the area. Though the sides tried early on to negotiate, each believed its alternatives to agreement to be quite favorable. Negotiations sputtered along until the environmentalists and farmers won a substantial court victory (quite unexpected by the power companies). In their turn, the power companies got strong indications of favorable congressional action—which could have overridden the court's action. With each side's perceptions of its alternatives to a negotiated agreement considerably less optimistic than at the outset, the stage was set for more fruitful negotiations, which ultimately resulted in a creative agreement for a smaller dam, stream flow guarantees, and a trust fund for preserving the habitats of the endangered whooping crane.

Many other examples could be presented of disputes that are not "ripe" for negotiation given the parties' inconsistently optimistic perceptions of their alternatives.[11] If "not ripe" is the diagnosis, however, getting people in a room together and employing all sorts of careful procedural means to foster negotiation will likely be to no avail. The basic condition for a negotiated agreement will not be met since possible agreements appear inferior to at least one side in comparison with its unilateral alternatives. When this is the case, strategy should focus *not* on the negotiation process but instead on actions *away* from the table that can reshape perceptions in a manner that generates a zone of possible agreement.

[10]See Fisher (1983).

[11]For example, Zartman and Berman (1982) give the example of fruitless negotiations in the Middle East preceding the Camp David accord and the changes in perceptions of no-agreement alternatives that stimulated the accord.

In each of these cases, then, negotiators should anticipate inflated perceptions of alternatives. The implied prescriptions are (1) be aware of and seek to counteract the biases of one's own role, and (2) where the sides have incompatible perceptions of the attractiveness of alternatives, focus negotiating strategy on altering those perceptions so that joint action will appear preferable by comparison.

Manipulating Alternatives Can
Influence Decentralized Bargaining

The potent effects of changing no-agreement alternatives go well beyond the bargain at hand and extend to a network of negotiations to be carried on by others. Quite frequently the rules, structures, conditions, or organizational systems imposed by others will heavily condition decentralized bargaining. Altering the rules or the structure within which others' negotiations occur may change the no-agreement alternatives of these negotiations and, often, their outcomes.

For example, in professional sports, a league representing team owners typically negotiates with a players' union over the players' rights to move to other teams and the teams' rights over the players. This overarching league-union agreement governs a large number of individual negotiations between players and teams. Under some earlier league rules, players were bound to one team and could not negotiate with others; thus, a player had *no* alternatives (except nonsports occupations). Predictably, this "reserve clause" system tilted the balance in favor of teams and yielded lower player salaries. At the other end of the rules spectrum, players may have the right to negotiate with *all* teams and play for the highest bidder. Under this "free agency" rule, the players have many alternatives and, not surprisingly, player salaries tend to be much higher.

Between free agency and the reserve clause lie many intermediate options that specify the player's alternatives in more balanced ways. For example, a since-replaced agreement in professional football specified that if a player did not reach agreement with his team, the player had to sit out for a year—without salary or experience—before entering unrestricted free agent status. Another set of rules might allow the player free negotiations but with a limited number of teams. The important point in this example is that the structure of rules governing a large number of decentralized bargains affects those bargains through the alternatives available to the parties.

A budgeting procedure used at IBM powerfully illustrates this point. In this very successful firm, certain budgets are constructed by negotiation among all interested divisions and departments. Each division or department has the option of concurring or not concurring with proposals of the others. "Nonconcurrences" that cannot be resolved by negotiation escalate through corporate ranks and finally reach a central management committee that renders a decision. Thus, top management stimulates a variety of constructive negotiations among the people in the company who are closest to the problems and who have the most expertise. High level "arbitration" here functions as the ultimate alternative to negotiated agreement among those who are under this budget procedure at IBM.

Beyond resolving individual disputes, top management affects perceptions in two ways by its pattern of decisions. First, by affecting employees' perceptions of the costs of disagreement, top management stimulates a large number of lower-level agreements. Second, it affects the *content* of lower-level agreements in ways that accord with key corporate objectives and policies. Recourse to the central management committee becomes a desirable alternative for those whose lower-level disagreement is for reasons that accord with preferred company strategy or norms. Similarly, the escalation alternative becomes unpleasant and very costly for those who disagree for reasons that are out of line with preferred policies. By carefully manipulating perceptions of alternatives to lower-level agreement, corporate management in this very successful firm effectively influences a large number of negotiations that are carried on throughout the company. Managers in many settings enjoy analogous possibilities.

Summary

Throughout this chapter, we have mainly treated negotiation as a means, albeit an important and promising one, to further desired ends. Because only agreements more valuable than the alternatives should be acceptable, the no-agreement alternatives should set each party's reservation value and thus establish the bargaining range or set. Hence, no-agreement alternatives set the limits of negotiation. As such, each negotiator should evaluate all sides' alternatives and, when his own no-agreement alternative seems superior to any agreement that can be reached, he should choose it.

Because tactical moves can favorably change perceptions of no-agreement alternatives and thus of the bargaining range, what goes on "away from the table" may be just as important as tactics "at the table." One is generally in a better negotiating position when one's alternatives improve and one's counterpart's alternatives erode. As Chapter Six elaborates, bargainers employ a variety of tactics to create the reality or impression that this is happening. By changing the no-agreement alternatives in decentralized bargains carried out by others, one can similarly affect the outcomes.

In certain classes of negotiations, many bargainers may tend to overlook and implicitly undervalue their no-agreement alternatives. In such cases, the advice to identify and evaluate alternatives should be helpful. In other situations, negotiators tend to be overconfident about their alternatives, and this often means that the dispute is not "ripe" for settlement. There, negotiators should focus on altering those perceptions so that, by comparison, joint action will appear preferable.

In short, negotiators often pay insufficient attention to their alternatives, which set the lower limits of value that any acceptable agreement must offer. But once they have evaluated their alternatives, the challenge is to find ways of cooperating to do even better. To do "better"—and even to evaluate alternatives—negotiators need yardsticks of value. So far we have discussed creating and claiming value, the *process* of negotiation, and alternatives to agreements, which imply its *limits*. It is now time to delve more deeply into the *measure* of negotiation, the parties' interests that are at stake. It is to interests that we turn in the next chapter.

CHAPTER FOUR

Interests: The Measure of Negotiation

PEOPLE NEGOTIATE to further their interests. And negotiation advisors urge attention to interests—often solemnly, as if the suggestion were original and surprising. Yet the classic admonition to "know thyself" surely scoops any late twentieth century advice of this sort. So, academic compulsiveness aside, why write a chapter on interests or, more to the point, why read one?

In part, negotiators often focus on interests, but conceive of them too narrowly; we will argue for a more expansive conception. But because interests often conflict, simply listing them without understanding their tradeoffs is a bit like writing out a recipe without including the proportions. Negotiators need ways to assess the relative importance of their various interests; we will try to clarify the logic of assessing tradeoffs.

As hard as it may be to sort out one's own interests, understanding how others see theirs—*their* subjective scheme of values are perceived through *their* peculiar psychological filters—can be extraordinarily difficult. Obviously, suggesting a stretch "in the other person's shoes" is good advice; equally obviously, it is only a starting point. In this chapter, we will try to go further.

An Expansive Conception of a Negotiator's Interests

In evaluating the interests at stake, a typical negotiator might focus on commodities that can be bought and sold or on concrete terms that can be written into a contract or treaty. And negotiators definitely have such interests: the crippled plaintiff desperately wants compensation; a sales manager cares intensely about prices, profit margins, return on investment, and his own compensation. Managers may derive value from seeing their particular product sweep the market or furthering some vision of the public interest.

Throughout this chapter, we assume that a negotiator wants to do well for himself. Of course, "doing well" is only measured with respect to the things he cares about, whether out of direct self-interest or concerns for others' welfare. Thus for a negotiator to do "better" need not imply that he presses for more money or a bigger share. Rather, it means advancing the totality of his interests, which may include money and other tangibles but also fairness, the well-being of his counterparts, and the collegiality of the process. Furthering Robert's interests may mean taking less money to obtain a fair settlement by a friendly process. By the same token, Helen may want only to humiliate her counterpart publicly and extract from him the very biggest check.

Especially in business negotiations, however, a common misconception is that one's counterpart's interests extend only to the bottom line. Yet imagine holding rigidly to this assumption when negotiating with the number two executive in a technical products company from the upper half of the Fortune 500. He echoed his firm's philosophy when he stated.

> Our most important goal is to do a good job. We don't have a specific growth target, but what we want to do is make a contribution. Not just a "me too" thing, but to develop technically superior products. Another goal is to earn our way, to grow from our own resources. A third goal is to make this an interesting and satisfactory place to work. The fourth goal . . . there must be a fourth goal. I mentioned it also in a speech at [a nearby university]. Oh yes, the fourth goal is to make a profit.[1]

Negotiators' interests can go beyond the obvious and tangible; take the simple pleasure one derives from being treated with respect, even in a one-time encounter. Self-esteem and "face" are often latent

[1]Donaldson and Lorsch (1984: 85).

interests; moves that cause loss of face or self-esteem can threaten the whole negotiation or at least make the obvious and tangible interests relatively less important. A stockbroker may want to develop her relationship with a customer for the future business it may bring; the plaintiff may feel anxious at the thought of a trial and may be willing to take a reduced settlement to avoid courtroom trauma. Negotiators have good reasons to be concerned with their reputations. A person who is widely known never to recede once he takes a position may rarely be called on for concessions. Fisher and Ury argue that a negotiator should seek to be known as reaching agreements only by means of "objective" principles; once achieved, among other effects, such a "principled" reputation may reduce the need to haggle.[2]

Beyond such concerns about reputation, relationship, and process, negotiators often care about subtle aspects of precedent. For example, Luther, a product manager in a fast-growing medical devices firm, had for the second time confronted his colleague Françoise with a vigorous demand for priority use of the firm's advertising department—even though Françoise had informally "reserved" this block of the ad department's time for her people. After analyzing her interests in this unexpected negotiation, Françoise balked at a few seemingly reasonable settlements that Luther suggested. Why? Françoise sought to avoid two undesirable precedents: (1) in the *substance* of the issue (her division needed to count absolutely on future ad department reservations) and (2) in the *procedure* set for raising a whole range of similar matters (she wanted to bolster the use of established policies). Concern with both types of precedent abounds in organizations and elsewhere.

Strategic interests are often at stake for managers. By this, we refer to the alignment of a particular decision with the manager's long-term personal or institutional strategy. Suppose that a prompt investment in the capacity to manage mutual funds appears likely to have high short-term potential for a firm whose long-term plan has been to develop expertise in real estate investments. Would a key manager's proposal now to devote substantial energy to mutual funds research and investment be wise? Recourse to strategic rather than short-term financial analysis may unravel the firm's best interests in this case.

Through her actions in one negotiation, a manager may have an interest in reducing the cost of later encounters and in affecting their outcomes. A manager may thus strive to instill in subordinates the

[2]Fisher and Ury (1981).

impression that explicit bargaining is impossible and that her commands must be obeyed. Perhaps the back-and-forth process has become too costly and inefficient for the task at hand. In such cases, paradoxically, a prime managerial interest in routine dealings may actually be to drive out future overt bargaining. It is exceedingly ironic that a powerful interest to be achieved through a determined pattern of negotiation may be to establish an impregnable image of rigid hierarchy, potent command, and iron control—that brooks *no* conscious negotiation. Especially in early encounters, say, between a freshly hired vice president and others in the firm, the new officer may see her central interest as establishing a pattern of deference by others to her "suggestions." Or she may strongly weigh the effects on her perceived track record or esteem as an expert so that others may be more likely to defer to her in the future.

Comparing obvious, "bottom line" interests with "others"—reputation, precedent, relationships, and the like—a very detailed study of corporate resource allocation in a multidivisional chemical company noted:

> These are the dimensions a manager takes into account when he makes his decisions. In some instances they far outweigh the importance of the substantive issues in his assessment of decision-making priorities.
>
> It is worth pausing to emphasize this point. There is a very strong tendency in financial or decision-making treatments of capital budgeting to regard the personal status of managers as noise, "a source of bias". . . . Theoreticians do not consider the problem a rational manager faces as he considers committing himself to a project over time. He has made other commitments in the past, other projects are competing for funds and engineering at the division level, and other managers are competing for the jobs he seeks. At the same time those same managers are his peers and friends. Whatever he does, he is more than likely going to have to live with those same men for a decade or more. While only some projects are technically or economically independent, all are organizationally interdependent.[3]

It is not always easy to know how to evaluate interests; sometimes they may derive from interactions too complex to understand directly. In such cases, carefully chosen proxy interests may help. For example, the President of the United States cannot possibly predict the effects of any particular negotiated outcome on all of his substan-

[3]Bower (1972: 302).

tive interests over the course of his term or beyond. Taking account of this, Richard Neustadt, in his classic bargaining manual, *Presidental Power*, counsels him to evaluate his dealings in terms of three particular interests.[4] The first is obvious: his interest in the substance of the immediate issue. Second, the President's professional reputation can heavily affect the reactions of important Washingtonians to his later concerns and actions. The President needs the resources and cooperation of these Washingtonians to carry out his programs. Thus, beyond the substance of the issue, Neustadt suggests, the effect of the current negotiation on the President's professional reputation among Washingtonians should be a proxy interest reflecting, in part, his ability to get the Washingtonians to act in accord with his subsequent desires. Third, Neustadt argues that the President should evaluate the effect of his actions on his popular prestige. High prestige reflects the strength of his mandate and influences Washingtonians. It is, in part, a proxy interest; actions that enhance his public prestige improve his chances favorably to influence subsequent outcomes of direct concern. A President may also value popular prestige for its own sake. As a negotiator, the President may well have to trade these interests off against each other; for example, he may yield somewhat on his substantive interest in the immediate issue to enhance his reputation and prestige elsewhere.

In many positions less complex than that of the President, negotiators' interests are difficult to enumerate because the link between actions and eventual outcomes is hazy. In such cases, a negotiator may benefit by finding proxies that indicate the negotiator's subsequent influence on outcomes of concern.

Some interests are latent in most negotiators. Negotiators' self-esteem and "face" are typically at stake. Tactics such as take-it-or-leave-it offers, forced linkages, commitment moves, threats, and preemptive moves are likely to induce loss of face if a negotiator attributes concessions to his weakness and his counterpart's strength. The newly included interests can sometimes swamp the ones previously felt to be at stake and begin a destructive cycle of hostile moves as the conflict escalates. Such moves are less likely to induce such a reaction if the negotiator can attribute his concessions instead to forces beyond the control of the negotiating parties.[5]

[4]Neustadt (1980).

[5]See Deutsch and Krauss (1962); Tedeschi, Schlenker, and Bonoma (1973); and Rubin and Brown (1975).

In short, interests include anything that the negotiator cares about, any concerns that are evoked by the issues discussed. Clarifying interests, however, can sometimes be difficult. We have often found that two distinctions can help.

INTERESTS, ISSUES, AND POSITIONS

Negotiators seek to reach agreement on specific *positions* on a specific set of *issues*. For example, a potential employee may initially demand $36,000 (her position) for her salary (the issue). Her underlying *interests* may be in financial security, enhanced lifestyle, organizational status, and advanced career prospects. Or, recall the last chapter's discussion of how the desire of a midwestern electric utility company to build a dam collided with farmers' needs for water and environmentalists' concern for the downstream habitat of endangered whooping cranes. Increased economic return, irrigated crops, and preserved species were the relevant *interests*; the parties conflicted over the *issue* of the dam's construction, and took *positions* for and against it.

interests. Of course, many different sets of issues may reflect the same interests: a country might seek to serve its interest in mineral development through negotiations with the same company over issues as varied as simple royalty concessions, joint ventures, or service contracts. Conceivably, the country's interest could be equally satisfied by different terms on each of these alternative issues. The issue at hand, however, may be only a proxy for imperfectly related interests. In the Paris peace talks the United States may have insisted on a round table and the North Vietnamese a rectangular one. The relevant compromise would hardly have been oval. The real interests were far from the rectangular versus round issue. Instead, they involved underlying questions of diplomatic standing and national resolve.

Many negotiators retard creativity by failing to distinguish the issues under discussion from their underlying interests. When the issues under discussion poorly match the interests at stake, modifications of the issues sometimes enable all parties to satisfy their interests better. For example, let us again refer to the conflict between the midwestern utility company that hoped to build a dam, the farmers concerned with downstream water flow, and the environmentalists who cared about the whooping crane habitat. After several years of costly and embittering litigation, the parties came to a resolution by a shift to issues that matched their underlying interests in a more fruitful manner. By moving from positions ("yes" and "no") on the issue of the dam's construction to discussions about the nature of downstream water guarantees, the amount of a trust fund to protect the whooping crane habitat, and the size of the dam, the parties reached an agreement that left all of them better off.

Negotiators who mistakenly see their interests as perfectly aligned with their positions on issues may be less likely to shift issues creatively. They might even suspiciously oppose proposals to modify the issues. Indeed, in attempting to protect their perceived interests, such negotiators may dig their heels in hard to avoid budging from their desired positions. In the above conflict over "dam versus no dam," positions could have hardened to a point where the grim determination of each side to prevail over the other—whatever the cost—would have ruled out any real search for preferable options. At a minimum, such rigid dealings can be frustrating and time-consuming; impasses or poor agreements often result.

The prevalence of hard-fought, time-consuming, unimaginative "positional" negotiations led Fisher and Ury to propose a general rule: "Focus on interests, not positions."[6] While we think that negotiators should always keep the distinction clearly in mind, focusing exclusively on interests may not always be wise. When the parties have deep and conflicting ideological differences, for example, satisfactory agreements on "smaller" issues may only be possible if ideological concerns do not arise. In such cases, the negotiations should focus on the issues or a much narrower set of interests—not the full set of underlying interests. For example, two hostile but neighboring countries may be embroiled in tribal, religious, or ideological conflict, but they may successfully settle a sewage problem on their common border by dealing only with this more limited issue. Or leftist guerilla leaders, each with an underlying interest in ruling the country, might unite on the issue of overthrowing the rightist dictator; an agreement that attempted to reconcile their underlying interests would likely be more difficult to achieve.

Moreover, a negotiator may choose to focus on an issue that, for legal or other reasons, provides greater leverage than do discussions of underlying interests. The nature-loving group that has an abiding interest in preventing land development may develop a sudden attachment to the issue of wetlands protection if the Wetlands Preser-

[6]Fisher and Ury (1981).

vation Act provides the strongest grounds for negotiating with and deterring developers.

At times, a tenacious focus on positions may yield desirable results. With a group of landowners, the CEO of a major mining company had negotiated the general outlines of a contract along with a few critical particulars. Then he turned the rest of the negotiations over to a company lawyer to finish in short order—before a hard-to-obtain environmental permit expired. One provision that the second group of negotiators inherited had not been extensively debated before. Yet its tentative resolution, while barely acceptable to the landowners, clearly would confer great benefits on the company. Though the landowners' representatives sought to focus on "interests" and "fairness" in order to undo the provision, the company's lawyer made a powerful commitment to it and turned a completely deaf ear to all argument, urging instead that they get on with "unresolved" matters. Though this tactic risked negative repercussions on the other issues, the lawyer's firm commitment to a position was an effective means of claiming value in this instance.

Thus interests should be distinguished from issues and positions.[7] Focusing on interests can help one develop a better understanding of mutual problems and invent creative solutions. But such a focus may not always be desirable when, for example, underlying interests are diametrically opposed or when a focus on particular issues or positions provides leverage. Whatever the focus, however, interests measure the value of any position or agreement.

INTRINSIC AND INSTRUMENTAL INTERESTS

It should be clear that negotiators may have many kinds of interests: in money and financial security, in a particular conception of

---

[7]More technically minded readers may find the following formulation helpful. Let u represent a negotiator's multiattribute utility function: the attributes of u are the negotiator's interests. Let p be a vector of positions taken on the issue vector i (.). Let f be a vector-valued function that reflects the negotiator's beliefs about how well an agreement with positions p on issues i advances his interests. Thus, an agreement p gives the negotiator utility $u(f(i(p)))$. Typically, of course, he will be uncertain about the relationship between issues and interests, which we might model by letting w represent the random variable reflecting relevant uncertain events and letting $f(i(p),w)$ reflect his beliefs about the relationship between issues and interests conditional on w. Thus, we might say that he wants to choose p to maximize $E_w[u(f(i(p),w))]$, where E_w is the expectation over the negotiator's subjective beliefs about w.

the public interest, in the quality of products, in enhancing a reputation as a skilled bargainer, in maintaining a working relationship, in precedents, and so on. However, one distinction—between intrinsic and instrumental interests—can provide an economical way to capture some important qualities of interests, call negotiators' attention to often-overlooked, sometimes subtle interests, and lead to improved agreements.

One's interest in an issue is instrumental if favorable terms on the issue are valued because of their effect on subsequent dealings. One's interest in an issue is intrinsic if one values favorable terms of settlement on the issue independent of any subsequent dealings. Thus, a divorcing parent's interest in gaining custody of his or her child, the farmer's interest in water rights, and a country's interest in secure borders can usefully be thought of as intrinsic interests. Such interests need not have any obvious or agreed-upon economic value. For example, a sixty-year-old venture capitalist was negotiating the dissolution of a strikingly successful technology partnership with a young, somewhat standoffish woman whom he had brought on as a partner two years before. At first he bargained very hard over the financial terms because, as it turned out, he saw them as indicating who had really contributed important ideas and skills to the venture's success. When the young woman belatedly acknowledged her genuine respect for his ideas and contributions, he became much less demanding on the financial issues. In this instance, it happened that the venture capitalist had a strong intrinsic interest in psychic gratification from acknowledgment of his role as mentor and father-figure.

Most issues affect both intrinsic and instrumental interests. Dealings with a subordinate who wants to hire an assistant can arouse an intrinsic interest in the overall size of the budget as well as concern with the perceived precedent this sets for the support his peers may expect—an instrumental interest. Recognizing the distinction may lead to improved agreements; the subordinate who can create a justifiable device to prevent decisions about his staff support from setting precedents may well receive authorization to hire a new assistant.

One of the central reasons we focus on the intrinsic-instrumental distinction is for the light it sheds on three often-misunderstood aspects of negotiation: interests in the process, in relationships, and in principles.

"Process" Interests—Intrinsic and Instrumental　Analysts often assume that negotiators evaluate agreements by measuring the value

obtained from the outcome. Yet, negotiators may care about the process of bargaining as well. Even with no prospect of further interaction, some would prefer a negotiated outcome reached by pleasant, cooperative discussion to the same outcome reached by abusive, threat-filled dealings. Others might derive value from a strident process that gives them the satisfied feeling of having extracted something from their opponents. Either way, negotiators can have intrinsic interests in the character of the negotiation process itself.

Beyond such intrinsic valuation, an unpleasant process can dramatically affect future dealings; the supplier who is berated and threatened may be unresponsive when his later cooperation would help. Indeed, negotiators often have strong instrumental interests in building trust and confidence early in the negotiation process in order to facilitate jointly beneficial agreements.

"Relationship" Interests—Intrinsic and Instrumental Negotiators often stress the value of their relationships; this interest sometimes achieves an almost transcendent status. For example, Fisher and Ury say that "every negotiator has two interests: in the substance and in the relationship."[8] Many negotiators derive intrinsic value from developing or furthering a pleasant relationship. Moreover, when repeated dealings are likely, most negotiators perceive the instrumental value of developing an effective working relationship. After studying hundreds of managers in many settings, John Kotter sensibly concluded that:

> Good working relationships based on some combination of respect, admiration, perceived need, obligation, and friendship are a critical source of power in helping to get things done. Without these relationships, even the best possible idea could be rejected or resisted in an environment where diversity breeds suspicion and interdependence precludes giving orders to most of the relevant players. Furthermore, since these relationships serve as important information channels, without them one may never be able to establish the information one needs to operate effectively.[9]

Of course, in the dissolution of a partnership or the divorce of a childless couple with few assets, the parties may find no instrumental value in furthering their relationship; that is, the parties would not be willing to trade substantive gains on, say, financial terms, to enhance

[8]Fisher and Ury (1981).
[9]Kotter (1985: 40).

their future dealings. In fact, a bitter divorcing couple may actually prefer a financial outcome that requires absolutely no future contact between them over another that is better for both in tax terms, say, but requires them to deal with each other in the future. Similarly, a division head with two valuable but constantly warring employees may have a keen interest in separating them organizationally, in effect to prevent any active relationship between them. And when dealing with an obnoxious salesperson who has come to the door or by the office, one's interest in the "relationship" may mainly be to terminate it.

Interests In "Principles"—Intrinsic and Instrumental Negotiators may discover shared norms or principles relevant to their bargaining problem. Such norms may include "equal division," more complex distributive judgments, historical or ethical rationales, objective or accepted standards, as well as notions that simply seem "fair" or are represented as such.[10] Acting in accord with such a norm or principle may be of intrinsic interest to one or more of the parties; for example, a settlement of $532 arrived at in accord with the mutually acknowledged principle, say, that each party should be paid in proportion to time worked, may be quite differently valued than the same dollar figure reached by haggling. Of course, an acknowledged norm need not be an absolute value in a negotiation: it may be partly or fully traded off against other interests.

Even when none of the parties derives intrinsic value from acting in accord with a particular principle, it may still guide agreement. Principles and simple notions often serve as focal points for choosing one settlement within the range of possible outcomes.[11] Equal division of a windfall may seem so irresistibly natural to the partners in a small firm that they would scarcely consider overt negotiation over who should get more.

The principles that guide agreement in the first of many related disputes may set a powerful precedent. Thus, negotiators may work hard to settle the first dispute on the basis of principles that they believe will yield favorable outcomes in subsequent disputes. They may take a loss with respect to intrinsic interests in the first negotiation in order to satisfy their instrumental interests in the principles used to guide the agreement.

[10]See Gulliver (1979) and Fisher and Ury (1981).
[11]Schelling (1960).

In short, with many less tangible interests such as process, relationships, or fairness, a negotiator should ask why they are valued. Distinguishing between their instrumental and intrinsic components can help. But even with these components sorted out, how can a negotiator go about assessing their relative importance? More generally, what logic guides setting priorities among conflicting interests?

Thinking About Tradeoffs

Listing one's interests as well as a best guess at those of others helps. But, difficult questions tend to arise in negotiations that force one to make sacrifices on some interests in order to gain on others. How much of a trade is desirable? In buying a seller-financed house, how should Ralph evaluate higher purchase prices compared to lower mortgage interest rates? How much more should a manufacturer be willing to pay for the next quality grade of components? How much should the sales manager trade on price for the prospects of a better relationship? How much should a manager be willing to give up on substance to secure a favorable precedent?

Thinking about tradeoffs is often excruciatingly difficult and done very badly. Yet, whether or not negotiators choose to ponder priorities, they effectively make tradeoffs by their choices and agreements in negotiation. We believe that negotiators benefit by being self-conscious and reflective about their interests and the tradeoffs they are willing to make among them. We therefore discuss several methods to illuminate tradeoffs. These methods draw primarily on judgment about interests, not about negotiating. The methods we consider help to convert developed substantive judgments into forms useful for analysis and practice. Finally, although these techniques have formal origins rooted in management science and technical economics,[12] we find that their prime value comes in their contribution to clear thinking rather than from their potential for quantification. While negotiators may often choose not to quantify their tradeoffs, they may benefit greatly by employing the same style of thought in comparing interests.

Certain tradeoffs are easy to specify. The present value or total cost of a loan is a well-known mathematical function of the amount and duration of the loan and the interest rate. Thus, beginning with a

[12]For example, see Raiffa (1982), Keeney and Raiffa (1976), Barclay and Peterson (1976), or Greenhalgh and Neslin (1981).

given price and interest rate for the self-financed home, Ralph can calculate precisely the benefit of a 1 percent decrease in the interest rate and how much of a price increase he would be willing to accept before he became indifferent to the original price and interest rate. Yet other tradeoffs may seem much harder to think about, especially ones that involve "intangibles" such as principles, anxiety about a process, or the relationship.

Assessing Tradeoffs Among Seemingly Intangible Interests Seemingly intangible tradeoffs can also be dealt with in analogous ways. The plaintiff crippled in a car accident wishes to negotiate an out-of-court settlement with an insurance company that is better than her alternative of a full court trial. Suppose that only taking trial uncertainties and legal fees into account, she would be willing to accept a settlement of $300,000. But, this analysis leaves her uncomfortable. The trial would cause her great anxiety. Yet her analysis so far does not take this anxiety into account. How should she take this into account in her preparation for negotiation? Perhaps she should lower her minimum requirements, but by how much? How can she even think about this?

After several anxious, inconclusive struggles with this assessment, someone asks her to vividly imagine the anxiety she would feel during a trial. He then asks her to imagine that a pharmacist offered to sell her a magic potion that would completely eliminate the feeling of anxiety from court proceedings. What would be the most she would pay for the potion before the trial? Would she pay $10? "That's silly. Of course." Would she pay $100? "Sure." $100,000? "Certainly not, that's one-third of my minimum settlement!" What about $50,000? "Probably not." $1000. "I think so." $10,000? "Well, that's a tough one. But, if push came to shove, the trial would be an awful experience so, probably yes." $25,000? "Maybe not, but I'm not sure." . . . And so on.

We want to stress our opinion that the important point in making such assessments is not quantitative precision. An absolutely precise cutoff would seem artificial. What is important is to get a sense of the order of magnitude of the value she places on avoiding anxiety. Here we see that she would pay between $10,000 and $25,000 or a little more to eliminate the anxiety. Thus, she should be willing to reduce her minimum settlement requirements by that amount because a negotiated settlement would avoid the anxiety. She should, of course, strive for more, but she can feel more comfortable knowing that her minimum requirements now roughly reflect her interest in avoiding trial anxiety.

Similarly, the insurance company executive may feel that going to trial against a plaintiff who evokes such sympathy will harm the firm's reputation. Yet how should he value this reputation damage and how should it affect his approach to the negotiation? As described in this thumbnail sketch, in comparing the court alternative to possible negotiated agreements, the executive sees two interests at stake—money and reputation. He could try to value the reputation damage directly by estimating the number of present and future customers he would lose and the financial loss this would create. If he finds such direct assessment difficult, he could attempt, like the plaintiff, to monetize the "intangible" interest. What is the most he would be willing to pay a public relations firm to completely undo the reputation damage? If at most he would be willing to pay $20,000, he could modify his maximum acceptable settlement and take this into account when negotiating with the plaintiff.

In some instances, concerns with precedent, prestige, anxiety, reputation, and similar interests loom large; negotiators focus on them and, finding them difficult to weigh, feel paralyzed with respect to their choices as a negotiator. After fretting inconclusively, the negotiator may ask himself how much he would be willing to pay to have the prestige conferred upon him by other means. He might discover that he values the prestige possibilities little relative to possible substantive gains. Or, by similar analytical introspection, he might discover that he would be willing to pay only a small sum to avoid an undesirable precedent. In such cases, the negotiator would have learned a great deal. First, the intangible interest is a second or third order concern rather than a first order one as he originally feared; he can now feel freer to make concessions on the less important interest if necessary. Second, unless the choice between packages becomes close, he may need to pay little attention to this interest. In short, much of the purpose of such assessments is more to discover the relative importance of different interests than to be painstakingly precise about monetary or other valuations.

In other instances, interests in precedent or reputation turn out on reflection to overwhelm the possible improvements in substantive outcome. Suppose that a lawyer working on a highly publicized class action suit against a corporation has an interest in his financial compensation and in the reputation he might develop by exceeding expectations for how favorable a settlement he can get for his clients. Even if he finds the range of possible financial compensation paltry, he may see that his interest in enhancing his reputation and political ambitions is extremely well-served by every increment he can obtain in the settlement. Thus, he may bargain tenaciously on his clients' behalf. In this case, the monetary interest was not the first-order concern. In other instances, simple self-assessment may suggest that the monetary and nonmonetary issues are roughly comparable concerns or, of course, that the monetary aspects predominate.

A More General Approach for Assessing Tradeoffs The judgment that one "cares more about quality than price" cannot be made independently of the range of possible values of quality and price. That is, in the abstract, the manufacturer may say that he cares more about quality than about price. However, the total increment in technologically feasible quality may well be small; the price differential necessary to achieve it may well be undesirably high. Relative to the feasible range of qualities, the manufacturer actually places greater weight on price. Similarly, the management negotiator who thinks that she cares more about obtaining productivity-enhancing changes in work rules than about wages must analyze the ranges of work rules and wages that are possible outcomes of this negotiation. Suppose wages could range from a minimum of $10 an hour to a maximum of $13 an hour—and that this increment would have a significant impact on her firm's competitiveness. Yet if the increment from the worst to best possible work rules was small and would only marginally affect her firm's competitiveness, she should give greater weight or importance to wages in this negotiation. Her rate of tradeoff should follow from comparing her valuation of the wage increment between $10 and $13 with her valuation of the benefit of moving from the worst to best work rules and not from the judgment that she "cares more" about one or the other issue in general.

This leads to a straightforward method for such assessments. Like the preceding examples, the purpose of this method is to help organize one's subjective judgments to get a clearer sense of the relative importance of various interests. Again, we are concerned with orders of magnitude rather than precise quantification. To illustrate the central elements of this approach, we shall work through the thought process in a highly stylized, simplified example and then discuss the more general lessons for thinking about tradeoffs.

ASSESSING LISA'S INTERESTS. Consider Lisa, a thirty-four year-old second-level manager who has been offered a position in another division of her firm as the supervisor of a soon-to-be-created department. She must soon negotiate with William, a long-time engineer who moved into senior management ranks seven years ago and has cautiously but steadily improved his division's results. Lisa has narrowed the issues she will have to negotiate to three: the salary, vacation time, and the number of staff for the new department. We will ask her to analyze her interests and then draw on her subjective judgment to assign 100 points to the issues in a way that reflects their relative importance to her.[13] To begin, she should assess the range of possibilities for each issue. Based on a variety of discussions with William and with others in the firm, and on the results of numerous feelers, Lisa has concluded that the salary could plausibly run from $32,000 to $40,000, the vacation from two weeks to four weeks, and the staff size from ten to twenty. Suppose that her current job pays her $32,000, gives her four weeks of vacation, and assigns her a staff of 10. (See Table 4.1.)

She should start by imagining the least appealing scenario: $32,000, two weeks of vacation, and a staff of ten. Lisa's next task is to assess her relative preferences on each issue. To do this, she must decide which one of the three incremental improvements she values most. That is, would she feel best with (1) $40,000 salary but only two weeks' vacation and ten subordinates; with (2) four weeks' vacation but only $32,000 salary and ten subordinates; or with (3) twenty subordinates but only $32,000 salary and two weeks of vacation? In making this evaluation, she examines her interests in money and the effects of a higher salary on her satisfaction, as well as the peace of mind and pleasure from longer vacations. On further reflection, she realizes that she must also consider her ability to do her job effectively and thus to improve her subsequent career prospects. A bigger staff could help her effectiveness directly; enhanced organizational status from a big staff and high salary may independently bolster her job prospects as well as add to her effectiveness. Suppose that after contemplating her interests in this way, Lisa decides that she prefers the salary increment to the other two increments, and, of the other two, she prefers the staff increment to the vacation possibilities.

Now comes a harder part. She must allocate 100 points—importance weights—among the three increments in a way that reflects her underlying subjective feelings. Would she prefer the package with the largest salary increment but minimum vacation and staff to the pack-

---

[13]The following example contains certain technical aspects that need not be mastered to understand the logic of assessing tradeoffs. As such, some readers may wish to skim this section and turn to the next section, "Assessing William's Interests."

TABLE 4.1
Lisa's Negotiation

ISSUES	RANGE
Salary	$32,000–40,000
Vacation	2–4 weeks
Staff	10–20 people

---

age with the lowest salary but maximum staff and vacation? If so, she should allocate more than 50 points to the salary increment. If she is indifferent between the two packages, she should allocate exactly 50 points to the salary increment.

Lisa decides that she slightly prefers the salary increment and assigns an importance weight of 60 points to the salary increment. Now, she can either assign importance weights to the staff and vacation increments or she can think about the relative value she places on each of the possible salaries. She begins with the latter and again compares ranges. How does she compare the salary increment from $32,000 to $35,000 with the increment between $35,000 and $40,000? The first increment would improve her housing and thus enhance her life in direct and important ways; the second increment, although larger, would go toward luxuries and saving. She thus feels indifferent between the first, smaller increment and the second, larger increment. In other words, she gives 30 of the 60 importance points to the increment between $32,000 and $35,000 and 30 to the remaining increment. Table 4.2 presents importance scores that reflect Lisa's preferences for salary; Figure 4.1 shows a plot of them. Interpreting this assessment, she would get no points if she received a salary of

---

TABLE 4.2
Lisa's Assessment of the Value of Different Salaries

SALARY	IMPORTANCE POINTS
$32,000	0
$33,000	10
$34,000	20
$35,000	30
$36,000	36
$37,000	42
$38,000	48
$39,000	54
$40,000	60

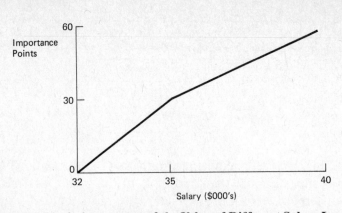

FIGURE 4.1:   Lisa's Assessment of the Value of Different Salary Levels

$32,000. If she managed to receive $35,000, she would receive 30 points, and she could move all the way up to 60 points if she were able to get a salary of $40,000. She must now assign points reflecting her comparative valuations of the vacation and staff increments. Naturally, making an assessment like this can feel like comparing apples and oranges—but Lisa will end up doing it either explicitly or implicitly.

She can assess her valuations of the other two issues by comparing their increments directly or by comparing one of the increments with her salary assessments. For example, how does the increment from ten to twenty subordinates compare with the salary increment from $32,000 to $35,000? If she is indifferent, she should assign 30 importance points to the staff increment and, thus, the remaining 10 points to the vacation increment.[14] She decides and continues in this manner, finishing the assessment by assigning 20 of the 30 importance points to the increment between ten and fifteen subordinates and 10 points to the remaining increment. Lastly, she assigns 8 of the 10 vacation points to getting the third week of vacation and 2 to the remaining week.

Table 4.3 shows a scoring system that reflects this assessment. From the table, a $35,000 salary, three weeks of vacation, and fifteen subordinates would be valued at $30 + 8 + 20 = 58$ points, whereas a salary of $37,500, two weeks of vacation and sixteen subordinates would be valued at $45 + 0 + 22 = 67$ points. If Lisa is comfortable with this assessment and the scoring system, she can use it as a shorthand

[14]To gain confidence in the assessment, she might also compare the value of the vacation investment with the values of various staff and salary increments and be sure that the assigned points are consistent with her actual preferences.

TABLE 4.3
Lisa's Assessment of the Importance of Salary, Vacation, and Staff Size

SALARY ($000)	IMPOR- TANCE POINTS	WEEKS OF VACATION	IMPOR- TANCE POINTS	STAFF SIZE	IMPOR- TANCE POINTS
32	0	2	0	10	0
33	10	3	8	15	20
34	20	4	10	20	30
35	30				
36	36				
37	42				
38	48				
39	54				
40	60				

means of evaluating and designing possible proposals and counter-proposals while preparing for and carrying out the negotiation.

It is worth noting that all the scoring is relative to an arbitrarily chosen zero point. That is, the "worst" agreement—$32,000, two weeks' vacation, and ten subordinates, the bottom of the range for each issue—receives a score of zero. All other possible agreements are scored relative to this "worst" agreement. The important comparison, though, is with her current job which, at a salary of $32,000, four weeks' vacation, and ten subordinates is valued at 10 points. Although any such scoring system is necessarily rough, Lisa can use it to evaluate possible agreements and to understand the tradeoffs she may have to make.

Comparing different increments can be difficult but a few tricks can sometimes facilitate the process. For example, Lisa might construct one package, say, of $32,000, two weeks' vacation, and twenty subordinates and another of $32,000, four weeks' vacation, and ten subordinates. But, how to compare them? Lisa might imagine that the phone rings and the call eliminates one of the options. Which option would feel worse to lose? Or, suppose that a coin flip will determine the choice of packages. Is a fifty-fifty chance of losing each appropriate? Or, would she prefer sixty-forty chances favoring one of the packages?

In helping Lisa construct this scoring system, we assumed that the value of an increment on one issue did not depend on how other issues were resolved; thus, scoring a package simply involves adding the points obtained on each issue. In some situations, though, the value of the outcome on one issue depends on how other issues are resolved.[15] For example, suppose that with a high salary Lisa would like a larger number of subordinates. With a low salary, however, she might feel aggrieved; a larger staff would mean more responsibility for which she was not compensated. Thus, how she values staff size could depend on her salary level. Such interdependent preferences could be assessed using more elaborate techniques, but the general logic of defining and comparing increments would remain roughly analogous.

ASSESSING WILLIAM'S INTERESTS.   As Lisa firms up the assessment of her own interests, she must, of course, do the same for her negotiating counterpart and potential supervisor, William. Her preliminary investigations had fairly confidently bounded the ranges of the issues, but now the question becomes how he sees his real interests in them. Tentative discussions with William left Lisa little doubt that he would prefer to pay less, allow shorter vacations, and get by with as few new staff as possible—in fact, in a meeting enthusiastically offering her the spot "in principle," William sketched the terms he felt were appropriate. There he said "a bit over $30,000, a few weeks' vacation, and only the staff she really needs." More than a little daunted by this less than forthcoming stance, Lisa feels a strong need to develop a much deeper understanding of his interests.

Asking around, she discovers that William is generally not at ease with "personnel" matters and that he tends to seek out whatever firm "policy" he can find for guidance. Fortunately for Lisa, little in the firm would be directly comparable to the new department she would head. But a few discreet inquiries turn up the fact that the supervisor of the firm's largest department makes around $39,000. Since the new department is an important endeavor, Lisa feels fairly certain that salary money will not be too tight, but that the other supervisor's compensation will make any salary above $39,000 very uncomfortable for William to consider.

Trying to ferret out his feelings about vacation, Lisa discovers that he has been a hard worker, seldom taking more than a few days or a week each year. Also he has mentioned the extreme importance of dedication and long hours during the uncertain startup of this new organizational unit. Lisa infers that the prospect of her taking extended vacations early on, while not at all uncommon elsewhere in the firm, would not sit at all well with William.

[15]The "additive scoring rule" constructed in this example is a simple case of multiattribute value or utility function. When interdependencies exist, non-additive, multi-attribute utility functions can be used in the assessment. (See Keeney and Raiffa, 1976.)

Finally, on the matter of staffing, Lisa thinks back to some comments William made during a long lunch they had together to explore the possibilities of her heading the new department. In the course of their conversation, he had mentioned two significant incidents from his career. First he recalled extreme pressure on the engineering group some years ago to come up with a new design. The group was simply too small to produce the needed results in time. Quality of work and quality of life "needlessly suffered" and, to William's mind, that kind of "economizing" makes no business or personal sense. Yet William also recounted an agonizing experience some years later when the engineering group had greatly expanded. A mild economic downturn and the loss of a major customer had forced him to lay off nearly a quarter of the group's engineers. Recalling the pain of that experience, he lamented that things would have been much better if most of those let go had never been hired, and instead, the others had worked somewhat longer hours. To Lisa, the implications of these incidents seemed obvious: William would have little problem giving her the staff that he believed she really needed but would be allergic to any perceived excess.

Lisa could then make this assessment much more precise, estimating importance weights for William. Already, however, the contours of a possible approach have begun to emerge as she considers her interests (recall Table 4.3) together with her insights into William's concerns. Lisa expects to press fairly hard for a salary toward the $39,000 range, perhaps conceding some vacation time for the last few thousand dollars. This makes sense because money is valuable to her and relatively "cheap" to him. Moreover, he cares a great deal about avoiding too much time being taken off and two extra weeks of vacation are not crucial to her. From her analysis so far of the new department's mission, Lisa has become increasingly sure that the job can be done with fifteen people, though twenty would certainly be nice. She plans to devote a great deal of time to developing and presenting a rock-solid justification of the need for fifteen.

We will not go further in exploring how William's interests might be more formally assessed or how his and Lisa's preferences could be better dovetailed.[16] And, of course, this rough assessment of an artificially simplified set of issues only starts the process. As Lisa learns more, relative valuations may be revised, issues may be reformulated, and new options invented. For example, her interests in "sal-

---

[16]Or for that matter, how to take the twin scoring systems for Lisa and William's values to produce a Pareto frontier. For a discussion of how to do this, see Raiffa (1982) or Barclay and Peterson (1976).

ary" could be expanded to include stock options, bonuses, and fringe and in-kind benefits. "Vacation" might encompass time to be taken in later years, a generous policy of accumulating unused vacation or turning it into salary, or leaves for various purposes like education. "Staff" may mean direct employees of various backgrounds and levels, "loans" from other departments, consultants, temporary help, or equipment to enhance the productivity of a given number of staff. But throughout, constant probing of each party's interests is the sine qua non of creating value by designing good negotiated agreements.

General Lessons for Assessing Interests

The most important lessons from this kind of assessment are those that help one think more clearly about the qualitative judgments that negotiators implicitly make all the time. Such evaluations are often made with respect to nominal issues rather than directly on underlying interests. Lisa's interests in money, lifestyle, peace of mind, career prospects, and organizational status are not perfectly aligned with the issues of salary, vacation limits, and staff size. When thinking about how well different packages satisfy her interests, the negotiator may discover reformulations that align more closely with her interests. If some of these "new" issues are easier to grant, they may form the basis for a better agreement.

During the process, the negotiator may learn about and change her perceptions about how well different positions on the issues serve her interests. As she learns, the relative importance of the increments on the issues may shift. If so, she should modify her assessments.

In contrast to the apparent crispness of the issues, interests are often vaguer. There may be no apparent scale with which to measure say, precedent or organizational status. Yet the same logic that is useful for making issue tradeoffs can apply to assuring the relative impact of interests. The generic steps are as follows:

- Identify the interests that may be at stake.
- For each interest, imagine the possible packages that serve it best and worst; for example, imagine the range of precedents that might follow from the negotiation. This roughly defines the increment of value associated with each interest.
- As with Lisa's job negotiations, the importance of each interest depends on the relative importance of its increment compared

to those of the other interests; for example, how does the gain from the worst to the best possible precedent compare with the gain from the worst to the best possible monetary outcome?

The currency of negotiation generally involves positions on issues but the results are measured by how well underlying interests are furthered. As such, it is helpful constantly to shuttle back and forth between abstract interests and more specific issues, both to check for consistency and to keep real concerns uppermost in mind.

Assessing the Interests of Others   Finally, it goes almost without saying that a negotiator should constantly assess his counterparts' interests and preferences. Obviously, careful listening and clear communication help this process. Uninvolved third parties can render insights not suspected by partisans wrapped up in the negotiation. Some negotiators find that, as part of preparing for the process, actually playing the other party's role can offer deepened perspectives. In various management programs at Harvard, for example, senior industrialists have been assigned the parts of environmentalists and vice versa. To simulate arms talks, high-level U.S. military officers and diplomats have been assigned to play Russian negotiators. Palestinians and Israelis have had to swap places. After some initial discomfort and reluctance, the most common reaction of participants in these exercises is surprise at how greatly such role playing enhances their understanding of each side's interests, of why others may seem intransigent, and of unexpected possibilities for agreement.

Beyond various ways of trying to put oneself in the other's shoes, assessment of another's interests may be improved by investigating:

- Past behavior in related settings, both in style and substance.
- Training and professional affiliation: engineers and financial analysts will often have quite difference modes of perception and approaches to potential conflict from, say, lawyers and insurance adjusters.
- Organizational position and affiliation. Those in the production department will often see long, predictable manufacturing runs as the company's dominant interest while marketers will opt for individual tailoring to customer specs and deep inventories for rapid deliveries. This is another example of the old and wise expression "where you stand depends on where you sit."
- Whom they admire, whose advice carries weight, and to whom they tend to defer on the kind of issues at stake.

In the end, interests are bound up with psychology and culture. Some settings breed rivalry; others instill group loyalty. Some people are altruists; others sociopaths. To some, ego looms large; to others, substance is all. Popular psychology designates Jungle Fighters, Appeasers, Win-Winners, and Win-Losers. Professionals label personality Types A and B along with victims of cathected libido. Others have spun out such classes, sometimes wisely, but for now we stress that perceived interests matter, that perceptions are subjective, and, thus, to assess interests is to probe psyches.

Summary

As a means of summarizing the main observations of this chapter, we have converted them into the following prescriptive checklist for analysts and practitioners:

ASSESSING WHICH INTERESTS ARE AT STAKE

- Beyond the obvious tangible interests that may be affected by issues to be discussed, consider subtler interests in reputation, precedent, relationships, strategy, fairness, and the like.
- Distinguish underlying interests from the issues under discussion and the positions taken on them.
- Distinguish between intrinsic and instrumental reasons for valuing interests, especially some of the subtler ones.
- In seeking to understand others' interests, remember that interests depend on perceptions, that perceptions are subjective, and thus that to assess interests is to probe psyches. This process can be aided by clear communication, the advice of third parties, role playing, and taking into account past behavior, training, professional affiliation, organizational position, as well as those to whom the others defer.
- Keep in mind that interests and issues can change on purpose or accidentally as the parties learn, events occur, or certain tactics are employed.

ASSESSING TRADEOFFS

- Tradeoffs are as important to interests as proportions are to recipes.
- To assess tradeoffs among intangible interests, it is sometimes helpful to imagine services one could buy otherwise to satisfy the same interests.

- To assess tradeoffs among issues:
  - —Specify the worst and best possible outcomes on each issue to define the possible increments.
  - —Compare the increments by thinking hard about underlying interests and which increments are most valued.
  - —Break the increments into smaller pieces and similarly compare their relative valuation.
  - —Change assessments as more is learned about how different positions on the issues affect interests.
  - —Assess interest tradeoffs using the same logic.

WHEN TO FOCUS ON INTERESTS AND WHEN ON ISSUES

- Focus the negotiation on interests to enhance creativity and break impasses by reformulating issues to align better with underlying interests.
- Focus the negotiation on positions, issues, or a narrower set of interests when underlying conflicts of ideology make agreement difficult or when a restricted focus is more advantageous for claiming value.

Negotiation is a process of potentially opportunistic interaction in which two or more parties with some apparently conflicting interests seek to do better by jointly decided action than they could otherwise. For evaluating alternatives and creating agreements, interests are the measure and raw material. The alternatives to negotiated agreement or what the parties could each do alone define the threshold of value that any agreement must exceed. The potential of negotiation is bounded only by the quality of the agreements that can be devised. The processes of negotiation are creating and claiming value. We can now focus more detailed attention on the first of these, namely, how value can be created from the parties' interests. In other words, we look hard at the real bases of joint gains.

CHAPTER FIVE

Creating Value
or
Where Do Joint Gains Really Come From?

AGREEMENTS EMBODY the potential of negotiation. In many cases the notion of agreement is very simple: a contract, a formal accord, a treaty. In organizational settings, however, the notion of "agreement" may become more complex, ranging from employment contracts and budget documents to understandings and accommodations, whether tacit or explicit. One vision of an organization is a complex network of agreements among its members and with "outside" parties. Thus seen, much of the manager's job consists of trying to create, influence, sustain, and alter parts of the organizational network of agreements.

People choose to act jointly—"agree" as we use the term—because it is more valuable to do so than not. But precisely why does joint action create value? Where do joint gains from cooperation really come from? This chapter seeks to answer these questions. Somewhat surprisingly, a very few principles underlie the creation of all joint gains. Stating them explicitly increases the chance for managers to make, improve, and sustain agreements.

Sometimes, the basis for agreement—the nature of the value created—is obvious. Suppose a stranger offers Joseph and Sally $100 if they can agree on how to divide it. In that case the only joint gain is reaching a deal on the division. Beyond the fact of an agreement where each gets more than nothing, their interests conflict diametricaly. Many negotiations have this character: does division A or division B pay that bill, or does Sam or Louis get the corner office? Much more frequently, as illustrated in Chapter Two, negotiators can fashion joint gains, that is, moves beyond simple agreement that benefit all parties. Equivalently, a joint gain represents an improvement from each party's point of view; one's gain need not be the other's loss.

We can now be more precise about what we mean by discovering joint gains and "creating value." By this, we have three kinds of actions in mind. First, reaching any agreement that exceeds the parties' no-agreement possibilities creates value relative to the alternatives. Second, negotiators create potential value with respect to one negotiated outcome by finding another that all prefer. And, third, negotiators create potential value by discovering that more is jointly feasible than previously was thought. That is, without necessarily reaching agreement, they discover a way—whether a new trade, a different option, a changed schedule of payments, or the like—to push the perceived Pareto frontier northeasterly, to reduce the apparent conflict of interest.

Negotiators can create two distinct kinds of value. This chapter will consider each in turn.

The first kind—what we will call "private value"—includes profits to be split, land to be parceled out, goods to be allocated, and, generally, results of negotiation that one party can consume, use, or enjoy while excluding others from the benefits. Those who mainly think of negotiation as the process of working out mutually beneficial exchanges have traditionally focused on private value. (In economic parlance, this is the kind of value conferred by "private goods.")

Yet negotiators can also create "common value," which is exceedingly important but often neglected in thinking about the process. Common value can be shared by all parties simultaneously; no one can be excluded unless all are. (To economists, "public goods" like clean air have this quality.) For example, suppose that two graphic designers are each committed to a different logo. They bargain for days over which one they will jointly recommend to top management. But suppose they discover a new logo that both prefer to their original choices. Their agreement to recommend it is good for both at the same time. In a more important case than so lucky a coincidence of interest, consider the value to two division heads of a greatly enhanced relationship that directly flows from their agreement on substantive issues. The improved relationship—which may be a central focus of the negotiation process—cannot be divided up for the separate use of each person. Many other tangible and intangible factors are likewise central to creating common value.

There would be little point to this chapter if all negotiating possibilities were fully known in advance. But this would be to assume away a crucial part of the problem. Particularly in organizations, many parties do not automatically know what opportunities for cooperative action there are to exploit. The parties must explore—imperfectly—the arrangements they may jointly be able to create. In practice many gains go unrealized. Inferior agreements are made. Impasse results and conflict escalates when cooperative action might have been far better for all. Understanding where private and common value really come from should make jointly creating it more likely. This chapter focuses on three primary sources: (1) the key role of *differences* among the participants in creating private (and common) value; (2) the often-misunderstood role of *shared interests* in creating common value; and (3) how *economies of scale* can create both kinds of value without requiring differences or shared interests.

In the analysis that follows, we examine the substantive basis of joint gains and do not dwell on the style of bargaining most likely to realize them. Near the end of the discussion, we will summarize the main points and show, perhaps surprisingly, how the principles we have described underlie *all* joint gains. Thus these principles, as illustrated by cases and anecdotes, are not merely important examples of the bases for creating value; instead, they constitute the full set of analytic building blocks needed for this process.

Creating Private Value: The Key Role of Differences

Gain from negotiation often exists because negotiators *differ* from one another. Since they are not identical—in tastes, forecasts, endowments, capabilities, or in other ways—they each have something to offer that is relatively less valuable to them than to those with whom they are bargaining. To take a trivial example, where something of Howard's is cheap to him and priceless to Eric, there is the basis for joint gain. Though rarely expressed as such, this "differences" idea is hardly new. It is implicit in the traditional description of the motivation for economic exchange as well as negotiation. What, then, is its special advantage?

In part, we focus on differences because they are often thought to cause bargaining friction or discord, especially compared to "common" interests. Consider the following familiar line of reasoning:

> When the many parties who are linked together interdependently are very diverse from one another, they will naturally have difficulty agreeing on what should be done, who should do it, and when. Differences in goals, values, stakes, and outlook will lead different people to different conclusions. The greater the diversity, and the greater the interdependence, the more differences of opinion there will be. . . . When there are a lot of people involved (lots of interdependence), and when the differences among the people are great (a high level of diversity), resolving conflicts in efficient and effective ways becomes much more difficult and complex.[1]

Likewise, the frequent diplomatic admonition about negotiation—first to reach a "common ground" of facts, assumptions, and forecasts, and then to bargain hard over this agreed terrain—may lead the process in the wrong direction. Instead, the observation that the set of *differences* among the negotiators is often the engine that drives their joint action may point them toward potential gains.

That differences lie at the heart of many joint gains follows readily from the fact that two utterly identical individuals may have no basis for *any* negotiation: neither has or wants anything that the other does not. If differences are admitted among many dimensions, however, negotiation opens up the prospect of joint gains. For example, gains may arise from differences in interests, in possessions, in forecasts, in aversion to risk, in attitudes toward the passage of time, in capabilities, in access to technology, and in other areas.

Since joint gains often derive from such differences, a primary orientation of managers, negotiators, and mediators should be toward discovering and dovetailing them. In line with this observation, this section will argue on behalf of two broad prescriptions:

1. When contemplating the potential gains from agreement, begin with a careful inventory of all the ways that the parties differ from one another—not how they are alike.
2. The basic principle underlying the realization of joint gains from differences is to match what one side finds or expects to be relatively costless with what the other finds or expects to be most valuable, and vice versa.

[1]Kotter (1985:18–19).

Of course, many good negotiators almost automatically seek to discern what is relatively important to each side—what are the parties' "real" interests. The best negotiators and mediators then find creative ways to weave these different strands into agreements of mutual benefit. The remainder of this section seeks to give form, precision, and prominence to the means of using common differences to create value.

DIFFERENCES OF INTEREST IMPLY EXCHANGES

If a vegetarian with some meat bargains with a carnivore who owns some vegetables, it is precisely the *difference* in their known preferences that can facilitate reaching an agreement. No one would counsel the vegetarian to persuade the carnivore of the zucchini's succulent taste. More complicated negotiations may concern several items. Although the parties may have opposing preferences on the settlement of each issue, they may feel most strongly about different issues. An overall agreement can reflect these different preferences by resolving the issues of relatively greater importance to one side more in favor of that side. A package or "horse trade" can be constructed this way so that, as a whole, all prefer it to no agreement.

Trading on Differences   This kind of negotiation is a special case of the economic theory of exchange wherein the parties "trade" differently valued items for mutual gain.[2] This theory applies not only to trading discrete things but also to constructing agreements that respond to different underlying interests. One party may primarily fear the precedential effects of a settlement; another may care about the

---

[2]Individuals and organizations may start with different endowments. They may also differ in their interests, that is, in their relative valuations of different arrangements of these items. Once interests and initial endowments are given, the economic theory of exchange indicates that "trading" opportunities will exist. Even if parties start with the same endowments, they may trade if they have different interests. Similarly, with identical interests they may trade if they start with different mixes of goods or resources. For mutually advantageous exchange it suffices that their combinations of endowments and interests differ. Then the basis for a quid pro quo exists. In other words, if the valuation of one "commodity" relative to the other—what economists call the marginal rate of substitution of the commodities—differs from one party to another, the two parties may trade with each other (at rates of substitution of the commodities that improve the welfare of each individual). Observing that it is precisely these underlying differences that provide the opportunity for mutual gains can lead to a systematic search for how to exploit them.

particulars of the current question; thus, both might profit by contriving a unique-looking agreement on the immediate issue. One side may be keen on a political "victory"; the other may want quiet accommodation for a particular constituency. Whether the differences are between vegetables and meat, form and substance, ideology and practice, reputation and results, or the intrinsic versus the instrumental qualities of a settlement, cleverly crafted agreements can often dovetail differences into joint gains.

From an economic viewpoint, then, differences in relative valuation can lead to the possibility of gain from exchange and thus can improve the likelihood of reaching agreement. This contention is consistent with the proposition of the noted analyst of social behavior, George Homans: "The more the items at stake can be divided into goods valued more by one party than they cost to the first, the greater the chances of a successful outcome."[3]

Unbundling Differences of Interest   It is an obvious enough prescription to "seek and dovetail asymmetries of interest." But frequently what appear to be zero-sum or purely distributive negotiations may conceal underlying differences that can be unbundled for joint gain.

Consider the homey story of two sisters arguing over the division of one orange, each claiming an absolute need for three-quarters of it. If however, their discussion reveals that one is hungry and the other wants the peel for a recipe, the negotiation could shift from where to cut the fruit to how to separate its different components.

In a more significant example, recall the midwestern utility that wanted to build a dam. The company had become embroiled in a dispute with farmers about downstream water flow and with conservationists worried about the effects of water diversion on the downstream habitat of the endangered whooping crane. After years of wrangling, the utility offered to guarantee downstream waterflow and to pay $7.5 million to purchase additional water rights or otherwise to protect the whooping crane habitat. Although both the utility and the conservationists saw the offer on the issue of financial compensation as generous, the utility was surprised that the conservationists rejected it.

After much more discussion, the utility came to understand that the conservationists' personal control over the money might make it

[3]George C. Homans, cited in Zartman (1976: 10).

appear as if they were being paid off and reduce their credibility with conservationist groups. An acceptable settlement had to unbundle the issue of financial compensation in a way that separated compensation and control. So, the parties created a $7.5 million trust fund to protect the whooping crane with a strict covenant that limited its trustees' control over the fund. To reach agreement, the parties needed to learn a great deal about the others' real interests. They had to identify differentially valued interests that were unnecessarily bundled. Then, they needed to invent ways to modify the issues and unbundle the interests to permit joint gains.

In short, where different interests are bundled into a negotiating issue, a good strategy can be to unbundle and seek creative ways to dovetail them. Many other differences beyond those of interest, however, also provide opportunities for joint gains. The next sections consider differences in probability assessments, time preference, and capability as means to create value.

PROBABILITY DIFFERENCES SUGGEST
CONTINGENT AGREEMENTS

At the heart of the sale of an investment property may be the buyer's belief that its price will rise and the seller's conviction that it will drop. The deal is facilitated by differences in belief about what will happen. Similarly, recall from Chapter Two the case of a singer at impasse with the owner of an auditorium over payment for a proposed concert. Since the singer expected the house to be filled while the owner projected only a half-capacity crowd, a contingent arrangement was ultimately agreed to in which the performer got a modest fixed fee plus a set percentage of the ticket receipts. Since the expected value of this agreement was greater to the performer than its expected cost to the owner, given their very different projections of attendance, the concert went ahead with both sides feeling better off and willing to accept whatever happened.

Probability assessments of uncertain events derive from the combination of prior beliefs and observed evidence; discrepancies in either of these factors may form the basis for contingent agreements. We have already observed that value differences can lead to horse trades. Analogously, for probabilities, Mark Twain noted that "it is difference of opinion that makes horse races." Two classes of situations suggest themselves in which contingent agreements based on different expectations may produce joint gains.

Issues Subject to Different Odds In the first case, outcomes of the event under discussion may be uncertain and subject to different probability estimates.[4] As with the concert hall example, economic arrangements frequently have this character. For example, an engineering firm had completed plans for a plant designed to burn garbage, to produce steam, and to convert it into electricity. The firm was negotiating with a medium-sized southern city over the sale of this electricity to the city. The city wanted to pay a lower price; the company insisted on a much higher one. As the discussions proceeded and then stalled, it became clear that the city representatives expected an oil glut and hence a drop in the price of the fuel most important to its electrical generation. The company believed that an oil price rise was much more likely. After protracted talks, the two sides could not agree on a set price for the sale of the plant's electricity to the city. Finally, however, they agreed to tie that price to the future cost of oil. Thus, the city expected to pay a lower price while the company expected to receive a higher price. When they also negotiated an upper and lower cap on the range of acceptable fluctuations, both sides could live with either outcome, and the plant went forward.

In a related example, Will, the managing partner and majority owner of a successful venture capital operation, listened to the almost-violent disagreements between two senior partners over the firm's strategic direction. One argued that it should maintain its traditional focus on advanced materials. The other saw a far brighter future in communication-related opportunties, especially after the recent breakup of the Bell system in the United States. Beyond discussion about their comparative technical advantage in either field, which could be argued effectively both ways, the partners' disagree-

---

[4]In theory, however, Harsanyi (1967–1968) argues that individuals share the same informational heritage, and thus that different assessments should be traceable exclusively to differences in observed information. Aumann (1976) shows that posterior probabilities should be identical for events that are "common knowledge." In fact, the assumption that prior distributions are common knowledge is extremely stringent; see Sebenius (1984: 177). But these results suggest a tendency and a prescription. The fact that someone is willing to accept the other side of a bet should lead one to think about what the other knows. And people do learn from others in this way, but the result is usually movement toward more similar posterior beliefs that are still far from identical. Because the differences in prior beliefs can come from different likelihood functions (different information partitions), convergence is not even necessary. For example, a Marxist and a neoclassicial economist might find it easy to bet after observing evidence of a downturn in the economy; the Marxist might interpret the data as evidence of the collapse of capitalism while the neoclassical economist might forecast a mild recession.

ment came from different projected returns from materials versus communications investments. As Will agonized over the choice, he realized that disagreements over the fundamental uncertainties contained the basis for a way out of his dilemma. He contemplated forming two separate divisions with a major part of compensation in each dependent solely on its performance. In effect, he devised a contingent agreement. In this way the partnership would receive the benefits of a hedge against the very real uncertainties, while each partner had the chance to raise additional money for and promote what for him seemed to be the most attractive opportunity. Before making the move, Will satisfied himself that each entity could be staffed by quality people. By making each such division responsible for its own added expenses, the firm itself would not expose itself to undue financial risks.

In each of these examples, contingent arrangements offer gains. They are often appropriate where the parties are dealing with uncertain quantities and actually or apparently differ in their assessments.

Different Assessments of the Attractiveness of Proposed Procedures Contingent agreements may be employed in a second common class of situations where the parties believe that they can positively affect the chances for favorable outcome of the uncertain event. Consider the voluntary submission of a dispute to arbitration. Firmly believing the persuasiveness of its position and highly confident in the quality of its representation before the tribunal, each side may feel that its chances of obtaining the desired outcome are very good. Their beliefs may, in fact, be incompatibly optimistic.[5] For this reason, the two parties may have been unable to negotiate their way to one or another specific proposed outcomes. With both sides nonetheless perceiving the value of a settlement, the parties might agree to arbitration, which is in effect, a contingent settlement. From each disputant's standpoint, the uncertain event is the arbitrator's decision. Other third party procedures may also be thought of as contingent agreements where the underlying probabilities differ.

Negotiations often leave much ambiguity with the tacit understanding that a definite resolution of the issue perhaps strongly favoring one party will later become necessary. In certain cases, leaving the ambiguity for resolution by a future mechanism that might be

[5]Raiffa (1982), Lax and Sebenius (1985), and Bazerman and Neale (1985) discuss studies that illustrate this type of consistent overconfidence.

subject to influence can be thought of as a contingent outcome where the probabilities differ. One thinks of the French saying "there could be no treaties without *conflicting* mental reservations."

If the uncertainty takes time to be resolved, moreover, other aspects of the agreed regime may settle into place making even a relatively adverse settlement of the formerly contentious issues at least tolerable to all sides. Forcing a resolution of one or more of these issues strongly in favor of one party during the initial negotiation may place unbearable strain on the overall settlement process. In some cases, leaving it for subsequent resolution in a more amenable future context can be a beneficial procedure.

Crafting a Contingent Agreement   Even when differences in probability seem great, crafting a mutually beneficial agreement that takes advantage of them can be tricky. In one case, a U.S. auto parts manufacturing firm and its union were at loggerheads over wages. The manufacturer wanted reductions because of "the new competitive environment;" the union wanted increases substantially beyond cost of living. A strike seemed likely. On probing, the manufacturer felt that foreign firms, especially from Japan and Korea, had begun to make inroads into the U.S. market and were likely over time to undercut U.S. competitors and take a dominant share of the U.S. market. Union members genuinely felt this scenario to be implausible and merely a way to scare it into concessions and givebacks. At first blush, given these differences, a contingent agreement for wages that stayed moderately high as long as foreign competition remained weak but that dropped to a base level if foreign competition intensified would have seemed jointly preferable to a strike.

Even when negotiators have discovered a difference in forecasts, however, considerable ingenuity may be required to find an appropriate uncertain event that all sides can observe and that no one can manipulate. Thus, management suggested that wages drop to a base wage if the firm's profit margins eroded past a certain level. The union countered that profit margins might drop for a wide variety of reasons other than foreign competition, including bad management and, worse, accountants juggling figures to arrive at low margins. Thus, the union could not agree to any such arrangement. After bargaining to set a base wage to be guaranteed under all circumstances, union leaders suggested that wages drop to that level if foreign sales exceeded 30 percent of the U.S. market—a fairly high share. In response, management argued first that market share figures come out months after the actual market penetration, and second, without the delay, by the time that foreign firms had a 30 percent share, all the damage would already have been done. A 10 percent share would be more like it. Of course, the union negotiator argued, a 10 percent threshold would benefit management but there would be no certainty that foreign share would rise much beyond 10 percent and the union members would merely be giving up hard-earned wages for more posh suburban estates for management. Moreover, they contended that it was only fair for union members to get especially high wages if foreign market share were to drop below its current level.

Ultimately the parties agreed on a base level to which wages would drop if foreign firms' prices fell a set percentage below the firm's current prices, and simultaneously, if foreign market share exceeded 10 percent. Wages would be boosted, however, if foreign market share declined. Thus, the negotiators found contingent events (foreign market share and relative prices) that were correlated with the eventuality that management feared (increased foreign competition), that both parties could observe, that were safe from tampering, and that would occur soon enough to allow a less than drastic response. More generally, each of these criteria can be a requirement for crafting feasible contingent contracts.

* * *

Thus, at least two kinds of situations exist in which contingent agreements add potential for joint gains. When the uncertain event itself is of interest, there are familiar economic contingent contracts with "betting" based on the probability differences. When the parties feel capable of influencing an uncertain event, making the negotiated outcome dependent on its resolution may be a good idea. Examples of this include voluntary arbitration, certain dispute settlement mechanisms, and occasionally, ambiguities in agreements.

Of course, contingent arrangements based on underlying differences are not a panacea. Crafting them effectively can be a high art. And once the outcome of the uncertain event is known, one party may have "won" and the other "lost." Whether the outcome will then be considered fair, wise, or even sustainable is an important question to be planned for in advance. We will take up this and related questions about the sustainability of agreements in Chapter Thirteen.

DIFFERENCES IN RISK AVERSION
LEAD TO RISK-SHARING SCHEMES

Suppose that two people agree on the probabilities of an uncertain prospect. Even so, they may still react differently to taking the risks involved. In such cases, they may devise a variety of ways to share the risk. In general, such mechanisms should shift more of the risk to the party who is less risk-averse than the other. For example, suppose that Mr. Broussard, a single, fairly wealthy, middle-aged accountant, and Ms. Armitage, a younger, less-well-off lawyer with significant family responsibilities, are planning to buy and operate a business together. The younger, more risk-averse Ms. Armitage may prefer to take a larger but fixed salary while Mr. Broussard may prefer a smaller set salary but much larger share of any profits. Though they may expect the same total amount of money to be paid in compensation, both parties are better off than had they, say, both chosen either fixed salaries or large contingent payments.

Different risk attitudes can be useful in fashioning negotiated settlements in a variety of such cases. Obviously, some individuals are simply more avid risk takers than others. This is often true in negotiations between small entrepreneurial companies and more established conservative firms. Similarly, if the parties are at different levels of their respective organizations, they may exhibit different risk attitudes. Different expected job mobility or career paths may also imply dissimilar risk preferences. A group of individuals facing a large risky project may be able to divide it up in such a way that each of the members takes on a more manageable piece of potential profits or losses. The group may thereby act in a considerably more neutral way toward the risk than do any of its individual members. Thus, in negotiations among different-sized groups, between a single firm and a consortium, or between a company and a national government, considerable scope for using risk differences may exist. Economists Kenneth Arrow and Robert Lind have shown that, under fairly general conditions, a large government should act in a risk-neutral manner when evaluating uncertain prospects.[6] Thus, inventing risk-shifting mechanisms may facilitate public/private negotiations, especially where the private body has a greater aversion to risk. Across these varied situations, the parties may construct advantageous agreements to reflect the differences.

[6]See Arrow and Lind (1970).

Consider an example. Different tax or contract terms—fixed fees, royalties, and profit shares—shift risk very differently. Suppose that the investment costs, operating costs, and revenues of an advanced plastics–forming plant are uncertain. Further, say that the investor undertaking it and the owner of the major patent critical to the process share the same beliefs about how these uncertainties are likely to turn out. If the investor agrees to pay the patent holder a large fixed fee, the investor bears the risk that returns will end up lower than expected while enjoying the prospect that higher profits may result. If the patent holder received a share of revenues (a royalty), his returns would be low when revenues were low and high when they were high, but the investor would fully bear the cost risks. If the two men agreed to share profits, all cost and revenue risks would be shared.

If the economic scenario that both parties expect in fact occurs, all three different combinations of fees, royalties, and profit shares could have been set to yield the same payment to the patent holder. Yet, since the actual outcome is uncertain and each type of contract has a different "upside potential" and "downside risk," a more risk-averse patent holder would prefer to receive a fee while a greater risk taker would prefer the profit-share.[7]

If two very risk-averse parties negotiate over an uncertain prospect, it may be possible to bring in someone who is risk-neutral to "buy the risk" from the original bargainers, thus facilitating their deliberations. For example, say that two fairly poor brothers have just inherited a working farm whose main crop has a volatile price. They might be wise to sell rights to the farm's output under a long-term contract for a fixed amount rather than bargaining over shares of an uncertain revenue stream. They may then be able to negotiate much more easily over the division of this known revenue.

Across these examples, the general principle is easy to state: different risk-sharing devices can allow joint gains to people who have differing attitudes toward risk.

DIFFERENCES IN TIME PREFERENCES
SUGGEST ALTERED PAYMENT PATTERNS

People may value the same event quite differently, depending on when it occurs. If one side is relatively less impatient than the other,

[7]However, if different combinations of these tax and contractual instruments have the same expected value, preferences among them may not be obvious. For an analysis, see Sebenius and Stan (1982).

mechanisms for optimally sharing the consequences over time may be devised.

A particularly simple form of time preference difference may be reflected in discount rates. Consider a highly stylized example. Suppose that Ms. Kanwate has a 10 percent discount rate, that Mr. Hurree's rate is 20 percent, and that each party cares about the present value of income.[8] Ms. Kanwate will receive $100 next year; Mr. Hurree is slated to receive $100 the year afterward. Thus the present value of her income is about $91 and his is $69.[9] The two could engineer a variety of profitable trades to dovetail this difference. Because Mr. Hurree values early income relatively more than does Ms. Kanwate, though, he should get the first year's $100. If, in the second year, Ms. Kanwate gets $100 plus $20 from him, the present value of her income rises from $91 in the original division to $99. The present value of Mr. Hurree's income stream (+ $100 in a year, − $20 in two years) remains at about $69. If he gave $10 to Ms. Kanwate in the second period, she could have the same present value as in the original division ($91), while the present value of his income would be $76 instead of the original $69. Any outcome in which he gets the first $100 and she gets between $110 and $120 in the second period is as good as or better than the original division for both parties.

Whenever time preference differences exist, the principle that future consequences can be beneficially rearranged in a way that gives earlier amounts to the more impatient party may be useful to negotiators and mediators. As with risk aversion, such characteristics occur in a variety of circumstances. Apart from ad hoc, individual differences, time attitudes may vary in cross-cultural dealings. Where the parties are of quite different ages or their opportunities to use money, say, are not the same, joint gains may be possible. People at different organizational levels or at different career stages can hold quite different time horizons for valuing the results of a negotiation. Time preference differences may be particularly important in some

---

[8]The "future value" of a present amount of money reflects the compounding of interest forward over time. The "present value" of a future amount of money reverses this process, "discounting" it back to the present amount that, if compounded forward at the same interest (or discount) rate, would just equal the future amount.

[9]That is, because Ms. Kanwate has alternative investment possibilities that return 10 percent, her getting $100 in a year is equivalent to placing $91 now in the alternative investment and taking out the $100 it will produce a year later. Similarly, for Mr. Hurree, getting $100 in two years is equivalent to putting $69 now in an investment that returns 20 percent and, two years hence, drawing the $100 produced by the investment.

public/private negotiations over projects with future ramifications; governments or public entities may weight benefits or costs to future generations more heavily than do their private counterparts. This state of affairs offers room for mutually advantageous sharing over time that enhances the possibilities of agreement.

COMPLEMENTARY CAPABILITIES CAN BE COMBINED

Organizations can be understood as networks of people with complementary capabilities. Managers are often vitally concerned with the agreements that link these parts into a productive whole. And just as differences in interest, probability, risk aversion, and time preference may imply gain, so may differences in capabilities, access to production opportunities, technology, or abilities to convert resources physically. In a simple example, Farmer Jones, with arid land and a tractor, may combine with Farmer Smith who has seeds and water rights. The more different the parties' original arrangements of stocks and production opportunities, the more different will be their joint production possibilities from those held by either individual.

Differences in capabilities can take many forms. Individuals may have differing access to technology, to the rights to use it, or to the physical, financial, or human capital needed to implement it. They may face differing costs of investment—for example, large organizations often have lower transactions costs in financial markets, may face lower costs of borrowing, or may have access to investment opportunities that yield higher rates of return. At any given moment, some individuals and organizations will have their assets in a more liquid form than others and will therefore be in a better position to take advantage of transient opportunities. One party may have access to better diversification possibilities. From the perspective of individual parties, differences in corporate and personal income tax status can generate opportunities for arrangements that produce higher after-tax income. Differences in legal, accounting, engineering, and sale talents can combine at the group, department, or organizational level to form the basis of productive agreements. Any such capability differences can form the basis for mutually profitable arrangements.

THE LARGEST MINING CONTRACT EVER NEGOTIATED: AN EXAMPLE OF DOVETAILED DIFFERENCES

A rich metallic ore carpets much of the deep seabed outside the limits of any nation's jurisdiction. Only developed countries have the technical, financial, and managerial potential to mine this rich resource. Lockheed, Amoco, U.S. Steel, Kennecott, INCO, Deepsea Ventures, Royal Dutch Shell, and many other companies have invested hundreds of millions of dollars in deep seabed mining research. At the same time, developing countries bordering key navigable straits and with large coastlines have the potential to decide whether traditional freedoms of the high seas will apply off their coastlines on a routine basis. This situation led to the international negotiations over the law of the sea during the 1970s and early 1980s. In the broadest sense, developed-country governments offered to share benefits from any deep seabed mining in return for guarantees of mobility rights for ships, planes, and submarines by the developing coastal countries and states that border navigable straits.[10]

One outcome of this process was potentially the largest mining contract ever negotiated internationally. In particular, part of the overall sea law negotiations came to concern a system of fees, royalties, and profit shares to be paid by future seabed miners to an international entity for the right to mine the deep seabed. The results of bargaining that was widely predicted to be intractable proved to be an arrangement that effectively exploited differences among the participants in probability, risk aversion, and time preference. Consider each difference.

First, a great deal of technical and economic uncertainty surrounded the prospects for deep ocean mining. Even after lengthy negotiations and the introduction of much common information, a strong divergence of opinion persisted between developed and developing countries about its likely economic profile. Developed countries saw mining as providing a new, lower-cost source of minerals. They argued that this industry would most likely show attractive but modest economic returns. Many negotiators from developing countries, however, felt that profitability prospects were very good indeed. In short, expectations diverged.

Second, any eventual revenue from seabed exploitation would be divided up among all treaty signatories and would not represent a major share of any country's national income. Thus, countries signing the treaty could be thought of as a large syndicate that should try to maximize expected income rather than trying to assure itself of a smaller, but steadier stream. Corporate investments in seabed mining operations, however, could represent significant portions of their assets. In particular, managers of the ocean mining divisions of these

[10]See Sebenius (1984) for a much fuller exposition of the checkered history of these mammoth negotiations and some of the lessons to be drawn from them.

companies were quite concerned with the potential impact of relatively fixed charges such as fees or royalties on the economic success of troubled projects. They seemed willing to share profits at high rates for successful projects in return for "low-end" protection of economically marginal ventures. Attitudes toward risk thus differed.

Finally, there was the question of timing. The companies' private, after-tax discount rates appeared to be higher than those implicitly used by the negotiators from developing countries, who saw themselves as setting up an enduring system. The welfare of future generations figured heavily in their negotiating statements and in their evaluations of proposals. The two sides' attitudes toward time seemed to differ with companies acting relatively less patiently than the countries.

An agreement was reached only after two years of difficult bargaining. The outcome dovetails these differences in probability, risk aversion, and time preference. Two sharing schedules were agreed upon, one with a low royalty and a low profit share, the other with much higher payment rates in each category. The low schedule is in effect until the overall cash flow of the operation, cumulated forward at an appropriate real interest rate, suffices to recover the preproduction investment costs (also cumulated forward with interest). Higher royalty and profit-sharing rates then take effect.

Negotiation of a single set of rates had proved extremely difficult, with any proposal either being opposed by the developed countries as too high or being opposed by the developing countries as being too low. The two negotiated schedules, however, use the differences in profitability estimates by giving each side an advantageous tax schedule for the economic outcome it portrayed as likely. Given the developing countries' expectations of high profits, negotiation of low rates for modestly successful projects was no great concession. Similarly, accepting high rates for bonanza projects was tenable for potential mining companies, given their lower profit forecasts. It was critical, however, that the low rates were neither so low nor the high rates so elevated that the ultimate result would be politically or economically unsustainable. The parties knew that they would have to live with and defend the outcome, however the profit uncertainties resolved themselves.

The agreement protects troubled or marginal projects against overly high fixed charges. In return for such lower rates, however, the miners face higher rates for successful projects than would likely have been otherwise negotiable. The signal for switching to the higher rates is based on the "accumulated" present value of a project's cash flows, that is, inflows and outflows cumulated forward with interest. Therefore, the higher rates apply only to projects whose risk—that the investment and its opportunity costs would go unrecovered—has substantially diminished. Differences in risk attitudes are dovetailed: the international community has a higher expected take, while the companies enjoy "low-end" protection. In effect, contingent high-end premiums are paid for contingent low-end insurance.

Finally, since the economic success of a project can normally be expected to increase over time, the stream of payments should be low at first and then much higher later. This matches the expressed attitudes toward the passage of time. Although this is hardly a claim for larger social optimality, this arrangement accords well with the espoused differences in time preference among the negotiators.

While it is not likely that any one of these differences by itself would have been sufficient to lead to a negotiated settlement, in combination they reinforced each other in pointing toward a solution. It is remarkable that this negotiation produced a new form of mineral taxation agreement designed to use differences among the participants to fashion joint gains. This novel outcome helped to avert the negotiating impasse on the financial issues that was widely predicted.

DOVETAILING OTHER DIFFERENCES

Important elements of negotiated agreements consist of creatively dovetailed differences. Thus far, we have examined five such qualities (value, expectation, capacity, risk-bearing attitude, and time preference) along with the characteristic ways of combining them. (See Table 5.1 below.) All these differences among negotiating parties—in what they have and under what conditions they have it, in what they want and when they want it, in what they think is likely and unlikely, in what they are capable of doing, and so forth—can be used separately or in concert to fashion mutually satisfying agreements. Generally, however, good negotiators can find ways to make use of many more differences—in the participants' criteria for success, in attitudes toward precedent and principle, in constituencies, in personal and organizational situations, in ideology, in conceptions of fairness, and so on. By this discussion, we hardly intend to produce an exhaustive enumeration, but instead, to convey the sense that differences are as varied as negotiators. If recognized, this truth carries a profoundly optimistic message for the process of creating value.

TABLE 5.1
The Technology of Dovetailing Differences to Create Value

DIFFERENCE	CHARACTERISTIC TYPE OF AGREEMENT
Valuation	
Simple	Exchange or trade
Bundled	Creative "unbundling"
Probability or forecast	
About event of interest	Contingent agreement or "bet"
About a resolution mechanism	Procedural agreement like arbitration
Risk aversion	Risk-spreading mechanism like insurance
Time preference	Altered pattern of payments or benefits over time
Other differences	Ad hoc arrangements giving that to each party which it values most and which costs the other party the least

Creating Common Value: The Role of Shared Interests

The negotiation lexicon abounds with potentially misleading concepts. We have discussed "differences"; now consider "shared" or "common" interests. By virtue of absolutely nothing more nor less than being in a negotiation together, parties could be said to have two "common interests":

1. The desire to improve on their respective alternatives to negotiated agreement: "We have a common interest in not breaking off our dealings."
2. The desire to realize all possible gains beyond doing marginally better than their alternatives to agreement: "Though our other interests may conflict, you and I have a common interest in profiting as much as we can from this deal."

But, in all negotiations, whether the bargainers wear Apache headdresses, fedoras, or gas masks, and whether the issues include pork bellies, parking spots, or ransom, realizing benefits and avoiding the costs of alternatives are minimal "shared interests."[11] Emphasizing this fact can certainly generate empathy. Yet used this way,

[11]We are not concerned with many of the other possible reasons for negotiation, such as spreading propaganda, gathering intelligence, influencing third parties, simply maintaining contact, or communicating on other matters entirely. For an extended discussion see footnote 1 in Chapter Three.

as it very frequently is, "common" or "shared" interest is an empty phrase, implying nothing more than that the parties are in a negotiation. As such, this usage would apply even to parties whose interests were diametrically opposed.

Yet there is a deeper and more useful meaning to the concept of "shared interest." Sometimes the resolution of a single issue in a particular manner—regardless of its relationship to a larger trade or package—simultaneously benefits all parties. Each side prefers the identical position on the issue. Since there is no conflict, no side's benefit from the settlement on this issue by itself comes at even the slightest expense of another's. In other cases, a range of settlement terms simultaneously furthers an identical interest of all the parties, In both instances, the value created by agreement on the issues in question cannot be exclusively "consumed" by any of the parties. We have called this kind of value "common" to distinguish it from the "private" value discussed in the last section.

Common Value to Parties Who Prefer the Identical Position
Consider a few situations in which a particular resolution of a *single* issue would yield simultaneous gains to all parties. Say that a divorcing couple deals with two main issues: the level of alimony and primary custody of the children. It may well be that one spouse genuinely desires custody and the other really does not, making that resolution potentially a simultaneous gain for both parties. Or, consider the new head of a government agency, whose organization has a large number of employees that she finds undesirable but that cannot be easily removed. In negotiations with the appropriating legislative body, the agency head and the committee chair may find a shared interest in a significant cut in funding to the agency. This resolution may be portrayed as evidence of fiscal responsibility by the legislator while serving as a surreptitious means for the agency head to clean house.

In certain instances, of course, the actual coincidence of interest may be unknown to at least one of the parties. This was the case in a contract negotiation between a police union and a city administration, which we discussed in Chapter Two. The city's mayor, in office only a few years, had run on a very liberal platform. She had the support of a number of community groups, had appointed a relatively progressive police commissioner, and had pushed such measures as a civilian review board. These moves were enormously popular among the mayor's political supporters.

Representatives of the police union, however, strongly preferred their old, more congenial commissioner and sought in negotiations to have the new commmissioner removed. In fact, members of the union would have considered it an enormous plus if the commissioner were ousted. Moreover, they would have been willing to trade off significant other issues—such as pay, vacation time, and the incidence of two-man patrol cars—for this result. Yet unbeknownst to the union, the mayor had found her vaunted commissioner to be an administrative disaster and would have liked nothing better than to have him replaced without suffering political damage. If the commissioner were to go, there was the potential for a pure joint gain.

Across these varied situations, coincidence of preference and identical resolution of a *single* issue benefit both sides. This is not, however, to say that one party cannot extract the value the other would gain—but to do so requires linking *another* issue or interest to the process. In fact, the temptation toward this kind of opportunistic issue manipulation can be almost overwhelming. Recall how the divorcing father, who might like nothing more than to be rid of responsibility for his children, may feign powerful parental instincts during divorce bargaining, hoping to "concede" custody in return for paying lower alimony. Sometimes, scheming of this kind causes costless joint gains to go unrealized.

Take, for instance, a case handled by Richard Neely, later made a judge in West Virginia, while he was still an attorney. His client, the husband, had had an affair, and the judge who would handle the wife's suit for divorce was known for requiring steep alimony and child support payments. In view of these circumstances, Neely sought to negotiate an inexpensive settlement. He told the husband to threaten the wife with a long, drawn-out fight for the custody of their children even though this "was 'the last thing he wanted from the divorce' and the likelihood of his getting custody was 'virtually nonexistent.'" It worked: the out-of-court settlement gave the wife custody but little alimony and child support. Neely concluded: " 'All we had needed to defeat her legitimate claim in the settlement process was a halfway credible threat of a protracted custody battle.' "[12]

Notice that for *differences* to create value, at least *two* issues must be involved. For example, two commodities or one of them plus money (which, here, functions as another "commodity") are required for an exchange. "Unbundling" typically converts one issue into more than one. Contingent agreements from differences in

[12]Rankin (1986).

probability or risk aversion generally require more issues than non-contingent deals—the parties must now negotiate over the payment to be made or the actions to be taken for each possible outcome of the uncertain event. And time-preference differences involve issues of what to do in each of more than one time period. By contrast, creating the kind of common value discussed in this section requires only one issue, taken by itself.

Common Value Across a Range of Settlements   A second kind of shared interest can come into play when a whole range of settlements on the issues under negotiation simultaneously furthers an identical interest of the parties, such as their relationship. Or consider a manager who is discussing with subordinates the allocation of a series of relatively unpleasant tasks. One outcome of this encounter might be resigned acceptance. Yet if the manager is convincingly able to portray these resulting obligations as steps in service of a shared organizational goal, the employees may regard them quite differently. Similarly, if a negotiator can make a common vision, ideology, symbol, creed, or purpose more salient and link it to virtually any resolution of the immediate issues under discussion, the parties may value the outcome more highly. The effect of this is analogous to settling a single issue in a way that all parties prefer. Both create common value, pushing the perceived Pareto frontier northeasterly. (Recall Figure 2.4.)

In some instances, the resolution of a single issue may be extremely difficult when that issue is considered in and of itself. Yet appeals to an ongoing and future relationship may render an agreement both easier *and* more valuable. For example, recall from Chapter Three the rancorous dispute between a group of states and the federal government over expenditures for social services that the states had made some years before. Accusations of bad faith and court suits had been legion over the dispute's history. This unpleasantness had also adversely affected a range of intergovernmental dealings. When a new administration came into office, a redoubled effort to settle the dispute became tangible evidence of improved relations between the federal government and the states. Making the relationship a visible and important aspect of the process clearly facilitated a settlement. In fact, the negotiated results did ease difficult federal-state dealings in many other areas over time.

In a series of intriguing experiments involving coalition bargaining, some students bargained face-to-face while others were assigned anonymous partners and bargained by computer.[13] A strikingly higher incidence of successful bargaining occurred in the face-to-face encounters. Many students reported that even the minimal relationship involved in their short, personal encounters induced more effective cooperation.

A number of other potentially shared interests may be made salient, increasing the potential value of an agreement and often making it more likely. For example, both sides may value a resolution that is perceived as "fair." Similarly, a "good" process of negotiation may add value to the substantive outcome. For example, suppose that a negotiation is carried on by a procedure that all parties perceive to be open, participative, and fair. The value of any substantive result may be enhanced in part by the intrinsic features of the process, in part by the procedural precedent it sets, and in part by the signal that subsequent dealings will likely have a similar character.

Sometimes, the very fact of agreement—across a range of possible terms—itself can become valuable to the parties and make resolution easier. This benefit may derive from a shared desire to set a good procedural precedent. Or it may be intended as a signal to others that this is a group that can work together and "do something." Congressional deadlocks are occasionally resolved, for example, by some action that will "show the people" that the legislature is in fact a potent body. Of course one of the most common pitfalls for negotiators, especially negotiating agents, involves giving too much value to the fact of agreement rather than to its content.

Finally we note several factors that may render a broad range of substantive agreements yet more valuable to the parties. Take, for example, mutual respect, approval, and acting in accord with the norms of an organizational or social culture. Some people find great value in being part of a group that is taking action together. This sense of belonging may complement the intrinsic rationale and purpose of the agreement. Similarly, some get altruistic value from an action because others value the action itself. Sometimes, the need to block or defeat a common enemy causes a range of settlements to be desirable to several parties.

A deeper meaning of "shared interests" thus goes beyond simply avoiding the alternatives or realizing possible gains. Sometimes the parties discover that they simply want the same resolution of an issue, though perhaps for different reasons. Moreover, when certain

[13]See Raiffa (1982).

interests are made salient they may add joint value to a range of settlements on the issues. Difficult negotiations may sometimes be eased by appeals to a higher goal, to intrinsic interest in the relationship, to fairness, to a good procedure, to group incentives, and even to the fact of agreement itself.

A number of these ostensibly shared interests can be used quite cynically. As such, they can at times be more accurately interpreted as differences to be dovetailed. Suppose something is of great value to you—for example, a higher vision, goal, fairness, or "the relationship"—but I could not care less about it. Say that is is cheap for me to make it salient. My doing so may cause you to go along with something else that in substance you would otherwise not choose. Independent of such manipulation, whatever its ethics, shared interests may add common value to a substantive agreement.

Differences Can Create Common Value   Mutual preference for the same position and pure shared interests are not the only tools for creating common value; differences can also create it. For example, several groups could decide to combine their complementary capabilities to defend themselves or to clean up their air. We chose to treat differences and private value together, however, because of their key practical connection. Yet there is still another means to create both private and common value, which we turn to in the next section.

Creating Value Without Differences or Shared Interests: Economies of Scale

There do exist joint gains not deriving from differences or pure shared interests. With scale economies, two absolutely identical parties may reach agreement even where no common value is to be created. Say that landowner has offered a large sum of money to have a heavy boulder moved. Harold cannot do it without his identical twin Harry, even by doubling his efforts or working twice as long. Yet both can, and may agree to move it, leading to a bargain between the twins over splitting the payment.

Scale economies underpin the private value created in many agreements. Instead of two organizations each setting up a health clinic in an underserved area, they might set up one, share overhead costs, and serve well more than twice the number of patients that either could have handled alone. Similarly, by merging, two firms can sometimes cut out redundancies, reap economies of scale in production, and enjoy volume discounts in purchases. Combined advertising may cost less than the sum of their individual efforts, but yield more than twice the sales of either one before.

Total cartel profits may go up faster and faster as more members of the industry agree to join—though splitting the additonal money and policing the agreement may be devilish. Paradoxically, each member of a group of risk lovers may increase his or her individual pleasure by creating a group risk. Each may forego a sure amount of money to create a large pool in which all have the same chance to win. A poker game can create this kind of pleasurable risk for some.

Finally there are cases in which identical people starting out with the same goods and tastes can also create private value through a peculiar version of scale economies. For example, if two people each have two half-sets of different patterns of china, they may trade so that each person has a much more useful complete set.

Scale economies can also create common value. Beyond the pleasure of taking the risk involved in poker is the pure fun of the game in which, like a party, six people may have ten times the fun of three. Moreover, the costs of an alliance to each member may decline with the number of members while the individual benefits increase. All may gain from lower chances of attack. (The costs, of course, must be divided.)[14]

In each of these situations, action becomes more potent or goods become more valuable at a rate higher than in simple proportion to the number of parties or items involved. By agreeing to exploit such economies of scale and number, private and common value can be created.

The Substance and Style of Cooperation

This chapter has focused on the substance of cooperation by laying out the remarkably few principles that underlie joint gains from agreement. We have not concentrated on the style of bargaining best suited to finding and realizing these joint gains. In part, this is because a great deal has already been written on aspects of effective cooperation (demeanor, ambiance, psychological orientation, commu-

[14]See Olson and Zeckhauser (1966).

nication, creativity, empathy, and the like).[15] Yet a few summary words on the requirements for creating value are in order.

To create value, a negotiator needs *to learn* about her counterparts' interests and perceptions, to help them learn about hers, to *foster ingenuity and creativity*, and to *blunt the escalation of conflict*. Learning typically requires listening and clear communication. Genuinely asking "Why?" and "Why not?" can help, as can intently listening to the answers.[16] One can often learn more about another's interests and concerns by trying hard to put oneself in the other's shoes and "testing" with the other side the accuracy of one's perceptions.

To enhance the likelihood of creative agreements, the cooperative negotiator may try to shift the bargaining from a stance "against each other across the table" to a posture that is "side by side against the problem." Brainstorming sessions may also be useful. In some versions of brainstorming, options can be proposed and improved upon but criticisms and decisions are not allowed—in order to stimulate the free flow of ideas and creativity.[17]

Likewise, the cooperative bargainer tries to prevent blowups that diminish the value of substantive agreement relative to concerns with self-esteem and precedents for future relationships; he may do so by "separating the people from the problem," being "hard on the problem but soft on the people," allowing counterparts to vent emotions, avoiding insults and offensive mannerisms, holding meetings in pleasant neutral settings, avoiding threats and final offers, and helping counterparts to save face when necessary.

Adherence to this cooperative style—mutual learning, creativity, preventing runaway conflict—can help a negotiator create value by realizing joint gains through well-constructed agreements. Yet, as this chapter has argued, the substantive building blocks for joint gains are differences, shared interests, and scale economies. It is a common error for some analysts and bargainers to focus on the *style*—"cooperative," say, in contrast to "competitive"—to the ex-

[15]Much has been written on this cooperative style, some of it quite insightful, on which we draw in the above discussion. See Walton and McKersie's (1965) discussion of integrative bargaining, Fisher and Ury's (1981) explanation of principled negotiation, as well as Pruitt (1981), Williams (1983), and Lewicki and Litterer (1985) on cooperative bargaining.

[16]In particular, using the technique of "active listening" which comes from work by Carl Rogers on nondirective psychotherapy.

[17]Fisher and Ury (1981) in particular offer a host of practical suggestions to enhance a creative cooperative ethos in bargaining.

clusion of the underlying *substantive* quest to create value. To err in this way is analogous to giving the prospective builder of a semiconductor factory advice on its landscaping, lighting, front office decor, employee dress code and working hours—without doubt, potentially valuable, but fatally incomplete without consideration of the physical inputs and engineering principles needed to make semiconductors.

Why This Chapter's Characterization of the Bases of Joint Gains Is Complete: A Technical Aside

Game theorists, economists, and other mathematically-minded analysts are able to fully characterize negotiators according to (1) their values and attitudes toward risk and time (represented by "utility functions"), (2) their beliefs and forecasts (represented by probability distributions), (3) what they originally possess (called initial endowments), and (4) their capabilities to produce (represented by "production functions"). Further, analysts distinguish between "private" and "public" goods. All joint gains derive from transactions involving various combinations of these four factors—but that can be summarized by simple and contingent trade and production agreements. The categories we have used in this chapter correspond exactly to this fully general characterization; hence the principles we have developed are not merely interesting or important special cases, but instead characterize the bases for all joint gains.[18] This distinguishes our analysis from much other work on "integrative," "mutual benefit," and "win-win" solutions that merely give examples or ad hoc taxonomies of joint gains.[19]

Summary

Agreements embody the potential of negotiation. If organizations can be thought of as networks of agreements, then much of the man-

[18]More technically, our underlying analysis utilizes von Neumann-Morgenstern expected utility as the measure of value. Private and common value correspond to private and public goods. The processes of value creation include not only exchange but production as well. Finally, subject to standard assumptions of mathematical "niceness," we allow the utility and production functions that underlie these processes to be concave or convex.

[19]See, for example, the discussion of various types of "integrative" agreements in Pruitt (1981)—all of which can be easily shown to be special cases of the more general principles developed in this chapter and elaborated in Chapter Nine.

ger's job consists of creating, influencing, sustaining, and, where appropriate, altering them. In general, there are two broad strategies to effect agreements: (1) to make the other party's alternatives to agreement worse or (2) to highlight and enhance the potential of joint action. In developing the second of these strategies this chapter has probed the underlying bases for creating private and common value, to explain the sources of joint gains. We have urged a focus on differences, shared interests, and scale economies. In particular:

- Differences in *relative valuation* can lead to exchanges, directly or by "unbundling" differently valued interests.
- Differences in *forecasts* can lead to contingent agreements when (1) the items under negotiation are uncertain and themselves subject to different probability estimates, or when (2) each party feels that it will fare well under and perhaps can influence a proposed contingent resolution procedure.
- Differences in *risk aversion* suggest insurance-like risk-sharing arrangements.
- Differences in *time preference* can lead to altered patterns of payments or actions over time.
- Different *capabilities* can be combined.
- Other differences (evaluation criteria, precedent and substance, constituencies, organizational situation, conceptions of fairness, and so on) can be fashioned into joint gains.
- *Mutually preferred positions* on single issues can create common value.
- *Shared interests* in a range of settlements can be made salient or linked to create common value.
- *Economies of scale* can lead to the creation of private and common value.

Intuition suggests that negotiations are likely to be more successful when they offer greater joint gains, or, equivalently, are more "integrative" or have lower conflict of interest. Indeed, in a series of carefully controlled experiments, investigators found that agreements took longer to achieve as the conflict of interest rose.[20] Others

[20]Robert Axelrod (1970) has shown that the "conflict of interest" in a negotiation can be described by an intuitive and unique measure that satisfies certain conditions. The measure can be obtained by (arbitrarily) setting the value of the alternatives to agreement for each party at zero, the maximum feasible value of an agreement to each party as one, and by drawing the Pareto frontier in the resulting unit square. His conflict of interest measure is then calculated to be the area above and to the right of the Pareto frontier and within the unit square. For a situation of

have found a strong positive relationship between conflict of interest in prisoners' dilemma situations and the probability of unilateral defection rather than mutually beneficial cooperation. Reviews of the social psychological literature lend support to the propositions that more integrative bargains (1) lead to speedier settlements, (2) have higher agreement probabilities, especially where aspiration levels and reservation prices are relatively high, (3) reduce the danger that one or more parties will repudiate the agreement, (4) tend to strengthen the relationship between the parties, thus facilitating later agreements, and (5) contribute to organizational effectiveness where subunits (individuals, work groups, departments) with distinct needs and values engage in intraorganizational bargaining.[21] Beyond offering an account of the nature of joint gains, therefore, the analysis of this chapter also points the way toward easier and more advantageous arrangements.

Let us review where we stand in our analysis. We have looked in detail at interests as the raw material and measure of negotiation. Alternatives to agreement imply the lower limits of value that any acceptable agreement must exceed. Negotiators can create value by fashioning agreements that dovetail differences, cultivate shared interests, and exploit economies of scale. Creating value is one crucial part of the negotiating process; the other, ultimately inseparable one involves claiming it, which is the subject of the next chapter.

---

maximal conflict, this measure is equal to one-half. Such a game might be called zero-sum or purely "distributive." Beyond simple agreement, interests conflict diametrically. If both parties can achieve their individually maximum outcomes simultaneously, there is zero conflict in Axelrod's sense. Loosely, the more the perceived possibilities set or Pareto frontier bulges up and to the right, the greater are the possible joint gains, the more integrative the bargaining, and the less the conflict of interest. The analysis throughout this chapter can be unified by considering it a guide to methods of reducing the conflict of interest in negotiation. Malouf and Roth (1981) found that agreements took longer to achieve as the conflict of interest rose.

[21]See Pruitt and Lewis (1977) and Pruitt (1983b, 1983c).

CHAPTER SIX

Claiming Value

THE YEAR 1912 is a good starting point for our exploration of tactics primarily intended to claim value. Teddy Roosevelt was nearing the end of a hard-fought and very close election campaign. Critical to his success was a final whistle-stop journey through the heartland of America. At each stop, Roosevelt planned to inspire the citizens with oratory, and leave each with a small pamphlet, three million of which had been printed. On the cover was a stern "Presidential" portrait; inisde was a stirring speech, "Confession of Faith." With luck, these would clinch the crucial votes. The final push was about to start when a campaign worker discovered a small line on each photograph that read "Moffett Studios—Chicago." Since Moffett held the copyright, unauthorized use of each photo could cost the campaign a dollar. The three million dollar price for distributing all the pamphlets greatly exceeded their resources. The campaign workers were in a tizzy. What to do?

Not using the pamphlets would badly damage reelection prospects. Yet if they went ahead without Moffett's authorization and were found out, they'd be branded lawbreakers and would be liable for an unaffordable amount. Quickly, the campaign workers reached a consensus: they would have to negotiate with Moffett. It is not hard for us to imagine their queasy feeling as they tried to plot strategy. It must have seemed a hopelessly weak position: approaching a small photographic studio, in an obvious hurry, pamphlets already packed in railroad cars, a potential three million dollar price tag, and nowhere near that amount in the till.

Dispirited, they approached George Perkins, noted financier and campaign manager. Perkins lost no time summoning his stenographer to dispatch the following cable: "We are planning to distribute many pamphlets with Roosevelt's picture on the cover. It will be great publicity for the studio whose photograph we use. How much will you pay us to use yours? Respond immediately." Shortly, he received this reply: "We've never done this before, but under the circumstances, we'd be pleased to offer you $250." Reportedly, Perkins accepted without asking for more.[1]

This story suggests a number of things about claiming value. First, many people readily assume that the bargaining range runs from the campaign paying nothing all the way up to three million dollars, or at least its total reserves. That the range could also include *Moffett's* paying anything rarely occurs to people. This exemplifies how incorrect assumptions often fence us in.

Second, this episode underlines the crucial role of information about each side's *perceptions* of its own and others' alternatives to agreement. If no agreement could be reached with Moffett, the campaign in fact would be in an awful bind—yet Perkins worded the cable carefully to suggest no problems if there were no deal, that they would merely use another photo. Perkins's omissions and suggestions masked *Moffett's* likely alternatives to agreement as well; and seemed to give them little time to find out. The studio was left with the impression that without a deal, life as usual would continue—not the fact that, if the campaign went ahead and used the already printed photos, Moffett could win a huge settlement in court. Moffett's awareness of either alternative to agreement could have dramatically improved their position in dealing with the campaign.

Finally, this anecdote leaves us with a feeling often experienced when claiming tactics are used in bargaining: ethical uncertainty.

Beyond these particular observations about tactics to claim value, this chapter examines general classes of such moves. At the end of the discussion, we try to evaluate some of the ethical issues raised.

[1]This example is drawn from Bacow and Wheeler (1984:73–74).

Shaping Perceptions of Alternatives

No-agreement alternatives set the lower limits on acceptable agreements. Key tactics for claiming value are intended to shape perceptions of these limits.

Such tactics are most clearly illustrated in rather simple, "distributive" bargains. A bargain is called distributive when more for one means less for the other, when no joint gains beyond simple agreement exist. The value that a negotiator would receive from his no-agreement alternatives is called his *reservation value*. As Chapter Three discussed, a negotiator should not accept any agreement worth less than this reservation value. After isolating the essence of claiming tactics in distributive bargains, we show how they function in bargains where joint gains are possible.

SHAPING PERCEPTIONS OF ALTERNATIVES IN DISTRIBUTIVE BARGAINS

A negotiator typically does not know his counterpart's reservation value.[2] For example, the high-tech firm preparing an offer to buy an industrial building whose asking price is $600,000 may only know that another group is interested, but not that the other group offered only $320,000. The high-tech firm is planning to convert it to office space, but unbeknownst to that firm's personnel, the other group plans to use it for nonprofit purposes. At the same time, the building's owner may know that the firm is considering another site but not how it rates the other building; in fact, it may be willing to pay up to $550,000 for his building.

The bargaining range or set runs from the seller's reservation value to the buyer's[3] (here, from $320,000 to $550,000, as depicted in Figure 6.1a). Of course, each negotiator is uncertain about the other's end of the range.

To claim value in a distributive bargain, each side tries to affect the other's perceptions of the bargaining range and where settlement

---

[2]In particular he does not know his counterpart's no-agreement alternatives. If he does know them, he is usually uncertain about how his counterpart values them relative to possible negotiated outcomes.

[3]In general, the bargaining range runs from the possible agreements that one negotiator considers equal in value to his alternatives to the possible agreements that the counterpart considers equivalent to hers.

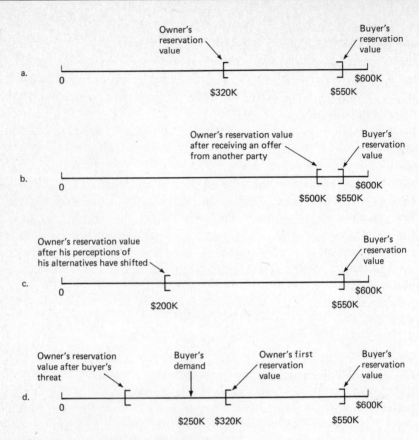

FIGURE 6.1:   The Changing Bargaining Set

is possible. For example, one side may claim that time is on her side, that no-agreement is quite tolerable, and that only an extremely favorable offer by her opponent can secure any agreement at all. The building's owner may bluff and portray the other group's offer as high, in the upper $400s, and attest to their willingness to pay up to $500,000. He may find another potential buyer willing to pay high prices, and then ask the high-tech firm to ante up. (See Figure 6.1b.) Or he may bluff, asking an associate to offer the real estate agent $500,000 for the building (with the understanding that the offer will just happen to fall through if the high-tech firm does not beat it) and having the agent make the new ''offer'' known to the high-tech firm. Thus, the essence of the owner's tactics has been to shift upwards the potential buyer's beliefs about the minimum the owner would take, either by persuasion about or by actually changing the owner's no-agreement alternatives. Changed beliefs, by either method, shrink the perceived bargaining set in a manner that favors the owner.

Tactics can also focus on the counterpart's alternatives: that they are bad and getting worse. Again, options run from shifting perceptions to shifting underlying realities. Thus, the high-tech firm can tell the building owner that the competing group is financially shaky, that it would require much longer to get financing, and that undesirable owner financing would be required. In other words, the owner should place a lesser value on his no-agreement alternative and thus his reservation value should be lower. Or, the firm might persuade the town's zoning board to rule out the competing group's uses. The firm could ask the competing group to withdraw its offer in return for a favorable long-term lease in the building if the firm can acquire it at a low price. In either case, the firm acts to shift the bargaining range (bargaining set) in its favor by reducing the value of the building owner's no-agreement alternatives. (See Figure 6.1c.)

The threat can be a potent weapon for claiming value. For example, if the firm's president were thought to be unscrupulous and well-connected to the zoning board, he might credibly threaten to work with the board to rule out any other buyers unless his offer of $250,000 were accepted. The threat, if believed, would lower the owner's reservation value to well below $250,000. The bargaining set as it is changed by the threat is depicted in Figure 6.1d. In general, a threat couples a demand with a commitment, often to worsen the opponent's no-agreement alternatives if the demand is not met.

SHAPING PERCEPTIONS OF ALTERNATIVES
IN BARGAINING WITH INTEGRATIVE POTENTIAL

When joint gains beyond simple agreement are possible, negotiators continue to use a variety of means to favorably shape perceptions of no-agreement alternatives.

For example, an engineering firm negotiating the sale of a new plant to a steel company might submit an initial offer that includes financial terms, technical specifications, responsibilities, performance requirements, penalties for failure to meet the requirements, and conditions and timing of installation. When negotiators for the two firms meet, Atkin, the steel company's representative, might state that the offer was not acceptable to the company and suggest areas for improving it, stressing price and some technical requirements over other issues. Then he might suggest another package that favored the steel company on all issues. Figure 6.2a illustrates the bargaining set (the set of all bargained outcomes that exceed both parties' reservation values), the reservation value that Atkin is feigning,

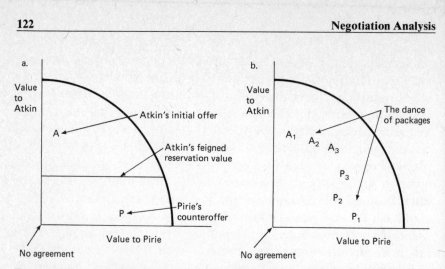

Figure 6.2: **Shaping Perceptions of Reservation Values in a Dance of Packages**

and the offer. The engineering firm negotiator, Pirie, would likely respond in kind, characterize Atkin's proposal as unacceptable, and offer a new package that is a bit better for Atkin but still retains the lion's share of benefits. As this process continues each negotiator may hold out well beyond the first proposal that actually surpasses his true reservation value—hoping to get much more from his counterpart.[4] Such a dance of packages would continue until one negotiator accepts the other's offer. (See Figure 6.2b for an illustration of their negotiation dance.)

When many issues are involved, the very complexity can make manipulating perceptions easier than in single-issue, distributive bargains. Tactics that alter no-agreement alternatives remain potent for claiming value. In all cases, such tactics shift perceptions of reservation values and thus shrink the bargaining set.

Commitments, Threats, and Focal Points[5]

The ability to convince a counterpart that one cannot be moved, that one can or will concede no further, is a crucial part of bargaining. One sometimes does this by conveying the impression, truthfully or not, that the proposed agreement is barely better than one's no-

---

[4]When there are many issues, a variety of possible packages may be equivalent in value to the best no-agreement alternative. The value of each such package is the reservation value.

[5]Much of this section comes from or has been stimulated by two seminal essays by Thomas Schelling (1961, 1966).

agreement alternatives. But, making a binding, credible, communicated commitment is a primary tactic for such persuasion.

Commitment tactics are most easily explained in extremely simple, intentionally artificial situations, but bear with us. The ability to make commitments, albeit much more subtly, is equally important in complex bargains of virtually all types as we shall later illustrate.

Let's begin with the simplest possible situation: a distributive bargain in which all reservation values are commonly known. Suppose that a buyer and a seller are bargaining about the price of a house; they will never see each other again. For example, the buyer and the seller both know that the seller has another buyer for $240,000 and that the buyer has found an equivalent house for sale at $260,000. The bargaining range or set thus runs from $240,000 to $260,000. Figure 6.3a illustrates the possible negotiated agreements. Here, claiming value means getting a better price for oneself.

Similarly, consider two equally senior law partners trying to decide which one gets the prestigious corner office overlooking the bay. Either Cadwalader or Botts will get the office if they can agree, but if they cannot, it will go to Stimson, an annoyingly aggressive junior partner. Because both senior partners want to maintain the traditional privileges and rewards for seniority and performance and because both detest Stimson, each prefers that either one take the office rather than let it fall to the upstart. Figure 6.4a illustrates the values each party places on each of the two possible negotiated outcomes. Because Cadwalader is a litigator and Botts is a tax man, they have

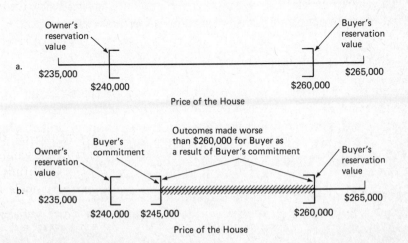

FIGURE 6.3: The Bargaining Set Before and After the House Buyer's Commitment

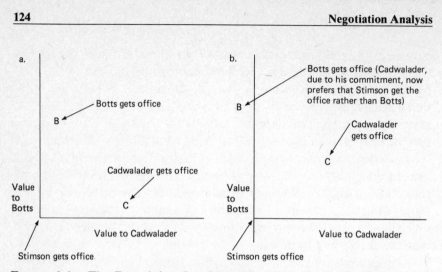

FIGURE 6.4: The Bargaining Set Over Who Gets the Office Before and After Cadwalader Makes a Commitment

no other real involvement and thus neither has a means to compensate the other for not taking the office. For either senior partner, successfully claiming value means getting the office for himself.

Knowing no more than this about the encounter, one should not be surprised to learn that either partner won the rights to the office. Or, with respect to the house example, that a house buyer and seller might divide the bargaining set evenly at $250,000, that the buyer was tenacious and paid $241,000, that the seller sold the house for $256,000, or that the two failed to reach any agreement at all. In this sense, these negotiations are indeterminate. The tactical issue, therefore, is how a negotiator can claim value when this is the case.

THE COMMITMENT

Such a distributive bargain can be "won" by the side that first commits credibly and irreversibly to a preferred settlement.

One bargainer commits to a point in the bargaining range by imposing large costs on herself for accepting settlements less attractive than this point. If these costs would make accepting any lesser settlement worse than her current alternatives, the other bargainer is stuck: he confronts a preordained choice between accepting the commitment point—which at least is in the bargaining set—or taking his own, less desirable alternative.

For example, suppose that Cadwalader, egged on in a rash moment by fellow litigators, makes a bet in the partners' dining room with a greedy but valued client: if Botts gets the office, Cadwalader will pay the client $50,000. If it bothers Cadwalader more to lose $50,000 than to see Stimson get the office, this bet changes his valuation of the outcomes: now he would rather let the office go to the upstart than agree to give it Botts. If Botts believes that the client will not led Cadwalader out of the bet, Botts must choose between giving Cadwalader the office and giving it to Stimson. If Botts does not fly into a rage at the way Cadwalader has rigged the situation, and if, on reflection, he really prefers to see the office occupied by one of the senior partners, he has no choice but to agree to give it to Cadwalader. Figure 6.4b shows how Cadwalader's commitment favorably changes the bargaining set.

Continuing to illustrate the point in the same simple manner, the buyer who claims that his wife will divorce him if he pays more than $245,000 may get the house for $245,000 if he can make his claim credible. Figure 6.3b shows how the commitment has shrunk the owner's perception of the bargaining range between buyer and seller. Regardless of the situation, a successful commitment favorably shifts perceptions of the bargaining range; the minimum one would apparently accept becomes more stringent.

MAKING COMMITMENTS STICK

But, making such a commitment binding, credible, visible, and irreversible is difficult. First, the claim might not be believed, even if true. The seller might doubt that the buyer's wife would divorce him over a house purchase despite all the buyer may do to persuade the seller of his wife's propensity for such behavior (and that he would prefer to stay married.) And, such commitments can sometimes be reversed. The house-seller might seek out the buyer's wife and attempt to persuade her that $255,000 is a reasonable price to pay for the house (or, politely, that her chosen course of action was nutty). Botts might attempt to persuade the client to repudiate his bet with Cadwalader for the health of the law firm and because it inappropriately alters the attorney–client relationship. In general, making commitments stick requires ingenuity and, often, a substantial investment of resources.

Even a successful commitment to a position may not obtain the desired agreement. First, if the negotiators make incompatible commitments from which they cannot back down, they will deadlock. If Botts simultaneously makes a similar agreement with his biggest client, and neither he nor Cadwalader budge, Stimson gets the office. Second, the commitment itself can change how the person on whom it has been sprung values the possible outcomes. For example, if Cadwalader's commitment angers Botts and causes him to crave revenge—by keeping Cadwalader from getting the office—more than the tradition that he originally valued, if Botts would feel publicly shamed by conceding, or if he believes that giving in to such tactics would set an intolerable precedent, Botts may come to prefer no agreement to letting Cadwalader win. If so, Cadwalader's commitment may only have been the first move in a destructive escalation of conflict.

FOCAL POINTS

It may be easier to commit credibly to some outcomes than others. The house buyer's attempt to commit arbitrarily to $251,968.40 may be called into question more readily than his resolve "not to take less than $250,000." Negotiations are often resolved at psychologically prominent "focal points." In addition to round numbers, people are attracted to outcomes that accord with simple formulas such as "equal division," "each person should be compensated on the basis of the number of hours worked," or other norms or principles of fairness. Even without commitments, both negotiators may well settle at such a focal point simply because doing so may be less costly than trying otherwise to resolve the indeterminate situation.[6]

Attempts to claim value often come disguised as appeals to fairness or reasonableness. Bargainers make commitments to appealing outcomes as well as to self-serving rationales and principles of "fairness." For example, the wily bazaar merchant may open with an exorbitant initial offer and then graciously offer to split the difference between his price and the buyer's reasonable first offer.

THE PREVALENCE OF COMMITMENTS

The artificiality of these examples should not obscure the practical importance of commitments. They are potent tactics in much

---

[6]In trying jointly to solve the indeterminate problem of where to settle in the bargaining range, a bargainer may move towards a focal point because he thinks his counterpart may be moving toward that point and that she thinks he might be doing the same thing. Bargainers may settle at such focal points because the costs of further bargaining exceed the expected value of pushing for more. See Schelling (1960).

more complex situations. For example, when a major investor attempted a hostile takeover of a large company, he included an interesting clause in agreements over the money he raised for the takeover: the interest rate he would be required to pay for this money would jump by 1.5 percent if he chose to make a counteroffer higher than his initial offer. Or, consider NATO's decision to put a significant number of American troops on the border of West and East Germany to commit the United States to respond to a Russian invasion of West Germany. Although the NATO forces would be unable to repel an invasion, it would necessarily kill American soldiers and a U.S. administration would incur huge political costs if it did not respond.

Less dramatic commitments abound. Kelno, a talented young associate at a management consulting firm, senses that Graham, a project director, is planning to pressure him to work on an undesirable study. To avoid this outcome when dealing with Graham, Kelno quickly arranges to join Voss's study, which is already in progress. When Graham begins the discussion, Kelno explains that he would love to work with him but that he is already working on Voss's study and does not feel he can jeopardize his relationship with Voss by pulling out now. Or, after the initial negotiating session with a vendor who asks for $13,000, a purchasing manager gets his boss to decree that purchases over $10,000 must go through a significant internal review. At the next session with the vendor, the purchasing manager says, "I am authorized to make purchases of up to $10,000 without approval; above that, the decision goes through a messy internal review. I went through two of them last month [not true] and cannot afford to go through another one this month. But, I think we can make a deal today if you can live with $10,000."

The costs incurred to make the commitment stick need not be external. To avoid conceding, a negotiator may invoke his undying need to maintain a firm reputation—for future bargains or even for later in the current negotiation. An administrator may refuse to make special exceptions to her policy by claiming that if she did, she would have to spend years considering other similar situations on a case-by-case basis.

UNDOING COMMITMENTS

Because of the prevalent use of commitments, negotiators learn ways to undo an opponent's commitment or prevent him from committing in the first place. To succeed, a commitment must be communicated (visible) and thus an opponent's attempt to commit may be thwarted by ignoring or pretending not to hear the attempt.[7] With the introduction of new information about the substance of the problem at hand, a party can defer to the new knowledge in moving from his commitment.[8] Because the commitment often specifies the concessions the opponent is being asked to make, changing the set of issues can sometimes undo the basis for the commitment.[9]

In addition, an attempt to commit frequently involves introducing a new interest into the negotiation that the opponent cannot satisfy and on which the negotiator will bear great costs unless the agreement exceeds some threshold. The negotiator who stresses his concern with his future reputation and the administrator who claims to be worried about having to deal with hundreds of others if she breaks long-established precedent are introducing interests only latent in the negotiation that their counterparts cannot apparently satisfy. The house-buyer whose wife will divorce him if he pays more than $245,000 is "adding" a party (his wife) and an interest (the relationship with his wife) that the seller cannot satisfy.

These sorts of commitments can often be undone by finding a way to satisfy the allegedly unsatisfied interests. By credibly promising never to tell anyone and thereby eliminating questions of reputation or by agreeing to intimate to the relevant public that the opponent did very well, one can sometimes undo a commitment based on reputation. Similarly, finding a reason that this case is "different" and therefore does not violate the precedent can undo commitments based on precedent. And, persuading the buyer's wife of the reasonableness of the $260,000 price satisfies the buyer's alleged interest in avoiding his wife's anger.

THREATS AS CONDITONAL COMMITMENTS

Negotiators sometimes threaten drastic consequences if their highly partisan demands are not met. A threat can be understood as a conditional commitment to do something undesirable if the threatened party does not comply. To take a farfetched example, suppose

[7]See Raiffa (1982) and Walton and McKersie (1965).

[8]See Walton and McKersie (1965) for a general discussion or Sebenius (1984) on how a computer model permitted a similar occurrence in a major international negotiation.

[9]Chapter Nine deals at length with moves intended to change the parties, interests, and other elements of a negotiation.

that a mild-mannered accountant threatens to blow up the seller's car if she does not sell it to him for a pittance. Suppose she refuses. What would motivate him to carry out the threat? It would be costly, messy, and dangerous for him and still he would not have the car. He has a serious credibility problem. Contrast his threat with the implied threat of co-CEO Lew Glucksman of Lehman Brothers to provoke internal upheaval and perhaps take the profitable trading operation to another firm if his abrupt demand to run Lehman by himself was not honored. Glucksman, with a reputation for volatile, vindictive, and even irrational actions, conveyed the powerful impression that his feet were "set in concrete"; he left little doubt that the apparent costs of executing his threat were meaningless to him and that he would act. In general, a threat tends to be more effective the more the underlying commitment to carry it out is binding, credible, visible, and irreversible.

THE RISKS OF COMMITMENTS

Making a commitment risks impasse if the other party becomes imcompatibly committed. Moreover, a negotiator usually does not know his counterpart's reservation value. With bad luck, too greedy a commitment may be unacceptable and, if irrevocable, will cause a breakdown.

Not surprisingly, some commitments, especially blunt ones, lead to bargaining explosions. The victim may not like the precedent being set for the style of future dealings. Or conceding to a blunt commitment may involve sufficient loss of face as to be undesirable; the commitment can start a destructive escalation of conflict.

Commitments based on "fair" principles and social norms are likely to be more effective than those made to apparently arbitrary positions. (Like committing to a position, one commits to a principle by imposing costs on oneself for abandoning that principle.) This may be true for reasons beyond any natural appeal of focal points.

A number of studies suggest that when a bargainer attributes his concession to his own weakness and the counterpart's strength, a blowup is likely. The bargainer would lose face or self-esteem by conceding. When this new interest (face) is included, he may find that no agreement, which retains self-esteem, is better than an agreement that seems to sacrifice it. This might well be the case for Botts when Cadwalader makes his bet or when someone stubbornly insists on an apparently arbitrarily chosen $104 settlement without any explanation. In contrast, when the bargainer can attribute the concession to something *outside* the two parties such as a mutually recognized norm, concession may not cause a loss of self-esteem. One might commit to refusing an employee a raise in various ways that do not risk his losing face in the dealing. For example, one may argue that such a raise would set an unacceptable precedent for all other employees in the same job grade or that one's boss would not accept it. Skillful commitments to norms and external standards are more likely to lead to concessions than commitments to more arbitrary points.[10]

Commitments and improvements in one's no-agreement alternatives are somewhat complementary tactics. Bargainers must normally expend resources to employ either. But commitments are risky because they are difficult to make credible, binding, visible, and irreversible and because they may fall outside the bargaining set. Finding a better alternative does not incur these liabilities. Moreover, one's commitment is vulnerable both to the other side's prior commitment and to an improvement in its alternative. An improvement in one's alternative, though, cannot be superseded by prior or subsequent commitments. A threat, of course, may hold the possibility of worsening the opponent's original (or even improved) alternatives. Bluffing a commitment or that one has an improved no-agreement alternative creates a risk that one will lose credibility if one's bluff is called or that, to maintain this credibility, one will forego an otherwise acceptable agreement. (And all these tactics raise ethical questions, with which we will soon deal.)

Shaping Aspirations

Doing better than one's alternatives to agreement is the point of negotiation, but how much more should one seek? More satisfaction of one's real interests is clearly better but, since the stars are unreachable, how high does one aim? And what effect do such "aspiration levels" have on the outcome of negotiation?

One important finding from experimental studies of bargaining is completely consistent with our experience on this question: higher aspirations tend to boost results. In some cases, the reason is obvious. Suppose that country lawyer Joe has inherited several acres of faraway rural property whose market value was appraised last year at $10,000. Say that the neighboring farmer calls and casually offers Joe $12,500 at a time when he had been thinking about selling and

[10]See Bacharach and Lawler (1981).

badly needs money. Almost at once, Joe thinks about accepting the offer since his bottom line is $10,000. But when a local real estate agent tells Joe that the nearby farmer desperately needs Joe's land as the critical link in a nearly completed major expansion plan, this information greatly increases Joe's aspiration level—and we are confident that he will end up with a much better price.

In some experiments, negotiators actually received the money corresponding to their settlements. Target settlements were suggested in their instructions—but in a way that did not change the money payoffs to subjects. In general, the higher the target *suggestions*, the more favorable the outcomes—despite the fact that the target suggestions did not change the money payoffs at all.[11] The reasons for this result are less clear to us than for Joe's negotiation—perhaps a specific dollar goal guides tactics better than the general desire to "get more," perhaps subjects seek to please the experimenter, perhaps something else. But the potent effect of higher aspirations is evident here and in many other settings.

Therefore, the behavioral importance of "aspiration levels" should be acknowledged, even if they seem somewhat arbitrary and lack the clear analytic basis of other key negotiation elements like reservation values. Even with this indeterminancy, bargainers need not set their aspiration levels capriciously. Clearly, one's aspirations increase with that one thinks possible. What is actually "possible," of course, depends on the other party's upper limit, which is determined by his alternatives to agreement. Once again, therefore, we see the absolutely critical importance of information about the other's alternatives—here it bears directly on setting aspiration levels. The studies suggest that higher is better, but plainly there are limits; two bargainers with stubbornly high, opposing aspirations will take time to reconcile them and may deadlock.

Moreover, in seeking to claim value, negotiators tenaciously try to lower their counterparts' aspirations. As the project head approaches his boss with a look that signals "budget increase request," the boss can be counted on to begin muttering about the tough year, the austerity directives from above, how the last four requests for increases were turned down, and so on. If successful, the boss will have lowered the project head's money aspirations. In general, the tools for accomplishing lowered aspirations are the same as those employed to affect perceptions of the bargaining set. Beyond run-of-the-mill arguments and efforts to persuade, these include moves to affect percep-

[11]See Siegel and Fouraker (1960).

tions of alternatives, where and how any commitments are attempted, as well as patterns of offers and concessions—a subject we treat in the next section.

Taking Positions

One common school of thought on how to choose offers is nicely expressed by Henry Kissinger:

> If agreement is usually found between two starting points, there is no point in making moderate offers. Good bargaining technique would suggest a point of departure far more extreme than what one is willing to accept. The more outrageous the initial proposition the better is the prospect that what one "really" wants will be considered a compromise.[12]

But, beyond the risk of souring the atmosphere, such tactics may stimulate equally extreme counteroffers that may simply cancel the intended effects and increase the chances of impasse. If one invests an extreme offer with a great deal of credibility, eventual movement may damage the credibility of subsequent "firm" stands.

If this is so and Kissinger's advice need not always apply, is there anything to guide the choice of offers?

CHOOSING OPENING OFFERS

Opening offers are often intended to influence perceptions of the bargaining set. Thus, the offer of $320,000 for the industrial building with an asking price of $600,000 was intended to convey to the building's owner that the buyer group aspired to a very low price, that they would not pay anywhere near $600,000, and that $600,000 was much higher than their alternative possibilities. In other words, the buyers hoped to cause a shift downward in the owner's perceptions of the bargaining set. They might well have accompanied this offer with arguments that other, potentially higher-paying buyers would not be able to get the zoning variances needed to make the building useful, and thus, that the owner's no-agreement alternatives were worse than he originally thought.

The choice of an effective opening offer and even the decision whether or not to make the first offer should also reflect a negotia-

[12]Kissinger (1961:205).

tor's perceptions about the counterpart's reservation value. When quite uncertain about the counterpart's reservation value, the negotiator may be better off letting the counterpart make the initial offer. Why? First, the negotiator hopes to gain information about the bargaining range from the offer. Second, the uncertainty inherently implies that there is a good chance a "moderate" opening offer would be too high or too low. An offer much worse than the counterpart's reservation value may provoke anger, sour the atmosphere, and raise questions of seriousness or good faith. For example, if the building owner's reservation value were much higher than the $320,000 offer, he might be offended by it and feel that the offering group is not really serious. Yet offering too high a price, say $550,000, runs the opposite risk: if the owner would have accepted $450,000, the buyers would have overpaid by $100,000. Thus, by refraining from making a first offer, a negotiator who is quite uncertain about the counterpart's reservation value avoids giving too much away and offering insultingly little.

But, the negotiator who defers when uncertain about the counterpart's reservation value bears another risk: his perceptions of the bargaining set may be manipulated by the opening offer. Thus, in this situation, many buyers make very low offers but try to make them seem soft or flexible. They hope to substantially reduce the counterpart's aspirations without being insulting, without unnecessarily giving up value, or risking committing to an unrealistic point.

By contrast, if the negotiator becomes fairly confident that the counterpart's reservation value lies in a small range, than he may clearly be best off making the opening offer. In this case, he does not expect to gain much information about the bargaining set from his counterpart's initial offer. Moreover, he is not likely to run the risks of either an insultingly low offer or an overly generous opening. For example, if the high-tech firm attempting to buy the building were fairly confident, after studying the market and the actual competing potential buyers, that the owner's reservation value was between $425,000 and $475,000, the firm might offer something below this range. For example, the firm might offer $400,000, which it feels has a 90 percent chance of being below the owner's reservation value; or it might go lower still. Given the high-tech firm's assessment, such an offer is likely to be outside the bargaining set, is unlikely to leave much profit for the owner, is close enought to entice him to bargain, and is chosen to guide the final agreement to a point just above the owner's reservation value.

Experimental results in distributive bargains suggest that, within limits, the higher the opening offer, the better the outcome.[13] But, what is acceptably high and what is insultingly extreme depends on the assumed norms. When making an offer to another member of the diamond industry in Switzerland, being 2 percent below the asking price might be insulting; when buying a used car in the United States, offers 20 to 40 percent below the asking price can be reasonable. Couching potentially extreme offers in "reasonable" trappings by appeal to "fair" principles and presenting them in a low-key manner may help mitigate the risk of adverse reaction. Finally, what is "high" depends on the degree of uncertainty about the counterpart's reservation value. Thus, a seller might choose an offer she thinks is 90 to 95 percent likely to be above the buyer's reservation value. The offer is likely to be much higher when she is more uncertain than when she is fairly confident.

ANCHORING

People often deal poorly with uncertainty.[14] Their cognitive deficiencies suggest tactics for claiming value. Consider the phenomenon of "anchoring" as it applies to judgments about reservation values and aspirations. When many people assess an uncertain quantity, they tend to jump to a point estimate of it and then adjust a bit around it to account for the uncertainty.[15] By influencing a counterpart's point estimate of the quantity, a negotiator can locate where the small range of uncertainty will lie. One can thus "anchor" another's beliefs about the quantity in a way favorable to one's bargaining position.

For example, in one experiment, groups of college students were asked to name the percentage of the countries in the United Nations that are African.[16] Before answering the question, a roulette wheel (modified to have the numbers one through one hundred) was spun in front of the students. For one typical group, the wheel stopped at 10

---

[13]See Siegel and Fouraker (1960), Sawyer and Guetzkow (1966), and Raiffa (1982).

[14]Kahneman and Tversky have done much striking work on people's deviations from decision-analytic or economic notions of rational decision making under uncertainty. (See Kahneman and Tversky, 1972, 1979; Kahneman and Tversky, 1974; Kahneman, Slovic, and Tversky, 1982). These cognitive limitations have begun to be studied in the context of negotiation by Bazerman (1983) and Bazerman and Neale (1983).

[15]See Kahneman and Tversky (1974).

[16]See Kahneman and Tversky (1974).

percent; for another group it landed at 65 percent. The first group was asked if the percentage of U.N. nations that are African was higher or lower than 10 percent (the number chosen by the spin of the wheel); the other group was asked whether the percentage was higher or lower than 65 percent. Then discussion was allowed to take place. In all other ways the groups were treated identically. Surprisingly, the first group's estimates were strikingly lower than those of the second: the mean of the first group's estimates was 24 percent while the mean of the second group's estimate was 45 percent! Thus, the clearly irrelevant piece of information—a randomly chosen starting point of 10 percent versus 65 percent—seemed strongly to anchor their perceptions about the proportion of U.N. member nations that are African.

A negotiator is typically uncertain about his counterpart's reservation value and aspirations. His own aspirations follow, in part, from these uncertain perceptions. And, although Chapter Three advised negotiators to assess their reservation values, social psychological experiments on "limits" (bottom lines or reservation values) suggest that "a bargainer without a limit seems totally plausible, especially in the earlier phases of the negotiation."[17] In practice, therefore, reservation values and aspirations sometimes have a lot of give.

When there is considerable uncertainty, a strong opening offer can sharply anchor perceptions of the bargaining set and aspirations.[18] Prenegotiation tactics, initial discussions, and opening offers by the counterparts can favorably anchor a negotiator's perception of these values, cause him to reduce his own aspirations, and alter his reservation value. The building owner who demands $600,000, argues forcefully that this price is fair and reasonable, refuses for weeks to listen to other offers, and keeps returning discussions to his $600,000 price may strongly anchor toward $600,000 potential buyers' perceptions of what the owner will accept. Their original aspiration to pay much less will also likely be revised.[19]

[17]Pruitt (1981:27).

[18]This application of the anchoring phenomenon is confirmed by a study on negotiating behavior unconcerned with anchoring. Liebert, Smith, Hill and Keiffer (1968) conclude that bargainers in a distributive bargain who had little information about the bargaining range tended to use the counterpart's opening bid to set their own aspirations while bargainers well-informed about the bargaining range used the counterpart's offer to assess the reasonableness of the counterpart's aspirations.

[19]A number of the cognitive deficiencies studied by Kahneman and Tversky (see Kahneman and Tversky, 1972, 1979; Kahneman and Tversky, 1974; Kahneman, Slovic, and Tversky, 1982) and by Bazerman (1983) and Bazerman and Neale (1983) have implications for offensive and defensive tactics. For example, people tend to be risk-averse when a gamble is presented as a potential gain and risk-prone when the

COUNTEROFFERS

Experiments by Howard Raiffa on distributive bargains suggest that the point midway between two opening offers is not a bad predictor of where a final negotiated settlement will fall—providing the midpoint lies inside the zone of possible agreement.[20] These results imply that a good response to an initial offer should be chosen so that the midpoint between the two offers is at the negotiator's aspiration level.

To prevent one's own perceptions from being unfavorably anchored, defensive tactics are called for. If the other party opens with an extreme offer, one should focus attention away from it. Rather than letting the offer shift one's aspirations, one should effectively dismiss it by directing discussion toward a much more favorable counteroffer.

Recall also that Raiffa's results had a caveat: that the "midway between opening offers" rough prediction did not generally hold where the midpoint fell outside the actual bargaining set. This may be because the extreme offeror necessarily had to make a disproportionate number of, or disproportionately large concessions to reach agreement at all. In the process, the apparent greed and manipulativeness may have tilted the psychological advantage to the other, more "reasonable" side. Thus in making the first counteroffer, one should take care that the midpoint between the offers is in the perceived bargaining set.

SEQUENCES OF OFFERS

The sequence in which one bargainer makes concessions can shape his counterpart's perceptions. A pattern of concessions that apparently converges to a particular point may give the impression that that point is the negotiator's reservation value. Similarly, the negotiator who exaggerates the cost of her own concessions and minimizes the benefits of her counterpart's movement also hopes to convince him to make "equally" costly, and thus larger, concessions.

---

same gamble is presented as a potential loss. Thus, framing a proposal as a possible gain for one's counterpart is desirable when one seeks risk-averse behavior; and framing it as a possible loss seems sensible if risk-prone behavior is desired. (See Tversky and Kahneman, 1981, for a discussion of framing and Kahneman and Tversky, 1979, on the switch from risk-averse to risk-prone behavior.)

[20]Raiffa (1982). See Pruitt (1981) for a survey of much social psychological experimentation on offers and concessions in distributive bargains.

TACIT SHAPING OF PERCEPTIONS

Although we have framed this discussion in terms of choosing offers, similar reasoning extends to a whole range of prenegotiation behaviors intended to favorably shape perceptions of the bargaining set. Consider the CEO who desperately desires to sell his company but feigns indifference and nonchalantly defers for a month a meeting to discuss a possible acquisition offer. Similarly, numerous American public statements announcing U.S. aspirations and castigating the Soviet Union's posture on arms control undoubtedly have the effect of shaping Soviet expectations; Soviet posturing no doubt has an equivalent effect on American perceptions. Opening statements, memos that stake out positions, statements to the press before formal negotiations begin, and detailed but clearly partisan analyses all are intended to favorably shape and anchor a counterpart's perceptions of the bargaining set.

Holding Prime Values Hostage

Imagine entering an antique store and covetously fondling an old brass clock for a quarter of an hour. Further, imagine telling the store owner how much you like the clock, and, turning it over and over in your hands, how it could be the *perfect* gift for your mother-in-law to make up for the bruising quarrel you had with her this morning. The world is not all bleak on all fronts, you idly continue, since you got an unexpected bonus two days ago; that helps things a bit. But this clock would absolutely turn things around with her, and, besides, you have no time to look elsewhere given your trip to Toledo late this afternoon. (You really mean all this.) Finally, ardently desiring the clock but trying to sound offhand, you ask the price. It seems very high, oddly, an iota less than your bonus, "yet very fair, sir, given the clock's truly unique qualities." "And," the shop owner intones firmly, but with a touch of sadness in his voice, "one does not haggle over things of such beauty."

Fortunately, this was only an unpleasant reverie. Yet it illustrates a venerable technique for claiming value: knowledge about how much an object or provision is worth to one party can allow the other to extract it all. In the above example, the clock and money were at issue; knowing your craving for the clock and sensing your relative indifference to money, it was simple for a greedy owner to press his advantage. The same phenomenon, which we have somewhat fancifully called "holding prime values hostage," can occur whether two or more issues are on the table. If a union negotiator discovers that management places enormous value on one provision of a complex contract, the union can hold that value "hostage" to concessions on the range of other linked issues.

The union's claiming tactic in this case is simple: having learned how much management cares about prevailing on this issue, the union commits to grant it only after substantial management concessions on the other issues. To gain its desired provision and thwart the union, the management may try several things. First, it will probably seek to downplay its real interest in the provision, hoping to win it at a lower cost. Second, it can try to *separate* negotiations over the provision from the other questions at issue, thereby depriving the union of another "currency" for payment. Separation could be accomplished if the provision were unconditionally settled first—and the other questions were only dealt with later and independently. Equivalently, if everything else was settled first, dealing with this provision at the end could separate it. Relegating it to a separate negotiating committee might also work. Needless to emphasize, the union will be pressing for linkage at every turn. Third, management could seek to undo the effect of the union's commitment to gaining concessions elsewhere. For example, management might make a countercommitment to give less, hoping this action would be more credible than the union's and that it would not lead to impasse.

The moral of all this is neither that cards should be played right next to one's chest nor that one should sneak a mirror behind one's opponent to see his cards; instead, we stress how potent such tactics can be for claiming value. But central to the Negotiator's Dilemma are the following two realities: understanding the other's values is essential to devising joint gains; yet exposed values can be taken hostage.

Linking to Claim

The first cousin to claiming value by means of an issue already on the table is to bring in new issues for the same purpose. When the Soviet Union had an especially bad grain harvest in 1975, Henry Kissinger sought to link continued U.S. grain sales to good Soviet behavior in the Middle East as well as to a price cut on Soviet oil that would hurt OPEC.

Such classic linkage ploys have a number of variants. Instead of negotiating directly over the extent of land development, an opposing group can link a variety of other issues to the process: suits over the standards required of an environmental impact statement, zoning laws, endangered species protections, and the like. If development costs can be sufficiently increased by switching issues this way, the whole project may be derailed.

A tactical shift to a matter where one has acknowledged expertise can be particularly effective. For example, consider an author negotiating to get his publisher to use and bear the cost of expensive nonstandard graphics in his forthcoming book. The author is ready with arguments about cost effectiveness and may be secretly prepared to concede on his royalty rate. Yet, the author might be completely stymied when the publisher says, "You want this to be recognized as a high-quality book, don't you? Can you think of any classy book that has this kind of graphics? People won't recognize the quality of your book." True or not, the publisher has gotten his way on the contested issue.

Some subordinates are very loyal and have strong conceptions of their roles. When trying to induce such a person to do an unpleasant job, some managers get their way by avoiding discussions on the merits of the task in question and linking other interests. For example, there may be appeals to the appropriate superior–subordinate relationship, the company's reliance on the person, and loyalty.

Managers and leaders can attempt to instill in others a deep psychological identification, that is, to want what the leader does simply because they want to be like him. Merely by making his wishes known, such an admired manager sometimes seems to transform conflict into pure shared interest. As a result, managers sometimes invest tremendous energy in cultivating identification, by letting it be known that they have access to and influence upon important people, by adopting the trappings of power, and by sheer force of personality. Whether the result of this is good for the organization or not, it certainly makes it easier for the manager's preferences to prevail.

In short, otherwise separate issues and interests can be linked to claim value. Even shared interests in the relationship, loyalty, norms of fairness and appropriate behavior, as well as broader common goals and visions, can be handy for this purpose.

Misleading

In their thirst to claim value, some negotiators mislead their counterparts. Several versions of this are especially common.

MALIGN PERSUASION AND EXPLOITING IGNORANCE

Suppose that a slightly senile widower brings a Stradivarius to a violin dealer or a diamond to a jeweler. Being told that, no, one is a fiddle and the other a rock (but, even so, they can be taken off his hands for a small price) would scarcely be unheard-of. Or take that valuable Arizona "ranch" with no water for miles, that supposedly meaningless "standard" clause whose addition reverses the thrust of an agreement, or that novice writer who signs a book contract lacking paperback, foreign, or film rights. All bear depressing witness to the sometime effectiveness of claiming value by lying or exploiting ignorance; we soon turn to the ethical side of tactical choice.

OVERSTATING AND UNDERSTATING

Recall the negotiations (from Chapter Two) over the terms of a cable television system. The mayor cared most strongly about the completion date but feigned primary interest in the subscriber price and the number of channels. By making the cable operator believe that his subsequent (modest) concession on price was very costly, the mayor hoped to induce a large concession on completion date in return. In other words, the mayor attempted to claim value by misleading the cable operator about his relative valuation of issues. Of course, the mayor might not actively mislead; he might merely be evasive or cagey and guide the cable operator to the same erroneous conclusions.

A more extreme example arises when the parties are not even sure about which interests their counterparts perceive to be at stake. By feigning a completely new interest, preferably annoying to the other party, the first party may hope to "concede" that interest in return for something of real value.

If one side discovers, unbeknownst to the other, that an interest is shared, the first side may use this knowledge to claim value. For example, recall the mayor negotiating a contract with the police union that has asked for the removal of the police commissioner. If the mayor secretly also wants to fire the commissioner, she may be able to "offer" this firing, but only in return for large concessions on salary and other issues. Even known shared interests can sometimes be manipulated this way. For example, two countries may be known to value a pleasant working relationship. Yet, one country may feign a lack of concern for it or even proclaim relations "damaged" hoping the other will "repair" it with concessions elsewhere.

Probabilities may also be distorted in order to claim value. To stimulate a high price, the seller of a small business may wax much more optimistic on its prospects than he actually believes to be the case. (We discuss appropriate countertactics in the next chapter.) And to get low tax rates, the sponsors of a zinc mine in a Third World country may go on and on to the local authorities about how modest profits are likely to be.

Negotiators are often uncertain about each other's interests, tradeoffs, attitudes toward risk and time, forecasts, technology, and so on. Misleading each other can become a significant element in the separate quests to claim value. Typically, interests are overstated with the intention of later "conceding" for a good price. Understatement to disguise actual valuation can prevent being squeezed. The lure of these tactics is individual gain; the victims are often foregone joint value—and ethical standards.

The Language of Claiming

Although the object of tactical action may be an opponent's perception of the bargaining set, the language by which value is claimed often has a moral ring. In many negotiations, positions are advanced and justified not by arguing that the negotiator desires them but rather that they are "right," morally, socially, or scientifically.[21] Distributive negotiations over who will get more are often carried out by a proxy discussion over who is more morally or factually correct. To argue for advantageous outcomes, negotiators draw on norms of justice and equity, institutional rules, consistency with past promises and performance, and appropriate social behavior.

Sometimes, the forceful assertion of a norm is sufficient to gain agreement: "It is only right that I pay you what the others are getting, not more." Even when one does not place intrinsic value on acting in accord with a certain norm, one may bear social costs for rejecting it outright.[22] For example, in response to an appeal to a widely accepted standard of fairness in dividing benefits, one may argue that the proposed rule is not applicable and propose another, more favorable one. By contrast, the response that "I do not want to

[21]See Gulliver (1979) for a clear discussion of the use of norms in negotiation. Fisher and Ury's (1981) approach to negotiation relies heavily on the prevalence and effectiveness of normative argument. Condlin (1985) provides an interesting discussion of argumentation in negotiation.

[22]See Gulliver (1979:192).

be fair, I want the biggest slice of the pie," can be costly. Thus, a negotiator is more likely to acknowledge the norm but argue that it is inappropriate to the situation at hand or that it has been applied incorrectly. Applied correctly, with the real facts about the real situation, the outcome would be quite different (and advantageous to the opponent). "Yes, fifty-fifty would be the right way to go, but I put in more work and am more senior."

Pressures to do the "right" thing can be applied not merely to the outcome but to behavior during the negotiation as well. For example, consider a restaurant chain owner who sought to expand her business in two new regions (the South and Southwest). She hoped to share the returns from the South with an early investor but retain for herself the profits from the more promising Southwest. The investor argued that because he invested early in the life of the chain, he deserved the same treatment from all of the chain's ventures. Accepting the norm in the discussion, she responded that she wanted to treat him in this way, but laid out the "insuperable" practical problems that prevented her from acting in this way. (In fact, she did not want to act in accord with the norm of equal treatment, but found baldly rejecting it hard; hence rejecting the "practical" aspects was her way to the same end.) When the investor suggested a way around these practical difficulties—which he had in fact had in the back of his mind from the start—the restauranteur found herself in a tricky position. Rather than violate a norm of consistency with her earlier statement in the negotiation—that equal treatment was the "right way to go"—she felt "morally" forced to accede even at a likely cost of several million dollars. Though this whole negotiation was carried out in terms of right and wrong, its effects were purely distributive.

The role of norms and normative argument goes well beyond cynical self-serving uses. As we have mentioned before, negotiators frequently derive value from acting in accord with social norms; this can be understood as an interest. The post-negotiation desire to justify the agreement to oneself and to explain the agreement to others also makes agreement in accord with norms desirable. At the same time, norms can also serve as the basis for nonantagonizing commitments and as focal points.

Because negotiators frequently find it costly to reject the suggestion that they should act consistently with norms of the group, introducing normative argument can limit the bargaining set to those outcomes that are "socially acceptable." Egregious demands that cannot find strong normative support can sometimes be ruled out.

In short, the language in which much negotiation is carried out and with which much value is claimed can be normative. Carefully working out normative arguments and counterarguments can be an important part of preparing for a negotiation.

Powerology: Power Clothes, Meals, Travel, Trappings, and Talk

We make a habit of reading books on how to get "power." We have learned about successful clothes: tan raincoats give one more power than blue ones; dark gray and navy suits give one more power than pale blues and green—and pinstripes really enhance one's power quotient; "Ivy League" ties and custom-made suits have similarly potent effects. We have read about "power lunches," in which a business executive conveys the impression of power by being known and respected enough by the restaurant staff to merit a "power" table, by arranging to have the staff come only at his request, and by ordering "power" food like steak and caviar rather than "wimp" food such as pasta or bouillabaisse. And we know not even to think of taking a cab or, heaven forfend, a subway; it is more powerful to arrive in a long limousine or a corporate jet, trailed by obsequious assistants. One's office can reflect power if it has the right trappings: a plush rug, a "masculine" desk and chair, a much lower chair for visitors, and so forth. Being interrupted by phone calls apparently from important people—senators, prominent CEOs, and the like—will also add to one's power quotient. And, we have learned that one can enhance one's power by speaking with a low voice, asking gruffly "What's the bottom line?" and using powerful body language.

What should one make of such tactics? How do they work? When effective, they function in a straightforward way. Each of us has a subconscious vision of the characteristics and trappings associated with a person who has power, gets what he wants, and can deliver what he promsies. If we do not consciously examine interests and no-agreement alternatives when dealing with such a person, we may aspire to less. We are sometimes even afraid to make requests. Hence the negotiator who drapes himself in powerful trappings may convince us that he is powerful, thus implicitly shaping our perceptions of *his* no-agreement alternatives (no doubt excellent, powerful people always have lots of options) and aspirations (he always get what he wants) and causing us to reduce ours. Thus, when successful, the powerologist shapes perceptions of the bargaining range.

Countertactics might involve responding in kind: imagine two business executives competing over whose "power" office will house their meeting, whose secretary can interrupt more frequently with calls apparently from "important people," or who can eat rarer meat. Yet the most effective response may well be awareness, bringing such tactics to a conscious level. Such tactics recognized may largely be tactics disarmed.

Though sometimes potent, these tactics are neither profound nor universal. Their effectiveness depends considerably on the culture in which they are used. In some settings, a nose ring, many wives, or a fleet of camels may well be more potent than a navy pinstripe suit; in others, apparent access to the supernatural may well have more useful connotations than claims of access to the White House.

Which brings us to the more general question of how culture affects negotiation.[23] While the particulars are not the province of this book, the cultural context gives strong clues to the participants about how to interpret the whole interaction from basic assumptions to communication (Does "yes" mean agreement?) to tactics (Does a small, early concession imply weakness or goodwill?).

Further, any culture has signals of hierarchy and status; emitting them can heavily affect expectations, and, as we have argued throughout, expectations play a central role in bargaining. Thus we do not mean to underestimate this effect by poking fun at some of the more flamboyant signals occasionally proposed. Certainly, we do not suppose that attempting to close a major real estate deal would best be done in a sweatsuit at a burger stand. When in Rome, one should do as a Roman,[24] and especially to the extent it usefully affects expectations. In general, the elements of negotiation on which we have focused—interests, alternatives, joint gains, and the processes of creating and claiming value—must be analyzed with the right cultural filter in place.

Summary Observations

We have looked at several classes of tactics for claiming value. These include shaping perception of alternatives, making commitments, in-

[23]For more on the role of culture in negotiation see Gulliver (1979), Hall (1959, 1960), or Fisher (1980).

[24]Figuratively. It would be silly and probably counterproductive for an American businessman to mimic a Saudi prince. It is not silly to pay attention to the characteristics that in Saudi eyes signal a "powerful" American.

fluencing aspirations, taking positions, manipulating patterns of concessions, holding prime values hostage, linking issues and interests, misleading other parties, as well as exploiting cultural expectations.

For expositional clarity, we have focused on explicit, acknowledged negotiations of brief duration. But analogous tactics apply to less well-acknowledged negotiations that are conducted tacitly over long periods of time. By using any of these tactics in any kind of negotiation, one party seeks advantage by influencing another's perception of the bargaining set. Virtually all these tactics involve distorting information in a way that risks impasse. Moreover, many of them risk negotiators becoming hostile, making threats and counterthreats, and the escalation of the conflict.

Many, if not most, bargaining situations contain significant potential for joint gain beyond simple agreement. But since claiming is as much a part of negotiation as creating and since the character of most claiming tactics is the opposite of those essential to creation, the risks of lost opportunity for joint gain are inherently very high.

The Ethical Dimension

The agent for a small grain seller reported the following telephone conversation, concerning a disagreement over grain contracted to be sold to General Mills:

> We're General Mills; and if you don't deliver this grain to us, why we'll have a battery of lawyers in there tomorrow morning to visit you, and then we are going to the North Dakota Public Service [Commission]; we're going to the Minneapolis Grain Exchange and we're going to the people in Montana and there will be no more Muschler Grain Company. We're going to take your license[.][25]

This chapter's discussion of such tactics mainly intended to claim value inescapably raises hard ethical issues. How should one evaluate moves that stake out positions, threaten another with walkout or worse, misrepresent values or beliefs, hold another person's wants hostage to claim value at his expense, or offer an "elegant" solution of undeniable joint benefit but constructed so that one side will get the lion's share?

One approach to these questions is denial—to believe, pretend, or wish that claiming value has no part in negotiation and hence such

[25]*Jamestown Farmers Elevator, Inc.* v. *General Mills*, 552 F.2d 1285, 1289 (8th Cir. 1977).

tactical choices are falsely posed: "If one really understood that the whole process was effective communication and joint problem solving, one could dispense with any unpleasant-seeming tactics, except to think about responding to their use by nasty opponents." Or one can admit that there are hard questions but deny they are relevant, as suggested by the following advice from a handbook on business negotiation:

> Many negotiators fail to understand the nature of negotiation and so find themselves attempting to reconcile conflicts between the requirements of negotiation and their own senses of personal integrity. An individual who confuses private ethics with business morality does not make an effective negotiator. A negotiator must learn to be objective in his negotiations and to subordinate his own personal sense of ethics to the prime purpose of securing the best deal possible for his principals.[26]

Obviously, we find simply denying that claiming is an essential part of negotiation to be conceptually flawed. And we are also uncomfortable with admitting that its characteristic tactics involve ethical questions but, along with the author of the above remark, judging them irrelevant. As with other interests, we find both intrinsic and instrumental reasons to be concerned with ethical issues in negotiation.[27]

Many people want to be "ethical" for intrinsic reasons—apart from the effect of such choices on future encounters. Why? Variously, because it simply feels better, because it may be psychologically healthier, because certain principles of good behavior are taken as moral or religious absolutes,[28] or for other reasons. Yet it is often hard in negotiation to decide what actions fit these criteria, especially when values or principles appear to conflict.

Ethical behavior may also have instrumental value. One hears that "it pays to be ethical" or "sound ethics is good business," meaning that if a negotiator does her calculations right, taking into account the long-run costs of overly shrewd behavior, profits will be higher. The eighteenth-century diplomat François de Callières made a more expansive version of this point:

[26]Beckman (1977).

[27]For an insightful, common-sense discussion of the reasons for being "moral," see Hospers (1961).

[28]If certain precepts are taken as Kantian categorical imperatives or as otherwise correct in an absolute sense, regardless of the consequences (the strong deontological position), the decision problem may be easy—unless more than one such principle appears to conflict.

It is a capital error, which prevails widely, that a clever negotiator must be a master of the art of deceit. . . . No doubt the art of lying has been practised with success in diplomacy; but unlike that honesty which here as elsewhere is the best policy, a lie always leaves a drop of poison behind, and even the most dazzling diplomatic success gained by dishonesty stands on an insecure foundation, for it awakes in the defeated party a sense of aggravation, a desire for vengeance, and a hatred which must always be a menace to his foe . . . the negotiator will perhaps bear in mind that he will be engaged throughout life upon affairs of diplomacy and that it is therefore his interest to establish a reputation for plain and fair dealing . . . [which] will give him a great advantage in other enterprises on which he embarks in the future.[29]

Of course, such justifications of ethics in terms of prudence rely on the calculations of its benefits turning out the right way: "Cast thy bread upon the waters," the Bible says, "and it shall return to thee after many days." The harder case, however, is when ethical behavior does *not* seem to pay—even after factoring in the long-term costs of reputation, credibility, how others may react, and any ill social effects.

Bargaining is fraught with such ethical issues. Three areas strike us as especially relevant: (1) the appropriateness of certain tactics, (2) the distribution of value created by agreement, and (3) the possible effects of negotiation on those not at the table (externalities). Without elaborating the philosophical frameworks within which such questions can be more fully addressed, we offer some thoughts on making these kinds of inescapable ethical choices.[30]

TACTICAL CHOICE

The essence of much bargaining involves changing another's perceptions of where in fact one would settle. Several kinds of tactics can lead to impressions that are at variance with the truth about one's actual position: persuasive rationales, commitments, references to other no-agreement alternatives, impressions intended by the pattern of concessions, failing to correct misperceptions, and the like. These tactics are tempting for obvious reasons: one side may claim value by causing the other to misperceive the bargaining range. And both sides are generally in this same boat.

[29]de Callières (1716:32).

[30]For a good informal discussion of these questions, especially the first, see Raiffa (1982:344–355).

Such misrepresentations about the bargaining set and about preferences should be distinguished from misrepresentation about the substance of the negotiation (whether the car has known difficulties that will require repair, whether the firm being acquired has important undiscussed liabilities, and so on). This latter category of tactics, which we earlier dubbed malign persuasion, more frequently fails the tests of ethical appropriateness that we suggest.

Are the "Rules" Known and Accepted?   Some people take the symmetry of negotiation as easing the difficulty of ethical choice. The British statesman Henry Taylor is reported to have said that "falsehood ceases to be falsehood when it is understood on all sides that the truth is not expected to be spoken." In other words, if these tactics are mutually accepted as within the "rules of the game," there is no problem. A good analogy is poker: bluffing is expected and thus permissible, while drawing a gun or kicking over the table are not. Yet often, the line is harder to draw.

A foreigner in Hong Kong may be aware that at least some tailors bargain routinely, but still be unsure whether a particular one—who insists he has fixed prices—is "just bargaining." Yet that tailor may reap considerable advantage if he in fact bargains but is persuasive that he does not. It is often self-servingly easy for the deceiver to assume that others know and accept the rules. And a worse problem is posed if our contention is right that many management situations are often not even recognized as negotiation, when in fact they are. If so, then how can any "rules" of the game meet this test?[31] By direct statement or by conduct indirectly, a manager can act in ways that try to make clear appropriate standards and expectations for conduct. But this does not address the question of what those standards should be.

Can the Situation Be Freely Entered and Left?   Ethicist Sissela Bok adds another criterion: for lying to be appropriate, not only must the rules be well-understood, but the participants must be able freely to enter *and* leave the situation.[32] Thus to the extent that mutually expected ritual flattery or a work of fiction involve "lying," there is little problem. To make an analogy between deception and violence: though a boxing match, which can involve rough moves,

[31]One response, consistent with this book, might be to widen understanding of the prevalence of negotiation.

[32]See Bok (1978:137–140).

meets this criterion, a duel, from which exit may be impossible, does not.

Yet this standard may be too high. We have argued that bargaining situations are far more widespread than bazaar-like encounters; in fact they pervade life inside and out of organizations. Hence free entry and exit may be impracticable. So if bargaining will go on and people will necessarily be involved in it, something else is required. When it is unclear whether a particular tactic is ethically appropriate, we find that a number of questions—beyond whether others know and accept it or may leave—can illuminate the choice.

• *Self-image*. Peter Drucker asks a basic question: when you look at yourself in the mirror the next morning, will you like the person you see?[33] And there are many such useful questions about self-image.[34] Would you be comfortable if your co-workers, colleagues, and friends were aware that you had used a particular tactic? Your spouse, children, or parents? If it came out on the front page of the *New York Times* or the *Wall Street Journal*? If it became known in ten years? Twenty? In the history books?

• *Reciprocity*. Does it accord with the Golden Rule? How would you feel if someone did it to you? To a younger colleague? A respected mentor? A member of your family? (Of course, saying that you would mind very much if it were done to another need not imply the tactic is unethical; that person may not be in your situation or have your experience—but figuring out the reason you would be bothered can give a clue to the ethics of the choice.)

• *Advising Others*. Would you be comfortable advising another to use this tactic? Instructing your agent to use it? How about if such advice became known?

• *Designing the System*. Imagine that you were completely outside the setting in which the tactic might be used, but that you were responsible for designing the situation itself: the number of people present, their stakes, the conventions governing the encounters, the range of permissible actions, and so on. The wrinkle is that you would be assigned a role in that setting *but* you would not know in advance the identity of the person whose role you would assume. Would you build in in the possibility for the kind of tactics you are now trying to evaluate?[35] A simpler version of this test is to ask how you

[33]Drucker (1981).

[34]This and the following questions are intended to clarify the appropriateness of the choice itself, not to ask about the possible consequences to you of different parties' being aware of your actions (firings, ostracism, etc.).

[35]This discussion draws from Rawls (1971).

would rule on this tactic if you were an arbitrator or even an elder in a small society.

• *Social Result.* What if everybody bargained this way? Would the resulting society be desirable? These questions may not have obvious answers. For example, hard, individual competition may seen dehumanizing. Yet many argue that it is precisely because it *is* encouraged that standards of living rise in free-market societies and that excellence flourishes.[36]

• *Alternative Tactics.* Are there alternative tactics available that have fewer ethical ambiguities or costs? Can the whole issue be avoided by following a different tack, even at a small cost elsewhere?

• *Taking a Broader View.* In agonizing over a tactic, say whether to shade values, it is often worth stepping back to take a broader perspective.

First, there is a powerful tendency for people to focus on conflict, see a "zero-sum" world, and thus confront the problems associated with claiming value in negotiation. Yet in developing the Negotiator's Dilemma, we showed that such a focus on claiming results from an inherent dynamic of the process, stunts creativity, and often causes significant joint gains to go unrealized. Is the real problem the ethical judgment call about a claiming tactic or a disproportionate focus on claiming itself? If so, the more fruitful question may be how to make creating value more salient.

Second, does the type of situation itself generate powerful tendencies toward the questionable tactics involved? If so, evaluating the acceptability of a given move may be less important than deciding (1) whether to leave the situation that inherently poses such choices, or (2) which actions could alter, even slightly, the prevalence of the questionable practices.

DISTRIBUTIONAL FAIRNESS

One reason that a tactical choice can be uncomfortable is its potential effect on the distribution of value created by agreement. If a "shrewd" move allows a large firm unmercifully to squeeze a small

---

[36]But, the welfare theorems of economics—that prove that competitive equilibria are Pareto-optimal and that Pareto-optimal allocations of goods and services are competitive equilibria—assume that bargaining is Pareto-efficient. The thrust of our argument about the Negotiator's Dilemma and the work on bargaining with incomplete information (Cramton, 1983, 1984a, 1984b, 1985; Fudenberg and Tirole, 1983; Rubinstein, 1983; Chatterjee, 1982; Myerson, 1985) is that bargained outcomes will tend to be inefficient since bargainers often act on the temptation to misrepresent.

merchant or an experienced negotiator to walk away with all the profit in dealing with a novice, something may seem wrong. Even when the nature of the tactics is not in question, the "fairness" of the outcome may be.

This difficulty is inherent in negotiation: since there is a bargaining set of agreements that are better for each person than his or her respective alternatives to agreement, value must necessarily be apportioned. Ultimately, when all joint gains have been discovered and common value created, more value for one party means less for another. But where should the split be? In microcosm, this is the age-old problem of "distributive justice," of what a just distribution of rewards and risks in a society should be. In the same way that this is a thorny, unresolved problem at the social level, so it is for individual negotiators—even when less well-recognized.[37] And this is why the ethical problem is so hard, and does not admit easy answers.

A classic problem among game theorists involves trying to develop fair criteria to arbitrate the division of $200 between two people.[38] An obvious norm involves an even split, $100 for each. But what if one is rich and the other poor? More for the poor man, right? "Not at all!" protests the rich woman, "You must look at *after-tax* revenue, even if you want a little more to end up going to the poor man. Moreover, you should really try to equalize the amount of good done for each of us—in which case $20 to him will improve his life much more than $180 will mine. Or look at it the other way: ask who can better afford to *lose* what amounts—and he can afford to lose $5 about as much as I can $195. Besides, he is a wino and completely on his own. I will sign this pledge to give the money to Mother Teresa, who will use it to help dozens of poor people. After all, that poor man *was* rich just two weeks ago, when he was convicted of fraud and had all his money confiscated to pay back his victims."

Who "should" get what in a negotiated agreement? This tongue-in-cheek discussion should not obscure the importance of distributional questions; certainly negotiators argue for this solution or that on the basis of "fairness" all the time. But the rich woman's objections should underscore how fragile and divisive conceptions of equity may be. One person's fairness may be another's outrage.

[37]In fact, bargaining is a time-honored way of resolving this dilemma, just as pure markets, legislative action, and judicial ruling are in other spheres where distributive issues must be settled. See Lindblom (1977).

[38]For a very clear look at how analysts have approached this kind of problem, see Raiffa (1982:235–255).

And fairness not only applies to the process of bargaining but to its underlying structure. Think of the wage "bargaining" between an illegal alien and the foreman who can have her deported at a moment's notice. Was the situation so loaded against one of the participants virtually to ensure that the results will be "unfairly" distributed? Can one consider the outcome "fair" if one believes that the management alternatives derive from a structure that one judges unfair?

Many times, by contrast, we will be comfortable answering that we do *not* care about the actual result, only that the process was within normal bounds, the participants intelligent and well-informed enough, and that no one outside the negotiation was harmed by the accord.

EXTERNALITIES

The last issue of others who are not at the bargaining table deserves some mention. If the Teamsters, major trucking firms, and a "captive" Interstate Commerce Commission informally bargained and agreed on higher rates, what about the interests of the unrepresented public? How do the children's interests figure into the divorce settlement hammered out by two adversarial lawyers who only know that each parent wants custody? Or suppose that a commission negotiates and decides dramatically to raise current Social Security benefits and pay for them by issuing very long-term bonds, the bulk of whose burden will fall on the next two generations?

It is often easy to "solve" the negotiation problem for those in the room at the expense of those who are not. If such parties cannot take part directly, one way to "internalize" this "externality" is consciously to keep their interests in mind or invite the participation or observation of those who can represent their interests, if only indirectly. Deciding that the process could be improved this way may not be too hard, though the mechanics of representation can be trickier. And even with "proper" representation, what about the actual outcome? We are back to questions akin to those in the last section on distribution.

Yet there is another, more subtle, external effect of the way in which ethical questions of bargaining are resolved. It involves the spillover of the way one person bargains into the pattern of dealings of others. Over time, each of us comes to hold assumptions about what is likely and appropriate in bargaining interactions. Each tactical choice shapes these expectations and reverberates throughout the circles we inhabit. And many people lament that the state of dealings in business and goverment is such that behavior we might prefer to avoid becomes almost irresistible, since others are doing it and overly idealistic actions could be very costly.

The overall choice of how to negotiate, whether to emphasize moves that create value or claim it, thus has implications beyond single encounters. The Negotiator's Dilemma we discussed has a larger social counterpart. Without choices that keep creative actions from being driven out, this larger social game tends toward an equilibrium where everyone claims, engages constantly in behavior that distorts information, and worse. Most people are willing to sacrifice something to avoid such outcomes and to improve the way people relate to each other in negotiation and beyond. The wider echoes of ethical choices made in negotiation can be forces for positive change. Each person must decide if individual risks are worth general improvement, even if such improvement is small, uncertain, or not likely to be visible. Yet a widespread disregard of ethics in negotiation would mark a long step down the road to a more cynical, Hobbesian world.

* * *

Bargaining in general and the process of claiming value in particular give rise to difficult ethical choices, especially with respect to tactics, distribution, and externalities. These choices can be especially poignant in organizations, where the bargaining itself is not obvious to all, and even where it is, exit from the bargaining can be costly.

The next chapter returns to the level of small groups negotiating. Yet its topic closely relates to this discussion. Claiming value is an essential aspect of bargaining, yet it constantly raises ethical questions in the small and in the large. How can its tension with moves to create value—which, admittedly claimers can exploit—be productively managed?

CHAPTER SEVEN

Managing the Negotiator's Dilemma

CREATING VALUE requires openness, communication, learning, ingenuity, joint problem solving, and preventing conflict escalation. Claiming value involves advantageously shaping opponents' perceptions of the bargaining range, often by manipulating alternatives and aspirations, making commitments, holding prime values hostage, misleading, and exploiting cultural expectations.

The last two chapters artificially separated creating from claiming value. Yet they are bound together. In discussing the Negotiator's Dilemma, we saw how each party may reason: "Approaches to creating value are vulnerable to claiming tactics; thus, if the other is creative, I can claim to great advantage. If the other claims, I must do the same to protect myself." Yet tactics to claim tend to impede creation. Rational choices by each to claim lead to poor outcomes for all.

Managing the Tension: Individual Responses

The way value is created affects the way it is divided. And how people seek to divide it affects its creation. Negotiators confront this tension by their general approach and choice of tactics. Some propose new ways to bargain. This chapter evaluates many ways of managing this dilemma. We start with the easiest individual response: denial.

DENIAL

The "Getting Yours and Most of Theirs Too" Philosophy   One current, popular school of thought offers an obvious, if myopic, way to eliminate the tension between creating and claiming value: Assume there is no potential to create value. The offerings of many an airport bookstore and the "win-lose" behavior of many participants in executive programs seem to deny the existence of joint gains. This belief neatly eliminates the tension. It may well have been learned from painful experiences with skilled practitioners of this school. Nonetheless, stubborn battles over small pies typically offer little for all.

The "Win-Win" Philosophy   A second popular school of thought eliminates the tension in an equally myopic way: it convinces followers that there is no claiming. Negotiators who adopt the "win-win philosophy" and search creatively for joint gains hope to forestall claiming and divisiveness by pretending or, actually believing, that claiming does not exist. Of course, wily practitioners may find that when negotiating with true believers, this philosophy provides the opportunity for remarkable joint gain: tremendous claiming with no hard feelings, since true believers' blinders can prevent the recognition of properly disguised claiming tactics. After extensively studying "cooperative" and "competitive" attorneys negotiating, Williams, no fan of hard bargaining, observes:

> [The cooperative strategy's] major disadvantage is its vulnerability to exploitation, a problem compounded by the apparent inability of some cooperative types to recognize it when it happens. When a cooperative negotiator attempts to establish a cooperative, trusting atmosphere, in a negotiation with a tough, noncooperative opponent, the cooperative attorney has an alarming tendency to ignore the lack of cooperation and to pursue his cooperative strategy unilaterally. . . . In this situation, the tough negotiator is free to accept all of this fairness and cooperation without giving anything in return.[1]

If one believes that negotiators' natural or learned tendencies lean toward claiming, then injecting them with win-win steroids may

[1]Williams (1983:54)

help for a while. The new vision and moral uplift may just barely off-set their propensity for excessive claiming and yield more jointly desirable agreements.

But, as a full conception of negotiation, the "win-win philosophy" is misleading and wrong. Even if two negotiators were fully open about their preferences, honest, and creative, they would not eliminate the distributive element of their bargain. In fact, they might enhance its salience.

With openness and creativity, they might invent the full set of jointly desirable agreements, the Pareto frontier. Beyond the issues, it would take into account their interests in fairness, in altruism, and in acting in accord with valued norms and principles. They might easily agree to eschew any outcomes below the frontier, since outcomes on the frontier would be better for both. But then, inevitably, deciding among outcomes on the frontier would involve a distributive bargain: an agreement better for one side must, by *definition*, worsen the other's outcome. And since this frontier would really reflect all their interests, each would *truly* prefer a more favorable point at the other's expense.

Appeals to fairness, principles, real communication, and the underlying goodness of humanity would be to no avail. Concern with fairness would already have been factored into the frontier. All useful real communication would already have taken place. The negotiators' interests here conflict diametrically; there is no getting around it. In choosing a point on the frontier, the negotiators would find themselves employing tactics for claiming value. Thus, the "win-win" description of negotiation is accurate only when there is no ultimate conflict, when the negotiators' interests are completely aligned.

A Doctorate in Economics or Game Theory   It is perhaps ironic that training in economics or game theory, two fields that rigorously develop theories of bargaining, has tended to breed a denial of the Negotiator's Dilemma, albeit of a more sophisticated sort. Economists and game theorists recognize the simultaneous existence of joint gains and distribution. But, under the assumption of complete information, negotiators are assumed to be omniscient, hyperrational beings who fully know what others value. In so doing, much of the problem is assumed away. Because these fully rational beings know the frontier of possible agreements, they will, of course, choose a Pareto-optimal agreement. What remains is simply a distributive bargain, and thus, the dilemma vanishes. Over the last two decades of game-theoretic and economic analysis of bargaining, the tension

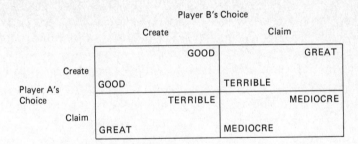

Player B's Choice

	Create	Claim

FIGURE 7.1: The Negotiator's Dilemma

NOTE: Player A's payoff is at the lower left in each cell.
      Player B's payoff is at the upper right in each cell.

between creating and claiming, when noticed, has generally been treated as one of many curiosities about bargaining and not a fundamental tension of the process.[2] Fortunately, recent work in game theory has made a significant advance by beginning to investigate bargains made without complete information. The general conclusions of this work support our conclusion that the tension between creating and claiming tends to lead to Pareto-inferior outcomes.[3]

CONDITIONAL OPENNESS

In our simplest formulation, two negotiators are trapped on the horns of a dilemma. Each would benefit if both worked to jointly create value but each might be even better off if he tried to claim individual value while the other pushed to create value. Not trusting the other, and for good reason, each pushes to claim value and both do poorly. Table 7.1 shows the payoffs two negotiators would receive given their choices to create or claim value.

[2]Relevant work includes the development of a number of special procedures that induce highly rational negotiators truthfully to reveal their preferences in a few, highly structured situations. These include the median procedure for voting (see Raiffa, 1982), the Groves mechanism for cost allocation problems (Groves and Ledyard, 1977), the Vickrey auction for allocating indivisible goods (Vickrey, 1961), the Steinhaus procedure for fair division (see Raiffa, 1982), and scoring rules for mediators that induce truthful revelation (Myerson, 1979).

[3]See for example, Cramton (1983, 1984a, 1984b, 1985), Fudenberg and Tirole (1983), Rubinstein (1983), Chatterjee (1982), Myerson (1985). Compared to the negotiations discussed in this book, these advances in game theory look at fairly restricted negotiations. One characteristic, such as the parties' discount rates or reservation prices is unknown to both sides; everything else including the distribution of this characteristic is common knowledge; and fairly heroic assumptions are made about negotiators' intellectual capacities. Under these assumptions, the lack of complete information combined with the negotiators' opportunistic behavior contributes to the negotiators' reaching a Pareto-inferior equilibrium. Thus, these recent game-theoretic advances support our conclusion that the tension between creating and claiming tends to lead to Pareto-inferior outcomes.

This representation can be improved. Negotiations usually take place in many steps. And, each tactical choice can be understood as having the structure of the Negotiator's Dilemma described by Table 7.1. By analogy, therefore, two negotiators can be roughly understood as playing an arbitrary number of rounds of this dilemma.

Robert Axelrod has recently performed several intriguing experiments on a game, called the Prisoner's Dilemma, whose structure (given by Table 7.2) is the same as the Negotiator's Dilemma.[4] In each round, two players choose, without communicating, either to cooperate (that is, to try to jointly create value)—or to defect (that is, to try to claim value). If they both cooperate, they each receive 3 points. If A cooperates and B defects, then B receives 5 points and A receives 0. Similarly, if B cooperates and A defects, then A claims 5 points and B gets none. If they both defect, each receives 1 point. Each pair plays a large number of rounds of the Prisoner's Dilemma. Each player's objective is to maximize the total number of points he receives by adding up his score in each of the rounds.[5]

Axelrod's striking results have received widespread notice and scientific praise. They suggest, by way of our analogy, a strategy for creating value while reducing one's vulnerability to others' attempts to claim it. Axelrod asked a number of specialists from a broad sweep of related disciplines to submit computer programs to participate in a tournament of repeated plays of the Prisoner's Dilemma. Each program would be pitted against every other program for a large number of plays of the Prisoner's Dilemma; each program or "strategy" would be rated according to the total number of points obtained against the strategies of all its opponents. The strategies range from the simple-RANDOM which flipped a coin to decide whether to cooperate or defect and TIT-FOR-TAT which cooperated on the first play and in subsequent rounds merely repeated its opponent's immediately previous move—to many devilishly exploitative schemes, including some that calculated the rate at which the opponent defected and then defected just a little bit more frequently.

[4]The game Axelrod analyzed has been studied extensively by psychologists, political scientists, game theorists, and others. Luce and Raiffa (1957) and Rapoport and Chammah (1965) provide important discussions of the Prisoner's Dilemma. In addition to reporting his results (Axelrod, 1980a, 1980b), Axelrod (1984) elaborates his results' implications for social and biological phenomena. Hofstadter (1983) provides a lucid summary of Axelrod's work.

[5]In Axelrod's work, each player may have a discount rate that causes the outcome of a future round to be worth a little less now than the same outcome in the current round; a player tries to maximize the present value of his scores in all rounds. Axelrod's results do not change if the players' discount rates are low enough.

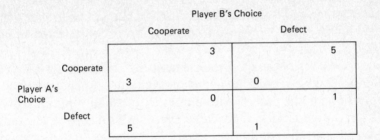

FIGURE 7.2: The Prisoner's Dilemma (with Payoffs as in Axelrod's Experiments)

NOTE: Player A's payoff is at the lower left in each cell.
Player B's payoff is at the upper right in each cell.

Axelrod's synthesis of his results is intriguing. First, the strategies that did well were "nice": they did not defect first. Second, they were "provocable" in that they punished a defection by defecting, at least on the next round. Third, they were "forgiving" in that after punishing a defection they gave the opponent the opportunity to resume cooperation. Thus, unlike other strategies that were less nice or forgiving, they did not become locked, after a defection, in a long series of mutual recriminations. Fourth, they were clear or "not too clever." Eliciting continued cooperation is sufficiently tricky that moves whose intentions were difficult to decipher tended to result in unproductive defections. Such strategies performed well because they were able to elicit cooperation and avoid gross exploitation. We call these strategies "conditionally open." The simplest of the submitted conditionally open strategies, TIT-FOR-TAT, actually won the tournament.

After disseminating these results, Axelrod ran a second tournament with a much larger number of participants. With TIT-FOR-TAT and other "nice" strategies as the contenders to beat, the second tournament brought forth a flood of even more clever, even more fiendish schemes. And, perhaps surprisingly, the best-performing strategies were conditionally open, and again, TIT-FOR-TAT won the tournament. The conclusions of these studies are of course only suggestive. The success of particular strategies depends on the population of submitted strategies.[6] Yet, the studies imply that being open

[6]One must question the robustness of Axelrod's conclusions about strategies for playing the repeated Prisoner's Dilemma. In his tournament, the population of particular strategies depended on the population of submitted strategies. The strategies that game theorists submitted may well be different from those that other people play. Indeed, some colleagues of ours report that strategies requiring more provocation before defecting and taking longer to forgive actually perform better than TIT-

in each round to cooperation conditional on an opponent's openness elicits payoffs from cooperation sufficient to offset the costs of occasional defections.

Axelrod's results suggest the elements of a strategy for managing the tension between creating and claiming value. A negotiator can attempt to divide the process into a number of small steps and to view each step as a round in a repeated Prisoner's Dilemma. He can attempt to be conditionally open, warily seeking mutual cooperation, ready to punish or claim value when his counterpart does so, but ultimately forgiving of transgressions. The attempt to create value is linked to an implicit threat to claim vigorously if the counterpart does, but also to the assurance that a repentant claimer will be allowed to return to good graces. Thus, both can avoid condemnation to endless mutual recriminations. Throughout the process, the negotiator may be better off if his moves are not mysterious.[7]

The Negotiator's Dilemma and the Prisoner's Dilemma are analogies to negotiation and as simplifications cannot be taken literally. In negotiation, one seeks ways of eliciting cooperation without becoming vulnerable to claiming tactics. In Axelrod's experiments, certain strategies were able to elicit this sort of cooperation. What characteristics were responsible? Can some negotiations in which these characteristics are not fully present be modified to exhibit them? In what ways do negotiations differ from Axelrod's game that make it easier to elicit cooperation?

What characteristics of the repeated Prisoner's Dilemma experiment, and potentially negotiation, enable this sort of cooperation?

Repetition   Players cooperate when they know that their current actions can affect their future payoffs, when they believe that a defection now will lead to sufficient defection by their opponent to make the initial move undesirable. Thus, when the repetition is about

---

FOR-TAT when played against a sample of people, who, unlike Axelrod's group, are untrained in game theory or related disciplines. Moreover, the symmetry of the payoffs in Axelrod's game may well make generalizations difficult. Although computer programs would not respond differently if the two players' payoffs were of different magnitudes but still in the right relative relationship, people playing such a version of the Prisoner's Dilemma might be less likely to play cooperatively when their payoffs are not symmetric.

[7]The presence of an implicit provocation may lead to distrust; the provoked response to claiming may be the second step in the escalation of the conflict. Thus, in attempting to follow the equivalent of a TIT-FOR-TAT negotiation strategy, one may be wise to blunt the potential for distrust and retaliation by explicit references in advance to norms of negotiating behavior and principles of fairness and honesty.

to end—as in the last play of the Prisoner's Dilemma—defections are likely.

In negotiations, repetition can take many forms. A negotiation can be broken into many stages by several means: for example, by separating issues, by writing a number of drafts, or by taking several meetings to reach agreement. Or, two actors may have to deal with each other on many matters over a long period; consider two managers who both expect to remain in the same company for a long time and will need each other's cooperation. Or, the repetition may come solely through linkage: although an individual may never negotiate with the same person again, his reputation as honest and reliable can circulate through the closely knit circle they inhabit. For example, a movie producer who is believed in the film-making community to have cheated some of his investors by creative accounting may have difficulty raising money from other backers.

But, not all negotiation involves meaningful repetition. There do exist important one-shot deals. And, at the end of many rounds of a negotiation, parties may not expect to have significant continued dealings with each other. Finally, whether or not there are to be more dealings can be a tactical choice. For example, Ralph may exploit trust and convenient legalities to fleece his long-time partner while setting in motion steps to dissolve their partnership. As we discuss later in this chapter, therefore common and suggested tactics for eliciting cooperation essentially involve enhancing the likelihood of repetition. And, many tactics for claiming value involve moves to eliminate meaningful repetition.

Readily Observable Defections   In the repeated Prisoner's Dilemma, each player knows at the end of the round whether the other defected. If Bob is prone to cooperation and Mary knows that he cannot recognize her defections—ever, or at least not before the end of their dealings—she will defect if her objective is to maximize her total score. Because Bob will not know when to punish, repetition will not save him. And, even if he finds out before the end of their relationship, the value she loses from his eleventh hour punishment may not offset her gains from an initial long string of defections.[8]

---

[8]Axelrod (1984) reran his experiment with a 1 percent chance that moves would be interpreted incorrectly and found that TIT-FOR-TAT was still the winner. But that result would likely change when 10 percent of defections could not be detected and certainly when half of defections went undetected. Moreover, reasonable ability to correctly interpret both cooperative and competitive moves seems essential to elicitating cooperation in many realistic settings. In most settings, there will be envi-

In long-term relationships where one party can observe the oth-er's compliance with agreements, defections may be observed in time for sufficient retaliation to deter. And, within a single negotiation, blunt claiming tactics are often obvious. When claiming is more likely to be detected, it is less likely to occur. Even when a negotiator believes the chances of detection are low, she may be deterred from misleading if the consequences are large. Suppose, that careful prep-aration allows her counterpart unexpectedly to recognize the decep-tion. If she becomes less certain about which misstatements will be caught but sure that negative consequences will follow if she is caught, she may be much more likely to cooperate. Even so, a great deal of clever misleading will go unrecognized. Do a counterpart's statements reveal accurate or misleading information? Are his hands really tied or is he craftily making a commitment?

A number of tactics that claim jointly created value involve clever means of making detection unlikely. Later in this chapter, we explore particular tactics for detecting and possibly punishing certain sus-pected attempts to mislead.

Appropriate Payoffs   Changes in the payoffs for a given round of Axelrod's tournament could enhance the likelihood of coopera-tion. (See Figure 7.2 for the values used.) As the 3-point payoff for joint cooperation is increased toward the 5-point payoff for exploit-ing a cooperator and as the payoff for mutual defection (1 point) edges downward toward the 0-point payoff for being exploited, the expected value of cooperating should climb compared to the expected value of defecting. Thus, cooperation should be more likely.

Moreover, the payoffs were the same in each round of Axelrod's tournament. Changes could affect the results. If one round were played with payoffs of 0, 100, 300, and 500 while all other rounds had payoffs of 0, 1, 3, and 5, a player would likely defect on the round with big payoffs because future punishments could not offset the potential gain. And, by the usual logic of the Prisoner's Di-lemma, both players would be likely to defect.

In negotiations, different rounds can have different payoffs; these payoffs are often uncertain and subject to manipulation. Some-times, the first round or the last may have payoffs significantly larger than other rounds. Sometimes, the timing of payoffs can be changed. For example, a negotiator may be able to arrange for much of the

---

ronmental noise that complicates detection. When player A mistakenly punishes B, player B may angrily retaliate, beginning a conflict spiral of mutual recriminations.

real payoff to come at the end by suddenly refusing to be bound by tentative interim agreements.

Given these possibilities, repetition can be a double-edged sword. A negotiator may cooperate because he fears punishment in future rounds. But the weight of future rounds may make the outcome of the current round vastly more important and push a negotiator toward deception and other forms of claiming. For example, suppose that a line manager can in effect arrange that this month's budget will set a precedent that governs budgetary allocations in the next thirty-six months. Especially with a less aware colleague, he may craftily push very hard to negotiate a favorable precedent this month.[9]

Later in this chapter, we dissect particular tactics that facilitate claiming by deceptively shifting value to one end of the process or the other. Of course, moves to change the payoffs within a round can also make cooperation more likely. We also discuss several devices intended to make moves to create value look more valuable than moves to claim it.

Is it easier to elicit cooperation in negotiation than in the Prisoner's Dilemma?

Apart from its characteristic payoffs, the Prisoner's Dilemma has two notable features: the players cannot communicate nor can they make binding commitments to choose in a particular way. If the players could do both, they could ensure cooperation. By contrast, negotiators *can* discuss future intentions. Moreover, they can sometimes credibly commit to cooperate or threaten to punish unless the other behaves appropriately. Even the partial ability to take these actions in negotiation can improve the likelihood of cooperation over that in the stylized version of the repeated Prisoner's Dilemma.

By their close ties to the Negotiator's Dilemma, Robert Axelrod's findings for maximizing one's results in the Prisoner's Dilemma suggest a potent strategy for managing the tension between creating and claiming: be nice but provocable, forgiving, and not too cute.[10]

---

[9]This can be understood as having one big payoff early and 36 small ones that follow. Another look may help. The Prisoner's Dilemma players' payoffs are assumed to be additive. Establishing a precedent in round one and then applying it for the next 36 rounds can be understood by seeing the payoffs as partly multiplicative (to be a bit simplistic, the player might receive his round 1 payoff multiplied by the value obtained in the next 36 rounds).

[10]Of course, our discussion of Axelrod's results does not "prove" their applicability and power in negotiation; that awaits further empirical testing and experience.

Looking behind this advice, however, we see that repetition, detection of claiming, and the relationship of payoffs within and among rounds of the Negotiator's Dilemma affect a negotiator's ability to elicit sufficient cooperation without making himself vulnerable.[11] The greater ability in certain settings to communicate and make binding commitments can also affect this objective. The next sections discuss tactics and approaches that manipulate all these factors to elicit mutual cooperation or, by eliciting the cooperation of another, to claim the lion's share of the gains so created.

MAKING CREATING VALUE SEEM BETTER THAN CLAIMING IT

If negotiators come to see cooperative moves as better than competitive ones, then the tension between creating and claiming can diminish. A variety of tactics aim at improving the expected payoffs from moves to create value relative to claiming actions.

Choice of Negotiating Philosophy   For example, instead of inviting others to announce their *positions* on the issues first, which could highlight distributive concerns and put everyone's credibility at stake, a negotiator might announce that she is only interested in a careful explanation of everyone's underlying *interests*. Or a session can be billed as "brainstorming," only to invent options, and with no criticism allowed. Such emphases may help create an ethos in which creative moves are the obvious and desirable choice.[12]

Breaking Up the Process and Channeling It Toward Cooperation   Because many negotiations involve a series of tactical choices, in effect, they take place in several steps. General discussions are followed by offers and counteroffers that are accompanied by principled justifications. The offers and counteroffers are interspersed with attempts to devise joint gains, to persuade, to make commitments, and so on. In tactical choices, negotiators face much the same dilemma at each step. They try to build "momentum" and trust by establishing a pleasant environment, making visible concessions on a

---

[11]Pruitt's proposed strategy of "flexible toughness" (1984), being flexible about the means to allow joint gains but tough on the ends to avoid being exploited, can also be understood as a guiding conception to manage the Negotiator's Dilemma. But the fact that uncertainty about preferences and beliefs, the raw materials for creating joint gain, also provides the means for claiming value adds a dimension to the negotiator's dilemma that is not easily handled by "flexible toughness."

[12]These are key elements of the approach espoused by Fisher and Ury (1981).

few issues early in the negotiations to show good faith. A strong dose of the appropriate cooperative attitudes early on may spill over to later phases so the negotiators can tackle the "hard" issues in a manner that facilitates jointly desirable agreements. Thus, negotiators create and highlight repetition that might otherwise have gone unnoticed in order to induce cooperative behavior.

Of course, settling the easy issues first to build momentum may eliminate potential for creating value by trades or logrolling between those issues and the remaining "hard" ones. Recall the negotiation between the mayor and the cable television operator and suppose that, unless the city agreed to a late completion date, no price acceptable to the city would provide sufficient return to the cable operator. If the two negotiators made a point of demonstrating cooperation and good faith early on by first amicably settling on a moderately early date, their negotiations over price would deadlock. When previously settled issues cannot easily be reopened, potential joint gain or even agreement itself may be foregone. On the other hand, to the extent that such tactics forestall claiming and allow for learning and ingenuity, the joint value created by more cooperative and trusting negotiators may more than offset this loss of potential joint value. The desirability of such tactics thus depends on one's assessment of the nature of the issues and the effect of such tactics on the other's attitudes.

Invoking Repeated Dealings   Embedding a negotiation in a series of repeated dealings can induce interests in trust and the relationship. It may also set expectations and precedents for cooperation. Since egregious claiming behavior can often be detected before the end of one or a series of negotiations, it may be mitigated. (Of course, if one party feels it can claim to advantage and remain secret, it may use the extended interaction for a long period of exploitation.)

When the negotiation is in fact one of many similar repeated encounters, negotiators may be able to mitigate claiming in subsequent rounds by agreeing initially on a principle for division of gains. For example, the partners of an investment bank may have agreed many years ago on a rule for allocating profits. In subsequent years, they need not bargain to divide the spoils; ideally their full energies could go to creating value. Such dividing rules, like much of an organization's structure, may evolve as an intended or unintended consequence of prior divisions. And those rules, like other agreements, can come up for renegotiation.

Making Cooperative Norms Salient   Negotiators often try to make norms for "appropriate" behavior more salient, in effect to penalize blatant claiming tactics. ("*What* is going on? We're engineers. Let's deal with this difference rationally." "Look, we're in this together. It's not fair to be selfish. We've got to find a better solution, one that works for *all* of us.")

Bringing in a respected third party known to share the norms can sometimes strengthen them. Or a neutral "process consultant," with authority over the process itself by which the disputes are handled, can be introduced.[13] Typically such a person first separates the parties, interviews them about their perceptions, interests, and the conflict's history. Then meetings are held on neutral ground for each to better understand the other and the problem. As an acknowledged custodian of the process, the consultant tries hard to keep conflict from escalating and the parties deeply engaged in problem solving. Though resolving the particular dispute at hand is important, the real point of this kind of process consultation is to teach the parties better ways to deal with each other, to improve the long-term relationship, and, in effect, to reinforce the norm of problem solving as the right way to handle differences.

Socialization   Over time, with repeated dealings and reinforcement of cooperative norms, negotiators' values can change so that egregious and even overt claiming tactics simply become undesirable. For example, the socialization of recruits into an organization may cause many to see that grossly competitive moves, which might seem appropriate in dealings with those outside the organization, are completely inappropriate in dealings within it. As is the case in many Japanese firms, by developing the ethos of cooperation and the relative illegitimacy of individual claiming, the acuteness of the dilemma may lessen.[14]

DUPLICITOUS CREATING

A number of tactics are intended to offer apparent or real joint gains in a way that confers great advantage to the offeror. Not surprisingly, the recipient often finds these hard to distinguish from moves to share information and create value.

[13]See Walton (1969).

[14]This is a key function of organizational "culture." For a first-rate discussion, see Schein (1985).

Using Cherished Principles with Advantageous Implications
Crafty bargainers select and argue on the basis of principles that their
opponents respect or value and that imply advantageous solutions.
The ringing proposal that the nodules of the deep seabed be considered the "common heritage of mankind" tapped deep and widespread feelings—shared interests. Yet, some industrial nations later
regretted their endorsement of this seemingly noble principle, which
ultimately came to imply an international enterprise for deep-sea
mining as well as substantial claims for royalties from private miners.
Some countries with private mining firms found both outcomes undesirable, but the need to remain consistent with their previous
stance cost them dearly. The less obvious the link between agreement
on principle and implied outcome and the greater the time between
agreement and consequences, the more likely this technique is to
work.[15]

Closing Quickly   When two rational economic negotiators discover a difference that allows them to create joint value, they should
realize that they face a distributive bargain over dividing the newly
created value. We have observed, however, the negotiators who discover a formula for joint gain after a protracted period of distributive wrangling will often settle at some minor modification of the
first creative proposal, rather than bargaining hard over the division
of the newly discovered gains. In short, people often settle too
quickly.

For example, a confident prospective employee and her superior
may have difficulty reaching agreement about her salary. To avoid in-
equities with comparable employees, the superior cannot offer a salary that is sufficiently high. After reaching an apparent impasse, the
superior offers a performance bonus and money from an educational
fund to help finance her plan to attend business school at night. Ea-
ger to find a way out of the impasse and to join the firm, she agrees
immediately. She might instead have seen that the boss offered her a
contingent agreement (the bonus) and a trade (the education money)
and wondered whether she could negotiate more favorable terms on
each. She might have learned that the boss would have been willing to
agree to a much larger bonus and to finance her entire business
school education with a semester's paid leave.

[15]This tactic is intended to shift the payoff to an early round of negotiation without the counterpart's detection. If successful, the subsequent repetition will not be
meaningful.

Much like the boss, sophisticated negotiators sometimes take advantage of this propensity to settle too quickly. They construct a trade or contingent deal that creates joint value, propose it in such a way that they claim a great deal of it, and close the dealings before the opponent realizes that more could have been gotten. This kind of tactic depends on the relief people frequently feel on finding any solution that solves a difficult problem. Experimental results seem to support this behavioral proposition.[16] They suggest that at any given time negotiators tend to think *either* about distributive concerns *or* about trying to find joint gains but not simultaneously about both. Negotiators who are jointly working to find a creative proposal that breaks a deadlocked bargain may find it unnatural to switch quickly to "distributive mode" when an acceptable, creative solution emerges.[17]

One-Sided "Cooperation"   Switching from a problem-solving orientation to a distributive one can be difficult.[18] A negotiator may feign cooperation to induce or merely allow her counterpart to try to engage in "joint" problem solving. She hopes that her counterpart—like the cooperative attorney who ignores signs that his cooperative behavior is not being reciprocated—will not see through the disguise. If so, value can be created but the duplicitous negotiator will likely claim most of it. This tactic relies on the counterpart's inability to recognize misleading behaviors.

Some negotiators do cooperate and carefully develop an aura of cooperation and sincerity during much of the negotiation. Later they argue sincerely and forcefully that only a highly favorable settlement would be acceptable. Because of their early cooperative behavior and the trust they have developed, their inflated last-minute claims may be accepted with less difficulty or resentment and no conflict spiral. Here the negotiator tries to bunch big payoffs at the end and then eliminate further negotiations.

Using a "Strategic" Negotiating Draft: Working to Create Value From a Highly Advantageous Starting Point   At the start of a cooperative problem-solving search for joint gain, a negotiator may claim great value by the careful choice of a highly favorable, initial

[16]McAllister, Bazerman, and Fader (1984).

[17]This tactic is thus intended to eliminate repetition at an advantageous point.

[18]See Walton and McKersie (1965: 167) and McAllister, Bazerman, and Fader (1984).

working draft. If the negotiators search to find improvements from this working draft, any agreement that they reach will give great benefit to its proposer. Such a proposal might be called a "strategic negotiating draft." Indeed, in complex merger negotiations, the opportunity to write the first draft can confer significant advantage.[19] The first proposal may, in addition, anchor the opponent's aspirations and perceptions of the bargaining range. Like gaining early agreement on principles with advantageous implications, this tactic relies on pushing much of the claiming to the front without the counterpart's detection.

Linking to Claim   When one party sees substantial value being created, he may try to claim it by linking new issues or interests to the process. While making a big show of creative problem solving, he may add new parts to the problem which skew the solution in his favor. Or, he may invoke higher goals, role-conceptions, feelings of loyalty, or identification to motivate others to yield most of the value created from the original issues. Or, with the same show of apparently cooperative behavior, he may shift ground to matters on which he has acknowledged expertise in order to explain to the others what is really good for them (but is certainly good for him).

Making Intentionally Insecure Agreements   Negotiators sometimes seek to get early benefits from an agreement and then hope to avoid living up to their half of the bargain. In some circumstances, a negotiator knows that legitimate excuses for breaking the agreement are likely to arise. For example, President Reagan's agreement with congressional leaders to negotiate seriously on arms control later in return for immediate funds for the MX missile is such an agreement; any number of legitimate reasons could be (and were) subsequently found to avoid serious arms negotiations. But the missiles were inexorably on the way. Similarly, the law firm partner who asks the associate to take on several especially difficult cases this month in return for an especially light load in the fall knows that the latter half of the trade can legitimately be violated if other circumstances allegedly press. Examples of intentionally insecure agreements abound.

INDIVIDUAL COUNTERTACTICS

Negotiators have developed countertactics to reduce their vulnerability when opponents mislead about their beliefs and preferences.

[19]See Freund (1975).

These countertactics sometimes induce more truthful revelations and can at other times punish a misleader.

"Petard" Tactics   Negotiators often mislead others about their beliefs, especially when anticipating a noncontingent agreement. The division head requests funds to build additional plant capacity insisting that demand will exceed capacity this year; the entrepreneur argues that the firm he is trying to sell will be dramatically profitable next year and thus a high sale price is critical and offers so far are unacceptable.

When asked how confident he is of his assertion and the justification for it, the seller may express complete confidence. If the buyer suspects that the assertion is misleading, a simple tactic can either induce more truthful forecasts or claim value from the misleader. Suppose that a *fixed* sale price has been under discussion and the seller has continued to extol the firm's supposedly fabulous future profits. The buyer might respond, "That's good to know. Because you don't think it can happen, you shouldn't mind a clause that substantially reduces later payments if the firm is less profitable than you say." Thus he constructs a contingent agreement through the back door. The seller has been hoisted on his own petard. If he really believes what he has been saying, then such a deal should be very attractive to him (if the firm can be monitored effectively and its accounts inspected). If the seller refuses the deal and red-facedly revises his forecast, he may lose credibility. Or, if he feels trapped into accepting the proposed terms, he preserves credibility but loses value.

We do not mean to imply that the countertactic is foolproof. The seller could respond: "Yes I still think the prospects are great; for you, my proposal is terrific. If all I were interested in was money, I would accept your contingent deal in a minute, but I need a set amount now. And, to move on effectively, I must have an absolutely clean break with my old business."

The analytical structure of such deals is simple: the negotiators discuss a single issue or set of issues (the sale price of the firm) that does not incorporate contingencies that reflect uncertainties (the firm's future profitability). By misleading about his beliefs concerning the uncertain event or by actually holding extreme, self-serving beliefs, one party seeks a favorable settlement on the issue (a high price). The expansion of the set of issues to include contingencies should his forecasts turn out to be incorrect (reducing the price if the firm is less profitable than forecast) can put him in a bind. Many skilled negotiators can sidestep such traps. Analytically, this is often done by adding still more interests to the discussion (in the above case, the need for certainty, early receipt of money, a clean break).

There may be another advantage to such petard tactics when what seems an uncertain event to one party is to some extent controlled by another. A general contractor may claim that the proposed building will certainly be completed by a certain date. If so, the prospective owner may ask for reduced payments (or, equivalently, penalties) for later completion. The contractor may then have to revise his predictions and accept a lower price or stick with his forecast and accept less money if he exceeds the agreed date. In the latter case, the contingent agreement also provides incentives for speedy completion. (In fact, even contingent agreements constructed without petard tactics often have this favorable incentive effect when one party has some control over the uncertain event.)

"Bait and Switch"   Other tactics operate on similar principles. A negotiator who is describing his interests, time preference, or attitude towards risk may intentionally mislead to claim value. If strongly suspected of misleading, he may be asked to stand behind his assertions. Suppose the mayor falsely claims that he values subscription price (which *is* most important to the operator) vastly more than completion date. The cable operator may bait him into making even stronger statements. Then the operator can switch, pressing the mayor to take substantial concessions on completion date in exchange for other concessions: "Because price is that important to you, Mr. Mayor, we are prepared to concede on that issue. Our new offer goes your way on price and gives us a break on the completion date and number of channels. [In fact, more than enough to compensate.] We think we have gone a long way towards meeting the concerns that you have expressed and expect to close this deal in short order." The mayor's credibility may be at stake. If he backs out, he confirms the operator's suspicions about his preferences and may damage his credibility. If he accepts the proposed terms, he maintains credibility but loses value. Certainly, such tactics are not foolproof; a wily mayor could find ways to wriggle out of the trap.

In general, exaggerated assertions can often be met by polite offers that take the assertions seriously and offer terms that could only be acceptable to someone whose assertions had been honest. By putting the asserter's credibility at stake, one hopes either to claim value or to gain information and discourage future misleading assertions.

Managing the Tension: Changing the Rules of the Game

Decisions to improve the apparent benefits of cooperating, to claim creatively, to employ tactics that counter opponents' attempts to gain by misleading, and to choose a strategy of conditional openness are individual decisions. Such decisions typically leave unchanged the accepted procedures for the interaction. Other decisions, joint and individual, can change the accepted procedures or rules of the encounter. In this section, we examine several proposals of this sort for improving the process of negotiating. In particular, we interpret and evaluate them as ways to manage the tension between creating and claiming value.

MEDIATION

A mediator is a third party who seeks to assist disputing parties in coming to a resolution. Unlike an arbitrator or judge, a mediator traditionally has no authority to impose a solution if the parties fail to reach agreement. Most common in labor relations, neutral mediators also participate in community and environmental disputes, and in alternatives to various legal processes (for example small claims court and divorce proceedings). And, as we will soon elaborate, managers often act much like mediators, but of a very special type, with an interest in the outcome and with various kinds of clout or muscle.[20] Mediation sometimes has the potential greatly to ease the tension between creating and claiming in negotiation.

Facilitating Information Flow, Communication, and Learning A skilled mediator can facilitate learning and communication. First, negotiators may be reluctant to reveal their preferences and beliefs because they fear that such disclosures will be exploited. A mediator or third party who enjoys the trust of the parties can enhance the flow of information by only passing on information that, in his judgement, will not hurt the other party. By acting as a selective conduit of information, a third party can reduce the expected or feared cost of disclosing information.

Second, as former Secretary of Labor and experienced mediator John Dunlop suggests, a mediator can also act as an advisor to one

[20]Donald Straus (1981) described Henry Kissinger as a "mediator with muscle" in the Middle East; Howard Raiffa (1982) introduced and emphasized the importance of the manager as a mediator with clout.

or more of the parties.[21] The mediator can help a negotiator more clearly understand his or her own interests. As advisor, the mediator can help a negotiator learn about key aspects of the subject matter at issue. And, the mediator can help a negotiator understand the interests and predicaments of the other negotiators.

Third, the shape of agreements depends on knowledge or information that the negotiators may not have or share. Because intentional or unintentional distortion of such information can confer substantial advantage to its provider, negotiators frequently distrust information and analysis provided by other negotiators. A third party can sometimes serve as a more neutral source or validator of facts and analyses.

Fourth, a mediator's careful attention to the process of the dealings may make the negotiators more comfortable with each other and thus better able to communicate.

Enhancing Ingenuity The mediator may also be able to enhance the negotiators' ingenuity and to put forward creative proposals himself. Private meetings, skill at the process, and encouragement can foster each negotiator's creativity at little or no risk. Moreover, because the mediator may know more about all the negotiator's preferences and beliefs than any single person does, he may be able to suggest mutually beneficial provisions that the others might not think possible. Mediators may float such proposals to the group as a whole or may attempt to persuade each negotiator individually of their potential benefits. Indeed, the mediator may want to press for rapid closure after proposing a jointly beneficial agreement rather than let the negotiators become enmeshed in dividing the newly created value. Finally, the mediator may have or develop sufficient standing to set the agenda, to link issues that allow trades, to separate others to prevent squeeze plays, to omit certain issues that would destroy chances for agreement, and to argue for principles that add joint value or point toward resolution.

Easing the Costs of Movement Negotiators may also be reluctant to propose compromises, even creative ones, because they fear loss of face or that their opponents may take the *fact* of the proposal as a signal that the proposer can be squeezed. By putting forth options that one of the negotiators would like to offer, the mediator can sometimes limit or eliminate such vulnerability.

An effective mediator can also reduce negotiators' vulnerability in the sometimes tricky endgame of negotiations. When all negotia-

[21]See Dunlop (1984).

tors think that the end is near as soon as one or the other makes a few crucial concessions, each party may wait for the others to concede. By conceding, a negotiator would be giving up real value; why shouldn't the other be the one to bear that cost? Whoever concedes may also make himself vulnerable. All now know that he could accept the compromise; presumably he still derives value from the proposed deal; the others may try to squeeze him still further, especially since he's shown that, when pressured, he'll give way. Negotiators may thus be reticent to make any offers at all. A skilled mediator can help forestall such a conclusion. He can privately ask each negotiator if he would accept a specific package if the others would do so. If each agrees to accept the package as long as the other does, the mediator then brings them all together, announces that they have an agreement, and asks them to sign. By changing the procedure for exchanging offers and information, the mediator can thus ameliorate the effects of excessive claiming at the negotiation's end.

Blunting Conflict Escalation   Finally, a mediator can help blunt possible conflict escalation, sometimes by separating the parties, sometimes by facilitating useful communication among them and, usually, by enhancing trust. He can also convey to each negotiator a more sympathetic understanding of his counterparts. Someone who understands a counterpart's situation and predicament may attribute the other's behavior more to the exigencies of the situation than to innate bad qualities. If so, future misperceptions and aggressive behavior may be avoided. Similarly, the mediator may enable each of the parties to attribute their concessions to him rather than to their own personal weaknesses or their opponent's strengths. And he may focus the discussion on external standards that tend to downplay attributions of personal strength or weakness. This can benefit both individuals and negotiators representing constituencies. Finally, a third party may facilitate trust and improve relationships by establishing a pleasant physical and social context. He may insist, sometimes effectively, on standards of civility, appropriate terms for the discussion, and norms for the interaction. If successful, such trust may prevent conflict escalation and enhance the prospects for learning and ingenuity.

The potential benefits of mediation require skillful execution. An incompetent mediator can negate any possible benefits and can easily exacerbate problems. For example, mediators who share damaging information given in confidence with the other side or somehow focus the parties on the pure claiming can easily be detrimental.

The Manager as Mediator   Managers often act as mediators when they want their subordinates to resolve problems among themselves in a productive manner. For example, consider the problem of planning a sales campaign or a design project and deciding who will take responsibility for which parts. Or, take the budgeting process of an extremely large computer firm in which budgets are constructed by negotiation among all interested divisions and departments. Only if each such division and department does not concur in the result is there an eventual top management "adjudication." But along the way, superiors act very much as skilled mediators. Unlike traditional labor mediators, however, managers in these situations are hardly disinterested or without subtle or direct means of intervention to influence the results. Thus, this kind of management by mediation can easily shade into management by negotiation, and may become management by arbitration.

Yet management by mediation can be desirable for several reasons, which are closely related to the appeal of mediation elsewhere. First, those closest to problems often can make use of their intimate knowledge to fashion solutions that are better than those imposed from above. Second, people frequently cooperate much more wholeheartedly with arrangements they themselves have devised and implemented. Third, a great deal of valuable management time can be saved if subordinates take responsibility for resolving their own problems and, if helped along the way by a skilled superior-mediator, they can learn patterns of doing so in a constructive manner. Finally, as we have discussed, the mutual dependence of managers and subordinates often limits the effectiveness of direct commands as the prime management tool.

Desirable or not, mediation is often the only practical alternative for managers who must depend on those outside the chain of command to resolve their disputes productively. Suppose that a problem between the engineering and production departments is causing headaches for the vice president of marketing. Effective mediation by the VP may break the logjam. And perceptive top management may greatly prefer the skilled intervention of the marketing VP to the alternatives of knocking heads or imposing a resolution. In fact, one of the most valued skills in public and private management is the ability of a respected but uninvolved manager to induce others to settle their differences productively. And, where a manager depends on others who are totally *outside* the organization to solve problems, mediation skills can be crucial.

For instance, a small personal computer manufacturer was dismayed by a sole supplier's delays in delivering the internal disk drives. On learning that the delays were due to a dispute between the disk drive manufacturer and one of its suppliers, he intervened, helped them reach an amicable settlement, and began receiving the necessary drives on schedule.

By changing the way in which the parties communicate and make suggestions and proposals, skilled manager-mediators can reduce the vulnerability that others may feel about conveying critical information and making creative proposals or any offers at all. When a manager takes the onus of concession-making from the participants, faster and more beneficial resolution of the conflict may occur. By virtue of organizational status, some managers can heavily influence the terms of discussion and interaction in a more productive direction. And managers enjoy some very special advantages rarely possessed by "other" kinds of mediators. A more expansive view of the organization and long experience will frequently equip a manager with information and perspective that can contribute in substance to a better resolution of others' problems. Often, managers can forge links between issues that were formerly thought to be separate. And if it looks as if one of the disputants will have to take an undesirable loss, it will often be possible for the manager to use this linkage power to "compensate" this person with something later or in another area. For example, an adverse budgetary result may be made more palatable by an independently desirable decrease in a transfer price or increase in personnel slots next year.

By modifying the rules of the game, mediators have the potential to lessen the tension between creating and claiming value. Managers in particular have special uses for the mediator's role and special tools to carry it out, including the ability to compensate parties on otherwise unrelated dimensions as we discussed above. Finally, the fact that a manager may choose to change from a mediator to a judge and commander can increase the disputing parties' incentives to search for a good situation.

SINGLE NEGOTIATING TEXT

The single negotiating text is a device used in international negotiations that has been adapted as a device to aid mediation of many kinds of negotiations.[22] Typically, a third party creates a draft agree-

---

[22]See Fisher and Ury (1981) and Raiffa (1982). Fisher attributes this device to Louis Sohn.

ment and asks the negotiating parties for criticism, but not evaluation or acceptance. The third party looks for creative ways to meet the interests that emerge from the criticism, revises the draft accordingly, and repeats the process of gathering criticism and suggestions. Eventually, when the draft is improved as much as the third party deems possible, all parties are asked for a single "up or down" decision.

The single negotiating text does not completely separate moves intended to claim and moves intended to create value. Each party may choose his criticisms of the draft in a way that he hopes will lead to a revised draft according him most of the improvements. Thus, he may well mislead in enumerating the current draft's shortcomings. Of course, excessive behavior of this sort increases the risk of no deal.

The virtue of a single negotiating text is simple: negotiators do not have to make concessions or commit to accept a text until they find it satisfactory. Normally a concession feels like a sure loss from one's position in return for an uncertain increase in the probability of ultimate agreement. Making concessions during the negotiation process can be costly, especially when external constituents critically scrutinize the negotiation and pounce on every supposed "sellout." Moreover, one's opponent may infer weakness from a concession. Similarly coming to interim agreements may involve posturing and hard-to-undo commitments along the way that prevent optimal—or even any—agreements. A single text can reduce these costs. Because each draft is constructed to offer joint gains with respect to the preceding draft, the negotiators may be induced to continue the process long beyond the point where negotiations without a third party would be deadlocked as a result of excessive claiming.

The single negotiating text seeks to avoid some of the destructive claiming associated with common positional bargaining. This proposed technique cedes the responsibility for creating value to the mediator, who must propose successive texts. Claiming, too, is in the third party's hands, since the interim and final drafts are his doing. The mediator, however, depends heavily on the parties for the information needed in the process. And since they are vitally interested in the results, they may still seek to claim by distortion and declarations of unacceptability—but at some remove from the kind of claiming characteristic of the familiar positional bargaining game. Of course, as we noted earlier, when the single negotiating text is shepherded through by a participant who prepares a highly partisan initial working draft, such a "strategic negotiating text" can be used to confer substantial individual advantage.

The informal use of single negotiating texts in nondiplomatic settings is not uncommon. For example, a committee chairman might, without naming it, use a single negotiating text by asking a staffer to draw up a rough proposal and send it around to the committee members before their first meeting. At the meeting and in writing, he takes their comments, revises accordingly, and repeats the process. After two or three meetings, the committee endorses the revised text.

SEPARATION OF INVENTING FROM DECIDING

Fisher and Ury argue that judgment hinders imagination and therefore that deciding on an outcome should be separated from the task of inventing a variety of possible outcomes. [23] They suggest that negotiators "invent first, decide later" by scheduling brainstorming meetings in which criticism and decision are ruled out of bounds. Later, the parties meet to decide among the invented options. Twenty years ago, Walton and McKersie proposed other ways of separating these two processes.[24]

Many of the difficulties with being creative result from the fundamental tension of negotiation. The prescription to invent first and decide later can thus be understood as an attempt to manage the inherent tension by doing all the creating first and deferring the claiming until later. The same parties can use time to separate inventing from deciding. For example, the department heads of a company division meet to inform each other about the projects they plan for the next year and try to discover synergies and improvements. They subsequently meet to decide on the budget allocations for each department.

One can also separate inventing from deciding by choosing separate people for each task. For example, rather than have department heads both suggest projects and make allocations, a firm may have a

[23]Fisher and Ury (1981).

[24]But they conclude in light of two dilemmas ("that information about what is minimally acceptable, which is revealed in problem solving, may provide the other with a bargaining advantage" and "that the information one reveals about his unfulfilled and existing dependencies becomes another source of weakness in the bargaining process") that separating the two processes cannot work unless the "bargaining phase can be completed before the problem-solving phase" (Walton and McKersie, 1966: 381–2). This is a special case of a proposal put forth by Raiffa that we evaluate in footnote 25.

budget office that presents analyses and proposals for a subsequent decision by the department heads. Firms sometimes hire consultants to serve such a role in deliberations over organizational strategy. The success of this sort of separation rests on the knowledge and ability of those chosen to help create joint value.

The success of such separation between creating and claiming rests on an implicit behavioral proposition. Negotiators are presumed to be unable to use the information and inventing sessions to affect the shape of ultimate outcome, whether by eliciting information about the other side's minimum requirements (undoubtedly couched in the language of "real needs"), misrepresenting preferences and beliefs, or by inventing proposals that create joint value but confer most of it to one of the parties.

We suspect that negotiators are less able to use the inventing process to claim value when the two processes are separated by a longer period of time, when the parties are less sophisticated, when the link between misrepresentation and desired outcomes is less clear, and when the inventing process is more skillfully structured and facilitated. However, when negotiators are sophisticated, are fluent in claiming behavior, and care intensely about the results, the temptation could be overwhelming to use the "invention" phase for duplicitous creating (see page 206) while really seeking unilateral advantage.

Successfully separating inventing from deciding does yield at least one irony. Suppose that negotiators successfully invent a wide array of possible outcomes. They then try jointly to improve each outcome in the original set they have invented until they have the Pareto frontier, bargaining along which is purely distributive. Happy invention may have unintentionally engendered bitter division.

In one case of this, two intensely competitive brothers, a businessman and a professor, inherited some very valuable items and argued over the way to split them up. They treated their problem as one of bitter division until they engaged a respected third party for help. The third party held a few exploratory sessions with the brothers, separately and together, and then unveiled a complex scheme that met their expressed needs far better than anything that had emerged from their bilateral wrangling. Initially the two were amazed and thrilled at the much more valuable possibility. Unfortunately, after the novelty wore off, even more vehement arguments began as both sides sought to gain by announcing strategically chosen changes in their preferences. The obvious duplicity threatened damage to their relationship. Later, the third party lamented that he had not let the two stew in their original problem for much longer so that the solution he invented would have been irresistible. Then he would have pressed for acceptance—before they discovered the underlying fact that, though inventing any joint gain improves on present possibilities, just as surely it presents new material for claiming.

POST-SETTLEMENT SETTLEMENTS

Howard Raiffa has developed an interesting twist on the notion of separating inventing from deciding: decide first, invent later.[25] When parties are hostile and suspicious, as when two partners seek to dissolve an acrimonious partnership, efforts to devise clever contractual terms may be undercut by attempts to claim value and the risk of conflict escalation. A fully complex contract may be unattainable. Raiffa suggests that the parties come to a simple settlement without attempting to create additional value and then engage the services of a third party to develop "post-settlement settlements." By interviewing the parties and performing careful analysis, the third party suggests outcomes that he believes to be better for each party than their initial agreement. Any party can veto the post-settlement settlements in favor of the initial settlement—which acts as the status quo. Thus, creating and claiming are separated by deferring further creation until the parties can only gain from it.

Unfortunately, the knowledge that the initial agreement will only serve as the starting point for later improvement may engender an even more bitter initial distributive bargain. With all subsequent creation in the third party's hands, claiming tactics may rage uninhibited by the usual need to create. Sophisticated negotiators may see the initial game as a purely adversarial contest to influence the starting—and hence ending—point of the creating game that follows.

With the security of an initial settlement—new reservation values—and nothing to lose, the post-settlement idea envisions that incentives to mislead the third party about beliefs and preferences will

---

[25]Raiffa (1984). Walton and McKersie (1966) proposed bargaining in advance, but limited their suggestion to bargaining first over the "share ratio" of joint gains and then problem solving. As stated, this seems to apply only when the issues are transformed by both parties into the same utility metric. Further, the utility involved must be transferable. This seems like a rare situation, since it would involve only tangible and divisible issues that are equally valued by both parties. This would rule out any issues like work rules in a union-management negotiation that are valued in different ways, issues that are indivisable, or issues that asymmetrically evoke concerns with reputation and the like.

be diminished. Of course, in normal bargaining, the fact that the parties have higher reservation values would not necessarily lead them to be fully forthcoming.

This incentive for even more bitter attempts to claim value may be balanced, however, by the momentum that agreement creates and the prospect of an ultimately superior post-settlement settlement—if the parties will cooperate enough so the third party can construct one. And the relief that they feel at finally having some agreement after an exhausting, bitter dispute may result in more accurate representations to the third party in the post-settlement phase.

Post-settlements do not require a third party; versions of them are common. For example, two CEOs might hammer out the outlines of a major deal between them and leave their accountants and attorney to "clean up the details"—a process that might greatly improve the deal for both. Or, the initial partnership agreement might state that the agreement would be reopened after a year for review; the revised agreement would include any changes approved by the partners' consensus. The separation between the initial agreement and the review might mitigate the after-effects of any hard feelings from original negotiation and foster some valuable creativity.

Summary

Earlier chapters laid out the Negotiator's Dilemma and explored its component parts: no-agreement alternatives as the lower limits of agreement, interests as the measure and raw material of negotiation, and agreements as the potential of negotiation. We then examined the bases for creating value and the tactics for claiming it. This chapter has returned to the Negotiator's Dilemma and taken its implications seriously. We examined many ways that negotiators can or might try to extricate themselves from it—or at least manage its inherent tensions.

The most powerful advice for managing the tension between creating and claiming value can be drawn from the results of Robert Axelrod's repeated Prisoner's Dilemma experiments. With many repetitions, immediate detection of claiming, and known, unchanging payoffs in each round, he found that conditionally open strategies—strategies that were "nice," "provocable," "forgiving," and "clear"—elicited sufficient cooperation without becoming vulnerable to excessive claiming. Under these conditions, strategies that sought to exploit opponents or that were too directly cooperative fared poorly. In drawing out the rough analogy between negotiation and the repeated Prisoner's Dilemma, we saw that repetition, detection, and known, unchanging payoffs are not guaranteed; in fact, each aspect was often the subject of tactical action, both to elicit mutual cooperation and to elicit another's cooperation in order to exploit it.

Throughout this chapter we have examined numerous ways to manage the creating-claiming tension, including variants of the following:

- Simple denial of the tension
- Conditional openness to guide negotiation strategy
- Ways to make creating value seem better than claiming it
- Duplicitous creating and various counter tactics
- Mediation, especially by managers in organizational settings
- Single negotiating texts
- Devices to separate creating from claiming
- Post-settlement settlements

Some of these tactics and approaches seek to enhance the mutual creation of value. Generally, they increase the likelihood and salience of repetition, allow claiming to be detected more readily, or seem to boost the relative payoffs for creative actions. Other approaches seek to enable one's lopsided claiming without sacrificing the benefits of the other's cooperation. Typically such efforts make detection less likely, end meaningful repetition at advantageous points, or shift large payoffs to certain rounds. Whether the approaches are individual, joint, or involve a third party, or whether they keep or alter the procedure by which negotiation is carried out, all respond to the inescapable tension of trying to create value while claiming it.

Now that we have examined the raw material, limits, potential, and basic processes of negotiation, it is a good time to see how these elements play themselves out in practice. In the next chapter we take a careful look at the bargaining process involved in annual budget planning for one division of a large company.

CHAPTER EIGHT

The Principles Applied: A Budget Negotiation

IN PRESENTING our approach to negotiation problems, we intend to provide a useful set of diagnostic and prescriptive tools. In the last six chapters we have offered many examples of explicit negotiations, such as those involving contracts between organizations. We now offer an extended illustration of how the framework as a whole can be applied to a more complex situation—a budget negotiation inside a firm.[1] Beyond making more tangible the relation between theory and practice, this example also helps to prepare the way for our later discussion of how a negotiation perspective gives insight into broader management tasks.

Background

In the late 1970s, the Dowponto Company introduced a new budgeting system company-wide. The system, called "Priority Resource

---

[1]The situation discussed in this chapter is an abbreviated version of a case documented by Professor Francis Aguilar of the Harvard Business School. The events, as well as the identities of the company, divisions, and managers, have been somewhat disguised for the sake of anonymity.

Budgeting'' or ''PRB,'' derived directly from the concept of zero-based budgeting (ZBB). The Texas Instruments Company first developed the ZBB method in 1969, and within a decade more than 100 large industrial companies were reported to be using it. Many levels and agencies of government also adopted brands of this system, most notably the entire federal government under the Carter administration.

Dowponto's PRB variant of the zero-base budgeting process was a simple concept—in theory. Starting at the lowest organizational levels, projects and proposed expenditures (''decision units'') were ranked in order of their priority, from the absolute minimum (the ''threshold'') level needed to sustain operations, through more ongoing projects and to more ''wish list'' ideas. The rankings of parallel lower-level (department) units were then aggregated at a higher (divisional) level and a composite ranking resulted. In turn, the rankings from the divisional level were merged and ranked at the corporate level. Top management then decided on a total amount of funding, which implied ''where the line would be drawn'' in the aggregate rankings. Higher-priority projects ''above the line'' would be funded

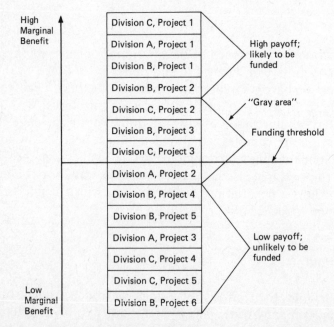

FIGURE 8.1a: Priority Resource Budgeting

Department heads rank their own projects according to marginal benefit. Then, in a ranking meeting, they merge their lists. A supervisor draws the funding threshold in the ''gray area'' where the desirability of the projects is arguable.

ORGANIZATIONAL LEVEL   ACTION

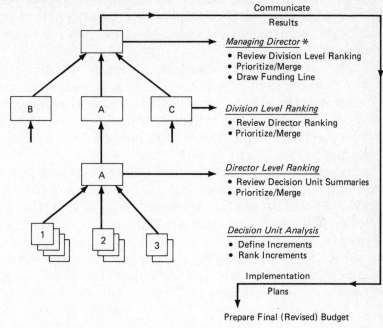

*Corporate management reviews the budget.

FIGURE 8.1b: The Priority Resource Budgeting Process

while lower-priority projects and expenditures "below the line" would not. (Figures 8.1a and 8.1b summarize the PRB concept.)

The following description and dialogue depict what took place in the Gamma Division of Dowponto shortly after the new system was presented. For convenience, we include a list of the involved managers.

Key Personnel of the Dowponto Division

Chris Hubbard, age 41, had worked at Dowponto for eighteen years. His first job had been as field salesman, but he was soon transferred into a product department and quickly became a department head. In 1977 he advanced to General Manager of Gamma. Hubbard was an intelligent, reasonable man with a low-key management style. He had worked hard to build team spirit among his managers.

Joe Roboh, age 45, had been at Dowponto for over twenty years, the entire time in R&D. His staff now numbered over sixty and along with most of them he shared an enthusiasm for basic research. He believed that most of Dowponto's R&D dollars had to be spent on immediately commercializable research, but as he told his people: "We do the commercial stuff because it pays the bills, but it's basic research that keeps us intellectually alive and secures the future of this company!"

Andy Dewing, age 57, had spent his career in manufacturing at Dowponto. Seven plant managers, and through them several thousand people, reported to him. Only his divisional headquarters staff was being ranked at this meeting; all the others would be ranked within their own plants. Dewing was thought to be hardnosed and was respected for his effectiveness.

Fred Ellis, age 35, had joined Dowponto in manufacturing in 1967. Four years later he moved to field sales, then to the marketing staff. He became a product department head in 1973. Ellis believed strongly that Gamma's growth would have to come from Consumer Products.

Norm Brewster, age 39, had joined Dowponto in the early 1960s as an engineer. After three years in a plant, he had taken a leave of absence to go to a well-known midwestern business school. On his return he had progressed rapidly and was one of the two product de-

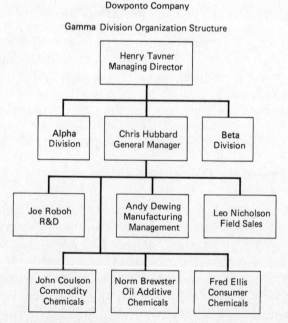

Dowponto Company

Gamma Division Organization Structure

FIGURE 8.2:   **Organization Chart**

partment heads. When the Oil Additive Chemicals Department was created, Brewster was put in charge of it.

John Coulson, age 37, had been at Dowponto for thirteen years. When Hubbard was promoted to general manager, Coulson took over the Commodity Chemicals Department. He was ambitious for his area and hoped that he could appeal for support to Hubbard. He had a somewhat excitable personality but was well liked and respected by his subordinates.

Leo Nicholson, age 35, was new to his job as manager of Gamma's field sales. Only two months before, he had headed up the Central Region Sales Office, where he had worked for almost thirteen years. He had made his reputation as a salesman, and his skills as an administrator were not yet fully tested.

Jack Eckert, age 29, was a first-level manager in Dowponto Chemical Commodities Company's Controller's Department. This was his first time as a PRB analyst, and he was somewhat unsure of himself. On the one hand he wanted the exposure; on the other hand he was frightened of making mistakes or antagonizing anyone.

A Case Study: Working Out the Budget for Dowponto's Gamma Division

"Well, all hell broke loose this morning. What do I have to do this afternoon to pull my group together and get some agreement?" Chris Hubbard asked himself. As General Manager of Dowponto's Gamma Division, Hubbard had spent the best part of the last day and a half with his immediate subordinates trying to get a consensus on next year's operating budget. After a rough morning, he had used lunch as an opportunity to get away and plan how he could resolve the issues that were blocking progress.

In the past, budgeting had been straightforward: the previous year's budget was adjusted according to the changes that Hubbard and his department managers agreed would be necessary. This year, however, the Gamma Division had been asked to employ a new budgeting process, Priority Resource Budgeting (PRB), as part of Dowponto's effort to improve cost management. The new process had proved to be far more time-consuming and complicated than the old.

During the past several months, Hubbard's department managers had worked with their subordinates to identify explicitly the tasks for which they were responsible and to attach specific estimates of benefits and costs to each task or activity. Each manager had then met with his key subordinates to rank the tasks ("increments," in PRB terms) from highest priority to lowest. The primary goal of this effort was to give priority to activities that supported the unit's tactical and strategic business plans.

Hubbard was now in the middle of his divisional ranking meeting. The goals of the meeting were the same as at the department level, but the task was more complex. While ranking increments within departments had often required that difficult decisions be made, the commonalities among the functional activities facilitated choices and tradeoffs. The "interfunctional" ranking in which they were now engaged seemed to produce an atmosphere of competition. Hubbard worried that the conflict would undermine his strenuous efforts over the past two years to develop a spirit of teamwork in his group.

"I've never seen John Coulson so angry," he reflected, "and his Commodities group produced three-quarters of last year's cash flow. And Sales really has me stumped. What is the right level of support for that function? I guess we are wrestling with some issues we should have confronted before, so things aren't all bad. But I'm sure of one thing—if we can't pull together on this budget, it's going to be a tough year."

THE DIVISION

The Gamma Division, of which Chris Hubbard was the General Manager, consisted of three departments. Hubbard had been promoted from the Commodity Chemicals Department, now headed by John Coulson. This unit, at $600 million in sales, was the largest of the three, but was projected to have the slowest growth. Norm Brewster managed the Oil Additive Chemicals Department, which was the second largest and was expected to grow at a medium rate. The smallest department, Consumer Chemicals, was expected to grow rapidly if it were adequately funded. Fred Ellis was its head. Market analysis and extensive discussions with upper Dowponto management had established the general strategy for the Gamma Division. Cash generated from Commodity Chemicals, and, to a lesser extent, Oil Additive Chemicals, would and should be used to fund the growth of Consumer Chemicals. Though the general strategic direction was clear, the Gamma Division itself had to determine the appropriate reallocations.

ONE-ON-ONE MEETINGS

"The seeds for what happened in the ranking meeting this morning were planted in the one-on-one review sessions I held with each of my managers over a week ago," Hubbard reflected. "Joe Roboh's was the easiest and most informative session. As soon as he knew I was committed to doing some basic research, he loosened up. I liked the results in his R&D ranking meeting because they fit our strategy. But I could see some potential problems coming from the big shift in research effort from Commodity Chemicals to Consumer Chemicals. I expected a backlash on that from John Coulson, and we sure got it.

"John is doing a good job with Commodity Chemicals, and his PRB analysis showed it. Still, I don't think he's fully taken to heart that he's in a mature market. He still thinks he can grow and resents all the attention Fred Ellis is getting with Consumer. 'Competent but defensive' is the way I'd characterize his behavior in our one-on-one meeting. He knew he wasn't going to get as much R&D as he wanted.

"The other men were about as I expected. Fred Ellis was well prepared and aggressive. He intends to grow and he can make a good case for it with Consumer. Norm Brewster was confident and protective. Too confident, maybe; Oil Additives has been so successful that they may only have looked at where they needed more resources. I'm not sure they checked to see which areas are fat, and some are, for sure. Andy Dewing, on the other hand, was a little discouraged. He didn't see that PRB made any sense for Manufacturing, and I think he still feels that way."

THE DIVISION RANKING MEETING: FIRST DAY

Hubbard's thoughts turned to the ranking meeting. Yesterday morning the ranking had seemed mechanical, easy—almost trivial. The thresholds reviewed in the one-on-one meetings were accepted without debate, except that Nicholson hadn't studied all the other guys' work and that slowed things down a bit. Andy got a laugh when he said, "Hell, Leo, you're in the big leagues now. You've got to read this stuff before you come to meetings." Ranking the items just after the threshold was no real problem, although during the later afternoon there were a few disagreements. As could be anticipated, most differences of opinion centered on the question of relative priorities of untried growth products versus proven and profitable mature products. Agreement was reached amicably in each case.

When the meeting broke up around four in the afternoon, Hubbard was confident that while the next day would bring some difficult issues, the group would continue to work well together to resolve them. "In retrospect," he mused, "I can see why those disagreements yesterday afternoon were so easily resolved. We were still well below what everyone figured to be the minimum funding level."

THE DIVISION RANKING MEETING: SECOND DAY

Trouble had started early in the morning. Hubbard remembered one exchange almost word for word. John Coulson, defending his interest, had thrown up his hand like a traffic cop to confront Joe Roboh on the ranking of the R&D increments.

"Wait a minute Joe, your next four increments all involve basic research aimed at Consumer products."

"Well, that's where the future is, John."

"But we're in the present and won't ever reach the future unless we pay our bills," Coulson said adamantly. "There's no support for my stuff!"

"Calm down. If we want to get to the future, we have to start now. Besides, we have applications research and production service for Commodity Chemicals in the threshold."

"But, that's just a tiny bit. Hell, my products pay the salaries around here, and we deserve a fair shake. I want those increments that have my stuff in them ranked now, before we spend all we've got on a future we're not sure exists."

At that point Fred Ellis broke in. "John, demand in your markets isn't growing, and competition may soon start to drive your margins down. I know you're producing most of the cash generated by Gamma, but we ought to use that cash to support the best opportunities we've got, and right now those opportunities are in Consumer. Besides, when you consider . . ."

Coulson interrupted, "That's bull! Our demand continues to grow and our competition won't change all that much. The fact of the matter is, Commodity Chemicals continues to be the mainstay of this division, and we'd be crazy to weaken it. Process improvements, and that means R&D, and hard-driving marketing are what it will take to keep this cash cow producing."

Hubbard recalled that he had interrupted at that point to get the facts straight. He had asked Joe Roboh exactly how much applications research and production support for Commodities was in the budget so far. Joe confirmed that production support was equal to 100 percent of the level expended during the past year. "I don't think we can change that since all our production is sold in advance and we have to be able to deliver," he said. But applications research had been cut to 30 percent of the current level for Commodities. For Oil Additive Chemicals, production support was at 120 percent and applications research at 140 percent. Consumer was at 140 percent and 100 percent, respectively. Roboh thought that more should be spent for Consumer applications research.

Hubbard wondered whether getting the facts helped, though. Coulson had just sat there without saying a word. Looking for a way to calm the situation down, Hubbard had turned to Andy Dewing.

"Tell me, Andy, what about you? What kind of manufacturing support do you have in the budget for John? Is it enough to see that all of his stuff is out the door on time?"

"Sure, just as long as I have my eight people. [Dewing's staff at headquarters consisted of eight people. The manufacturing line personnel in the plants were not included in these deliberations.] Frankly, Chris, I think this whole thing is dumb. We know how to run our business. I sure as hell know how I run my end of it. This is just another system trying to tell us what to do. And you know, I told that guy, that PRB, ABC alphabet soup guy that was supposed to help me with this, 'I only have one increment. Eight people and ten years on the job has taught me that eight is the right number.' But no, he made me play games, and now I have four levels of increments or whatever they're called, and who knows or cares what's in them? You want the plants to produce on time and at spec? I need eight guys, no more, no less. And no matter how many increments or whatever you cut that into, it adds up the same. I can't guarantee anything until I get *all* my men."

Hubbard remembered being flustered a bit by that. "You mean you can't operate with less than eight?" he queried Andy.

"I mean I can't say what will happen with less than eight. It all depends on the risk you want to take. Four may be enough, or two, or none if you're lucky."

Hubbard had become angry at that. "Well, why isn't your threshold eight people? What are we fooling with less for?"

"Don't ask me. I tried to do the right thing and make it eight. Ask him," Andy said, and pointed at Jack Eckert, the PRB coordinator. "It was my PRB analyst who said I couldn't have eight in my threshold."

"Wait a minute, Andy," replied a very much on-the-spot Eckert. "I wasn't at your sessions when you did your original analysis, but I suspect that the guy who worked with you said that the threshold could not be equal to the current level. That's a basic assumption in PRB. You have just told us how to view your department: the major issue is risk. How willing is Gamma to risk a production delay or quality-control problem? For which products? Which customers? What are the costs of a delay?"

"We can't take those risks and keep our customers. How much risk do you say we should take, Jack?" countered Andy.

"You have to make that decision," Jack replied. "My job here is to facilitate the process, not to make operating or budgeting decisions. You have to make that decision, and you have made it, year after year. All the system does is help you attach different prices to different levels of risk. The choice is yours."

Andy smiled ironically. "You say that like it's easy."

"I don't mean it to sound easy," Eckert said, looking around the room.

Coulson spoke up, "I think we should give Andy all of his men right now. All these management systems sound fine, but we know what's going to happen if the plants back up. We need the same amount of production as last year, and his staff worked full time then."

Nodding his head, Brewster called out, "I agree with John, let Andy have his people next."

Hubbard moved to get closure. "I think that's right. Anyone disagree? . . . No? Then Andy, we'll accept all your other increments now."

Relaxing, Andy responded, "Good! That finishes my part. Can I get back to work now, Chris?"

"No, I want you involved in the rest of the ranking. A lot of the decisions we still have to make could indirectly affect your department."

Hubbard now wondered whether he had moved for closure too soon. Andy's impassioned complaint had interrupted the flow of the meeting, and Hubbard had wanted to return to the question of how much research support to devote to Commodity Chemicals.

Coulson raised the point immediately. "We still haven't answered the question we began with. I still think I should get more support from R&D."

Hubbard nodded. "Joe, where is the rest of John's support?"

"Spread across my last eight increments, numbers sixty-eight to seventy-four."

"O.K., John," Hubbard said as he turned to examine the display that explained what was in each of those increments, "if you could have two of those, which would they be?"

"I'll need three. Number sixty-seven is the area where we have the best opportunity, but it alone doesn't do much for us. Increments sixty-eight and seventy-one will give that project the punch it needs to produce some applications we can take to the market."

Brewster broke in, "Remember, Chris, we haven't yet funded any of those new Oil Additives projects I spoke to you about, and . . ."

Coulson interrupted. "We've already ranked three of your exploratory research projects, Norm. The increments you have left look like long shots to me, and my projects have pretty clear near-term benefits."

"These new projects have a lot of potential," Brewster countered, "and I think the results we've gotten in my group over the last five years show that investments in R&D for our business pay off."

Dewing spoke up. "Look, why don't we give John one of his increments, then Norm one of his, then John, and so on?"

Coulson responded before anyone could reply. "But aren't we supposed to rank each increment with the idea that it really is the most important thing available, and not simply trade around? My projects are critical and should go in the budget now!"

Everyone started speaking at once. After some fifteen minutes of spirited argument, Hubbard intervened. "Look, we're getting nowhere on this one. Let's move on to something else for awhile and come back to this later."

The group made good progress on several items until Norm Brewster got upset. At the time, the group was discussing advertising, and the debate was whether Oil Additive Chemicals' increment should come before Consumer Chemicals.

"Right now I've got 90 percent of current advertising expense in the budget," Brewster said. "Rates will go up at least 15 percent, and if we take my next increment I'll be just short of my current level in advertising purchase power. If we take Consumer's increment, Fred will be at 160 percent of current. I don't even understand why we're wasting time talking about it."

"Maybe it's time to start cutting your advertising," Hubbard explained. "You've been spending at high levels, but you dominate the market now and you keep telling me you get terrific word of mouth.

You haven't convinced me that this advertising increment will have much effect on either your share or profitability."

"I'm the one who needs the advertising," Fred Ellis interrupted. "Consumer is right where you were a few years ago. We're at 'take-off.' We have terrific products in a growth market, and we have to get out there and establish a dominant position. Right now, getting more awareness and supporting our distributors is critical."

Brewster looked straight at Hubbard. "If our ad budget gets cut, I can't promise the profits we've delivered in the past. We've been damn successful, and our advertising has been an important part of our marketing program. It doesn't make any sense to change a successful strategy."

Hubbard wasn't sure whether he was grateful that Nicholson interrupted at this point, or whether it would have been better if they had resolved the ad question.

"Here we are talking about advertising," Leo Nicholson interjected, "and we don't even have enough guys in the field to take orders. Right now the budget only gives me skeleton crews in three sales offices. We don't have anyone out traveling around."

"You mean we haven't ranked your whole staff yet?" Coulson asked in amazement.

"No."

Coulson sat up straight, exasperated. "That means that the whole ranking is screwed up! What are we supposed to do now?"

Hubbard broke in, "Leo, if you were going to add a man to those ranked so far, what office would you do it in?"

"There's no way to answer that, Chris. We may sell in the East, but then again the East could be slow and all our sales could come from the West or Central. There's no way to tell."

Coulson chimed in, "We've just never gotten a handle on how to judge the marginal utility of a salesman. There's no useful information."

"What you mean," said Ellis, "is that we don't know what information is useful."

Leo replied, with a look that said he had been through all this before, "Whichever, we don't have it. We know we need to add salesmen, and that means we need to add them everywhere."

That comment led to an extended discussion about how many salesmen were needed. The discussion produced lots of ideas but no resolution. Eventually everyone agreed that the Gamma sales force could not be cut, and that probably Nicholson should be given budget for two new salesmen to be added where necessary.

Then came the issue of where the sales force should fit in the ranking. Should it simply be added now, or should it be inserted among increments ranked earlier in the meeting? The group decided to put it in earlier, but after twenty minutes of discussion they still had not decided where.

"This is a mess," Coulson protested. "There's no way to compare Leo's need for salesmen with my need for more R&D and for more guys on my commerical staff. How are we supposed to compare one against the other? They're apples and oranges."

"I don't think there's any easy way," Hubbard replied.

"I don't want an easy way—just a way!" Coulson was pushing.

"But you know, John," said Ellis, "this is the first time we've sat down together and really talked about all our departments in this much detail."

"How is the talk helping?" asked Coulson.

"That's a good question, John," Chris said. "Why don't you guys try to answer it over lunch, and let's meet again at one thirty."

Problem Solving and Conflicting Interests

Before analyzing Hubbard's specific situation, it is useful to summarize how the system was supposed to function:

> Top management set corporate objectives and policies. Given these statements, Dowponto's senior operating managers produced explicit statements of strategy ("Direction Papers"). Operating companies and similar units then produced "Summary Long-Range Plans," followed by more detailed statements of strategies and tactics, "Operational Plans." Next, individual managers identified the results they must achieve, the "Management by Results Program" to support the Operational Plans. The budgeting process was then to develop explicit statements of organizational goals and resource commitments for a one-year period.

The PRB system was the method used to facilitate this process. Its designers seemed to envision a clean, rational, problem-solving process: with all the participants wanting to maximize net present value, they would exchange information, rank the projects, agree on a total amount to be spent, and implement their decisions. Of course, this problem-solving model crashed into the reality of a hard bargaining process, where different interests and perceptions generated conflict and opportunistic interaction.

At this point in our example, the divisional strategy does not appear salient. The PRB process itself is in tatters, conflict among the participants has been exacerbated, and whatever shared interests might unify the group seem all but invisible.

Hubbard might dredge up a series of negotiation nuggets. (Maybe now is a good time for a power lunch. Adopt a win-win orientation. Be creative. The keys are power, time, and information. It's all psychology. Exchange your leisure suit for a powerful gray one with pinstripes.) What he really needs, however, is a general approach and a way to choose specific next steps. Should he open the afternoon meeting with an impassioned brief for cooperation? Should he be stern, threatening, or even suggest that the participants lock themselves up until they can reach an agreement? Should he bring a higher up, such as Tavner, into the process? Should he do the budget himself this year and merely put it out in a PRB format? Or, should he take another tack?

We will approach this problem by self-consciously applying our framework to get an idea of the general structure of the situation. This will enable us to evaluate more particularly what has happened and to suggest specific next steps in line with a broader strategy.

First Cut Analysis: Elements of the Negotiation

Hubbard is charged with using the PRB process to develop a divisional budget that reflects a larger strategic concept. The results of the process will be his division's input to the next level of budget discussions, in which Hubbard, other divisional managers, and top executives will work out resource allocations and marching orders for the year. In short, Hubbard is in the midst of working out the financial mandate for the Gamma Division's productive activities. In the just-ended meeting, Hubbard was in the midst of an analogous process—working out process, resources, and expectations for each department head. His position, at the nexus of these linked negotiations, divisional and corporate, heavily shapes his interests.

Interests   The PRB process appears to present a single *issue*: the budget rankings. Everyone's *position* on the issue seems predictable: "More for my division." A closer look, however, shows that Hubbard has at least four deeper *interests* in this encounter.

His first interest is strategic. He wants the budget allocations to align with his division's strategic mission, and he will need information from each department for this purpose.

Second, Hubbard has an interest in legitimating and institutionalizing the PRB process. He wants it to generate good information, and result in rankings agreed to by all participants. Obviously the more effectively his division uses the new PRB process, the better the resulting allocations will fare at the corporate level—where a lot rides on the success of the new budgeting method.

It is worth noting that Hubbard has chosen to go along with the PRB process. And, it is a significant choice. He has allied himself with his superiors, agreed to accept the system, and to try to gain his subordinates' acceptance. He might easily have chosen instead to form a more or less tacit alliance with his subordinates against PRB. If so, he might have gone back to Tavner and argued against its applicability or use in his division. He might have gained considerable support from his subordinates for his defense of their perceived interests. But his decision implies his interest in strengthening the PRB process.

Hubbard's third interest lies in developing a team spirit among the department heads. He has expended a great deal of effort trying to foster this interest so that his subordinates will work better together, coordinate their activities, and function more effectively as a unit. Ideally, he would like to enhance this spirit throughout his division by use of the PRB process. In particular, he does not want the experience to demoralize any of his managers. He prefers to work in an atmosphere of high esprit de corps for its own sake (an intrinsic interest) and for its salutory effects on his division's output (an instrumental interest).

Finally, Hubbard has an interest in the effect of this budget encounter on his personal standing and reputation, with his peers, subordinates, and superiors. He would like to appear effective, credible, and fair both for intrinsic reasons and for the effects of this perception on subsequent dealings.

His subordinates appear to have roughly comparable interests. Each seeks to protect and enhance his own share of the budget. With a bigger budget, it is easier to produce results. Perhaps more importantly, there appears to be a corporate ethos that bigger implies more important, and thus, better opportunities for promotion, more interesting jobs, and higher compensation. Each of Hubbard's subordinates also has an interest in his own personal reputation and standing, seeking to look good to Hubbard (though this may be weaker for Dewing and Roboh), to his subordinates, and to important peers. Third, each subordinate has intrinsic and instrumental interests in the spirit of teamwork and cooperation that prevails in the division. Fourth, they share an interest in success of the division's strategy, and therefore, in a strategically appropriate allocation of resources. This interest derives from a desire for the Gamma Division to look good at the corporate level, and hence, have higher status and collectively to be in line for more resources. But the departmental position of each manager fosters a belief that divisional success is contingent on increases, at least in part, in his own unit's funding. Finally, each subordinate has some interest in the character of the budget process, preferring one that is open, fair, and sensible to an alternative lacking these characteristics.

If we were to speculate on the relative weights that Hubbard and his subordinates place on these various interests, we would probably find that each subordinate puts the heaviest weight on the protection and enhancement of his own department's budget share as well as on his personal reputation and standing. Hubbard would place a far higher weight on overall divisional success and the PRB process. It is difficult to assess the value each might ascribe to divisional esprit de corps. (If we were directly advising Hubbard, we would spend a fair amount of time trying to understand his interests and assess the relative weights he would give to each of them.)

Alternatives to Agreement   To Hubbard, the alternatives to negotiated agreement are either (1) to continue this painful process or (2) to order an allocation. If the process drags on for too long, it runs the risks of destroying any spirit of teamwork and looking very bad to corporate superiors. Should he feel obliged to order a budget allocation, his subordinates would have little choice but to accept it; however, they might well try to sabotage it by various means at their disposal. For Hubbard, imposing a set of allocations risks significant loss relative to arriving at the same allocation by consensus. That route would defeat the ostensible purpose of the PRB process and would surely damage the possibilities of its future use in the division. Depending on the manner in which Hubbard imposed the allocation, he would also risk demoralizing key subordinates and harming a spirit of teamwork. He also would risk a loss in the eyes of top management, who have made a substantial commitment to PRB's success.

Hubbard's subordinates can continue this process, cooperatively or uncooperatively, without agreement on rankings. They may stay with this alternative to agreement until a budget is imposed, at which point they will have the options of going along or taking actions to sabotage the result. Any subordinate who refuses to "agree" risks an ultimately unfavorable budget allocation. (Of course, too quick agreement may also yield a shrunken budget.) Defiantly withholding consent may also result in considerable costs to reputation and standing. In any case, protracted wrangling may deal a blow to a valuable spirit of teamwork.

Agreements   Here, overall "agreement" means broad consensus on a budget ranking to be sent upstairs. From Hubbard's viewpoint, however, a series of bilateral budget agreements between him and various department heads may make the overall agreement more possible.

We explained in Chapter Five how differences and shared interests can combine to make agreement superior to the alternatives in the eyes of the participants. Both factors are potentially at work here.

At least two sets of complementary differences will be woven into a broad agreement. Hubbard cares deeply about the division producing in line with the agreed strategy and using the PRB process to arrive at an appropriate allocation. He has the ability to get resources for the division and the prerogative to rank each department head as good, effective, cooperative, or not. Individually and severally, Hubbard's subordinates care about their standing with him as well as obtaining the resources required for their departments. The subordinates have the ability to go along in good faith with the PRB process, to agree on strategically sensible allocations, and to produce in line with their agreements. These different capacities can dovetail with Hubbard's ability to get resources and his prerogatives to judge and reward their performance. Together these complementary differences contain the basis for broad agreement.

Although apparently submerged in the meeting, a number of shared interests also exist that could be realized in an agreement and make it more valuable. All other things being equal, division members would prefer that "the best strategy" be adopted in the sense that the division as a whole is most profitable. And even if such a "best" strategy is not adopted, anything that makes the division look better to others in Dowponto can redound to the credit of its members. They will find this intrinsically valuable—it feels good to be in a top-notch division. It is also instrumentally valuable in terms of its potential for, at a minimum, increased prospects for resources from above as well as possibilities for prestige and promotion. Further, division members share interests in an enhanced spirit of teamwork and in an allocation process that appears to be fair, open, and sensible.

Creating and Claiming   Broad differences between Hubbard and his subordinates thus provide the basis for an overall agreement. Hubbard wants—and his subordinates can provide—acceptance and use of the PRB process as well as production more or less in line with the division's strategy. His subordinates want—and he can provide— resources for doing this along with a positive evaluation of their managerial performance. Though some version of this large-scale "exchange" between Hubbard and the subordinates will almost certainly be realized and thus some of the potential joint value created, its terms will be contested. In particular, they will vie over the amounts of money for each purpose, how much production of each type will be expected, how closely aligned is the overall mix of division activity with the overall strategy, and the degree to which Hubbard's opinion of his subordinates' behavior is diminished or enhanced.

The strongest "claiming" behavior, however, is not likely to be between Hubbard and any department manager. Instead, the most divisive and competitive actions so far have been exhibited among the department managers over the issues of relative budget rankings or departmental shares. The tension became acute as the perception heightened on the second day that the cut-off amount was near and the bargaining was mainly distributive. In particular, the group's common interests in the best strategy, a good budget process, the division's image, and an atmosphere of positive teamwork have, to put it mildly, not been evident. If dissension rages unchecked, this behavior could further damage a number of shared values.

In short, the value from the broad "trade" between Hubbard and the others is likely to be realized with some "claiming" behavior over its terms. The greatest conflict, however, will come in the rankings among subordinates. It threatens to overwhelm the shared values that would make any agreement more valuable to all parties.

Evaluation of the Negotiation So Far

Thus far, we have presented the case itself along with the major elements of our framework applied to bring out the encounter's general configuration. We may now look much more closely at the intersection of the case and framework, both to evaluate much more particularly what has happened and to prescribe a series of next steps.

Hubbard acted as if he understood that the process would be most valuable if it resulted in a consensus. He did not act in an unfair or heavy-handed way, apparently appreciating the need for cooperation, information transfer, and a team spirit. Before the meeting, he had assuaged some fears and built commitment to the strategy and PRB process, in particular with Joe Roboh. And, in our judgment, stopping for lunch was a very good idea.

In general, however, Hubbard acted as if he believed in (or was fooled by) the nominal rationale for the PRB process. He seemed to think that, with the most profitable divisional strategy in mind and a mutual desire to reach it, his subordinates would smoothly exchange information and arrive at an optimal set of rankings. He acted more like a passive steward of a problem-solving process, almost as a computer attendant faced with a slightly cantankerous machine. He did not see a need for an active mediator, one who might make the inevitable conflict productive. Instead, he acted as if the naive vision of the process was right and the elements of conflict would take care of themselves.

In fact, Hubbard did not seem to anticipate and was surprised by the conflict that was generated. Arguably, he exacerbated this conflict by leaving powerful shared interests in the background and his subordinates in a situation that they experienced as one of virtually pure conflict. He had a strong interest in the discussion proceeding according to the PRB process and toward an allocation that lined up with his preferred strategy. Somehow, as the meeting progressed, this interest seemed to melt into the background.

It is striking, given Hubbard's interests in strategic funding reallocation and the legitimacy of the PRB process, that neither consideration played much of an overt role in the ranking discussion. He could have made these considerations the nominal criteria for his subordinates to apply in framing all requests, thereby setting or heavily influencing the terms of the discussion. Yet, he did not typically insist that requests be justified either in line with the requirements of PRB or in terms of the substance of his strategic conception.

In fact, some of Hubbard's actions actively undercut the PRB process itself and, by implication, his strategic vision for the Gamma Division. Consider an incident which seems to represent a turning point in the negotiation. Near the beginning of the reported dialogue, when Coulson and Ellis were squaring off over R&D funds, Hubbard recognized the impasse and turned to Andy Dewing, the Manufacturing Manager. Dewing appeared badly prepared and was both unable and willing to justify his submissions. In fact, he derided and attacked the PRB process itself and ended up with a know-nothing plea for the status quo. Significantly, Coulson and Brewster then joined in the chorus for Dewing to get his increments. The charitable face of this action might be that they saw and understood Dewing's justification even if it was inarticulately expressed. Instead, they appeared to be tacitly conspiring with Dewing to form an alliance against the PRB process. When Hubbard "rewarded" Dewing with his full increment, thus implicitly sanctioning the violation of the PRB process, Dewing in turn "rewarded" him with the request to leave the meeting and "get to work." In so doing, Dewing effectively undercut yet another intended feature of the process, that of interchange of information among the senior managers for more effective coordination.

In a later dispute between Brewster and Ellis over advertising increment allocation, Leo Nicholson, the Sales Manager, interrupted, breaking the news that he had not ranked all his people. The ensuing discussion revealed that Nicholson had not adequately prepared in other key areas. Hubbard's subsequent decision to award Nicholson last year's base personnel level plus two additional salesmen further weakened the PRB process, which, by this time, seemed only a charade.

A number of interests underlay the overall episode, some apparently in direct conflict, others easily compatible, and still others shared. Yet Hubbard did not seem to expect that his subordinates would focus on the distributive issues, those of apparent pure conflict that would generate adversarial "claiming" activity. In fact, in each of the incidents just discussed, Hubbard seemed to reinforce the idea that it was one department *versus* another by referring to "Norm's increments" and "John's increments" and heightening the sense of competition. When things became tense, he implicitly acknowledged the competitive tension by switching issues.

A better approach at this point might have been to diffuse the X versus Y aspect by demanding a justification of the request in terms of the divisional strategy and by means of the PRB process requirements. If the issues had been "which justification better serves the agreed divisional interest" rather than "who will win this standoff," the questions of lost face and imputation of weakness to the "loser" might have been mitigated. This was an opportunity for Hubbard to "teach" the importance of process and strategy rather than be visibly uncomfortable about and in fact exacerbate an apparently distributive confrontation.

Somehow, also lost in these encounters was the set of shared interests that would go along with constructive resolution of the issues: finding the best strategy, looking good as a division, working together as a team, and collectively constructing a good process. If these common interests had been more salient in the specific encounters at the group meeting and in the previous one-on-one sessions, the conflict might have been mitigated by the clearly enhanced value to all of agreement on "legitimate" terms.

One can, of course, argue that this meeting never should have been held. Given that one of its major purposes was to exchange information necessary for cross-departmental understanding and ultimate budget ranking, then combining the information revelation and decision allocation functions in a single meeting almost certainly confounded the twin aims. All participants understood that information could be used "against them." At a minimum, a meeting solely called to exchange information could have been held following the one-on-one meetings and well before a session to agree on allocations.

Prescription: A General Approach for Hubbard

Taking stock of the situation, there seemed to be four major problems: (1) the divisional strategy lacked salience; (2) the PRB process was in tatters; (3) the conflict from apparently incompatible claims had been exacerbated; and (4) the shared interests latent in this situation seemed virtually invisible. In this section we outline a general approach to each of these problems. We will then be in a position to propose and evaluate a number of specific steps.

Make the Strategy Salient   Hubbard needs to articulate carefully the divisional strategy and to affirm his and others' commitment to it. He should insist that the budget requests and justifications be framed in terms of the strategy. If he succeeds in setting the terms of the discussion in this way, he is more likely to get his preferred reallocation (thus effectively claiming—getting close to his optimum—while creating—improving overall divisional standing). To the extent that his strategic vision becomes the shared premise for the discussion, he has the opportunity to convert what now appear to be "*X* versus *Y*" clashes of interest into contests over who can best match the strategy. The "losers" in such contests need not attribute the outcome to personal weakness, having given up, or having lost face, but rather to an external norm—the strategy—that is intended to provide joint benefit. Moreover, to the extent that furthering the strategy becomes a common problem for the group to solve, team spirit should be enhanced.

Strengthen the PRB Process   By word and deed, Chris Hubbard should reaffirm his commitment to the PRB process and, at every turn, act to enhance its rationale, legitimacy, and standing. Further, he should underline his intent to support requests that are justified in terms of the strategy by means of the PRB process and look with disfavor upon them otherwise.

Why would his appeal to adopt the PRB method (and the strategic concept) have a chance of working? In part, Hubbard's public and private commitment to it would link his subordinates' keen interest in their standing with him to a variety of present and future issues. Moreover, all concede his formal authority and the legitimacy of his request in this matter. Further, the discussion so far has been chaotic and it would be helpful if someone imposed an orderly set of terms on it. Hubbard—as the nominal leader—is the prominent candidate for the job. Finally, in tandem with these factors, his subordinates simply expect requests to emanate from the person occupying his role. All these factors increase the likelihood that others will heed Hubbard's insistence on a particular "legitimate" set of terms for the discussion. Incidentally, the more the PRB process and his strategic concept become the terms of discussion, the closer the final outcome is likely be to Hubbard's preferred one.

It is important to note here that conferring "legitimacy" on congruence with division strategy but not on explicit concern with one's career advancement prospects may breed future problems. Subordinates who perceive that their honesty this year was exploited by less honest peers may choose more opportunistic behavior next year.

Even this year, those who worry that their promotion prospects are not being considered as "legitimate" may learn to argue for what they want in the language of PRB. Such discussion is unlikely to yield accurate information that will lead to budget allocations that Hubbard will find desirable.

Thus, Hubbard should make clear, perhaps in one-on-one meetings, his empathy for his subordinates' concerns for their advancement. For example, he might tell Coulson that if he were in Coulson's shoes, he would be concerned about the effects on his career prospects of getting behind the division strategy. Having legitimated these concerns, Hubbard should then seek to reduce the perceptions of conflict between individual long-run advancement and convergence on a budget in line with division strategy developed by a PRB process.

Reduce Focus on Interdepartmental Conflict   The PRB meeting revealed that the participants felt engaged in a situation of pure conflict. Each acted as if his real interest lay with a larger departmental budget. The rationale underlying this perception is not obscure: with a larger budget it is easier to produce; the corporate ethos seems to suggest that bigger is better; compensation, promotion, and general evaluation appear highly correlated with size of department. Hence the strife, the haggling atmosphere, and the prevalent zero-sum imagery that even Hubbard reinforced in the meeting. If it remains dominant, this perception will be deadly for Hubbard.

But if Hubbard's (and top management's) strategic vision for Gamma is correct, the division should become far *more* profitable after the budget reallocation. Thus, given an appropriate incentive system, budget reallocations should lead to tangible joint gains. Hubbard needs to change the perceived relationship between the *issue* of the budget ranking and his subordinates' real *interests*. If the proposed new strategy really is successful, everyone ultimately should be able to be amply compensated. Even if the economic results are uncertain or take time to become clear, Hubbard can offer many other forms of reward and compensation.

To change their current conflict-generating perceptions would require Coulson and, to a lesser extent, Brewster to be rewarded explicitly for managing cash yield from the more mature parts of the division. This new role might even be collectively understood by the Gamma Division management team as "managing the (very) profitable decline of Commodity Chemicals." Hubbard needs to reach both private and public understandings with Brewster and Coulson that their jobs and most significant rewards lie in effectively generating cash from their departments and thereby supporting overall divisional growth. Publicly and privately Hubbard can press for changed "psychological contracts," the perceived agreement between superior and subordinate about desired performance and behavior. Through the "Management by Results" program, he may be able to alter their compensation to be rewarded specifically for efficiency and cash generation, even as their departments decline in size. In addition, much of their compensation should be tied to overall divisional profitability over time. The psychological contracts as well as tangible incentives and measures need to be realigned for these vital players to embrace the new strategy. And Hubbard, having once occupied Coulson's current position, can credibly suggest paths to promotion via the proposed new strategy.

Even if Hubbard is effective, he is unlikely to reverse completely the perceptions that a budget in line with division strategy will hurt some subordinates' promotion prospects. The views of others outside the division that those with bigger budgets are more powerful, influential, or ascendant ought to weigh in the subordinates' calculations. But, by legitimating these conflicting interests, Hubbard can bring them to the surface rather than have them appear in a negotiation over self-interest carried out in the proxy language of PRB and strategy.

Heighten Salience of Shared Interests   Hubbard should take every opportunity both publicly and privately to get his subordinates to perceive and embrace the set of shared interests that are latent in their interaction. The value of any settlement that evokes those interests will thereby be increased for all parties and each can derive value beyond the substance of the settlement from the "best" strategy, looking good as a division, enhancing esprit de corps, and participating in the development of a good process for the future. The value each would derive from these interests may reinforce their solidarity in trying to achieve them.

Specific Steps for Hubbard

Continue the Meeting?   If Chris Hubbard decides to resume the meeting after lunch, it will be difficult to follow any of these approaches very far. He may offer a plea for unity, seek to make the shared interests salient, and outline the importance of the strategic concept. Given the previous encounter and the limited time, however, this is not likely to be effective on all counts. Instead, if Chris continues the meeting, he will need to decide whether his interest in teamwork or his interests in the PRB process and the new strategy are more important. If teamwork is more important, he may have to trade off better strategic allocation for it. And if the strategy dominates his values, teamwork may simply have to suffer if the meeting is to achieve closure.

Some argue that Hubbard should reconvene the meeting, closet the group until they finish, and ask everyone to be open about their interests and concerns. He should then turn the meeting into a session in which he and the group consider their Dowponto superiors (as well as the strategy and PRB) as common enemies and keep talking until they have worked out a budget. This focus on the group as a team, it is hoped, will rebuild the somewhat shattered feelings of team spirit.

While the group might "bite the bullet" and build esprit de corps, several experienced resolvers of such disputes were horrified at this suggested approach. And indeed, the suggestion is not much different from what has already been done. Our analysis suggests that such a meeting is more likely to lead members to focus squarely on what so far have seemed to be pure conflicts among them.

Cancel the Meeting?   A more promising approach might be for Hubbard dramatically to cancel the afternoon meeting, signaling that henceforth, things would be different. He might then hold a series of one-on-one meetings with his department heads to build a coalition behind the strategic process and in line with the PRB process. His approach in each of these one-on-one meetings should be composed of several elements. He should reaffirm his commitment to the PRB process and the strategic concept and insist on appropriate preparation of information in line with PRB process requirements, as well as justification of all requests in terms of the PRB process and the chosen strategy. He should stress the group's shared interest in agreement on an appropriate set of rankings. Hubbard can subtly affect the expectations of what each participant will get from this process by his manner and the substance of the assessments he offers. And where appropriate, particularly with Brewster and Coulson, Hubbard needs to work hard to alter the psychological factors that now seem to equate greater divisional size and budget allocation with more value. Having worked on expectations and the value of agreement, Hubbard should let his subordinates know that *not* going along with the new strategy and process will probably result in a drop in his and his peers' esteem as well as a likely lack of resource support.

Hubbard should give some care to the order in which he holds these meetings. His aim should be to get the "easy" people on board first and use their concurrence as a resource in subsequent encounters, appealing to a norm of solidarity. Joe Roboh should be easy to bring around as should Fred Ellis. Hubbard may have to work a little harder on Leo Nicholson and Andy Dewing, but getting them to prepare and take the system seriously should not be difficult if Hubbard makes a strong and visible commitment to this result. Norm Brewster and John Coulson will probably be the hardest. Though Hubbard can point to the others lined up behind the new strategy, Brewster and Coulson will each almost certainly feel a serious threat to his department. Hubbard will need to persuade each one that his welfare, reputation, and evaluation are not dependent on increased resource allocation to his department, but instead depend on the whole-hearted management of their product lines in accord with the strategy. Hubbard needs to work hard on each man's perceptions of what Hubbard sees as desirable behavior and performance as well as on changes in the compensation system that align each man's economic interest with the chosen strategy. Beyond psychological expectations and tangible rewards tied to cash generation from their departments and the division's overall profitability, Hubbard may offer some help with their subordinates who may experience dismay and loss of confidence in their department heads if their budgets are shrunk.

Hold an Information Meeting?　After obtaining commitments to remedy the holes in their submissions, it may be a good idea to have an "information-only" meeting wherein the department heads present and justify their rankings but do not attempt to aggregate them or establish overall priorities. Separating the informational and decision phases of the process may result in less noisy and distorted signals. Before a larger subsequent meeting for rankings, Hubbard might have an assistant, perhaps Jack Eckert (the PRB Coordinator), prepare a tentative set of rankings. He might use this as a single negotiating text: taking it around to each department head, emphasizing that it is merely a draft, and asking for their comments, criticism, and suggestions for improvement. Having generated a fair amount of information outside the head-to-head competitive environment that prevailed at the last large meeting, Chris Hubbard may have generated a far better starting point for decision making. Use of a draft may also shape expectations about ultimate rankings in a more compatible manner than the initial attempt.

Hold a Ranking Meeting for the Division? With this preparation, a larger meeting is far more likely to be productive and conducive to consensus. With the terms of the discussion largely agreed in advance and shared interests more salient, Hubbard should expect a more constructive interchange. The prepared draft, as well, may take some of the onus from his subordinates' having to "concede" to one another about relative rankings. Instead, Hubbard would be tacitly taking some of that responsibility on himself and diffusing adversarial attitudes among his subordinates. When conflicts arise, rather then ducking them or changing the issue, Hubbard may decisively press for resolution, but in terms of the division strategy. If he anticipates that both the PRB process and the strategy need a further boost, he may arrange for Tavner, his superior, to drop into the meeting for friendly observation and a possible pep talk. In making such a request of Tavner, of course, Hubbard would speak of his division's hard work with the demanding new process rather than allude to his own inability or bungling. For example, he might say that the first time around his people are a little bit uneasy with the process and that it could use a boost from Tavner.

What Chris Hubbard Should Have Done

We think that Hubbard, by straightforward analysis, could have anticipated many of the problems that did come up. What we advocate at this point in the process does not differ greatly from what we would have advised him before the ill-fated meeting. The steps involved in preventing the destructive manifestation of these problems need not have been much more time consuming than the steps he took. More carefully thought out one-on-one and informational meetings, perhaps a draft budget, and an overall meeting with Hubbard actively mediating would have been required for the revised approach. This would have improved the odds for an agreement to emerge that Hubbard and his subordinates would be able to live with and even like. A little bit of prior analysis could have gone a long way.

Next Moves

Preparation for the Corporate Meeting   Once Hubbard has his division's proposed budget rankings in hand, he needs to think hard about the meeting with higher-level corporate officials. He should certainly meet with each of his subordinates to smooth ruffled feathers, to fill in gaps in his understanding, and to fashion arguments that will be responsive to the likely criteria in the higher-level meeting. He will also want to learn what his own peers' divisional experiences with PRB have been; for this, he may speak with them directly, or he may discuss with PRB analysts throughout Dowponto how the process has gone. He also needs to gain a sense of whether his peers have been padding their budgets or playing other games with the system.

His most important preparation for the higher meeting will be a session with Henry Tavner to explain his situation so far, to understand Tavner's interests and his expectations for the upcoming meeting, and perhaps to win the right to make certain budget adjustments himself if "the line is drawn," so that it cuts off certain of his division's increments. For example, though Hubbard's ultimate ranking may be faithful with respect to his division's strategic objectives, unexpectedly large cuts that disproportionately fell on certain of his managers might be more evenly spread to avoid demoralizing the most heavily affected managers.

Depending on how his team arrived at their ultimate budget submission, Hubbard should press more or less hard for additional divisional funds. If the Gamma group had gone through a wrenching process in which they honestly shared information, Hubbard may argue persuasively for a generous budget from corporate headquarters. In this way, subordinates concerned with the effects of the process given their honesty might be rewarded. Such allocations could make subsequent cooperation with the system more likely.

Longer-Term Moves   It may be that a divisional reorganization would facilitate the new strategy and be more compatible with the inclinations of the current departmental managers. If this were true, and, for example, Coulson appeared temperamentally unable to manage a declining department, he might be moved to a newly combined sales, R&D, and manufacturing department with the implicit lure of Hubbard's general managerial job if all works out. Brewster might preside over a consolidated commodities and oil additive chemicals department, a much bigger fiefdom but one now to be managed for cash generation. Of course, Ellis's department would have already received a boost from the budget reallocations. The rub, of course, would be with Joe Roboh, Leo Nicholson, and Andy Dewing. Each of them would still have his department, but each would fall under another manager. Conceivably, a new R&D applications task force could be formed with Roboh in the chair and strong visible backing from Hubbard and Tavner. If this new configuration lined up better with the inclinations of the managers and with the chosen strategy in a way that fostered its realization, the move could be appropriate. Of course, if this action, other reorganizations, or different incentive plans were understood as attempts merely to "buy off" current difficult disputes, they would be shortsighted and unwise in the extreme.

But, regardless of new incentives or structures, Hubbard needs to convey the impression that the PRB process is not merely a year-to-year activity, but that successive iterations are linked and that people's performances will be monitored and evaluated over time. Hubbard needs to make sure that his managers do not regard PRB as a one-shot game in which misrepresentation or exaggeration could yield advantage. The future needs a longer than one-year tie to the past.

What Happened

For what it is worth, Hubbard apparently took relatively little of this advice. The afternoon meeting was held as scheduled, agreement was painfully forged, and the Gamma Division's overall increase was virtually identical to that of last year though there was some reallocation. On the plus side, the strategy had become more explicit and the management team had taken a relatively hard look at some of what before had been implicit priorities. Some reallocation in line with the new strategy took place, some information was exchanged, and a modest sense of "ownership" of the result prevailed. It appears, though, that this system exacted a price in the valued harmony and team spirit of the division. Coulson, having lost ground, was embittered and may have lost standing in the eyes of his subordinates. Brewster, if anything, appeared more defensive and protective of his turf. A divisional "win-lose orientation" with an implied power struggle appeared to be in the offing, and Hubbard wondered whether his managers might behave in self-serving ways in future years.

Conclusions

The PRB system effectively structures a bargaining process among advocates for various divisions and departments. Its requirement for ranking one budget increment ahead of others tends to lead to a perception that the interaction is one of pure "claiming"; that is, that each side's apparent interests conflict with those of all others. With each side seeking to claim value—understood as obtaining more favorably ranked increments—the appropriate tactics are those of distributive bargains. An adversarial atmosphere tends to be generated, information and analyses are subject to misrepresentation and exaggeration, people seek to commit to positions, and a suspicious, tense atmosphere often ensues. The only joint gains possible under such a system of perceived pure conflict seem to lie in reaching any collective agreement that is better than the alternatives. In this case, the alternatives were to continue the process and ultimately perhaps accept a budget imposed by Hubbard or, conceivably, by those higher up.

If the purpose of PRB is to generate enough information to make beneficial reallocations across divisions, the results can lead to the creation of substantial gain. Ways may be found to share the gain, and hence make it in people's interests to realize. As implemented in this case, however, the PRB process emphasized the claiming of immediately evident value at the expense of creating much greater future value by adopting a budget in line with the preferable strategy. Rather than cooperatively and cleverly expanding the pie, the parties' attention focused on dividing up the existing one in individually advantageous ways.

But if the ultimate purpose of PRB was the creation of gains large enough to make all parties better off, Hubbard's continuing problem was to make those creative aspects salient. He needed to emphasize the collective value of the long-run strategy, the shared purposes, the long-term value of the PRB process, and each individual's stake in the division's outcome. Not only should Hubbard have worked on his subordinates' perceptions, but he should also have sought to realign the psychic and financial compensation systems and measures by which people felt evaluated. In this way, the new strategy and its concomitant budget reallocations would lead to reward for the participants.

The PRB system in effect assumes that the parties have identical perceived interests in maximizing organizational value. Thus the ranking process should be a problem-solving one, a search for truth, an exchange of good information. Since PRB's real effect is to structure a bargaining game among the participants, however, this search for truth is often confounded by a quest for individual advantage. In this case, the urge to win dominated possibilities for learning.

It is quite common in the public and private sectors to adopt new systems for budgeting, control, and policy development. For example, building on Robert McNamara's experience in the Pentagon and at the Ford Motor Company, Lyndon Johnson instituted a government-wide "Program Planning and Budgeting System" that ultimately foundered, as did Richard Nixon's attempt to institute "Management By Objectives" and, later, Jimmy Carter's efforts to implement "Zero-Based Budgeting." If a new system is overlaid on an entire existing set of old incentives, the result is virtually bound to be dissonant. If new systems seek to generate good analysis and information on the implicit assumption that all sides have identical interests—and yet what the system does, in effect, is to structure a new bargaining relationship among the parties—results similar to those in the Gamma Division can be expected. Problem-solving processes intending to generate knowledge will malfunction as advocates seek to advance their interests.

Managers like Chris Hubbard play distinct roles in such processes. The manager, in part, is a negotiator even among his or her subordinates. But the role can be better understood as a special kind of mediator, one with a strong substantive interest in the outcome, much as the United States had in its mediating role with respect to the Egyptian–Israeli negotiations. So the manager is not a neutral mediator but instead an interested mediator and, further, a mediator with considerable potential clout. This mediator can significantly shape the terms of the discussion—what is an acceptable justification and what is not—and ultimately, should the result be unsatisfactory, he may impose a settlement. Of course, imposing a settlement may run against some of the manager's important interests in fostering teamwork and a sense of ownership of the results among subordinates. But that possibility is always in the background and can heavily affect subordinates' negotiating behavior.

Chris Hubbard's experience underlines the critical need for analysis and preparation on the part of such an interested manager-negotiator-mediator with clout. The odds against successfully "winging it" can be great. Such a manager needs to understand how cooperative moves to create value are entwined with competitive ones to claim it. His or her task is to emphasize shared purposes and joint possibilities to create value, to provide the participants with incentives and structures that line up with ultimately desired results, and to shape the manner and terms of discussion so that favorable agreements become more likely.

Previous chapters developed the kinds of analysis and tools needed for this task. Yet one major gap remains in this basic approach. So far, our discussion has mainly assumed that the elements of the negotiation are mainly "fixed" or given. But what about the case in which the game itself changes or could be changed? It is to this question that we now turn.

CHAPTER NINE

Changing the Game:
The Evolution of Negotiation

INTERESTS ARE THE MEASURE of negotiation. Alternatives to agreement set the standard of value that any possible agreement must exceed. Interests, alternatives, and agreements together compose a static picture of a negotiation. Within it, the competing needs to create and claim value shape the outcome. So far we have described a "configuration" and a process that takes it as given. By the configuration of the negotiation—or "game" as we will call it—we have meant: a set of parties, the issues and underlying interests, a notion of the relationship between them, the perceived alternatives to agreement, and the governing rules or procedures. But how does a negotiation or game come to be "configured" in the first place? How does the game change?

Analysts such as economists, game theorists, or management scientists are at their most powerful in analyzing a situation that has been carefully specified. Thus far we have mainly followed this tradition, holding the game relatively fixed and examining the processes of creating and claiming within it. Now we examine moves intended to alter the game itself. In so doing, we add an evolutionary dimension to the analysis.

To proceed, we need to ask precisely what determines the configuration of a game?

The answer to us seems simple, yet it has deep implications for the analysis and practice of negotiation. *The game is that which the parties act as if it is.* There is no a priori reason why this issue or that should be included or why this party or that interest is excluded. If the parties in fact deal with a particular set of issues, alternatives, and possible agreements, then, those issues make up part of that game.

One party will sometimes try to act as if a particular item is on the agenda. Other parties may strenuously resist including it. Such situations can result in a tacit or explicit negotiation over the game itself. To analyze this larger or "meta" encounter, our standard questions apply: What are the parties' respective interests in including or excluding the item? Their alternatives to including it? (Ignoring the other's demands? Walking out?) The set of possible agreements? (Agreement to include? Exclude? Include with concessions on an earlier issue? Include only if yet another issue is added?) And so on.

If we are right that the game is merely what people act as if it is, negotiators enjoy great freedom of action in trying to change it. This chapter first examines certain key *elements* that are common subjects of such action.

The *issues* make up one such element. Of course, the agenda itself is often a key initial and ongoing question. And even when it is set, questions arise about which of its issues will be packaged and which will be handled individually.

Like the issues, the *parties* in a negotiation are key elements that may be changed. The question of who participates or who might be prevented from participating at each stage of the process is obviously vital. In some cases, procedures like elections determine the parties. In other settings such as environmental or facility siting negotiations, the full set of parties may not even be identified until well into the process. Sometimes bargaining agents or ratifying bodies may become involved. And so on.

Other elements of the configuration are also candidates for change. Widely different *interests* may be evoked or downplayed. In Chapter Three we discussed moves to change perceived *alternatives* to agreement. In some cases the parties look after and buttress their own alternatives; in others, parties worsen opponents' alternatives. In still other cases, parties agree early on as to mutual alternatives; for example, the parties may choose binding arbitration if no substantive accord is reached. And the question of which body serves to appeal lower level disagreement is at the heart of negotiations in many budgeting and policy systems.

Beyond these specific *elements* of the game—about which we will have much more to say soon—we will focus on a number of *processes* by which people revise their beliefs about the game. Of course, the *negotiation* process itself influences perceptions of the game: that is, where alternatives to agreement lie, what the parties' real interests may be, whether a commitment in fact binds, and the like. From each party's vantage, such moves aim at making salient an advantageous portion of the zone of possible agreement.

Yet in tandem with this kind of negotiation process are other processes intended to change perceptions of the game. For example, moves to persuade another that the situation is different than it appears to be, or that a particular proposed agreement really does meet another's interest, can change the perceived game. So closely entwined are negotiation and persuasion that Richard Neustadt argued that the essence of presidential power is the "power to persuade" and that "the power to persuade is the power to bargain." Similar processes include learning and attempts to "teach." One party may seek to inspire, lead others, or to give a situation new meaning. And of course, one may try to obtain agreement by changing another's values. We examine these widely studied processes—persuading, learning, inspiring, leading, transforming, value changing, and so on— from the standpoint of how they can affect perceptions of the game.

Just as conventional analysis may help design moves within a game, a more supple kind of analysis can be applied to moves to change it. Because each element of the game can become an issue to be negotiated, we may apply the tools of negotiation analysis. In doing this, we address at least two classes of important negotiation problems.

First, given a well-configured game, when is it advantageous to change one of its elements, that is, add or subtract an issue or party, evoke another interest, or seek to alter the rules of procedure?

The second class of problems starts at an earlier stage. Suppose a manager-negotiator has envisioned an agreement or set of possible agreements that she would like to bring about. What configuration of interests, issues, alternatives, and so forth is most likely to achieve this preferred outcome? Critical questions must be addressed about who should be included and excluded, on what terms, which issues will be dealt with, in what order, and by what set of procedures. This might be understood as the problem of "negotiation design."

In exploring these questions, this chapter first considers certain key elements of a negotiation's configuration—issues, interests, parties. Then we examine some of the processes closely related to negotiation—persuading, learning, transforming, changing values—by which people revise their conception of the game.

Altering the Issues

One or more parties to a negotiation may seek to "add" an issue to the currently accepted configuration, or to "subtract" one. The process may be formal or informal, express or implied. In one case, a manufacturing vice president might simply raise a new item of concern in dealing with a long-time supplier, thus expanding the agenda. Of course, the supplier might object and urge that the question be ignored or dropped. And issue "subtraction" is common in advanced rounds of collective bargaining, when initially lengthy lists of issues (often more than one hundred in large negotiations) are pared by mutual consent to the "real" twenty-five or so.

Issues are said to be "added," combined, or linked when they are simultaneously discussed for joint settlement. "Package deals" and "single negotiating texts" are examples. When issues are joined at "summit" conferences, rather than being treated separately at lower bureaucratic echelons, we say that issue addition occurs.

Issue "subtraction" or separation takes place when each issue is evaluated without respect to others or excluded from consideration. Wholly different people or organizations may address different issues. At one time NATO and the OECD (Organization for Economic Cooperation and Development) effectively separated the military and economic issues faced by the industrialized countries. Issues may be separated by considering them at different times, by distinct subgroups of negotiators, or one at a time without the possibility of trades. Tacit or overt agreement not to take up a question or drop another are examples. The acceptability of possible settlements on each issue may be strictly "on the merits."

In the following section, we first focus on moves to add or subtract issues whose emphasis is on creating value. We then look at analogous actions that focus on claiming value.

Creating Value by Adding Issues   In this section we look at three distinct ways that adding issues can create value for the parties.

1. CREATING OR ENHANCING A ZONE OF AGREEMENT BY ADDING DIFFERENTIALLY VALUED, UNRELATED ISSUES.   A U.S. tin mining com-

pany operating in South America had been involved in a long wrangle with the Ministry of Labor over the degree to which the firm should and could employ nationals of the country to operate its ten-year-old mine. Negotiations had been deadlocked with the company preferring to hire fewer nationals and the ministry demanding more. At the same time, but completely separately, the firm had been negotiating fruitlessly with the Mining Ministry over the concession to develop a new mine in a rural part of the country. There the problem concerned prospective royalty rates. Taken by itself, each negotiation was at impasse. Yet the company was very concerned with royalties while local hiring practices were becoming a much hotter political issue in the country. When a high government official brought the two separate ministries together with a senior company executive, the deadlock was easily broken—somewhat lower royalties for the new mine, more local labor at both, and an engineer who was a national of the country to be the first mine's manager.

The point is easily stated: adding differently valued issues together can create or enhance zones of agreement where none would be possible if separate negotiations took place and the outcome of each such negotiation were separately evaluated for acceptability. This might be called changing the game to dovetail differences of value. Adding an issue as a side payment can work for the same reason.

2. ADDING ISSUES TO EXPLOIT THEIR DEPENDENCIES.   The analysis so far has proceeded under the implicit assumption that each party evaluated each issue identically whether the issue was taken by itself or combined with another. Yet sometimes there are positive dependencies or "synergies" among the evaluations of issues when the issues are taken up together. Positive dependence shows up simply in the case of economic complements: pencils and papers may be worth more in combination than the sum of their values taken independently; the same may be true of coffee and sugar. If such positive interactions exist, combining issues may create value.

Another kind of dependency can be exploited by adding issues in the same way that portfolio diversification can reduce investment risk. Suppose that an entrepreneur owns two businesses on a tourist island, one with the concession for rain umbrellas, the other with the rights to sell suntan oil. He is negotiating the sale of each business to a different party. Neither is willing to pay the entrepreneur's price, partly because each business by itself is quite risky. When the sun shines, the suntan oil concession flourishes while the umbrella business languishes. When it rains, the reverse happens. A potential buyer in each negotiation has lowered her offer to compensate for this specific risk. Yet, if the negotiations could be combined, the two potential buyers could form a partnership to buy both concessions, which together would have a much less variable cash flow than either single business. The price offered for both together may well exceed the sum of the offers for the separate components. Combining the issues enhances the possibilities of agreement. [1]

3. ADDING ISSUES TO ACCOMMODATE DIFFERENCES: UNBUNDLING AND DECOMPOSITION.   Say that an engineering firm is negotiating with a city over the sale of a plant to burn garbage and make steam for electricity. The company is highly certain of its recently developed technology; the city has less faith in the innovatively engineered design. The firm demands an unacceptably high price (to the city) for this state-of-the-art venture; the city, fearful of failure, offers too low an amount (to the firm). Our previous discussion of creating joint gain through differences suggests an obvious strategy: add new issues to the bargain, that is, make an arrangement for each contingency of concern about whose chances the parties differ. Given their expectations and concerns, both sides could gain by expanding the issue from "price" to "price if success" and "price if failure," with a high price in the former case and a lower one in the latter.

Analogous advice applies to situations in which a single issue conceals underlying differences of interest: as we have previously discussed, unbundling the differentially valued interests by expanding or adding new issues can yield gains. Similarly, the issue of the *amount* of a one-time payment may be beneficially expanded to the *amounts* of each of several payments over time. And so on. The general principle is again easy to state: where differences such as those of valuation, probability, and time or risk attitude are present, adding new issues to the bargaining by unbundling or allowing contingent arrangements may create value.

The overall proposition—that adding issues can yield joint gains that create or enhance a zone of possible agreement—is thus true for at least three types of situations: first, where unrelated but differentially valued issues can be combined; second, where actual dependencies (complementarities or synergies) among issues can be exploited by their combination; and third, where unbundling or decomposition is possible.

One can take these points as arguments for simultaneous rather than separate or sequential consideration of issues. For instance, if

[1]More complex examples of this can be found in Sebenius (1984).

formulating a government's "bottom line" in negotiating instructions is done on an issue-by-issue basis, with only the contested items referred to a higher bureaucratic level, beneficial agreements may be inadvertently ruled out. What appears to be a bare minimum on one issue taken by itself may in fact be flexible—from the vantage point of a higher-up—when this issue is considered together with favorable settlements on other questions.

The use of a "single negotiating text" can facilitate the simultaneous consideration of several issues. "Package deals" can result in similar advantages. The social-psychological literature lends experimental support to the proposition that juggling multiple issues together can lead to settlements that are jointly preferred to those obtained by bargaining on an issue-by-issue basis.[2]

It is but a short step from stressing the value of simultaneous consideration of issues to the argument that as many issues as possible should be added together so that the best possible settlement may occur after "trading."[3] Yet adding issues together is *not* always desirable as the next set of propositions seeks to demonstrate.

Adding Issues Can Reduce or Destroy a Possible Zone of Agreement; Thus, Subtracting, Avoiding, or Separating Issues Can Help Parties to Create Value Adding issues together, with the requirement of simultaneous explicit agreement on all of them, may reduce the chances for a successfully negotiated outcome. It is useful to distinguish between cases in which some of the included issues may have no separate solutions and those in which all the issues are resolvable individually until combined.

1. ADDING ISSUES THAT THEMSELVES HAVE NO ZONE OF AGREEMENT MAY DESTROY OVERALL CHANCES OF A SETTLEMENT ON OTHER ISSUES. We have shown that combining issues that are individually impossible to resolve may facilitate agreement. But it is possible to go too far. Adding a sufficiently divisive issue to less contentious questions *and* requiring joint resolution of them all may render agreement impossible. Requiring that the status of Jerusalem be resolved at the first stage of a possible Middle Eastern accord, for example, might overburden a set of other issues that potentially could be settled. If

---

[2]Rubin and Brown (1975:275–277).

[3]Tollison and Willett (1976:98) make the same point in general terms. When the Pareto frontier "is clear and well understood by all parties," they state, "the aggregation of issues is quite helpful to the process of reaching international agreement. A multiplicity of issues creates more possibilities for indirect trades leading to productive agreements."

the negotiation agenda initially included Jerusalem, the parties might profitably agree to "subtract" it and perhaps to take it up later if benefits from agreement on the other issues had strengthened their relationship enough.

An instinctive response to a situation like this is to drop the requirement of simultaneous settlement, especially if both sides prefer a resolution of the remaining topics to no agreement. Yet agreement to drop or postpone the settlement of an issue can affect the outcome of the questions still in the negotiation. Consider an arms control example:

> Excluding underground tests from the nuclear test ban treaty surely facilitated agreement. But until the summer of 1963, Khruschev vigorously opposed this separation of issues. He must have realized that once a partial treaty had been signed, the western powers would feel under much less pressure to accept his minimal detection arrangements for banning underground tests.[4]

Despite its obvious appeal, the separation of extremely divisive issues from other questions that by themselves do have mutually beneficial settlements is sometimes difficult or impossible. Appropriations bills in the U.S. Congress must sometimes be signed or vetoed in their entirety. Executive–legislative budget negotiations may deadlock because of a single, divisive item. Otherwise acceptable compromises are often lost in this manner.

2. ADDING ISSUES WITH INDIVIDUAL ZONES OF POSSIBLE AGREEMENT MAY DESTROY OR REDUCE A COMBINED ZONE OF AGREEMENT. A more interesting case involves issues that could be resolved individually but that cannot be settled when considered together. This can happen when a "smaller" issue takes on some of the attributes of a "larger," difficult, but potentially solvable question.[5] Consider a proposed trade deal between two countries that are engaged in drawn out, inconclusive, expensive hostilities. Both the hostilities and the economic action may have outcomes preferable to the current situation. But it may be impossible to consummate the trade deal unless the hostilities are settled. Even a jointly desired agreement not to mistreat the other's prisoners or not to use particular tactics or weapons may be impossible to reach because of its symbolic overtones. Or consider an example that underlies the subjective construction of the

[4]Iklé (1964:224).

[5]See Sebenius (1984) for a variety of other examples of where and why this may occur.

negotiation: "In August, 1961, a civil aviation agreement between the United States and the Soviet Union was negotiated. The United States might have signed the agreement, treating it as a separate matter. We chose, however, to decline to sign it, and considered the matter related to [Soviet actions with respect to] Berlin."[6]

To avoid adding such issues together, they may be considered at a lower bureaucratic level. Sharing of the fur seals on the Alaska–Siberia border in the 1950s, at the height of the Cold War, was easily handled by relegating the question to low-level officials. In another case, meteorologists in the Weather Bureau were able to maintain the common interest in exchanging weather data with Cuban stations even during the Cuban missile crisis.

In the discussion so far we have considered numerous ways in which adding or subtracting issues at various stages of a negotiation can create value or enhance a zone of possible agreement in negotiation. Yet moves to alter issues may also have the primary intention of claiming value.

Adding or Subtracting Issues May Be Devices For Claiming Value As one observer of foreign relations observed, "linkage between unrelated or only loosely related issues in order to gain increased leverage in negotiation is an ancient and accepted aspect of diplomacy."[7] One side may force a new issue onto the negotiating agenda by the exercise of otherwise unexploited power.[8]

1. TRADITIONAL "LEVERAGE." Suppose a transnational mining company felt compelled to enter negotiations on building hospitals and schools in a host country less the financial terms of its contract be unfavorably revised. In such a case, the threat to a different issue in the "larger" game among the parties could be used as the lever to force the linkage.

Where "forced" linkages are involved, the party desiring the linkage need not actually be able to carry out the threat. Its effectiveness is a function of the threatened party's attitude toward taking risks, its evaluation of the magnitude of the consequences, and the credibility of the threat. A very risk-averse party might respond to a large threat that has only a small chance of actual occurrence.

[6]Fisher (1964:93)

[7]Wallace (1976:164)

[8]Of course, rather than being used to force linkage, the same power might compel a particular settlement of an existing issue.

Analogous moves to subtract issues or avoid linkages are often the responses to attempts at claiming value by adding issues. "That is a separate question. Let's deal with it later (in a different forum) (strictly on its own merits)" are standard countering gambits. Or threatening further issue escalation can keep items off the agenda. Suppose that a purchasing agent raises the issue of nonstandard delivery terms for one product from a firm that supplies him with many other products. The agent may fail in his attempt if the supplier insists that opening this additional issue would require a reconsideration of pricing and delivery policies over the whole array of products.[9]

2. ADDING ISSUES CAN SOLIDIFY COALITIONS. Adding issues to a negotiation may be a way to strengthen a coalition by offering an inducement for preserving solidarity. A national labor union may bargain primarily over such issues as wages that concern all its members. Adding several issues that particularly concern different local unions, however, may earn their more enthusiastic support in a contest with management. Because there may be considerable uncertainty as to the resolution of these issues, the actual effects of a settlement, and the ultimate distribution of any benefits generated, including a number of such issues may be a way to hold coalition members together.[10]

Complicating Considerations in the Addition and Subtraction of Issues There are several qualifications to this discussion of adding and subtracting issues. First, there is the question of complexity. As issues are aggregated, the amount of information a negotiator requires increases and the negotiation itself becomes more cumbersome. Tradeoffs among more diverse areas may need to be made at ever higher levels of the organizational structure. The issues themselves may be technically complex, while rationality and attention spans are limited.

[9]A related and negative "second face of power"—to keep issues off the agenda in the first place—is often important. See Bachrach and Baratz (1962:947–952).

[10]The developing countries' organization across many international conferences—called the Group of 77—has displayed a remarkable solidarity even when internal divisions of interest were present. Part of the reason for this solidarity may consist of the large number of issues—terms of trade, technology transfer, debt relief, sovereignty over natural resources, and the like—that promise widely distributed but uncertain benefits if the group succeeds. The issues may have very poorly understood cause-and-effect connections. The likelihood of achieving success on any of these items, however, appears lower if overall solidarity is not maintained. Ernst Haas (1980:373) calls this phenomenon "fragmented linkage," in which "uncertainty about outcomes is part of the glue that holds the coalition together."

Relationships among diverse issues may be complicated. Putting questions together to make bargaining tradeoffs may be unintentionally harmful. Roger Fisher and Bill Ury argue for the separation of issues and individual settlement "on the merits." They use an example in which

> a contractor in a negotiation with the owner of a building in the works said "Go along with me on putting less cement in the foundations because I went along with you on stronger girders in the roof." No owner in his right mind would yield. Nor would he yield if the contractor threatened to make the owner's brother-in-law lose his job or offered the owner a special favor.[11]

Adding issues together for bargaining purposes while ignoring their real interdependence (in this example, it is physical) would be a bad idea. But all interdependencies are not so obvious. To add issues is to run the risk of increasing complexity, causing overload, or fear of unintended consequences. Subtracting or separating them can have opposite influences.

Attempts to force linkage may poison the negotiating atmosphere and add new, undesirable attributes. The victim may regard the move as illegitimate and unethical. It may backfire. Of such moves, a shrewd eighteenth-century diplomat noted, "Menaces always do harm to negotiation, and they frequently push one party to extremities to which they would not have resorted without provocation. It is well known that injured vanity frequently drives men to courses which a sober estimate of their own interests would lead them to avoid."[12] As a practical matter, it is generally easier to sustain a linkage that has a substantive connection either with the other (voluntary) subjects of negotiation or, at least, with the recognized goals of one party.

Even proposing issues for addition that may enhance a zone of possible agreement can cause problems. Such issues may transform a simple, tractable bargain into a complex, uncertain one. Proposing trades among unrelated issues may engender more such suggestions, escalating the negotiation to include all possible aspects of a common relationship. This may make small, desirable deals unlikely.

This tendency may also lead to the creation of a stingy trading atmosphere, which becomes "I won't do anything for you unless I get something in return." In negotiation over various forms of European

[11]Fisher and Ury (1979:106)
[12]de Callières (1716:125)

integration, diplomat Jean Monnet actively encouraged a "community spirit";[13] common interests were to be the focus rather than logrolling, package deals, or trades based on conflicting interests in separate areas. He tried to induce joint problem solving and to build long-term relationships rather than to foster the habitual use of bartered deals for immediate advantage. Of course, apparent concessions now may be accompanied by the expectation that they will be reciprocated later. Recognizing that the relative importance of issues to each side changes over time may be the basis for building longer-term relationships.

The addition of issues, along with changing the substantive focus of a negotiation, may also have the effect of adding new parties whose primary concern is with the new issue. Indeed, changing the parties may be part of the reason for adding the issue. For example, the entry of a different, supposedly more reasonable group of bureaucrats may be triggered.[14] Of course, a particularly obnoxious set of negotiators may leave the bargaining if "their" issue is dropped or postponed.

Legal officers of two corporations, working out a primarily legal agreement, may add the financial staffs to the negotiations by adding financial aspects to the original bargain. Conversely, one way the House Merchant Marine Committee could ensure that the House Ways and Means Committee members were not able to leave their specific imprint on a bill to authorize U.S. companies to mine the seabed would be to take great care not to add a minor tax provision to the bill. It is easy to imagine cases in which a party brought in with an issue might have still another useful relationship or connection with one of the original negotiators; likewise, omitting an issue to get rid of its associated party is a common tactic. The next section takes up the general question of changing the parties.

Altering the Parties

So far we have generally held the parties constant in order to look at changing the set of issues under negotiation. In a marketplace analogy, we might imagine the same traders acting to force or entice each other into considering fewer or more types of commodities. We now

[13]His efforts are noted by Iklé (1964:119).

[14]This "new party effect" could have accompanied many of the instances of issue addition discussed earlier.

keep the commodities the same in order to look at some of the means and ends of adding or subtracting traders.

Parties may be brought in or ejected by unilateral action of one side, by unanimous agreement or by suitable votes of the original negotiators. Such parties also may be able to force their way into the dialogue by means of their leverage over the existing players or their stakes in the issues under negotiation. Their participation may be explicit or it may be tacit. Their assent may or may not be required for a settlement but their influence during the deliberations may be significant. Sometimes such parties are brought in as a consequence of added or subtracted issues.[15]

Several fairly straightforward reasons for changing the parties in a negotiation merit brief mention. If one is seeking a nonproliferation agreement or a division of market shares, those players with a tangible influence on and interest in any ultimate deal will normally enter the game at some stage.

One side may bring in a third-party ally with influence on a current bargaining partner. The Japanese automaker Nissan was negotiating unsuccessfully with the Mexican government for permission to manufacture in Mexico. Bringing in the Japanese government as an ally was a useful ploy. Since Mexico's largest foreign-exchange earner at that time was cotton and Japan absorbed 70 percent of Mexican cotton exports, the implied threat to cut imports was sufficient to assure Nissan the necessary license.[16] It is not necessary, of course, that an additional party have unrelated, unexploited power. Before the 1963 newspaper strike in New York, the publishers of nine newspapers formed a Publishers' Association to bargain with the newly forged "blood brotherhood" of several unions in the Newspaper Guild.[17]

Third parties with other relationships to the negotiators may be used to strengthen commitments arising from the negotiation. If either negotiator were to renege on their agreement, the third-party agreement would be affected as well, possibly with adverse conse-

[15]The number of participants in a negotiation may vary for other reasons. The size of a delegation may change; it may acquire or discharge advisers; or the negotiators may create or draw on outside bodies—secretariats, technical commissions, consultants, and the like. Though these situations are of independent interest, the rest of the above discussion on the addition or subtraction of parties takes the point of view of those who themselves can be considered direct or indirect "principals" in the bargaining.

[16]Bennett and Sharpe (1979).

[17]Raskin (1976).

quences. A commitment within a negotiation not to accept less than some settlement amount may be buttressed by a link to future or parallel negotiating parties (as was the case with issues). It is also possible to bring in parties to solidify an agreement, to add legitimacy to a bargain or aid in its implementation.

The more parties (and issues), the higher the costs, the longer the time, and the greater the informational requirements tend to be for settlement. But the number of parties can be radically reduced to allow agreement among a smaller group. The Soviet-U.S. Test Ban Treaty, for example, came about only after an eighteen-nation disarmament conference gave way to bilateral negotiations.

Recall the discussion in Chapter Three on alternatives to agreement. We described the example of Malta, which "added" the Soviets and Libyans to its naval base negotiations with Great Britain. In doing this, Malta not only improved its alternative to an agreement with Britain, but made Britain's no-agreement alternative (in which the Russians or Libyans would get the base) seem much worse to NATO than a neutral Malta. Similarly Kennecott "added" customers, banks, and governments to its side prior to negotiations with Chile over copper mine expropriation. By whatever means, changing the parties can be a potent means of changing alternatives.

We devote the remainder of this section's analysis to three ways in which changing the players can significantly alter the zone of possible agreement among the original parties.[18]

1. ADDING OR SUBTRACTING PARTIES WHO HAVE AN INTEREST IN A SETTLEMENT MAY ALTER THE ORIGINAL ZONE OF AGREEMENT.   If the settlement of a dispute has value to outside parties, the original negotiators may try to appropriate some of that value. Involving the other parties is one method. The added value may be a windfall to the original parties, if they would have agreed anyway, or it may significantly increase the inducement for them to come to terms. In either case, party addition is likely.

Imagine two young brothers loudly arguing over a single ice-cream cone and deciding to risk its summary confiscation by appealing to Daddy. Their hope is that Daddy will oblige by getting them a second cone to buy peace. An externality in the original situation (the noise of their quarrel) provides the basis for the desired (or undesired) entry of other parties.

The United States clearly perceives a strong interest in Egypt's

---

[18]In Chapter Fifteen, we discuss related issues concerning bargaining agents or bodies that must ratify the results of negotiation.

and Israel's settling their differences. Thus it is hardly surprising that the United States interjected itself into the Middle East negotiations along with substantial offers of economic and military assistance. If an existing party—the Soviet Union, for example—is perceived as having an interest in *no* settlement, it may be frozen out of the negotiation for analogous reasons.

2. ADDING PARTIES MAY SPREAD OR ELIMINATE RISKS FROM THE BARGAIN OF THE ORIGINAL PARTICIPANTS.   An earlier section considered the possible advantages of adding issues to exploit risk dependencies. Separate negotiations on rain umbrella and suntan oil concessions could be combined; the resulting "diversified" issue in a single negotiation would be worth more to all parties than when the questions were separate. Now, consider the reverse situation in which the issues (which involve uncertainty) are held constant while parties are added to spread or eliminate original risks.

Suppose that two companies are negotiating over constructing a risky experimental energy technology with an agreed chance of success estimated at one-half. Assume that each company's risk attitude toward such a project can be described simply: each would be willing to risk losing $250 million for a possible $500 million gain but an even chance of losing $375 million against a $750 million gain is too much risk for either to bear. Say that the project's costs are known to be $750 million, and its benefits (if successful) would be $1.5 billion over cost. Under such circumstances the two-company bargaining would be inconclusive, while the addition of a third similar firm could spread the risk in a way that would be beneficial to all. Each project sponsor would then be happy with a $250 million cost balanced by a $500 million share of potential benefits. Adding the third party would allow agreement.

Negotiation of the financial terms of mineral agreements in developing countries is often rendered very difficult by the price uncertainty of the product. In a market slump, large losses could result; a boom may send profits to extreme levels. The mining taxation system can significantly affect the risk. Trying in advance to decide the proper tax mixture and level of relatively fixed charges (which shift price risk to the company) or contingent charges (such as profit shares, which tend to shift price risk to the country) may be extraordinarily difficult if both parties are risk-averse. One solution to this problem is to sell bonds to less risk-averse third parties in specially created markets. These bonds could be denominated in the price of the commodity. The (certain) proceeds of the sale could then be the subject of bargaining. Each side, of course, might elect to hold some proportion of the bonds. But by indirectly involving others, such bonds could mitigate the price risk inherent in the agreement, thus opening or widening a zone of agreement.

3. ADDING OR SUBTRACTING PARTIES IN A NEGOTIATION WHERE SCALE ECONOMIES ARE PRESENT MAY ALTER THE ZONE OF AGREEMENT FOR THE ORIGINAL PARTICIPANTS. Scale economies (or diseconomies) associated with negotiating issues may make including (or excluding) parties desirable. Consider three examples:

Negotiators trying to set up or share the costs of a defense alliance, for example, confront such a situation. Alliance benefits—defense against an attack—may readily be extended to like-minded countries. Barring cases of special added geographic vulnerability, new members should lower the costs to other members. A larger alliance may also reduce the probability of attack. The addition of as many parties as possible may enhance a zone of agreement in such a situation by lowering costs and increasing benefits.[19]

Several states or nations in a region may be negotiating to build a regional power-generating plant. Economies of scale tend to be considerable in power generation. In order to enjoy the lowest average costs, the group may seek to add members in the early stages. Their presence may facilitate agreement.

Finally, consider an ongoing, tacit negotiation in a small cartel that dominates a market. Say that fewer members mean fewer enforcement problems and disproportionately larger profit shares for those involved. With this "diseconomy of scale," the participants would like to have as few members as possible and perhaps would seek to drive smaller rivals out of the ongoing bargain and erect barriers to entry.[20]

---

[19]Olson and Zeckhauser (1966).

[20]Two observations about Cases 2 and 3 are worth making. First, the "added" parties could be new active participants or they could be passively involved, possibly through some outside connection to one of the original negotiators. Second, the rationale offered for adding parties could equally well serve as a reason for expanding the coalition if the original negotiation were defined to include potential participants. One necessary condition for the success of a coalition is usually taken to be that it can do better ("create more value") than can its members individually or in competing coalitions. The economic factors of Cases 2 and 3 may create potential for the addition of parties that for some reason were not regarded as part of the original game's configuration. The phrase "for some reason," which may refer to psychological, institutional, political, historical, or other factors, is defined to include these potential participants. Whether this phenomenon is regarded as adding parties or aligning members in coalitions, the same underlying factors are at work.

Evoking and Avoiding Interests

At the beginning of this chapter, we observed that the configuration of a game is merely that which the negotiators act as if it is. A priori, there is no reason why any element of the interaction—party, issue, alternative, interest—should or should not be present. By their actions, negotiators "construct" their encounter. With this in mind, we considered some of the effects of moves intended to alter the issues and parties. But one of the most powerful implications of this observation about how a negotiation comes to be configured lies in the set of interests seen to be at stake. Much of the bargaining process consists of conscious or unconscious moves by the parties to shape the set of involved interests.[21]

Two broad principles guide the art of advantageously shaping the set of evoked interests. First, to create or enhance value, a negotiator should seek to "add," evoke, or emphasize shared interests that are latent in the interaction. To avoid destroying value, damaging or harmful interests should be downplayed ("subtracted" or "sheared off"). The second broad principle concerns moves primarily intended to claim value. To accomplish this, negotiators often try to gain acceptance of their terms without evoking interests and interpretations that the other side would find unappealing. Similarly, value claimers try to evoke self-serving principles, rationales, and interpretations. In exploring these principles, we do not investigate the social or psychological mechanisms by which the joint negotiating reality is "constructed." Rather, we seek to illustrate the importance of the phenomenon and provide examples of some of the ways that interests evolve and are changed.

Evoking or Avoiding Interests to Create Value Consider three important classes of such moves.

EVOKING INTERESTS THAT CREATE COMMON VALUE. When elements of conflict are present, shared visions, superordinate goals, overarching purposes, ideologies, norms, and fairness principles are

---

[21]Many of the points we made earlier—especially in the chapters on envisioning agreements and creating and claiming value—really depended on moves intended to evoke or avoid interests that otherwise would not be present in the interaction. In this sense, we violated the logic of our presentation, which was first to investigate moves within the configuration and then to examine means of changing it. Our purpose in this section is to place such actions in tighter logical relation to the rest of our approach and to offer some further ways of evoking and avoiding interests.

often overlooked. Yet what might in itself be an onerous proposal—say, to work solidly through a holiday weekend—may be cheerfully agreed to if it is seen to further a valued cause. But it is the connection with the larger interest that overcomes the negative, distributive features of the chore.

Sometimes a manager can evoke such interests simply by raising them or habitually couching discussions in terms of them (though the obligatory "win one for the Gipper" speech before each task is more likely to evoke yawns). Raising the salience of relationships and, in effect, linking them to the task at hand may be effective. The perception that procedures are "fair" can be of great value, often eclipsing in importance their actual results. A manager sensitive to this fact may be able to create considerable common value, seemingly "out of nothing." (Of course, this may be done cynically and as a tactic mainly to claim value—which we discuss below.) A very senior manager or other high-status figure may be brought in to emphasize the larger issues and inspire people to look "beyond" the seeming conflict. Analytically, such moves simply push the perceived Pareto frontier northeasterly.

PROCEDURES TO SHEAR OFF NEGATIVE INTERESTS. As a function of history, the situation, or negotiating dynamics, a variety of destructive characteristics may come to encrust a bargaining encounter and make agreement difficult. As we discussed in Chapter Four, forcing a person to attribute his concession to his weakness and his counterpart's strength can cause a loss of face and begin the escalation of conflict. Sometimes, appeal to a mechanism that is outside the control of the parties offers a way out. For example, negotiation over a minor issue like who should do the dishes may rapidly escalate to involve a much broader set of questions about the relationship—who is right, wrong, aggrieved, powerful, and so on. A simple procedure, such as a coin flip, however, may shear off this whole set of other questions and solve the problem.

Organizational disagreements with similar, if more consequential, characters may sometimes be kept more tractable by an appeal to authority, precedent, or long-standing procedure. "Giving in" to such considerations often does not carry with it an attribution of personal weakness or loss of face. Similarly, if both sides discover what seems to be an "objective" principle, it may offer a way out of otherwise more tangled dealings.

In some cases, the *fact* of agreement—as opposed to its substance—may be costly to one or more of the parties. For example, two state governors may be quite willing to live with any of a number of negotiated resolutions of a boundary dispute. Given vocal constituents, however, one or the other of them may find any reasonable outcome politically damaging to endorse. The governors may avoid the onus of such a decision, however, by submitting it to binding arbitration, in which the arbitrator takes responsibility for the outcome.

Similarly, consider a newly introduced budgeting system like that examined in the last chapter. The system requires a meeting in which the affected managers are supposed to rank the entire unit's proposed expenditures for the year. Requiring agreement on such a ranking—that Joe's project is the most important, while Andy's is number fourteen—could produce extraordinarily divisive, adversarial reactions. In such a case, it may be far better for the boss to take responsibility for the final rankings and thus shear off negative aspects of forcing agreement among the parties. Either way, the managers may be quite able to live with the budget outcome; the process may be the problem.

WORKING ON ANOTHER'S PROBLEM TO AVOID NEGATIVE ROLE INTERESTS.　Associated with habitual roles may be a large number of conflict-producing factors and attitudes. Particularly where disputes have continued for a while, destructive hostility and suspicion may lie barely below the surface. Sometimes, however, it is possible to find the means for the parties to escape their accustomed roles and work on a problem related to their own. In the process, they may go a long way toward resolving the difficult issues between them. Consider two instances, both suggested by Howard Raiffa. About the "British colliery" experience, he writes:

> In the 1940s the collieries in England were in a deplorable state. Internal labor strife within each colliery was severe and resisted management's efforts toward improvement, until a new management leader named Reginald Revans devised and executed a brilliant scheme. He had each colliery organize a team whose members ranged from lowly workers to top managers. The team from Colliery A was given the task of writing a report on how to achieve better managerial rapport not within their own colliery but within Colliery B! The Colliery B team was assigned to do a similar task for Colliery C; Colliery C for D; and so on, returning finally to A. Colliery B, for example, would profit somewhat from the advice given by Colliery A. But more, much more, would be accomplished from the nonthreatening interactions among the members of Colliery B's team as they discussed the problems of C. The Revans Plan was de-

signed to foster communication within each team by focusing members' attention on a problem that was removed from their own, but related enough so that the lessons articulated about that problem could trigger insights into their own. Apparently, the plan was a success.[22]

Consider a second case in which bad relations hindered a settlement. By 1974, the Tyrolean village of Obergurgl in Austria had enjoyed some three decades of economic growth, albeit in a haphazard fashion. Hotels were crowding out bottom land, which was essential for farming, and there was extreme pressure from tourism in the summer as well as during the winter skiing season. Future development plans and their potential impact on both the village itself and its fragile alpine ecosystem had for some time been the heated subject of local negotiations.

At this time, research groups from Vienna's International Institute for Applied Systems Analysis (IIASA) were concerned with the substance of such ecological problems but, more critically, with how to bring together modelers and users. A team from IIASA with interests in adaptive approaches to environmental management was dispatched to organize a series of workshops designed to explore the village's interrelated problems. Howard Raiffa, then the head of IIASA, recently evaluated the process.

> The first workshop brought together for a week a small group of ecological modelers, computer specialists, experts on alpine regions, and economists with businessmen, hotel managers, town and regional officials, and some just plain villagers. They joined together to build a model . . . as can be expected (and was expected) the first weeks' work was a fiasco and the model that was developed had to be scrapped . . . The group tried again and again (for shorter periods of time). The model changed only slightly, but something important happened: the nonscientific contributors from Obergurgl began to talk and to listen to each other. They gained new deep insights into their problems and they demonstrated that these insights could be translated into operational policies. They began to communicate not *via* the model but *around* the model and they felt the effort was worth their while. (The Obergurglians treated the foreign scientists most hospitably). . . . Months later, Austria's President Kirschlager, when reviewing IIASA's impact on the country, praised the organization for the way that it had fostered communication in Obergurgl. . . . The exercise even won over some skeptical observers from Czechoslovakia, who expressed interest in using similar methods in their own country.[23]

[22]Raiffa (1982:339).
[23]Raiffa (1982:338).

The Obergurgl experience is an illustration of the principle that it may be far easier to work on another's related problem than to tackle one's own problem directly. With adversarial elements more in the background than they would be during a direct negotiation, the flow of communication may be improved substantially. In working on the IIASA team's problem of building the model, the villagers were in fact helping to solve their own. The independence of the IIASA group was important to the process, but the actual results of the modeling were relatively incidental. In fact, the analytic tool served more as a quiet group therapist than a computational wizard.

DESIGNING THE NEGOTIATION TO EVOKE COMMON VALUE AND DOWN-PLAY CONFLICT.   In some cases, undesirable interests and attributes may be downplayed by careful design of the encounter. Recall the negotiations between the federal government and a group of states (from Chapter Three) over the level of reimbursement of state claims for prior social service expenditures. While the issue was of a purely distributive character, the underlying interests of the sides involved both money *and* the relationship, which had markedly deteriorated in many areas, in part as a consequence of the unhappy dealings. The federal officials in particular saw the many components of an "improved relationship"—for regulation writing and promulgation, for support of legislative initiatives, and so on—as important interests to be fostered by a negotiated, out-of-court settlement of the claims.

After some extremely complicated bargaining within the executive branch, the federal official in charge of the negotiations was able to make a fairly generous aggregate offer to the states. He made the offer on a take-it-or-leave it basis, provided that the states could agree on the allocation *among themselves*. Normally, such an inflexible stance risks angering the other side.[24] Here, however, the offer to the states transformed what would have been a relatively adversarial, distributive bargain *between* the federal government and the individual states into a distributive bargain *among* the states.

From the federal point of view, the tactical choice had the effect of highlighting the most desired attribute of the settlement—the relationship—and displacing the most destructive aspects of claiming value—division of the money—to a squabble among the states. More

---

[24]The tactic even has a name—Boulwarism—after the General Electric industrial relations official who in the 1950s made a policy of first and final offers to the union. This practice, incidentally, ushered in a stormy period of labor relations for GE. The tactic has since been associated with unfair labor practices, "refusals to bargain in good faith."

generally, unwanted attributes of negotiation processes can sometimes be avoided by the design of the encounter.

Evoking or Avoiding Interests Mainly to Claim Value

CHANGING THE "FACE" OF THE ISSUE.   A congressional negotiation over Food Stamps, ostensibly in a welfare context, may be dramatically converted by a focus on its implications for farmers. While a liberal and a conservative senator may be at each other's throats on welfare questions, treating Food Stamps as a farm issue may make agreement between the senators possible, especially if each is from a rural state. Changing the so-called face that an issue wears can be understood as affecting the interests evoked by the process.[25] This technique may be invaluable to the negotiator-advocate.

The same issue may be dealt with quite differently if posed as a budget or economic item as opposed to a defense or national security one. In the negotiations over the international regulation of data flows across borders, the United States' response is likely to be considerably different if the computer data at issue is treated as a "commodity"—and subject to the usual sorts of trade regulation—than if it is treated as "information"—thus raising all kinds of questions of free speech, censorship, and the like. The contest to define the nature of the issues at hand may be one of the keenest in the quest to claim value.

COMMITTING BY ADDING INTERESTS.   As we noted before, committing to an advantageous position involves introducing interests not previously salient in the negotiation. Commitments often aim to link the resolution of the issue at hand to a supposedly similar parallel or future set of issues. If agreed wage levels in one setting will be focal points for other negotiations; if the terms of the latest Third World mineral contract with a mining company will be applied to its other operations; or if these consequences can be presented as likely enough (whether in fact they are or not)—then negotiators may credibly make a commitment not to accept certain terms. In short, if a negotiator persuades others that he will incur real costs elsewhere if he accepts certain settlements of the current issues, he may favorably narrow the zone of possible agreement.

Linking interests in one negotiation to those of another one may squeeze the first zone of agreement favorably. A negotiator may link

[25]See Neustadt (1980).

her conduct or concession-making behavior to her "bargaining reputation" and claim grave future harm for taking an action now that appears in substance to be quite acceptable. Invoking one's future credibility, reputation with others, the cost of supposedly adverse procedural or substantive precedents, and the like are all devices intended to persuade one's counterpart that movement would be very costly in terms of these newly added interests. By being costly, movement is intended to appear unlikely. Hence the commitment gains credibility.

SEEMING CREATION.   Since the processes of creation and claiming are so closely entwined, it should not be surprising that each of the tactics discussed above to create value by evoking or avoiding interests has the potential to be used for unilateral gain. When faced with tough negotiations in substance, one may cynically evoke the relationship, principles of fairness, or superordinate goals of genuine value to the other parties. Then, one may seek to appropriate the lion's share of the total value so created by demanding large concessions on the linked substantive issue. By appearing to put the relationship at stake, feigning anger, insult, or hurt, one party may effectively "offer" restored relations or forgiveness in "return" for substantive concessions. A similar intention may be behind appeals to conscience, duty, self-image, approval of the other parties, and norms.

Related Processes That Change the Game

Thus far, we have examined some effects of changes in a game's key elements—parties, issues, interests, alternatives to agreement. Much of the negotiation process consists of each side seeking to influence the other's perceptions of these elements—what would actually be possible through joint action, its real value, what would likely happen absent agreement, how good or bad that would be, and so on. A variety of tactics to create and claim value within the game are intended to affect these perceptions; other negotiating moves attempt the same thing by working on perceptions of the game itself. By stressing perceptions, we do not mean to downplay objective changes in issues, parties, or the like; reality is often, though by no means always, the most convincing factor. But entwined with what we might most naturally call the "negotiation" process are a variety of closely related processes whose intent is to change perceptions of the game and the relationships among its elements.[26]

Persuading Much of the "art of bargaining" consists of trying to convince another party that what you want is in his or her real self-interest. In our terms, this is equivalent to changing beliefs about the relationship between the issues at hand and underlying interests. The issue between a Third World country and a multinational mining firm may be the level of royalties. The country, wanting more money, argues for the level to be high; the company prefers it to be low. Yet much of the negotiation may consist in the company's claiming that "Yes, you want the level higher because you want more money. If rates reach a certain level, however, we'll have to invest less, other companies will be scared off, and you will end up losing in terms of your monetary interests. Therefore, you should retreat on the issue." And the country will counter in its turn.

Suppose a lobbyist is trying to convince a member of Congress to agree to vote for a bill to aid minorities. Suppose further that the member's primary interest is in re-election. One route to persuasion would be factual. Arguing that there are many more minority voters in his district than was previously thought would be an attempt to change the relationship between his position on the issue of support for the bill and his interest in re-election. Or, without attempting to change what the member believes about the composition of his district, one might instead argue that the relationship between the issue and his interest is different. Thus the case might be made that support for this bill will win a great deal of liberal backing in the district. But whether on the basis of facts, the nature of the issue-interest rela-

[26]What is the role of persuasion, for example? One of the most astute students of the Presidency, Richard Neustadt, argued that Presidential power "is the power to persuade, and the power to persuade is the power to bargain." Should we therefore conclude that bargaining and persuasion are one and the same? Should we try to unravel the conceptual distinction and be fastidious about our usage? And how about learning, inspiration, leadership, as well as factors that change our own and other's values?

Early on, we characterized negotiation as a process of potentially opportunistic interaction by which two or more people with at least some conflicting interests seek to do better by jointly decided action than they could otherwise. We then examined basic elements of the process. Rather than now trying to work out mutually exclusive characteristics of related processes like persuasion, we will try to relate their common meanings to the elements of negotiation that we have discussed. By describing the connections, we hope to enhance the usefulness and precision of the previous discussion. Ideally, we would like to help prepare the way for insights from studies of each of these processes to find useful application in the others.

tionship, or the probabilities of either one, successful persuasion of this sort depends on a desired agreement lining up with the congressman's perceived self-interest.

There are other routes to persuasion beyond *direct* explanation and argument on the basis of self-interest. (We are ignoring direct bribes or logrolling.) The lobbyist may observe that another party or group is in favor of the desired policy. If the congressman defers to their judgment, this may be sufficient. Deference may be on the basis of at least three distinct, though complementary factors. First, the congressman may simply trust the judgment of certain other people or groups.[27] When he learns their opinion, he is more likely to go along. Second, if enough of the "right" people are thought to hold this belief, the congressman may feel social pressure to concur in the group's view. Third, deference now to the opinions of another group may be in the expectation of reciprocity later. Persuasion in this case would merely be an implicitly linked trade over time.

An issue can display, on its face, many possible interests. As countless observers have stressed, a key to persuasive appeal lies in emphasizing the face most in line with the target person's interests. Does the proposal represent a "handout" or a "hand up?" Is it an "operational detail" or a "bold strategic initiative"? A mere "personnel" action or "a message to the sales department"? A "budget" matter or a matter of "science policy"? A question to be decided on the basis of "costs and benefits" or "principle, morality, and larger duty"? In each of these cases, the presentation or emphasis seeks to give more weight to some aspects of the decision while giving less to or completely obscuring others.

Persuasive moves seek to change the game by altering the "mapping" from interests to issues and positions. Such moves may appeal to facts, belief about the issue-interest relationship, deference, or the face of the issue. In practice, persuasion is hard to separate from negotiation.

Changing Values   Recall the reluctant congressman whose mind we were seeking to change on a bill favoring minority rights. Beyond the value of supporting the bill in re-election terms, it is plausible that various other factors might operate over time to cause the congressman to give higher intrinsic value to minority advancement. Causes might include greater personal exposure to the problem, changing so-

[27]In particular, the factual, prudential, or moral content of their judgment.

cial mores, sustained moral suasion on the part of some whom he respects, or other factors.[28]

It is not our purpose here to investigate the mechanisms by which "values" might be said to change. Rather, we will suggest some fairly typical instances in which people appear to evaluate given positions on issues quite differently. Imagine a charismatic leader whose followers seem to identify with his purposes and constantly press for their realization. We might observe the same phenomenon between an inspiring organizational superior and her subordinates who come to take keen pleasure in successfully furthering her mission.[29]

It has become fashionable to discuss the potent effects of "organizational culture" on the motivation, productivity, and satisfaction of employees.[30] A number of firms go to great pains to "socialize" new workers into the culture of the firm. Over time, powerful social and economic measures can result in the entrant's strong identification with and valuation of the organization's purposes and procedures. (If these measures do not "take," the deviants may be edged out or choose to leave.)

A more homogeneous culture within an organization can facilitate the large number of "agreements" needed among the employees. More weight given to shared interests makes agreement more valuable to the involved parties, hence easier to achieve and sustain. But acculturation that really changes values generally takes a long time, much longer than any single bargaining encounter. (And value change in organizations is a special case of a much larger phenomenon by which values, attitudes, and role expectations of members of social units—families, armies, countries, professional disciplines, and so on—come to be shaped.)

Learning, Teaching, Inspiring, Leading, and Transforming   We treat these important processes briefly and in the same section since

[28]We might imagine much of the previous discussion on evoking interests functioning as if there were a latent preference or interest "map," parts of which were "illuminated" as the result of tactical moves in the negotiation. At any given point, some areas are highlighted, while others are barely if at all visible. It is quite possible, however, to imagine that the actual values held by the parties to a negotiation undergo changes. Whether, at some deep level, there exists an underlying primitive "preference order" or set of more or less fixed values is less interesting for our purposes than whether the utility "yardstick" by which negotiators appear to evaluate the inherent desirability of a set of positions on issues appears to change.

[29]The concept of identification has a long history in psychological literature which need not concern us here except to validate the existence of its effects.

[30]See, for example, Ouchi (1981), Sathe (1985), or, especially, Schein (1985).

they function similarly within the framework we have outlined for negotiation. Each of these processes can cause interests to change or can alter beliefs about the relationship between positions, issues, and interests. In some cases, these processes lead to envisioning new possibilities that creatively rearrange existing elements of the game. In other cases, new pieces, new understandings of relationships, and with them, new visions may become apparent.[31]

The collective sense of possibility, aspiration, and even expectation may change dramatically. Agreements for joint action that seemed impossible in the old game may be realized in the newly perceived one.

* * *

Negotiators try to change the game in advantageous ways. But their moves are often contested and lead to new negotiations. In exploring such moves, we first considered attempts to manipulate key elements of a negotiation's configuration—the issues, interests, and parties. Then we looked at some of the processes closely related to negotiation—persuasion, learning, transforming the sense of the possible or desirable, changing values—by which people seek to alter perceptions of the game.

This analysis bears on three types of questions: whether and how to change one element of a well-configured game, how to design a configuration that is more likely to result in a desired set of agreements, and ways to put into place or alter a preferred network of linked agreements.

Since the game is simply that which the parties *act* as if it is, its elements—including one's *own* beliefs, interests, and understandings—need not be fixed and unchanging. Abandoning a static view simply unveils many more opportunities to create and claim value.

---

[31]So-called "transactional" leaders arrange trades with their followers or subordinates; a crude example would be an exchange of salary and status for obedience. "Transformational" leaders, on the other hand, change others' perceptions of the nature and potential of the situation, thereby inspiring or influencing the others to act in the ways desired by the leader. For a discussion of the differences, see Bass (1985).

CHAPTER TEN

The Approach as a Whole and So-Called Power in Bargaining

THE PRINCIPLES we have developed so far explain and make use of the underlying reasons why people agree to joint action, where such agreements are appropriate, where not, and some of the possibilities and perils of the processes for reaching them. We now pull together the elements of this approach into a small number of recommendations for negotiators and analysts. For each element, we recapitulate some of the main points developed in earlier chapters. When taken together, these elements form an overall logic. Once we summarize it, we look at its relation to the subject of negotiating "power," which, perhaps puzzlingly, we have so far ignored.

Elements of the Approach

STATIC ELEMENTS OF THE GAME

The configuration of important elements common to negotiating situations includes an enumeration of the parties, their underlying interests, the issues, the parties' beliefs about how issues affect their interests, their alternatives to reaching agreement, and some notion of the "rules of the game." In approaching any negotiation, we recommend first focusing particular attention on interests, alternatives, and potential agreements.

Interests   To make sense of a negotiation, one must first understand all the parties' interests. If a side is monolithic—that is, it has no internal divisions—this task is equivalent to ferreting out its full set of interests and specifying the ways in which tradeoffs among them will be made. In negotiations over erecting a building, the relevant interests may be cost, time, and quality; in a more complex setting, they may include less tangible aspects such as precedent, reputation, fairness and the relationship among the parties. In general, an interest is anything that a negotiator cares about.

Intrinsic interests—those of concern in and of themselves—should be distinguished from *instrumental* ones—those that provide a means to intrinsically valued ends. Many methods exist to help weigh the various interests against each other and make tradeoffs. When individuals or groups with different concerns constitute a negotiating "side," it is no longer possible in general to specify overall tradeoffs; however, carefully tracing which set of interests is ascendant in the internal bargaining may continue to provide insights.

It is often important to distinguish parties' underlying *interests* from the *issues* under negotiation, on which *positions* or stands are often vehemently taken. The connections among positions on issues and interests is rarely a simple one. Sometimes a focus on deeper interests can unblock a stubborn impasse over positions that relate only partially to the parties' real concerns; in other cases, emphasizing interests will only generate hopeless conflict when mutually beneficial agreement on certain overt issues could be reached. And focusing on issues and positions can be tactically advantageous. In all cases, though, a vital first step is to probe deeply for interests, distinguish them from issues and positions, and carefully assess tradeoffs.

Alternatives to Negotiated Agreement   Parties generally engage in negotiation with the expectation that their interests will be better served by a jointly decided action than by the unilateral alternatives each side would pursue absent agreement. This observation focuses central attention on the parties' perceived alternatives to negotiation and to negotiated agreements. The extent to which no agreement serves a party's interest provides the benchmark against which any proposed accord must be compared. The more favorably that negotiators perceive and portray their best alternative course of action—whether this means a course that is less costly, more efficient, less risky, with earlier benefits, with more desirable linked attributes (such as reputation) or fewer undesirable ones (such as bad precedents)—the smaller is their ostensible need for the negotiation and the higher the standard of value that any proposed accord must reach to be acceptable.

Different alternatives may imply very different kinds of dealing: negotiations with a union (that may strike) may hardly resemble those with a subordinate (who may "only" withhold key information, tap allies, engage in foot dragging, resist covertly, or quit). But in both cases, all sides seek joint action as a means of doing better than the solo alternatives. And, of course, one corollary of these observations is that the alternatives will sometimes compare favorably to joint possibilities. Negotiated accommodations will give way to firings, recourse to other suppliers, and other versions of walking away from the table.

As this discussion indicates, alternatives to agreement may take many forms: they may have one attribute or many; they may be certain or uncertain; they may be static or changing; they may be unilateral or coalitional; they may involve simply leaving the negotiation to an independent *status quo ante;* or they may critically depend on moves and countermoves among the original negotiators as it becomes clear that no agreement will result. Regardless of these characteristics, comparison of the expected utility of agreement with that of no agreement can heavily influence the way a party acts in the process. Careful monitoring of bargainers' perceived unilateral alternatives reveals the limits of any joint action and thus implies boundaries to the bargaining set.

Potential Agreements   The lure of joint action lies in the prospect of doing better than the alternatives. It is therefore crucial to understand the bases for joint gains and to envision possible agreements. Three distinct classes of factors are at the core of all possible mutual benefits from cooperation.

First, on some issues, negotiators want the same settlement, and their mere agreement can produce it. Furthering their relationship, or acting in accord with an identical interest, such as a shared vision, ideology, or norm of equity, may also add "common value" to an agreement.

Second, where economies of scale, collective goods, alliances, or requirements for a minimum number of parties exist, agreement among similar bargainers can create value.

Less well understood is the third fact that differences among the participants—in relative valuation, forecasts, risk aversion, time preference, technical capacity, tax status, and so forth—often constitute the raw material for creating "private value" for all parties.[1] Each type of difference has a characteristic type of agreement that makes possible its conversion into mutual benefit. For example, value differences suggest trades and "unbundling," probability and risk-aversion differences suggest contingent agreements, differences in time preference suggest altering schedules of payments and other actions.

In short, negotiated agreements may improve on the alternatives by: (1) dovetailing differences, (2) cultivating shared interests, and (3) exploiting scale economies.

THE PROCESS: CREATING AND CLAIMING VALUE

With these elements in mind, negotiators should focus on the dynamic aspects of negotiation, the *process* of creating and claiming value.

In most managerial negotiation, the potential value of joint action is not fully obvious at the outset. Creating value—that is, reaching mutually beneficial agreements, improving them, and preventing conflict escalation—requires an approach often associated with "win-win," "integrative," or "variable-sum" encounters. To generate gainful options, information must be openly shared, communication enhanced, creativity spurred, joint problem solving emphasized, and hostilities productively channeled.

Some negotiations are primarily "distributive," "win-lose," or constant-sum; that is, increased value claimed by one party implies less for others. Although value is created by merely reaching an accord in these cases, the parties' interests conflict diametrically over the terms. And where value can be created beyond simple agreement, that value still must be apportioned. We explored several broad classes of tactics for claiming value in these kinds of bargains. These

---

[1]To be a bit more precise, recall that scale economies and differences can create both private and common value.

include shaping perceptions of alternatives, making commitments, influencing aspirations, taking positions, manipulating patterns of concessions, holding prime values hostage, linking issues and interests, misleading other parties, as well as exploiting cultural expectations. By using these tactics, one party seeks advantage by influencing another's perception of the bargaining range.

If the processes of creating and claiming value were separable, we could recommend a distinct approach to each task. Unfortunately, they are not. Tactics to claim value are poorly suited to the task of creating it. Many claiming tactics involve distorting information and risk inferior agreements, impasses, threats, counterthreats, and conflict. Yet one side's genuine openness can leave it exposed and vulnerable. The resulting Negotiator's Dilemma explains why moves to claim value so frequently drive out moves to create more of it.

This tension between cooperative moves to create value and individual moves to claim it manifests itself across most negotiating interactions. Bargainers adopt many devices that deny, cope with, or exploit this tension; we described several approaches to manage it by individual strategies (conditional openness, making creating seem better than claiming, etc.) or by other means (third parties, single texts, post-settlement settlements, etc.).

CHANGING THE GAME

Thus far in the approach, the parties, the issues, and the evaluations of the issues were mainly treated as fixed. Yet in setting an agenda, including or excluding groups from the bargaining, or seeking to link or separate different interests or issues, these "givens" may become variable. The parties' attempts to change the game's "configuration" by varying one or more of these aspects are analytically equivalent to moves in a fixed game.

Like tactics within a fixed game, tactics that change the game itself are intended to create and claim value. As the process evolves, as new information becomes available, and as the parties learn, there are opportunities to create and claim value by changing beliefs about how issues relate to interests, by manipulating rules and alternatives to agreement, as well as adding and subtracting interests, issues, and parties.

Before the overt process even starts, moves to shape the negotiation itself can heavily affect eventual outcomes. For example, terms of discussion can be chosen or the agenda defined so that some issues never come up, some interests are never evoked, or some parties never take part.

But most important, a game's configuration is simply that which the parties act as if it is. The way they will act is often influenced by norms and precedents. Still, disagreements over a game's configuration must themselves be resolved by negotiation.

The Approach as a Whole

Suppose that a manager-negotiator has thought hard about her underlying interests in different settlements of the issues. Further, she has clarified her tradeoffs—perhaps assigning "importance weights"—among the intrinsic and instrumental interests at stake, and has compared them to the value of the best no-agreement alternative. She has also carried out a similar excercise from her counterpart's viewpoint. Finally, she has carefully envisioned a set of possible agreements. Her counterpart has done the same thing.

Assume that we were privy to the results of such evaluations by both sides. The situation might be represented, familiarly, by now, as in Figure 10.1.[2] The origin (point "O") represents the value of failing to reach agreement; each side's best alternative to agreement implies the location of this point. The curve in the northeast part of the graph—the perceived possibilities or Pareto frontier—represents the evaluations of the set of those possible agreements on the issues that could not be improved on from the standpoint of either party without harming the other. In general, neither side knows the location of the frontier, only theoretically that it is there. The entire shaded region—bounded by the two axes and the frontier—is the bargaining set. Each party has his own perceptions of it. Since this graphical representation is quite general, it can encompass the whole range of possible interests, alternatives, and agreements.

Our first focus—on all parties' interests—furnishes basic data for analysis; interests are the measure of negotiation. The second—on evaluating alternatives to agreement—implies the hurdle that any joint action must surmount to be acceptable; in locating the origin,

---

[2] Recall that value to Party 1 increases away from the origin (point 0) on the horizontal axis; value to Party 2 goes up with higher points on the vertical axis. Of course, no comparison of how Party 1 ranks things relative to Party 2 is implied; the value of any settlement for each party is independently compared with that of other settlements and with no deal. Then the two sides' values for each possible agreement are plotted as points in the plane.

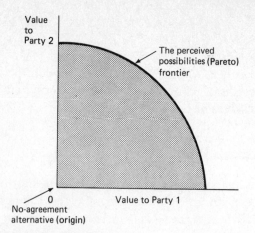

FIGURE 10.1:   **The Bargaining Set**

alternatives set the limits of negotiation. Our third recommendation—to envision potential agreements—highlights the potential for
negotiated agreement to do better than (be northeast of) the non-
cooperative alternatives (the origin).

Within this setup, the basic process takes place. Since the parties
do not normally know what is possible (where the frontier lies), their
joint problem is to invent means of moving northeast to "get to the
frontier" (create value). Yet how they move influences their individual problems of where they end up on the frontier (claim value). Cooperative moves to create value vie with competitive ones to claim it.

And the parties need not limit themselves to creating and claiming within this fixed configuration; they often move to change the
game itself. By changing alternatives, the origin will shift. For example, an improvement in Party 1's alternative shifts the vertical axis to
the right, leaving the bargaining set generally more favorable to her.
If Party 2's no agreement alternative worsens, the horizontal axis
shifts down, worsening his prospects. A successful commitment cuts
off an undesired part of the set for the party who makes it. A new,
mutually beneficial option causes the frontier to bulge upward and to
the right, reducing the parties' conflict of interest. When issues
change or other aspects of the game vary, each side's perception of
the basic picture in Figure 10.1, the bargaining set, will be transformed. These possibilities add evolutionary elements to the analysis.

Figure 10.1 summarizes the extended analytic metaphor that we
have been developing. The prescriptions we have laid out bear on

each part of this "model" of possible joint action. Interests provide the basis and the measure; alternatives imply the limits; agreements hold out the potential; within this configuration, the process consists of creating and claiming value; yet, the elements of the interaction may themselves evolve or be intentionally changed. In this sense, the elements of the approach form a whole.

In developing this logic of negotiation, we have not stressed the many useful ideas that arise from focusing on interpersonal and cultural styles, on atmosphere and logistics, on personality and psychoanalytic motivation, or on a host of other aspects. Yet because the logic is general, it can profitably accommodate insights from other approaches as well as from experience.

Setting the Search for Negotiating "Power" on a New Path

What about "negotiating power"? Nine and one-half chapters on negotiation have passed with scarcely a mention of it. Why? The concept is notoriously slippery. Seeking to understand the sources of power has mired many in plausible but incorrect generalizations.

Consider a few common notions of what gives power.

"One party has power if it can inflict harm on another, especially if it can inflict 'more' harm than it will suffer." Yet the United States' unquestioned capacity for the nuclear annihilation of North Vietnam did not yield Vietnamese submission before or during the peace talks.

"Having more resources gives one power." But, if a rich person's child is kidnapped, having much accessible money may not help in the negotiation; that person may merely pay more.

"Having someone in your debt gives power." The borrower who owes the bank $450,000, is six months behind on house payments, and has a very sick wife may think he has problems, but it may be his banker who is really in trouble.

"Being rational and persuasive gives one power." Yet a bargainer who refuses to listen to an eminently reasonable argument and "irrationally" insists on having his demands met "or else" will sometimes succeed.

"Having full authority and control over one's organization is power." Yet the union leader who can line his people up behind almost any agreement may get a less favorable settlement than the leader whose flexibility is limited by a powerful, militant faction.

In each of these cases, the supposedly "powerful" party's interests do not appear to have been advanced. The common generalizations do not quite work.

Attempts to define power often lead into tautological quicksand. For example, one widely cited definition reads, "A has power over B to the extent that he can get B to do something that he would not otherwise do."[3] In other words, if A has power over B, he can get an extremely good deal in negotiations with B. But how can we tell that A is more powerful? Well, he got a good outcome from B. Power defined this way and negotiated outcomes themselves cannot be distinguished. Schelling has commented on such common slides into tautology:

> "Bargaining power," "bargaining strength," bargaining skill" suggest that the advantage goes to the powerful, the strong, the skillful. It does, of course, if those qualities are defined to mean only that negotiations are won by those who win. But, if the terms imply that it is an advantage to be more skilled in debate, or to have more financial resources, more physical strength, more military potency, or more ability to withstand losses, then the term does a disservice. Those qualities are by no means universal advantages in bargaining situations; they often have a contrary value.[4]

How can those who pursue the meaning and nature of bargaining "power" miss the mark in the way Schelling describes? We suspect that it is because they focus on power as an absolute, abstract entity. The flaws in statements about power's meaning and nature suggest a new focus.

ASSOCIATING POWER WITH FAVORABLE CHANGES IN THE BARGAINING SET

We observe that the things thought to give "power" seem to succeed when they advantageously change perceptions of the bargaining set and to fail when they do not. We argue that "power" is associated with the ability to favorably change the bargaining set.

What "a favorable change in the bargaining set" means is a bit trickier than it may seem at first blush. Given his current situation, a

---

[3]Dahl (1957). For an extensive survey of definitions, see Bacharach and Lawler (1981:10–26). See also Gulliver (1979:186–190) for other references to and definitions of bargaining power.

[4]Schelling (1960:22). See also Wrong (1968).

negotiator can assess a probability distribution over the possible outcomes. If a new tactic were employed, the likelihoods of different outcomes would change; thus he has a revised probability distribution of outcomes given the new tactic. If he prefers the revised probability distribution to the original, we say that he has favorably changed the bargaining set. While this change need not guarantee him a more favorable outcome, he thinks it more likely.[5] We now recall a number of tactics that, given our experience, observation, and experimental studies, typically result in favorable shifts in the bargaining set.

Many tactics for claiming value function by shifting no-agreement alternatives, thus favorably altering the bargaining set. By his opening offer, concessions, normative justifications, and appeals to precedent, Bill attempts to persuade his counterpart that his no-agreement alternatives are better than she thought and that hers are worse. As we have described, his commitment favorably reduces the bargaining set by making the unfavorable part unacceptable and thus

[5]To be more precise, we must be a bit technical.

To see if using certain tactics favorably changes the bargaining set, we must compare the negotiator's subjective distribution of beliefs about the negotiated outcome conditional on using the new tactics, with his subjective distribution of beliefs about the outcome conditional on not using them. The change is favorable if the former distribution gives him higher expected utility than the latter. That the changed distribution of outcomes gives higher expected utility than the original still need not mean that the negotiator will get a better outcome than he would have by eschewing the tactics. A random draw from the changed distribution will, with some probability, be worse than a random draw from the original one. But a more favorable outcome is likely.

Specifying these distributions requires an internalized and admittedly subjective model of the bargaining process in the given situation. No such general model exists. In most settings, for example, visibly improving one's no-agreement alternatives will improve one's outcomes; the many examples we have cited, our experiences, and our laboratory experiments provide empirical support for our intuition. Yet, we can construct instances in which this will not be the case. In a marriage, finding a potential replacement mate might seriously damage how one's spouse values the marriage. Or, a disgruntled subordinate whose boss is known to value loyalty might be better off if he did not generate other offers before going to his boss to improve his job; the breach of loyalty would reduce the boss's sense of obligation to keep his employee happy.

Similarly, the many examples of moves that simultaneously offer joint gains and claim them, as well as our experience, suggest that such moves typically but not unfailingly lead to better outcomes. Moves to worsen a counterpart's no-agreement alternatives that do not provoke an escalation of the conflict often but not always improve the outcome; if conflict escalates, though, the change in the distribution of outcomes is likely to be undesirable. Because no general model exists of how such tactics affect the distribution of outcomes, we must rely on experience, limited empirical evidence, and logic.

inaccessible. If the tactics succeed, the set of remaining possible outcomes is more favorable for Bill than the original set. A credible
threat may make his counterpart's no-agreement alternative worse
and advantageously shape the set of possible agreements.

Tactics that simultaneously offer joint gains and claim most of
the newly created value push the possibilities frontier northeasterly
while focusing consideration only on individually advantageous
agreements. Similarly, moves that change the game by adding favorable issues and interests as well as helpful parties, blocking unfavorable linkages, and shaping the terms of debate to exclude unfavorable issues, if they succeed, advantageously shape the bargaining set.
That the bargaining set has improved, however, need not mean that
the negotiator will necessarily get a better outcome as a result of his
tactical success, though it is likely.

INTERPRETING SOME COMMON IDEAS OF POWER

With this focus on the bargaining set, let us return to some of the
supposed sources of power and see when they succeed and fail.

The United States' capacity for nuclear attack did not determine
Vietnamese choices because the threat to do so was not credible; having the capacity without the credible threat of using it did not change
Vietnamese perceptions of their alternatives to agreement on preferred American terms, and hence, the way they saw the bargaining
set. The ability to inflict harm may also fail to influence bargaining
if it goes unnoticed or cannot be communicated; the hornet flying
toward you may not move out of your path even though you explain
that you will kill it if it stings you. And, the capacity for harm can
fail if what *seems* harmful in fact is not. The threat to kill someone
who aspires to martyrdom may not lead to cooperation. And, inflict-
ing harm often fails to yield desired outcomes when it provokes conflict escalation.

In these cases, the ability to harm failed because the moves did
not advantageously change the bargaining set, because they were not
credible, not communicated or not actually harmful, or because they
brought in harmful new interests that swamped what was originally
at stake.

This is not to deny the effect of the ability to harm another on
bargaining. To take but one example, countless managers have paid
countless millions of dollars in "greenmail." Say that a corporate
raider buys a large block of the firm's stock and credibly threatens to
acquire a controlling share and dismember the firm unless his shares

are purchased from him at an inflated price. The firm's managers often grant his demands. His threat has shifted their perceptions of their no-agreement alternatives—if they do not respond, they may lose their jobs following the acquistion. The implicit threats of firing, of the withdrawal of college tuition, of physical harm if money is not handed over, and the like, when credible and known, frequently change the bargaining range in "favorable" ways.[6]

By the same token, the available wealth of the kidnapped child's rich parents unfavorably changes the bargaining set relative to having less accessible money.[7] The government could seek favorably to change the bargaining range if it immediately impounded the parents' assets the moment the kidnapping became known. Of course, more resources can certainly lead to favorable changes in the bargaining set. An executive with considerable resources may gain others' cooperation because they hope that she will reward them in future encounters; she may never do so, but the potential reward shapes the others' perceptions of the current bargaining set. (And greater resources may translate into greater capacity to impose sanctions.)

The negotiation between the banker and her strapped borrower over rescheduling the loan is trickier. Because she can foreclose and ruin the borrower's valued credit rating, his no-agreement alternatives are undesirable. In contrast, if the borrower feels certain that he will lose his rating anyway, his no-agreement alternatives would be unchanged by the banker's action and he may feel much less cooperative about repayment.[8]

[6]As we noted (see Lax and Sebenius, 1985), a credible threat or a move that worsens the opponent's no-agreement alternatives still does not guarantee an outcome at the desirable end of the bargaining set. A prior commitment by the threatened party just above the threatener's reservation value may make the threat ineffectual. If successful, such a commitment will determine the outcome, whatever has been done to the opponent's no-agreement alternatives.

[7]In this example, the negotiators do not shift the bargaining range by their actions. Instead, we are examining counterfactual situations: how the distribution of outcomes would differ if the situation were changed. This counterfactual comparison accords with common usage: "I would be more powerful if my father were president of the company" or "I'm powerful because the other guy can't afford to go to court." No matter how a perceived change in the bargaining set was produced—by a tactic or by a counterfactual situation—the question of whether "power" increases depends on whether the change produces a distribution of outcomes that yields higher expected utility.

[8]That the borrower's no-agreement alternatives are much worse when he will not lose his credit rating for other reasons need not mean that the banker would end up with favorable terms when the foreclosure really hurts, but we think it is likely in

But this looks only at the foreclosure's effect on the borrower and not on the banker. If foreclosing is quite costly for the banker, her no-agreement alternative (foreclosure) will be much worse than in the case where it is not costly. Our guess would be that this condition would be reflected in an easier negotiated repayment schedule. In short, having someone in one's debt need not give "power." What matters here are the parties' perceptions of their no-agreement alternatives.

In our earlier example, the "irrational" person effectively removed from consideration an unfavorable part of the bargaining set by successfully refusing to hear about or discuss it. But, forsaking rational discussion may mean missing the possibility of agreement at all if the "irrational" person commits to a point that is outside the bargaining set. Possibilites for expanding the bargaining set by rational problem solving are foregone. Moreover, such behavior may unfavorably alter the bargaining set by bringing in new interests (e.g., appropriate behavior, revenge) that swamp the original interests at stake.

Similarly, not having full authority and control over his organization helped the union leader; his militant faction made it impossible to accept certain agreements, thus eliminating them from the bargaining set. In other circumstances, on the other hand, having full authority and control over one's organization is associated with "power." The executive whose firm always delivers on his promises may be able to expand the perceived bargaining set in many encounters.

EVERYBODY HAS A LIST

These examples do not begin to exhaust the possible sources of "power." Without trying, anyone could spin out a long list of candidates: having someone depend on you for resources; having a great deal of formal authority; owning the last parcel of land needed for a major development to start; knowing the maitre d'; possessing the secret of a new process; being able to withstand pain or delay; hearing

---

practice that she would. The borrower could make a commitment in both cases to a point just acceptable to the banker and end up with the same outcome regardless of whether or not the banker can make his no-agreement alternatives worse. But, as we mentioned in a previous footnote, our experience, surveys of various negotiations, and experimental evidence suggest that the banker is likely to do better because the foreclosure promises to hurt the debtor "more."

about someone else's checkered past; enjoying a reputation for unswerving principle; having an uncle in the plumber's union; being owed a string of favors; having figured out a clever solution; being chauffered by helicopter; and on and on.

It is easy to examine these and other potential sources for their effects on the bargaining range. For instance, "dependency" usually implies that someone can withhold resources or information (worsening no-agreement alternatives, unfavorably shifting the range) or grant them (improving the value of agreement in a mutually beneficial way, pushing out the Pareto frontier). Advancing item by item in this way through the full list of power candidates is obviously impossible.[9] Thus, to advance the discussion of power beyond particular cases, we need a more general approach.

Fortunately, the underlying bases of "power" in such particular cases have been extensively studied and summarized in terms of five basic factors.[10] A quick look at each suggests that, where each class of factors is indeed associated with improved odds of better outcomes, it functions by changing the perceived bargaining range.

• *Coercion.* This generally represents the capacity to change no-agreement alternatives. As our discussion of the use of force suggests, such a change can often, but by no means always, favorably shift the bargaining set.

---

[9]It is worth taking a quick look at five bases of a subordinate's power discussed by Kotter (1985:82):(1) skills that are difficult to replace quickly or easily; (2) important specialized information or knowledge that others do not have; (3) good personal relationships, which make it difficult to reprimand or replace a subordinate without incurring the wrath of those other people; (4) the centrality of the job a subordinate holds to the boss's agenda and therefore the large impact of a subordinate's performance on the boss's performance; (5) job-related interdependencies between a subordinate's job and other jobs or people that are important, which make the boss indirectly dependent on the subordinate. Relative to dealing with a subordinate who does not have one of these assets, the boss's no-agreement alternative in a negotiation with a subordinate who does possess the asset is worse or the possibility of joint gain is greater. For example, compare two subordinates who have the same important information but, in one case, another subordinate also has it; the boss's no-agreement alternative with the subordinate who has monopoly control of the information would likely be worse. Or, compared to a subordinate who does not have the information, the possibilities frontier is not bowed out as far. Thus, Kotter's list of bases of subordinate power, which is similar to several others, is consistent with our argument.

[10]We rely in particular on French and Raven (1959), Raven (1974), Etzioni (1961), and Pettigrew (1973) for these categories. Interestingly, none of these explicitly associate the capacity to improve one's own no-agreement alternatives with a better distribution of outcomes.

• *Remuneration.* This is a special case of the ability to create value and reduce conflict of interest. In its simplest form, remuneration can set up "trading" opportunities that offer some consideration in return for desired action. (Of course, we have developed much more extensive ways to favorably expand the bargaining set.)

• *Identification.* As we discussed in chapters on claiming value and changing the game, identification with a charismatic person can cause people to want what that person wants and take his judgment as superior. If genuine, these changes cause followers to perceive the bargaining set differently, in a way that makes agreement with the person's preferences much more likely.

• *Normative Conformity.* Claims that one's position is right, legitimate, and principled can carry weight in negotiation.[11] For some people, acting in such a manner has intrinsic value and improves potential agreements that are normatively "correct." And pressing for positions that arguably are principled or legitimate may impose costs on other parties who would go against them. As anthropologist P. H. Gulliver wrote:

> Even if negotiators themselves are unimpressed by normative conformity—and the evidence does not support so gross a conclusion—they are often constrained to conform, or at least to conform more than they otherwise might, because they need to appear to accept and adhere to the rules, standards, and values of their society.[12]

To the extent that such constraints are effective, they limit the bargaining set in a way favorable to the person who invoked the principle.

Moreover, to the extent that such principles derive from the larger society, arguments about them can escape the implication that one party is stronger and the other weaker. Recourse to external standards is one way to avoid attributions of weakness and loss of face, ingredients that can worsen the bargaining set from the standpoint of all parties.

Often people discuss principle as if it were a question of right versus might. To us, the real question involves how invoking it does or does not change perceptions of the bargaining set. Strong evidence

---

[11]This is the basis of the method of "principled negotiation" advanced in Fisher and Ury (1981).

[12]Gulliver (1979:192).

that norms can have this effect comes from observing the extent to which people employ them, genuinely or cynically. Again, as Gulliver observed:

> Thus a party attempts to persuade his opponent of the legitimacy and morality of his demands and to gain outsiders' approval and support. This does not, of course, deny the obvious possibility of the deliberate (and also unconscious) manipulation of norms; for instance, by selective emphasis on those that seem most supportive, by particular interpretation and biased application, by virtually inventing a norm to fit the demand ex post facto, and by the exploitation of attitudes and emotions associated with the symbolism of the norms.[13]

• *Knowledge*. Sometimes knowledge is a resource to be granted or withheld (each of which changes the bargaining set in ways we have discussed). Some information can change understanding of how an issue relates to an underlying interest and thus, can bear on the desirability of possible agreements.[14] Acknowledged expertise and other forms of persuasion can directly shape perceptions of the bargaining set in ways favorable to the expert or persuader.

* * *

In short, where these bases of "power" have their supposed effects, they do so by advantageously changing the bargaining set. Yet as the examples at the beginning of this section suggest, seemingly "powerful" conditions can lead to naught when they do not cause such changes. It is easy to explain why this is so by examining "powerful" factors to see how they limit the bargaining set (for example, through alternatives or commitments), expand it (by conceiving of new trades, options, or evoking shared interests, and so on), or otherwise revise understanding of it.

Analyzing "power" in and of itself has often proved to be a sterile exercise. However, directly focusing on factors that can change perceptions of the bargaining set and the ways that such changes influence outcomes seems more fruitful for both theory and practice. By no means is this different approach likely to be a panacea; the bargaining range is a subjective concept and the relationship between alterations in it and eventual agreements is hardly certain.

[13]Gulliver (1979:192).

[14]Knowledge of some kinds can keep issues or parties out of the interaction entirely.

Some years ago, William Zartman took stock of the extent to which power was understood. This tricky concept, he judged, had been "recognized, typologized, summarized, and left hanging in midair in pieces—a great half step forward."[15] Translating ambiguous statements about power into more precise statements about the bargaining set does not complete the step, but it suggests a new path around the old obstacles.

*   *   *

We started this book with a discussion of the intimate connections between negotiation and management. Negotiation, we argued in Chapter One, is a useful skill for important occasions, but also central to the manager's job. Having laid out a general approach throughout Part I that applies directly to the most familiar, acknowledged negotiations, it is now time to see how these same elements pervade organizational life.

Part II develops negotiation analysis in an organizational context. Three of its chapters, however, should be of special interest to readers more concerned with general negotiation principles than with their management applications. The first such chapter (Thirteen) considers how agreements that might come up for renegotiation can be made more sustainable. Second, after discussing organizational hierarchies, we analyze the general problem of negotiations carried out through agents (Chapter Fifteen). And, after considering organizational networks, we analyze the very common situation in which a negotiator is at the nexus of two linked bargains; take, for example, the company purchasing agent who must negotiate "internally" for authorization and "externally" with a supplier. Our concluding chapter (Seventeen) analyzes the dynamics of such situations.

[15]Zartman, (1974:396).

PART II

NEGOTIATION AND MANAGEMENT

CHAPTER ELEVEN

What Does Any Manager Have to Worry About?

IN VIRTUALLY ANY function, position, or type of organization, a manager has at least three related concerns about a goal he or she hopes to accomplish: (1) Is it inherently a good idea? (2) Can it attract and sustain support? (3) Can it be administratively realized?

A great deal of substantive analysis and judgment goes into figuring out whether a proposed action is a good idea. Will the market accept it? Does it make sense given the competitive environment? Does the ratio of benefits to costs appear favorable? Is it otherwise economically feasible? Will it actually solve the problem? Any manager should worry about substance.

However appealing to the manager personally, embarking on and sustaining a given course of action generally requires the support of others. Grants of authority and resources typically depend on others' views of the manager's purposes and plans. And managers modify their most preferred programs and plans in response to the concerns of others. Though the overt need for garnering support varies from setting to setting, and over the life of projects, all managers need to worry about sustained authorization and resources.

To be worth anything, even an independently great idea that can attract and hold support needs to be implemented. Thus, the inclinations and potential capabilities of those who are supposed to carry out the desired action should be of primary concern. It is certainly not news that managers need to worry about production.

A variety of tools and disciplines seek to advise managers on each of these new concerns. To determine whether something is inherently a good idea, various kinds of business and economic analysis can be applied. Industry and competitive analysis examines the viability of positions within industries, marketing determines whether a product has a market, production engineering whether a product can be made at an appropriate price, and so on. Sophisticated methods for analyzing public policies and techniques of program evaluation likewise address this question of *substantive desirability*. Common sense, experience, and the judgements of outside experts can help to assess the independent merits of a proposal. With depressing frequency, however, practitioners of these disciplines discover that what appears to be a good idea on paper cannot be "sold" to those who count. Even if it can, "details" of administration sometimes prevent its realization.

Similarly, attracting and retaining needed authority and support both inside the organization and in the larger world is the province of *political analysis*. Those whose specialty lies in getting others to support their ideas often discover, to everyone's dismay, that substance in fact matters and that "implementation" cannot be taken for granted.

Tools and techniques from public and business *administration* address the production concerns of managers. Yet the ranks of unsuccessful managers are strewn with those who looked no further than to grimly efficient administration of their units—whether they made losing products, oversaw badly flawed programs, or had needed authorization and support cut out from under them.

In short, any manager needs to be concerned in some measure with goals, authorization and support, and production. Equivalently, we might say that all managers deal with aspects of substance, politics, and administration. Together, these considerations shape the job. Ideally, each should be compatible with and reinforce the others.

One characterization in particular takes these three dimensions of a manager's job into account.[1] It employs the concepts of "mandate," "production," and "strategy."[2]

---

[1]This characterization is due to Moore (1982).

[2]To see how and where the negotiation perspective applies within an organization, we need a characterization of managerial functions that is amenable to the

A manager in virtually any type of organization, position, or functional area needs to obtain, shape, and protect a *mandate*, that is, a combination of the substantive purposes to be accomplished, the authority and resources to be employed, and the conditions and expectations for their use. The purposes embodied in a mandate typi-

---

task. Such a description should allow the negotiation-related parts of the manager's job to emerge and should not, by its formulation, downplay and obscure them. Unfortunately, many traditional descriptions of managers' duties, while useful for other purposes, tend to have precisely the latter effect. For example, if public or business administration is defined in terms of management control, information systems, organizational structure, capital budgeting procedures, competitive strategic analysis, and the like, we find ourselves implicitly adopting deterministic or hierarchical notions. As a prerequisite for prescriptive progress, the very definitions we use of managerial functions should admit and not hide the fact that much organizational life involves negotiation.

To get around this problem, we might be tempted to develop specific "applications" of our general negotiation technology—consummating a merger, closing a sale, procuring goods and services, arriving at a union contract, settling out of court. Each of these and other such tasks has its own special characteristics that call for working out. But the sheer number of such kinds of negotiation would preclude us from saying much of general applicability. To avoid this pitfall, we might choose to examine standard functional specialties. We could then look at negotiations in finance, marketing, in service delivery, in personnel, in logistical coordination, in industrial relations, and so on. We could also examine managerial negotiations by different types of organization. We might then investigate the role of negotiations in public agencies versus private firms. Or we could contrast manufacturing with service, petroleum with agriculture, regulation with defense, or insurance with financial services. We could compare single-product with multi-product firms, or decentralized with centrally managed operations. We might contrast technology-driven with marketing-intensive organizations. Another approach would look to the nature of particular managerial positions to tell us about the general roles of negotiation in management. Positions, though, may range from high to medium to low in a hierarchy, from line to staff, from general to functional management, from political to career, and along many other such dimensions. And beyond these cuts at the problem, everyone seems to have his or her favorite conception of the manager's job or the absolutely critical distinctions for a task like this. For quite a discussion of similar issues, see Mintzberg (1973).

We think that studying the place and particular characteristics of negotiation according to each of these organizing conceptions would yield real rewards. We even hope to add to the stimulus for such investigations. Still, the extreme variability we see when describing mangerial jobs by specific application, by function, by type of organization, or by nature of position, poses serious problems for our efforts to make generally applicable observations about the role of negotiation in management. For this quest, we need an economical characterization of the manager's essential tasks that is nonetheless robust to their diversity. Beyond economy, this approach should highlight the consistently important dimensions of managerial responsibilities and help distinguish what is critical from what is less so. And, it should be cast in a way that allows prescriptive negotiation insights to find ready application in a variety of settings. Moore's (1982) characterization, of which we make liberal use, fits the bill.

cally require the manager to obtain *production*, often of goods and services but sometimes of less tangible outputs. Production may be carried out directly through one's organization or indirectly through other entities. But wherever the locus of production, the manager is in some measure accountable for the results. Mandates and productive capacity are brought into alignment by the concept of *strategy*, which is intended to integrate substance, authority and resources, and administration. A good strategy offers a "fit" among these factors; it is a statement of purposes and plans that have substantive merit, that can attract and retain support, and that can be administratively realized.

Before we developed the key concepts and methods of "negotiation analysis," the first chapter of this book showed that negotiation is inherent in managerial tasks involving superiors, subordinates, and those outside the chain of command. Identical arguments imply that managers negotiate with organizational and other superiors over purposes, authority, and resources (mandates) and that they negotiate with subordinates and those outside the chain of command to produce desired results. The manager is at the nexus of two evolving networks of linked agreements—one over mandates, the other over production. A good strategy requires that these sets of agreements be consistent with each other. In fact, this consistency criterion gives operational meaning to the sometimes blurry notion of strategic "fit." It is now time to revisit these topics from a negotiation perspective.

Strategy: Consistent Networks of Linked Agreements

By now it is commonplace that exclusive managerial focus on any one of substance, politics, or administration can founder on the shoals of the other, neglected ones. Hence the need for a good manager to take all three into account. This proposition is easily stated and heads around the table will solemnly nod their assent. But how can this advice be made operational? What is available to integrate these separate areas, especially when each has lifetimes of specialized knowledge within its purview?[3]

[3]A number of valuable, if partial, answers to these questions have been developed. Chandler (1962) explored the relation between the firm's competitve approach (its "strategy") and its organizational "structure." Lawrence and Lorsch (1967a,b)

A viable organizational strategy embodies a "good goal" and is both "authorizable" and "producible." When a purpose and plans to achieve it possess all three qualities simultaneously, it is said to possess a good "fit." The notion of "fit," while quite suggestive and often used, is only loosely defined. Hence the process of integrating the different required factors is iterative, somewhat ad hoc, and even requires a kind of esthetic judgment. But, by art, science, or luck, one's "mandate" (purposes, authority, and resources) should be compatible with one's direct or indirect "productive capacity" if one is to have a good strategy.[4]

A simple picture (Figure 11.1) can help clarify this conception.[5] The upper circle represents the purposes and plans that the manager finds potentially attractive and substantively sound. The leftmost circle corresponds to the purposes on whose behalf authorizing bodies will grant authority and resources. Mandate negotiations should conclude in the overlapping part of these regions.

The purposes that are possible given the preferences and capabilities of those who will produce are represented by the circle on the right. Again, there is some overlap with other circles. It is in this overlap that the network of direct and indirect production agreements should be struck.

---

looked at the "fit" between the firm's internal organization and aspects of its environment. A number of business strategists (e.g., Andrews, 1971) focused on the match or mismatch between what a firm wants to do or is doing and its actual or potential areas of "distinctive competence." Porter (1980, 1981) took a more explicitly external view, suggesting more or less generic "strategies" that different kinds of firms might use in markets with various product and competitive characteristics. Significant insights have come from each of these and many related studies. With a view to public sector organizations, Moore (1982) argued for an idea of "strategy" that is compatible with the above conceptions although it is somewhat more encompassing. We have taken it as a point of departure for what follows.

[4]As a diagnostic device, this concept of strategy allows the analyst or manager to scrutinize an organization's purpose and plans simultaneously with respect to all three required elements (Inherently a good idea? Supportable? Producible?). If any aspects are out of line, the strategy concept becomes prescriptive: change course or bring the elements into simultaneous alignment. If a change in the environment occurs or a new purpose, source of support, or organizational change is proposed, good strategic thinking immediately considers its compatibility with other elements.

A clear idea of strategy can also provide a shorthand means for assessing the many opportunities presented by the environment. If an option is compatible with the strategy, consider adopting it; if not, spurn it and stay with central pursuits (or plan for major changes on all fronts). Moreover, to the extent that the "goal" portion of the overall strategic concept can be simply stated, it can communicate a sense of purpose, motivation, and identity to people inside and outside the organization.

[5]This representation was suggested by Herman Leonard.

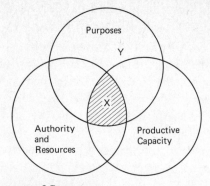

FIGURE 11.1: Elements of Strategy

Bargaining should focus on the set of feasible strategies, those that lie in the crosshatched intersection of the three circles. Often, many potential agreements are consistent. Therefore, choosing among them requires balancing their appeal to the manager and others, their sustainability, and how easily they may be altered to accommodate environmental changes.

The inevitability of change, moreover, suggests that a good strategy will include a function that monitors and gathers information. Changes in the environment will often require renegotiation of mandate and production agreements. Thus, one of a manager's interests in early negotiations should be the later ease of renegotiation. The apparent success of certain Japanese enterprises in adapting to change lies in the perception common to workers and management that no one will lose from changes—workers have secure employment and will be retrained as part of revised productive arrangements. As a result, renegotiation of arrangements is much easier than when layoffs are the expected result of change. In fact, the more that organization members truly share interests, the easier it will likely be to reach, sustain, and change agreements that further those interests.[6]

Suppose, for example, that the manager chose to attempt a move from a current set of deals in the cross-hatched region, say point X, to a new strategy, represented by Y. To do this would require changes in resources and productive capacity. In the picture, the lower two circles would have to be moved up and to the right so that their intersection included Y.

Of course, this picture is only intended to evoke the tasks required for a manager to negotiate in accord with a strategic conception. For

[6]As we discuss in Chapter Fourteen, shared interests in purposes can be reinforced by selection and "socialization" processes, and cultivated by a variety of other means.

any proposal or desired action, questions of substance, authority and resources, and administrative feasibility immediately present themselves. Associated with each such question is a set of people with whom to negotiate or renegotiate. Over time, an immense number of possible negotiations present themselves. A carefully thought-through strategic perspective is intended as a guide for quick evaluation of choices, as a key for deciding what is critical and what is less so, and as a means for selecting which negotiations to undertake.

Negotiating Mandates, Production, and Strategy: An Overview of Part II

The remainder of the book investigates several negotiation problems that recur in management situations. The material is roughly organized around mandates, direct and indirect production, and strategy. This section provides a more specific overview of the upcoming chapters.

MANDATES AND THE SUSTAINABILITY OF AGREEMENTS

Managers must negotiate and renegotiate over purposes, support, authority, and resources. Chapter Twelve lays out important features of these special negotiations over mandates. Because agreements within organizations are typically insecure or renegotiable, Chapter Thirteen examines the factors that may cause agreements to come up for renegotiation. It then discusses ways to make agreements more secure as well as how to open them up for renegotiation when this is desirable.

DIRECT AND INDIRECT PRODUCTION: NEGOTIATING THROUGH AGENTS

The point of management is to produce—whether tangible goods and services, a portfolio of them, or elusive entities like coordination or public safety.[7]

In the most common vision, a manager produces through subordinates in his unit. We call this "direct management" or "direct production." In this hierarchical image, a manager's accountability matches his authority and resources; that is, the expectations for his performance are reasonable given his authority and resources. Much

---

[7]We use the term production rather than implementation, which is perhaps more common. "Implementation" suggests the somewhat cut-and-dried execution of a carefully conceived master plan that merely needs to be carried out. We are trying to characterize a more organic process in which new information arises, resistance appears, new deals are cut, and so on.

has been written about direct management and its tools—authority, management systems, and socialization. We supplement this work on direct management by highlighting in Chapter Fourteen the role of negotiation and mediation in hierarchies and by underscoring the fundamental link between negotiation and authority.

So far, we have cast the manager as an agent (negotiating with principals for a mandate) and as a principal (getting "agents" to produce). In Chapter Fifteen, we take a closer look at the characteristics of negotiation in the principal-agent relationship—the most elementary and yet extremely important form of organization. Because many conventional negotiations are carried out through agents, this topic also applies directly to many nonmanagerial negotiations.

We then resume our more specific look at management, contrasting "direct management" with "indirect management" (or "indirect production"), in which a manager's accountability is concentrated while critical authority or resources are *shared*. Managers are increasingly held accountable for production carried out by other organizational units or organizations. To meet expectations, such a manager depends on the sharers of his authority or resources. He finds himself enmeshed in a network of linked agreements. Negotiation becomes an absolutely necessary course of action in most such indirect management situations. Chapter Sixteen examines the nature and extent of indirect management and discusses two broad strategies for negotiating in networks.

THE NEGOTIATOR IN THE MIDDLE:
LINKED BARGAINS AND STRATEGY

In this section, we add a layer of complexity to the topic of negotiating through agents. Managers are in the middle of linked negotiations when they try to keep mandate and production agreements in good strategic alignment. They face another version of this pervasive bargaining form when representing their organizations in negotiations with external parties. Negotiators who must deal with constituencies likewise fall in the middle of linked bargains. In Chapter Seventeen, we examine key tactical choices of "negotiators in the middle" and certain dynamic aspects of linked bargains. The analysis applies to negotiations in hierarchies and networks, to some kinds of mediation, and to synchronizing external negotiations with internal ones. Perhaps most importantly, it develops the negotiating link between the major parts of a manager's job, how to deal simultaneously "upwards and downwards," "side to side," as well as "inside the organization and out."

CHAPTER TWELVE

Negotiating for Purposes, Authority, and Resources:
A Manager's Need for a Mandate

FAILURE TO OBTAIN and bolster support for one's initiatives frequently dooms well-intentioned efforts to failure. Interestingly enough, once the initial go-ahead for a project is granted, the need for carefully maintaining support for it is often ignored.[1] This chapter examines the components of what we have called "mandates" and some characteristics of negotiations over them.

A mandate consists of a combination of substantive purposes to be accomplished, resources to be used, along with attached conditions and expectations. Normally, managers must work out generalized or specific mandates with superiors, creditors, boards of directors, and legislative units, as well as other interested parties who can grant or withhold needed resources.

Purposes

Purposes can be very specific. A manager might be asked to reach a target rate of return, to increase the level of city procurement from

---

[1] This topic certainly does not make up a major part of management curricula at most management schools.

minority firms, to slash budgets. Purposes can also be quite general—to boost divisional morale, to protect the environment, to invent something commercially useful.

A manager may have preferences for different objectives on the basis of personal interest or vision, as the result of careful economic analysis, or based on an interpretation of legislative intent or historical precedent. However compelling personally, a manager's preferred goals normally need to be reconciled with those of authorizing entities. Sometimes all parties want virtually the same things to be accomplished, disagreeing only on the means. More often, there is resolvable conflict. For example, an entrepreneur's appetite for a risky shot at the big time may collide with the conservatism of some of his financial backers; they may ultimately settle on a somewhat less risky but still adventurous plan. In certain instances, the clash is so severe that no agreement is possible and resignation results—think of a manager who is pressed to gut a cherished program or take actions that he or she finds immoral or illegal.

Authority and Resources

Formal authority granted as part of a mandate usually extends to a specified set of decisions; many kinds of productive resources can be involved.[2] For example, Bill was made the head of the medical testing equipment division of a large firm. He was given authority to hire and fire, to set prices, to change reporting relationships, and to allocate resources within a set budget. In addition to the budget, the CEO promised support in dealings with a recalcitrant marketing group and that the division's progress would be one of his high priorities. Later Bill found that he needed authorizations from the VP for finance and from the capital budgeting committee; in accepting the job, these necessary parts of his mandate had not been discussed. He subsequently had to negotiate with these parties. Unfortunately, the CEO's implied support was not always there when Bill needed it.

Managers do not typically need special authorization for each action they contemplate; they should, however, watch whether they

---

[2]Formal authority usually extends to a specified set of decisions, whether personnel, budget or resource allocation, organization structure, or a class of policies such as pricing, financial structure, marketing, or program design. Productive resources can include financial capital, people, quiet or overt backing, charters, licenses, permissions, or even agreements to ignore or not to attack a program, policy, or unit.

are operating within the express or implied limits of their mandates. Bill's attempt to initiate large capital investments without approval would have been taken as an attempt to usurp ungranted authority.

Because the manager holds out the promise of achieving desired purposes, overseers share an interest in providing sufficient resources and authority. Typically, the more that overseers' purposes seem likely to be furthered, the more generous they will be with grants of authority and resources. But interpretations of how much is appropriate are almost always subject to disagreement. Managers want to be able to produce as promised but also to have some margin for contingencies and discretionary purposes. Overseers, however, want the highest return for their "investment"—in terms of *their* purposes.

Conditions and Expectations

Hand in hand with purposes and resources go conditions, expectations for performance, and accountability. Sometimes conditions such as loan covenants are quite explicit. Frequently, though, important expectations remain unstated. Bill and the CEO had worked out a few targets for the medical testing division's performance after six months, one year, and two years, but many other expectations about what Bill should accomplish went unstated; for example, Bill was taken to task for a morale crisis when morale had never been discussed. Similarly, both had unstated expectations that Bill would quickly convey any important information to the CEO.

These conditions and expectations are often part of a "measurement system." For example, a series of milestones may be jointly worked out in a "management by objectives" program. Because a manager's performance may be assessed by comparing results to previously established expectations, considerable conflict and negotiation—however tacit or masked—often accompanies their development. Failure to meet expectations may lead to reduced discretion and authority; in fact, Bill's failure to meet initial unstated sales targets led to greater supervision by the CEO. Similarly, officers of a small firm threatened by insolvency are likely to lose much of their control to creditors.

A manager may thus have powerful incentives to "lowball," that is, to establish expectations that can almost certainly be exceeded, while his superior may hope to coax peak effort by establishing objectives that will be difficult to achieve. Sometimes, though, "selling" an idea requires overpromising. Then backpedaling, lowering expectations, finding good excuses, and disappointment become the order of the day.

There are almost always unstated expectations of "good conduct" and behavior befitting a faithful agent. For example, a good manager is generally not supposed to incur significant obligations for his superiors or to act in ways that quietly but dramatically reduce their future flexibility.

A manager who, over the course of his tenure, proves to be a faithful "agent" of authorizing bodies is likely to enjoy increased discretion. Some managers (like Robert Moses or Harold Geneen) can at times accumulate sufficient authority and resources that "outside" control or accountability seem like empty formalities.

Richard Neustadt counsels the President to pay close attention to "teaching" the public; that is, to align expectations with possibilities.[3] Prestige and public support, he argues, are more a function of meeting or exceeding expectations than of the absolute level of performance. When Gerald Ford was prodded by health officials to appear on television to announce that, come fall 1976, safe shots would be available to every American man, woman, and child to protect against the possibility of deadly swine influenza, he set up the expectations by which this program would be judged. He elevated them even further later when he publicly got his shot. When sufficient vaccine turned out to be unavailable and bad side effects were linked to immunization, Ford and the program were badly tarnished. Suppose that, without respect to the merits of universal coverage, the program for all had never been announced by the President. Instead, had the Centers for Disease Control mounted a campaign of immunization only for high risk groups, the identical substantive result would almost certainly have been less politically damaging.[4]

Though most executives do not face the President's public, negotiating expectations and conditions that are compatible with agreed purposes and resources remains important. Failure to set such expectations may necessitate even more time-consuming negotiations later. For example, Bob Furz, the manager of a Brazilian subsidiary of a London-based multinational office air-conditioning manufacturer, persuaded headquarters, after considerable effort, to allow him to shift the subsidiary's strategy. For years, it had been known as a high-quality, custom-made, premium-priced manufacturer; Bob Furz was

---

[3]Neustadt (1980).
[4]Fineberg and Neustadt (1982).

convinced that a higher-volume, discount approach offered superior potential in a changed environment. By this shift, he hoped to take over the South American market.

Though London agreed to the new purposes, milestones appropriate to the new plan were not negotiated. By habit, London expected the steady high margins and few cash demands associated with the higher-quality approach. The initial losses, mounting debts, and quality complaints, which the Brazilian subsidiary had expected would initially accompany the new course, clashed with London's expectations and were read there as a disaster in the making. Bob Furz had carefully negotiated the new strategy with an attractive vision of the end result. Yet the lack of agreed-on interim milestones compatible with other elements of his new approach doomed him to a debilitating battle with London over "staying the course"; his job was constantly at stake.

Building a Coalition Behind a Mandate   A mandate frequently depends on the outcome of a group meeting or process: the capital investment committee, a troika of the administrator and two key deputies, the domestic policy group, the board of directors. In preparing for the formal process, a manager in search of a particular mandate may need to build a coalition of support behind the proposed initiative. To do this, she should think hard about her real interests in the initiative. Then she should carefully enumerate the parties who will be involved, their likely interests, their alternatives to going along with her ideas, potential agreements with each, and, thus, who will likely be helpful and to whom she will be vulnerable. She will probably be able to appeal to each party on the basis of different factors: the merits, shared or complementary interests, valued principles or precedents, aspects of the process, and who else supports the idea.

Now she must choose a sequence for approaching those involved. If the manager can discern "patterns of deference" among needed parties—who defers to whom—it can become clearer whose support is critical early on and, thus, where real persuasive effort and investment would be most valuable. It is best to start with the parties whose assent will be influential in later dealings with others.

With this preparation, it is possible to plan a sequence for approaching each needed party and obtaining their agreement. Frequently the natural allies of a proposal are easy to identify and quietly bring on board first. A useful exercise for thinking through the rest of the problem often consists of "mapping backward" from the person or group whose agreement appears the most difficult to obtain.[5]

Once identified, another question becomes apt. What collection of previous commitments to the proposal and agreements to back it would make most probable the agreement of the most difficult person or group? To whose judgment do the reluctant ones defer or at least give some weight? With these parties targeted, the manager should repeat this process of backward mapping until at least one promising order of approach emerges (in effect the most advantageous "configuration" for yielding the desired agreement). Then one has a carefully set pattern of standing dominoes; when the first is pushed over, the rest will fall in line. Of course, even with such careful planning, obtaining agreement can be tricky; conditions required by one early party may rule out a later party's agreement.

In general, keeping the initiative and dealing with likely opponents separately runs the least risk of the process unraveling. As the manager begins to build a coalition of support, she will learn better what is needed to secure the others' agreement. Her approach may change accordingly.

Of course, a manager engages in many such support-building processes. Many of the reactions encountered will depend on past relationships and patterns. Similarly, future efforts will be affected by this one. As such, a manager's interests in each encounter extend to the web of issues and parties involved with one another over time.

Special Topics in Mandate Negotiations   For the simplest sort of mandate negotiation, one between a middle manager who has proposed a project and her immediate superior, we have identified the generic issues and some likely interests. The logic of negotiation analysis developed in Chapters Two through Nine applies directly. Yet a number of further topics have special relevance to mandates.

By agreeing to grant a mandate to a subordinate, a manager creates an agent. In turn, the subordinate may negotiate partly on his own behalf, in effect, acting as principal. In Chapter Fifteen, we examine several ways that divergences of interest between principal and agent can benefit or hurt the principal.

Mandate negotiations often occur without anyone admitting that there is conflict or even that in fact there is negotiation. Rather, all

[5]See Elmore (1979) for a discussion of backward mapping as a policy implementation tool.

hew to the fiction of purely "common" interests and shared purposes. Adroitness in such fake "problem solving"—when purposes in fact are being hammered out—can substantially alter the actual outcome. We discuss this sort of bargaining by proxy in Chapter Fourteen.

Often, the mandating body consists of different parties who can grant different kinds of required authority and resources—a superior gives the formal go-ahead, hiring authority, and a budget; the R&D department head agrees to provide bench time and two engineers for a month; the sales department consults on design, carries out marketing studies, and tests market prototypes, and so on. In such cases, the process of obtaining a mandate typically requires a series of linked bilateral negotiations, each to be analyzed and carried out as we have often outlined. In Chapter Seventeen, we will look more closely at the logic of linked bargains.

Finally, agreements over mandates that seem secure today may come up for renegotiation tomorrow. New parties or events may intrude; some element of the measurement system may flash caution; a factor implicitly held constant may change; or rivals may simply make an opportunistic play for a new, more favorable deal. The manager's job consists not only in obtaining and shaping a mandate but also in protecting and appropriately altering it.

In Chapter Thirteen, we take an extended look at the sustainability of agreements. We look more closely at why agreements come up for renegotiation and which might be broken. Because mandates are often insecure, we offer prescriptions to strengthen them. This is not to suggest that a manager's stance should be habitually conservative and defensive; it is often desirable to reopen and change a mandate— sometimes drastically. Knowledge, conditions, and opportunities evolve; so, too, should purposes, resources, and expectations.

CHAPTER THIRTEEN

Sustaining Agreements

AGREEMENTS are not forever. Whether it is the Chinese ninety-nine year treaty with Britain over Hong Kong, a tacit agreement between major airlines not to cut their New York–Los Angeles fares, or a manager's mandate, accords typically have finite lives. In his famous sociological study of the "negotiated order" within organizations, Anselm Strauss and his colleagues observed:

> The shared agreements, the binding contracts—which constitute the grounds for an expectable, nonsurprising, taken-for-granted, even ruled orderliness—are not binding and shared for all time. Contracts, understandings, agreements, rules—all have appended to them a temporal clause. That clause may or may not be explicitly discussed by the contracting parties, and the terminal date may or may not be made specific; but none can be binding forever—even if the parties believe it so, unforeseen consequences of acting on the agreements would force eventual confrontation. Review is called for, whether the outcome of review be rejection or revision, or whatnot. In short, the bases of concerted action (social order) must be reconstituted continually.[1]

[1]Strauss et al. (1963:148).

For many negotiators, a central concern is that their agreements, contracts, or understandings will not hold. Within organizations, agreements are frequently not recorded and thus are subject to reinterpretation. Moreover, mechanisms for enforcing such understandings often do not exist. Thus, a manager needs to take special care to secure agreements, for say, authority and resources, that she fears are unstable. At other times, flexibility will be important and ensuring that renegotiation is later possible may require advance planning. This chapter examines conditions under which renegotiation or repudiation become likely, and ways to lessen the chances of this happening undesirably.

When Do Agreements Come Up for Renegotiation?

Renegotiations often occur when new parties come on the scene and do not feel bound by old contracts. For example, a country's government may change and feel justified in repudiating prior commercial agreements. Or, a company may be taken over and new management installed. The new group may feel quite free to override old understandings, even firmly held ones.

Many contracts have an agreed set of conditions under which they will be reviewed or renegotiated. This may take the form of a five-year lease with an option for either side to renew, and incidentally to renegotiate terms. Or, specific conditions, covenants, and expectations may be built into an agreement. If they are violated, the whole accord may be reconsidered. For example, a real estate developer may fail during a recession to meet certain of his loan covenants specifying minimum rent and vacancy rates in an office building, thereby calling the rest of the agreement into question. Or, after getting approval to embark on a new product strategy, a manager may not meet agreed profitability targets, or he might fall short of a set of implicit expectations about his progress if, for example, his group is several months slow in getting the product to market. This may cause the overall agreement to be reopened and, possibly, repudiated. These observations underscore the critical importance of whatever "measurement system"—covenants, profit targets, milestones, other expectations—is explicitly or implicitly a part of the original agreement.

Agreements are frequently reviewed when one of the parties asks for a change in some provision. For example, a computer manufacturing plant had received exceedingly favorable tax treatment from a city government early in the city's campaign to attract industry. Later, after the campaign enjoyed success, and even spawned worries about "excessive" growth in the local area, the company would be quite ill-advised to ask to extend the favorable tax treatment to an additional plant it hoped to build nearby. The old arrangement might endure if undisturbed, whereas a new request or even a request for a minor alteration might spur an overall review of whether *any* continued tax breaks—let alone new ones—were justified.

In many instances of negotiated agreement, however, the legitimacy of particular *outcomes* may be an issue. Even though the parties agreed to a set of terms, some outcomes may not be viewed as acceptable or "fair" after the fact. For example, a U.S. firm's mining venture in Latin America ended up a bonanza even though it had been portrayed as incredibly risky and was subject to fairly light taxation as a result. With the "sunk risks" forgotten, and original misrepresentation by the company suspected, the costs to the host government of leaving the contract intact—especially with a vocal political opposition—appeared higher than the cost of demanding new terms. If, during the initial negotiation, this lopsided result could have been anticipated as sufficiently likely, then leaving it as a possible contractual outcome seems questionable (unless, of course, ulterior motives were involved).

Beyond such distributional grounds for regarding an outcome as illegitimate, other aspects of the process of reaching an agreement or resolving subsequent uncertainties may taint the result. Surprises such as oil price shocks may leave an agreement nominally workable but with radically changed effects on the parties from those originally contemplated. Assumptions of "all other things being equal" may have been implicit in the initial accord. Adherence to an agreement may be tacitly conditional on the observance of certain conventions or norms. One side may perceive the other as having concealed relevant information in the negotiation, as having cheated in some way, or as having improperly influenced the resolution of an uncertain event that was the basis for agreement. One side may feel tricked and hence justified in repudiating the accord.

In general, an individual is likely to press to break or change an agreement when the value of keeping it seems lower than the value of not doing so, when the benefits of noncompliance exceed the costs. The costs of not complying may come from legal fees, damage to reputation and future dealings, feelings of unfairness, and so forth.

Two kinds of situations deserve special attention. Despite our emphasis in Chapter Five on the possible virtues of contingent agreements—that is, agreements to do one thing if an uncertain event comes out one way and another if the event comes out otherwise— poorly designed contingent agreements can lead to renegotiation. The second situation, which we call "insecure contracts," arises where enforcement is difficult and one party has an incentive to violate an agreement as soon the other has made an irrevocable commitment to it.

The Sustainability of Contingent Agreements

One common reaction to the suggested use of contingent agreements is: "That's all fine to do before the fact, but what about afterwards when the uncertainty is resolved and one party is relatively worse off than the other." Suppose, for example, that a third party had induced the warring factions in a divided country to agree to a cease fire and to hold an election. Suppose that this agreement were possible primarily because each side had an over-optimistic estimate of its chances to win. Once the election was held, high *expected* utility would be replaced by a declared winner and an army of angry losers. Was thought given, for example, to how after the election a dominant coalition might form? Otherwise, the losers may find that abiding by the agreement and being ruled by the winners is worse for them than their alternative to continued agreement, which is to start fighting again.

Such questions about the parties' relationship once uncertainties are resolved might be called "morning after" problems. The first thing to ask is whether there will be a morning after; that is, whether the agreement was explicitly one-shot, or whether the parties have already carried out their agreed actions and the question of "backing out" is moot since the consequences are all that remain to be suffered or enjoyed. Because many, if not most, negotiated arrangements require some continuing involvement of the parties, sustainability once uncertainties are resolved deserves analysis before reaching agreement. One should ask how different agreements will be valued relative to the alternatives under various contingencies.

When the outcome of a contingent bargain turns out badly for a negotiator, what motivates him to abide by the agreement? For example, if Raoul agrees to split the expenses of maintaining Mary's car in return for the right to use it for the year and then a problem requires a repair much more expensive than either anticipated, what might cause him to pay his half of the repair cost? Had he known that the car would need such extensive repairs, he would not have entered into the agreement in the first place. But, refusing a particular outcome beforehand may be quite different from reneging on the same outcome after a contingent agreement has been made. Once having made the contingent agreement, breaking it might result in powerful sanctions—the permanent loss of Mary's friendship and affection, a reputation as untrustworthy, a lawsuit, and the like—which could make abiding by the agreement better than the alternative. To be effective, the costs incurred for not complying—in terms of the bargainer's perceived interests—must exceed the benefit of reneging; otherwise the bargainer may happily renege. If all Raoul actually would suffer for reneging is Mary's unhappiness for a week, he might refuse to pay, especially if his finances are tight and he cares mightily about money. Thus, a negotiator should beware of contingent agreements that can have worse results for one party than reneging, even after taking into account the full costs of doing so.

Insecure Contracts

In certain bargaining situations, the "walkaway" conditions may themselves change in a predictable way following an initial agreement. For example, before a mining company makes a large fixed investment in a country it may have great leverage over the contractual terms by threatening not to build the mine. Afterwards it cannot as convincingly threaten to leave and the host country's new prerogatives may be exercised. That is, after signing a contract and investing, the company's alternatives to continued agreement are much worse than its no-agreement alternative prior to investing. Similarly, the host country's alternatives to continued agreement are much better after the company has invested.

The essence of this situation can be captured by a sequence of decisions with three possible outcomes: investment followed by renegotiation, investment without renegotiation, and no investment. The mining company prefers investing without renegotiation over staying at home and ranks renegotiation last. The host country, on the other hand, wants investment and may try to attract it by promising not to renegotiate. Should the company decide to invest, however, the country may have lesser incentives to abide by its original contract. Knowing this, a wary company may choose to stay home. The company and the country may both suffer as a result.

Analogous insecurities reside in the structure of many non-mining bargains. The Israelis might wish to return the strategic Golan Heights to Syria in exchange for a promise of peace. They may fear, however, that the promise could not be enforced should the Syrians later resume hostilities. Similarly, after a few years as the sole source on a vital defense contract, a large contractor may be in a powerful position to demand more lucrative terms from the government, which may have to accede or risk a costly switch of contractors and likely project failure. Or, after leaving his old job and moving to a new part of the country, an employee who finds that his new job is not as was promised may be powerless to correct the situation. An agreement to have a child only if the father shares its care may evaporate once the baby is born, with all the responsibility falling to the mother. Each of these ''contracts'' is insecure because one party's incentives to abide by its terms are reduced after the other party has made an irrevocable first move (e.g., digging the mine, giving up the Golan Heights, making the sole source contract award, moving across the country, or having the child).

The following brief discussion suggests three different ways to secure insecure contracts.[2] For illustrative purposes, the approaches are cast in terms of the mining example. To enhance their general applicability the suggestions deal only with the principles involved, ignoring the specifics of implementation.

Securing an insecure contract requires a change in the relative magnitudes of the payoffs for different courses of action. In the case of mining, only if the value to the country of not renegotiating exceeds its value for doing so will a rational host government be less likely to renegotiate; that likelihood is critical for the company. If a renegotiation does occur, despite the company's prior perception of its probability, the firm can be compensated by raising its payoff in that case.

Solution 1: A Performance Bond   One obvious way for the country to commit itself convincingly to the terms of a contract is to post a bond valued higher than the proposed investment with a

_____

[2]See Lax and Sebenius (1981) for a much more extended discussion of the problem of insecure contracts.

trusted third party. If the terms are abrogated, the bond would revert to the company. Both company and host payoffs would thereby be changed. Two separate effects of this idealized solution are important: (1) the company would be compensated in the event of adverse action, while (2) because the host would have to pay this compensation, its incentive to renegotiate would decrease. The firm's perceived probability of such a change is greatly reduced. In principle, this sort of performance bond would do the trick of securing this insecure contract.[3]

Solution 2: Linkage   If the host country believes that forcing a renegotiation would hurt other parties who would be likely to retaliate, the host may be less likely to take such measures in the first place. That is, the direct linkage between a renegotiation with one firm and other companies' or governments' actions could reduce the host's relevant payoff for renegotiation. This kind of linkage, however, does not increase the company's payoff in the event of renegotiation. A company considering investment in a country also might wish to use a variety of financial and contractual mechanisms indirectly to link parties (such as banks, corporations, and other governments that have dealings with the host) to the successful completion of the project. Investors sometimes go to extraordinary lengths to set up indirect links that raise the cost to the host in other spheres of a forced renegotiation. By simultaneously linking this investment to dealings with other parties and taking out insurance, a company can affect both the country's and its own renegotiation payoffs, thus simulating the effect of a performance bond. (In a later section, we will review how Kennecott sought to employ this kind of linkage in its Chilean copper operations.)

Solution 3: Prevention   One of the easiest ways to avoid the insecure contract problem is to prevent its occurrence by reducing the disparity between the country's valuations of abiding by the agreement and of renegotiating. While this may not be entirely achievable, measures such as fiscal provisions that have higher tax rates when profits are high can reduce the apparent gain from renegotiation over holding to the original terms. Other measures that increase

---

[3]See Lax and Sebenius (1981) for reasons that a performance bond would be impractical in this international setting. It can be quite useful in many other settings.

the host's control and participation can also prevent too wide a gulf from seeming to open between the payoffs for renegotiation and those for not doing so. Of course, a contingent agreement that results in strikingly high company profits may still result in a renegotiation. A party may also take direct steps now to worsen a potential reneger's alternatives to continued agreement. For example, by acquiring control of downstream processing, aluminum companies have substantially reduced the value of expropriating mining operations.

The equivalents of performance bonds, linkage, insurance,[4] and prevention can often be implemented in non-mining settings. If by these means, one succeeds in causing the value of continued agreement to exceed the value of renegotiating, the problem should be solved. Otherwise, one should evaluate the likelihood of renegotiation and the value of a renegotiated agreement and compare these prospects with the value of one's initial no-agreement alternatives. Not entering into an initial agreement should be a salient possibility.

Of course, parties may wish to conclude certain agreements—say, on arms control—even though they can foresee circumstances that would render the agreement unworkable. The odds of these circumstances occurring may be seen as low enough that they are offset by the expected value of making an agreement. Compliance need not be an absolute certainty for an agreement to be better than no agreement.

Crafting More Secure Agreements   Considerable ingenuity and effort are often required to make renegotiation less likely and to improve the renegotiated outcome if renegotiation cannot be prevented. Recall our example from Chapter Three in which, during the early 1960s, Chilean expropriation of Kennecott Copper's El Teniente mine seemed increasingly likely.[5] In preparing to negotiate the terms of the renegotiation such as the timing, compensation, and any continued management involvement with the mine, Kennecott attempted to link to the agreement a variety of other parties to worsen Chile's alternatives to continued agreement. The company voluntarily sold a majority interest in the mine to Chile and then arranged a loan from the U.S. Export-Import Bank. It used both this sale of equity and the

---

[4]Companies often take out "political risk" insurance to insure against expropriation. Such insurance need not affect the probability of repudiation because it does not necessarily affect the country's payoffs for doing so. See Lax and Sebenius (1981).

[5]Smith and Wells (1975).

loan to finance an expansion of the mine in line with Chilean interests. The Chilean government guaranteed this loan and agreed to make the guarantee subject to New York State law. Kennecott then insured as much as possible of its remaining assets under a U.S. guarantee against expropriation. Finally, Kenecott sold the mine's output under long-term contracts to Asian and European customers and the collection rights for these contracts to a consortium of European banks and Japanese institutions.[6]

When negotiations began, customers, the U.S. and other governments, and major creditors with whom Chile had a range of interactions would have been damaged by moves to expropriate Kennecott's stake in the mine. Thus, Kennecott's preparations worsened Chile's alternatives to continued agreement. Moreover, the guarantees and insurance partially compensated Kennecott in the event of expropriation. Although the mine was ultimately nationalized in a wave of such nationalizations, Kennecott fared better in the dealings than similar companies that had not taken such measures.

A manager who suspects that agreements may be broken by others may not be able to use performance bonds or linkage inside his firm. One way to secure agreements is to make others' alternatives to continued agreement worse than continuing to cooperate with him. Recall Bob Furz, who, as the new head of the Brazilian subsidiary of a British multinational, persuaded his parent board of directors to centralize South American operations and to move away from the previous strategy of customized products to a mass standardized approach. Selling his strategy had been a long battle, and he had made numerous enemies at British corporate headquarters in London. Though he was the nominal head for the new South American organization, he had only limited authority over certain key decisions. Many of the formerly autonomous country managers resented his new status. The sales force preferred the old customer relationships and higher-quality image. The company's South American engineers liked their prerogatives of individual design. Though Bob Furz took some steps toward implementing his new strategy, he needed to obtain the more wholehearted cooperation of key South American players to act in accord with his policies. But, at the early stages of the new strategy, each South American group's alternative to "agreeing" to act in accord with the new strategic vision was simply to ignore the

[6]See Fruhan (1978) for other, related examples.

new head or make end runs around him to the British headquarters. London had simply not given Furz the tools to force compliance.

At the outset of his new venture, he was thus only able to tempt each critical South American group into "agreement" with him by holding out the lure of joint gain from the new strategy. He offered a certain new status to country managers; he offered higher volume and profits to the sales force; and he challenged the company's engineers with new design problems. But Bob Furz's strategy was designed in such a way that, once embarked on, it involved the entire South American group in a price war with competitors and destroyed the old ways of doing business. In short, the South Americans' alternative to continued agreement, once the strategy was under way, was a very much worse situation than had earlier prevailed. This kept the entire group on board and worked against the incentives and opportunities to resist, not to go along, or to defect. As it happened, the strategy was exceedingly successful, and all parties in South America as well as Britain shared in enormous profits. But as the new manager, Furz had carefully designed his strategy such that, once implemented, the alternative to continued agreement with him always appeared worse for the parties than the cooperation he sought to obtain. Because his strategy had the side effect of worsening the other parties' alternatives to continued agreement over time, Bob Furz kept other parties acting in line with his strategic vision. Although linkage and performance bonds were not available tools, his complex strategy prevented the alternatives from becoming more attractive than continued agreement.

Insecure Agreements with Oneself People sometimes make the equivalent of insecure contracts with themselves. Imagine parents with a nine-year-old boy agreeing solemnly among themselves to take in an adorable, healthy looking stray puppy for "one week only" before turning it over to an animal shelter. As with other such arrangements, a first move creates conditions under which the odds drop that next, agreed-on steps will be taken. Though measures exist to help bind oneself to fulfillment, advance recognition of the situation can be a potent deterrent to being caught in such an insecure contract. As with the preceding example, prevention is often the best cure.

One such instance occurred when a diversified medium-sized manufacturing firm, which we will call Deltex, spotted what looked like a good acquisition in a small specialty chemical company producing rayon. The market served by the potential acquisition was gradually shrinking as competitive products gained dominance. Still, the small company's niche seemed to promise a good, though diminishing cash flow over time. With the aid of management consultants, Deltex had decided on a strategy to make the acquisition worthwhile. If favorable enough purchase terms could be negotiated, then the right course of action would be to invest nothing in the smaller firm's operations, but instead to "milk" it for maximum cash flow. At some point, what was left of the small firm would be sold.

After the sale price had been bargained down to a very attractive level, Deltex decided to make the purchase. As a condition of the merger, however, the smaller firm's president obtained a seat on the Deltex board and was appointed to membership on the Capital Investments Committee. It should not be surprising that, after three years of returning substantial cash flow to Deltex, the chemical subsidiary made urgent requests to the Capital Investments Committee for a large amount of funds to "modernize and regain lost market share" in rayon. It should also be no surprise that the requests were taken seriously and, ultimately, granted. Before and since the takeover, the subsidiary's president had become good friends and socially involved with a number of Deltex's managers—now his co-managers—and with his fellow board members. The stern divestiture plan based on careful strategic analysis was somehow forgotten even though the analysis ultimately proved correct: the subsidiary subsequently became a big drain on Deltex's cash flow. Did the acquiring management understand that by placing the chemical company president on the board it might be making an insecure contract with itself?

A related case occurred in MIC, a small professional company owned by a group of its senior officers. Two of its most able vice presidents advocated radically different future directions for the firm. One vice president, George, argued strenuously for the firm's traditional activities to be continued. The other, Ken, pressed for a very different strategic vision and used every means at his disposal, such as pulling employees off major projects to work on his unauthorized tasks, to edge the firm toward it. Ken's strategy almost certainly would have produced significant short-term gains but its longer-term prospects were most uncertain. Kirk, the firm's president, found the choice between the recommended strategies agonizing; the merits were unclear. Given the economic uncertainty facing the firm, he felt that choosing one direction or the other entailed significant risks.

As Kirk pondered his problem, he realized that, since a difference of probabilities about the future lay beneath the strategy disagreement, a contingent agreement might offer joint gains over the choice of one or the other course. He began to envision two entirely separate divisions, each headed by one of the vice presidents. The divisions could then pursue their preferred courses of action. In effect, this would allow each VP to "bet" on the activity he believed most strongly would succeed. This solution seemed to promise twin benefits to the overall firm. It would provide an economic hedge against an uncertain business future and it would retain both highly able VPs.

Yet, on reflection, he rejected this strategy as containing the elements of an insecure contract. He felt that the Ken would almost certainly use the short-term glamour of his strategy to lure others in the firm—owners and key employees—to his division. Given a short supply of experienced people in the firm, this could present a real problem. Kirk judged it almost organizationally impossible—especially given Ken's known history of almost ruthless advocacy—to keep the traditional division intact. Thus, the *organizational* risks of diluted effort from the insecurity of the arrangement would outweigh the *economic* benefits of the hedge. If he were to go forward at all with the new division, it would have to be headed by another person. In fact, he chose to fire Ken. In this instance, staying away from such an insecure agreement was likely the wisest course of action.

Creating Flexibility

Change is a given. The environment, the organization, the needs of other actors, and all manner of unforeseen circumstances can sometimes require that agreements be modified. Renegotiation may be avoided if the initial agreement includes a way to handle unforeseen contingencies. For example, negotiators can agree to submit disputes that arise during the life of the agreement—about others' compliance with it or about unanticipated changes in external conditions—to an arbitral panel or a committee. Foreseeable but unlikely events can also be treated in this way.

Moreover, one can seek contingent agreements that are robust in a variety of external circumstances. Compare a division head whose bonus is tied to his division's profitability with one whose bonus depends on outperforming his industry average. When the whole industry is in a slump, a very capable division head may feel under-rewarded and seek to renegotiate the profitability-based bonus. By contrast, the more robust bonus, based on industry comparisons, would not require modification.

Perhaps the most effective contingent mechanism is a long-term relationship in which the parties trust each other. Needed changes can be renegotiated in the context of their many dealings over time.

Even with more flexible agreements, negotiators may still wish to modify or break their agreements. How do they do this? Reference to unforeseen events (a new boss, pressing constraints, etc.), "better" analysis or evidence, or even a fervent change of heart can be used to contend that fully following the agreement would now be imprudent. Simple inaction, despite the best apparent intentions, also serves the purpose. And one party can break an informal understanding by misinterpreting or merely failing to remember it. Of course, in such cases, breaking an agreement may reduce trust between the parties and lessen the likelihood of full cooperation in later dealings.

Summary

In general, the sustainability of an agreement depends on how binding a commitment the parties make to it and the advantages that flow from adherence. Typically, the degree of commitment to an agreement is established by incurring costs if one fails to comply with its terms. The larger these costs are expected to be relative to the cost of keeping the agreement, the more the other side will regard the commitment as binding. The costs of holding to the agreement in all contingencies include perceptions of unfairness—distributionally, in process, from surprises, and from treachery, for example. If the parties can anticipate these factors, they should be considered for inclusion in the original agreement.

The costs incurred for not complying should thus be carefully analyzed in advance. In market or other economic transactions carried out under an accepted legal framework, sanctions may be obvious and accepted; parties may thus have a strong commitment to agreement. But, even there, if legal help is expensive, it may not be worth bringing a reneger to court over small matters; thus noncompliance on such matters becomes more likely. And, when means of enforcement are only partially effective, as in some mineral agreements or international relations, both contingent and noncontingent agreements are likely to be insecure.

When constructing an agreement, then, the parties should anticipate the possible later problems. They should carefully analyze the chances of self-destruction from considerations of ex-post unfairness, surprises, new information, illegitimacy, or changed alternatives. They should compare the value of continued agreement for all parties with the value of alternatives to continued agreement under a variety of possible contingencies. Variations on performance bonds, linkage, prevention, and insurance may make continued agreement superior to reneging. If incentives for renegotiation still appear large enough and its consequences sufficiently bad, a negotiator should seriously consider not making the initial agreement.

*   *   *

We began Part II of this book with an examination of the manager's job in terms of mandates, production, and strategy. So far we have taken a closer look at mandates and at the sustainability of agreements, an especially relevant topic. In the next chapter, we return to a basic managerial task, namely "direct production."

CHAPTER FOURTEEN

Negotiating in Hierarchies: Direct Management

PRODUCING THROUGH the efforts of one's subordinates is the oldest topic in management. Reams have been written on the subject, describing "scientific management," "management-by-objectives," and "quality circles," to pick a few. In this chapter we supplement basic work on direct management by highlighting the role of negotiation and authority.

Given the idea of a product, the manager seeking to have his organizational unit produce it should ask two questions. First, who will actually make it? Second, what is the network of linked negotiations and decisions that leads from managerial intent to organizational output? Direct management involves shaping and modifying this network of agreements to achieve desired outcomes. The manager has essentially three avenues for influencing the negotiated outcomes.

First, he can negotiate and influence decisions within the existing network. The manager's explicit negotiation and mediation are accompanied by tacit bargaining in the use of commands and the exercise and expansion of authority.

Second, he can attempt to change the network, for example, by implementing management systems. Such attempts frequently engender their own negotiations.

Finally, he can seek to influence others to place greater weight on common interests. If he succeeds, his preferred agreements will offer greater joint benefit and may thus become more likely.

We take up each avenue in turn. Many systems designed to gather information and control behavior pose a serious problem for managers that extends beyond the organizational context: those who have developed or otherwise possess information have an interest in the outcomes of decisions based on it. Thus they have an incentive to distort what they know. We examine bargaining in which this problem occurs, where knowledge and interest intermingle in management systems. We conclude the chapter by highlighting the evolutionary quality of agreements, systems, and precedents in organizations.

Negotiation, Mediation, Command, and Authority

Negotiation   In Chapter One, we showed how managers negotiate with subordinates to get things done. To further his purposes, a manager delegates parts of his mandate, and as our discussion of mandate negotiations makes clear, each element of the mandate is negotiable and, typically, renegotiable.

Mediation   Much like Chris Hubbard in Chapter Eight, a manager can help settle disputes among subordinates. Unlike traditional, supposedly neutral mediators who facilitate agreements, the manager-mediator generally has interests in the content of the agreement as well. And, he often has clout. In fact, the manager-mediator is a special kind of negotiator with an interest in the *fact* of agreement among his subordinates. He must weigh this interest against his interests in the *content* of their agreement.

Lawrence and Lorsch underscore the importance of the manager's role as mediator in a particular class of jobs that involves "resolving interdepartmental conflicts and facilitating decisions, including not only such major decisions as large capital investments, but also the thousands of smaller ones regarding product features, quality standards, output, cost targets, schedules, and so on."[1] They argue that this "definition reads much like the customary job description of any company general manager or divisional manager who has 'line' authority over all the major functional departments." But beyond general and divisional managers, many other positions involve

[1]Lawrence and Lorsch (1967a, 1967b).

integrating and coordinating without full authority, among a variety of departments—including production control people who resolve schedule conflicts between production and sales, budget officers who resolve interdepartmental conflicts over the allocation of funds, product managers, brand managers, program coordinators, planning directors, and so forth.

The existence of these "integrator" positions arises as an increasingly complex environment requires a specialization of tasks and skills. An integrator is needed to mediate among the specialists while directing their agreements to desired outcomes. Lawrence and Lorsch argue that the increasing rate of market and technological change is leading to a proliferation of such positions.

The manager as mediator can often help others on budget matters, career paths, and compensation. At the same time, his ongoing relationships with those he needs to influence restrict the range of his actions. A manager-mediator cares about his standing with those whom he coordinates: he needs to enhance and maintain his professional reputation and standing by mediating effectively, appearing fair, possessing expertise, and using information judiciously.

It is worth noting that our prescription to an integrator would not be to mediate merely by bringing conflicting parties together in a room to hash it out. As our prescription for Chris Hubbard and our more general negotiation analysis implies, mediation requires preparation, analysis of interests, alternatives, and possible agreements, as well as, sometimes, careful sequencing of meetings, and so on.

Commands   Explicit negotiation and mediation are often supplemented by commands, requests that function as commands, and the use of formal authority. Indeed, we have sometimes been told that the fact that managers give orders reduces the nature and importance of managerial negotiation. To the contrary, we argue that giving a command is a bargaining tactic, that authority generally derives from agreement, and that it is often changed by renegotiation.

In the bargaining range between superior and subordinate, a command is a take-it-or-leave-it offer, a commitment to a position. Like a take-it-or-leave-it offer, a command is sometimes taken or accepted. Acceptance can increase the credibility of subsequent commands. But, again like take-it-or-leave-it offers, commands can be left, ignored, or rejected.

When the subordinate does not comply with the command, the commander faces a tricky decision. She can back down and continue negotiating with her subordinate, probably damaging her credibility.

Or, she can back up the command by threatening sanctions; success-fully enforcing the command may bolster her credibility, reinforcing a pattern of obedience.

A crafty manager may pick his spots opportunistically: he may give orders on matters that hold little intrinsic value for him because he believes that the orders will be accepted and thereby improve his subsequent credibility; he may avoid giving commands that he sees as likely to be rejected. And there is often a fine line between a "sugges-tion," "request," "firm request," and "command"; the ambiguity is often deftly exploited by all sides to imply a commitment without some of the risks or to escape one without the costs.

Merely giving an order may evoke hostility or defensiveness and call into question the nature of a seemingly cooperative relationship. Even though explicit orders may be obeyed for a while, the benefits to the commander may be offset by a progressive tearing of the fabric of the relationship.[2]

Formal Authority   An explicit negotiation dance can be com-plex, time-consuming, and expensive. The manager who constantly engages in this dance, sharing information and exchanging pro-posals, can be afflicted by "bargaining overload." Thus managers should and do seek to reduce the costs of explicit negotiation.

As we have noted, there are several ways for a manager to reduce the costs of explicit bargaining. He can use current negotiations to establish precedents that will more efficiently settle future encoun-ters.[3] He may seek a reputation as a fearsome or effective bargainer, to whom it is better to acquiesce on matters of mutual concern. Or, he can develop particular expertise to which others defer.

The manager may strike an overarching agreement with a subor-dinate in which she grants him permission to make a range of deci-sions affecting her. The overarching agreement establishes a range, sometimes fuzzy, of acceptable commands. Within the range, a com-

[2]The alternative to the superior-subordinate agreement is merely what would happen otherwise; the *status quo ante*, a deterioration of relations, or merely contin-ued negotiation. The implicit threat of sanctions worsens a subordinate's alterna-tives. In principle, agreement at the ordered point should be more likely. But, by calling into question the nature of the relationship—evoking a latent interest—com-mands can make compliance worse for the subordinate than absorbing the sanc-tions. Sanctions may follow; conflict may escalate and the working relationship may be seriously impaired.

[3]The manager can sometimes introduce precedents into the organization's for-mal procedures and systems.

mand is likely to be accepted; negotiations can thus be concluded at small cost.

By this sort of agreement, the subordinate gives the superior the authority to decide or command. This brings us to what some might have expected to be the first topic in a book concerning managers: authority.[4]

If enough people tacitly or explicitly agree or think that a person has a right to make a certain class of decisions for them, then that person has the authority to make such decisions. Often giving such authority follows from an exchange among the parties. Early on, for example, we characterized the decision to join a firm as just such an exchange. A similar situation obtains when venture capital investors give management a grant of authority to invest money on their behalf.[5]

The authority relation between subordinate and superior often makes bargaining relatively costless. But having formal authority need not imply that exercising it will be effective. The civil servants may all believe that the Secretary of Commerce has authority to impose management control systems; yet such an authoritative command may never result in the successful implementation of information and control systems. Why? Because we are back to the uncertain effectiveness of take-it-or-leave-it offers (commands).[6]

The range of decisions over which formal rights are given in authority relations is rarely clear. It is often tested and tacitly renegoti-

[4]Precisely defining authority has been the subject of a long-standing, thorny intellectual debate that we do not propose to resolve. Rather, by examining the relationship between negotiation and one characterization of authority, we hope to illuminate the role of negotiation and agreement in the exercise, construction, and expansion of authority. The characterization of authority that we adopt is similar to Lindblom's (1977).

[5]Of course, giving someone the formal right to make certain decisions may follow from any of the ways that agreement might appear better than no agreement. In addition to exchange based on differences, the grant of authority may follow from shared interests or scale economies. Someone may be persuaded that the grant is in his interests, or, acculturation may shift his values to make the grant of authority desirable. Finally, agreeing to grant authority may follow from coercion, from threats to dramatically worsen an individual's no-agreement alternatives; this last category may be more prevalent in political settings and in economic relations with unskilled laborers but seems less important in dealings among managers. For a discussion of coercion and authority, see Lindblom (1977).

[6]It is more likely to be effective when the value of going along appears to exceed that of not going along. Going along will be more likely when: (1) the command falls clearly in the range of rights granted by the subordinate; (2) the command is not taken as an affront; (3) the threat of sanctions for noncompliance is credible; (4) role

ated by all parties. Successful exercise of authority—in tandem with a fuller range of negotiating tactics—may expand the range of decisions over which others act as if one has authority. As our discussion of mandates suggests, a manager can also negotiate directly with authorizing bodies to obtain greater grants of authority over specific decisions such as pricing, hiring, and firing.

In summary, agreements form the basis of authority, these agreements are frequently modified and renegotiated, and commands can be understood as bargaining moves.

Systems

We have characterized direct management as influencing the outcome of a network of linked negotiations. What gives structure to these negotiations?

To monitor and influence organizationally and geographically distant units; to monitor, motivate, and control the performance of managers; and to integrate the decisions of people in specialized positions, direct managers have a variety of systems at their disposal. Beyond control over the organization's structure and reporting relationships, management systems can include (1) a personnel management system that "recruits, selects, socializes, trains, rewards, punishes, and exits [sic] the organization's"[7] personnel; (2) information systems that include operating and capital budgets, accounts, reports and statistical systems, performance appraisals, product and program evaluations, audits, and quality controls; as well as (3) systems for strategy formulation and policy development.

Much has been written about how to design and manage such systems. By viewing management systems through a negotiation lens, we hope to shed some new light on an old and important subject and

---

conceptions and norms that one should obey authority are ingrained and salient. A failure to comply might call into question many of the aspects of the original agreement, thereby worsening both sides' no-agreement alternatives. As we have seen, this cuts both ways.

Acceptance of an authoritative order is by no means certain. Formal authority is but one of many means for affecting the outcomes of negotiations. Civil servants often have good no-agreement alternatives. Scientists control specialized knowledge. Control of material resources and information, strong allies and external constituencies, obligations from previous favors, ability to link issues and broker deals, and capacity to persuade and shape values all can affect bargained outcomes.

[7]Allison (1979).

to pose some new questions. First, we shall look at the ways that management systems structure negotiations. Second, we shall examine the often tacit negotiations involved in inducing someone to adopt and comply with a management system.

DIFFERENT MANAGEMENT SYSTEMS SET UP DIFFERENT NEGOTIATIONS

Different management systems create negotiations or affect negotiations by altering issues, interests, no-agreement alternatives, parties, and perceived links between issues and interests. As we noted in Chapter Nine, such changes in the game can dramatically alter the outcomes.

For example, think of the contrasts among the issues discussed and the parties present in Chapter Eight, where a zero-base budgeting system was adopted by a firm that had used incremental budgeting. In that situation, negotiations occurred among the department heads and their division head, then among division heads (likely with their director), and so on. The issues in the negotiations were rankings of proposed projects in each division. By comparison, managers engaged in incremental budgeting would discuss increments over last year's budget (the issues), and the negotiations might largely take the form of bilateral dealings between each department head and the relevant division head.

The choice of administrative system can affect which issues are linked and which will be separated. For example, the 1975 U.S.-Soviet grain deal might have been the province only of the Agriculture and State departments if it had occurred during a more centralized Presidency. In the "multiple advocacy" system of policy development used in the Ford White House, however, all Cabinet secretaries were given a formal voice on issues, whether or not the issues otherwise fell within their purview. Thus, a range of maritime and foreign policy issues that were nominally separated from the grain deal became linked to it for a time. As we discussed earlier, linking issues can facilitate joint gains from trade, logrolling, and synergy, but can also complicate what should be simple, clean agreements.[8]

---

[8]The interests and expertise represented can be affected by organizational structure. In a decentralized firm, each department head bargaining over the rights to produce and sell a revolutionary new technology, may see the issues as operational and evaluate the opportunity with respect to his own department's production and

And what are the no-agreement alternatives given the participants by the organization's structure and procedures? Do contested issues in negotiations among subordinates rise to superiors? If so, the "easy" issues may be settled first at lower levels. A subset of all the issues, predominantly ones with small or no zones of agreement on their own, will be kicked up to the next level. Thus, the potential for logrolling and joint gains from trade between easy and hard issues may well be lost when the superior confronts only the issues on which there is lower-level disagreement.

How are the different negotiations themselves linked? Must superiors "ratify" agreements by subordinates? If several layers of sequential ratification are required, this structure may induce the equivalent of organizational risk aversion. If there is a cost to the original proposer of her idea being turned down, and a long sequence of intermediate agreements are required for final "agreement," we would expect to see few proposals offered, fewer still accepted, and fewer of those on terms preferred by the originator. In short, this kind of organizational structure can produce timid employees at lower levels and considerable bureaucratic inertia.

CONFLICTS OVER THE IMPOSITION OF NEW SYSTEMS

To be useful in monitoring or coordinating, any system must be adopted by the relevant managers. The designers of such systems and, frequently, the system's advocates often presume that the authority relations existing in the organization are sufficient to ensure compliance with the system. Thus, information systems are frequently imposed by edict—a memo that goes out informing managers of their responsibilities in setting up and complying with a new system—and all too often are ignored. And, even when general cooperation is obtained, conflict over the specifics of required actions is frequent.

---

distribution capabilities. In an organization with a different structure, interests in the firm's *overall* strategy and the products' potential for synergy *across* the firm might be represented. Moreover, systems and organizational structure can create or induce interests. Merely being part of the production department, for instance, can heavily affect what one considers important. Having agreed to adopt a budgeting system, a manager may acquire an interest in convincing others to do the same and, instrumentally, in others' perceptions of its fairness. He may feel compelled to sacrifice other interests, at least to some degree, in order to enhance the perceived legitimacy and equity of the procedure.

Implementing a system can induce its own network of linked negotiations. Compliance with these systems can scarcely be taken for granted since managers must in effect agree to act in accord with them. Ignoring them completely may be a far preferable alternative. For example, the decision of a company president to adopt a zero-base budgeting system (see Chapter Eight) set in motion dealings between the president and the managing director, between the managing director and the division heads including Hubbard, between Hubbard and the department heads, and so on. In particular, Hubbard needed both to induce Nicholson to agree to adopt the system in the first place, as well as to negotiate with Dewing, Coulson, and others over the terms of the system.

Those hoping to implement such systems should thus ask a few simple questions: Who must agree to adopt the system? What are their interests in doing so? What are their alternatives to agreement? (The *status quo ante*? Sanctions for failure to comply? Merely being ordered to fill out the paperwork and go through the motions?) What private and common value will induce agreement? How can the value of agreement be enhanced or the value of no agreement worsened? When the negotiations cascade down the hierarchy, subordinates can be understood as one's bargaining agents. How can one help these agents in their negotiating task?

Knowledge and Interest Bargaining[9]

This difficulty with the adoption of management systems raises an important question: Why do those who resist feel that their interests are better served by not complying in part or at all? When managers are asked to provide information and forecasts that will serve as targets for their performance and then will later serve as the basis for rewards and punishments, they have an incentive not to provide the information or to distort it (often to set easily exceeded targets). More generally, since those with knowledge often have an interest in the outcomes of decisions that will be based on that knowledge, they may use their positions to influence the decisions favorably by selectively providing or withholding information.

---

[9]Arthur Applbaum has highlighted the importance of the many situations in which one party's knowledge, if shared, would change another party's valuation of possible agreements and no-agreement alternatives.

That good managers constantly seek to acquire information of all sorts is not news.[10] It may not be clear which discrete decisions, if any, the information will aid. Rather, the paths that lead from individual action to organizational outcome are often quite uncertain and unexpected. Unanticipated shocks can change a manager's understandings. Thus, snippets of information, facts, forecasts, and gossip help a manager piece together a complex and shifting mosaic, an understanding that is consistent with available data. In almost all encounters, therefore, managers have an interest in gathering information, in learning.

But, managers as negotiators need both to learn and to do well for themselves. The tension between these dual needs becomes more complex when bargainers hope to learn the real connections between their actions and desired outcomes, in addition to learning about the others' interests. Because others have knowledge that might affect how a bargainer values the possible outcomes and no-agreement alternatives, those with such knowledge can use it to their advantage.

Because most managers who are asked to comply with information systems face this apparent incentive to use proprietary knowledge to advantage, we expect the information generated by many management information systems to be of poor quality. Negotiations over who gets a bigger budget are often carried out as "factual" discussions about the returns from various investment strategies. Or, a manager's forecasts of next month's sales are carefully chosen to be less than his real expectations. In general, the organizational processes intended to generate knowledge cannot easily be separated from those that confer relative advantage.

Knowledge and interest can be sufficiently entangled that some information-gathering systems provide essentially no information. Consider capital budgeting decisions in a firm whose experience is not uncommon. To get a new project funded, a manager presents extensive analyses and projections that estimate the project's expected rate of return. The capital budgeting review committee is reputed to reject projects whose estimated rates of return are below some known threshold and to seriously question projects with forecasted returns much higher than the threshold. Unsurprisingly, the committee thus receives an array of interesting projects, all with essentially the same predicted rate of return. At its grand culmination, the complex system of gathering and analyzing information provides the capital

[10]See Kotter (1985), Mintzberg (1973), Neustadt (1980).

budgeting review committee with little real information. In practice, therefore, the committee does not distinguish between projects on the basis of forecasted rate of return but rather, decisions to fund depend on the track record or credibility of the individual proposing the project.

Bower's advice, after his detailed study of resource allocation, was consistent with the committee's actions: trust people and not information.[11] Yet this reliance on managers' past performance has several undesirable ramifications. Often, short-term information does not tell much about long-term success. Managers with short time horizons may act risk prone because they expect to have moved on long before the actual results will be in and their performance reliably assessed. Or, because a good *decision* leading to a bad *outcome* could drastically reduce a manager's credibility, managers may become extremely risk-averse in choosing which projects to submit. If so, they may suppress projects that the committee would have been willing to fund. In general, a committee's reliance on each manager's credibility when it makes capital budgeting decisions leaves the committee vulnerable to all sorts of opportunistic behavior by project sponsors.

The apparent opportunism may be only partially intentional. In Chapter Three, we counseled negotiators to "anticipate inflated perceptions of no-agreement alternatives." Recall Raiffa's experiment in which students and executives were given a firm's financial data and then asked to estimate the true value of the firm.[12] Those assigned the role of buyer estimated substantially lower values than those chosen to be sellers while those assigned no role estimated values in between. Advocates who provide self-serving information may have similarly biased perceptions.

For example, a key concern during the 1975 negotiations with the Soviet Union over a possible grain sale was the possible effect of a grain sale on inflation. The analyses of the Agriculture Department, whose constituents strongly supported the sale, unsurprisingly predicted minimal effects on inflation. The analyses of the Wage and Price Stabilization Committee, whose chief concern was fighting inflation, predictably forecast a substantial increase in inflation.[13] Separating the opportunism from the natural biases of advocates would have been quite difficult.

[11]Bower (1972).

[12]Raiffa (1982).

[13]See Roger Porter (1980).

Systems for strategy formulation or policy development, intended to provide and develop informed judgment about the outside environment and the organization's capacity, are often similarly afflicted. Because those involved in negotiations over such issues often have tremendous amounts at stake, opportunistic behavior is common.

GETTING RELIABLE INFORMATION

How can a manager get reliable information from systems intended to generate it? The concerned manager should reframe the question: How can I get others to *agree* to provide good information and unbiased judgment? Others will agree to do this if the apparent value of doing so exceeds that of not complying. Thus, the manager can try to improve the lure of compliance or decrease the lure of the no-agreement alternative. She can try to increase the value others place on the organization's success relative to what seems to be in their own individual interest.

In principle, she might monitor the others' forecasts and actions, and punish those who are not providing good data. If monitoring increases the perceived chances that noncompliance will be detected, the no-agreement alternatives become worse relative to providing good information. Moreover, providing information is only one facet of the ongoing give-and-take between the manager and her subordinates. If that manager can detect both self-serving reports and omissions, then the subordinate may avoid these practices in order to elicit the manager's later cooperation. Unfortunately, effective monitoring is typically quite difficult. The event of interest may take place much later and a great deal can happen in the meantime that reduces one's ability to tie actions to outcomes.

Some managers ruthlessly hold subordinates to short-term forecasts regardless of mitigating circumstances. Placing this risk on the subordinates may well improve performance by increasing their efforts to control the manageable risks, but also, this practice may encourage them to set conservative targets. Ensuring realistic targets then becomes the problem, but doing so, ironically, requires managers to develop the knowledge they sought in the first place.

Creating properly controlled conflict and competition can sometimes yield good information. Franklin Roosevelt strengthened his subordinates' incentives to provide reliable information by his pattern of setting a number of aides—unbeknownst to each other, in any specific case—after the same story or facts.

Conflicts in organizations sometimes follow from differences in judgment. If the disputants must try to persuade a superior of the merits of their positions, the process may generate considerable information. For example, transfer pricing rules that generate conflict between division managers may generate valuable information if resolution requires each manager to prepare substantial documentation of his arguments and to take the dispute to a superior.[14] In certain parts of IBM, disagreements about budgets rise successively through the organization until they are settled; the disagreement can help inform higher-level managers. The conflicting responsibilities of managers in matrix organizations may have similar effects.

Further, managers can create "agents" with an interest in getting good information: outside auditors, consultants, and strategic planners often play this role. Indeed, some firms have staff people who make their own forecasts and push line managers to be more realistic about projections (and, sometimes, more ambitious in their goals).

Top managers may also seek to foster interests in and widespread normative justification for providing high-quality analysis. Perceptions that the knowledge-generating systems work fairly over time may help. Executives may make sacrifices on strategic and substantive interests in order to bolster their interests in the successful working of strategy formulation and policy development systems. The consequence of neglecting these systems may be a diminished capacity to generate reliable information.

For example, the chairman of the board of a state-owned steel corporation favored a major capital investment for external political reasons although he would have to justify the decision to the board on purely economic grounds. The planning department's implicit mandate was to perform high-quality but narrow financial analyses that did not factor in political considerations. The planners' preliminary financial analyses did not favor the investment. Because of the mismatch between his actual interests and ostensible decision criteria, the chairman pressured the planners into juggling the numbers in their report to the board. By savaging the planning department's reputation for fairness and technical quality, he demoralized the planners and diminished the future information-generating capacity of

[14]See Eccles (1985).

the policy development process. Its functioning became straightforward: "find out what the chairman wants and argue for it."[15] To prevent strategy formulation systems from merely justifying top managers' impulses, executives have a strong interest in enhancing general perceptions of the fairness and quality expectations of these systems.

Shaping Values

Personnel systems and a range of top management actions are sometimes intended to shape perceptions and values. It follows from our earlier observations (Chapters Six and Nine) that if all of a firm's managers give greater weight to a shared interest such as the success of the firm, a common goal like "customer service," or even to a collectively preferred process for handling certain issues, managers may be able to find more joint gains in their internal negotiations. From top management's perspective, this makes both agreements and favorable outcomes more likely. Top management's attempts to shift values to common precepts or norms of behavior may be effective in influencing agreements even when they do not affect managers' valuations. These norms and precepts may still serve as focal points and thus yield favorable outcomes (from top management's standpoint).[16] It is worth noting that these sorts of changes are probably difficult to realize, slow to take effect, and difficult to change once established.

Attempts to shape perceptions and values may follow a systematic plan; many organizations pay careful attention to socializing "recruits" into the corporate or agency's culture. More ad hoc means for this often present themselves in the context of administering one or another management system. In Chapter Eight, for example, Chris Hubbard did not take the opportunity to "teach" his subordinates about the appropriate way to handle budget negotiations—by strong reference to firm strategy and to the PRB system.[17]

[15]Similarly, the CEO at a major U.S. bank was once known to believe that interest rates would fall. Despite scepticism elsewhere, the bank's economists almost unanimously predicted declining interest rates. Planning and major decisions on the basis of these assumptions resulted in enormous losses when interest rates shot up.

[16]See Kreps (1984).

Evolutionary Nature of the Negotiated Order in Organizations

Finally, it is important to emphasize the evolutionary nature of systems, procedures, and structure. Although they configure bargaining, these formal administrative tools are typically brought into existence and changed by negotiation. Procedural and substantive precedents may be intended or unintended by-products of negotiations. For example, the way that the first budget request of a certain type is handled may set a precedent for the handling of similar subsequent requests. This precedent may gradually become formalized and incorporated into the budgeting system. And, when the joint benefits of linkage across areas are considerable, these linkages may well become institutionalized in the structure of the organization or its management systems.

In a study of hospital administration, sociologist Anselm Strauss and his colleagues describe how informally negotiated rules, procedures, and policies eventually become a major part of the hospital "structure."[18] Subsequently, they make use of the concept of a "negotiated order." Their findings are fully compatible with ours: systems and structure configure bargaining; bargaining affects systems; and everything evolves.

Summary

This chapter has assumed a negotiation perspective to examine the problems of direct management: the tight links between negotiation, mediation, command, and authority; production through systems of agreements; the special quandary resulting from the conflict between revealing generally useful knowledge and distorting it for reasons of individual interest; the possibilities and reasons for shaping values in organizations; and how the "negotiated order" evolves.

*   *   *

[17]Peters (1978) suggests a variety of ways that managers can signal their concerns and shape values: careful praise of actions they favor, singling out analyses that just happen to support major concerns, random but careful probes of subordinates' work that signal "how we deal with things" and indicate the sort of understanding of issues that is expected of managers up and down the line.

[18]See Anselm Strauss et al. (1963).

In our investigation of the manager's job so far, we have looked at mandates and direct production. The simplest mandate situation is that of a principal working out purposes, resources, authority, and expectations with an agent. Likewise, the simplest possible direct management arrangement is that between a principal (the manager) and her agent (the subordinate who is to produce). In fact, entire complex organizations can be interpreted as linked principal-agent units. Thus, the negotiation side of this important relationship deserves a closer look. That is the task of Chapter Fifteen.

Agents and Ratification

IN VIRTUALLY ANY management situation, negotiations are carried out by someone who acts as an agent for his or her division, immediate superior, or the organization at large. Thus far we have seen the relevance of the agency relationship to negotiations over mandates and direct production. Sometimes the situation virtually dictates that an agent be used. An ambassador negotiates on behalf of the President and, ultimately, as an agent of the Senate. In contract talks, a bargaining agent or union official represents the rank and file, whose vote ultimately determines whether an agreement is reached. And the company's board of directors is represented by an industrial relations official or another corporate "agent."

At other times, one has a choice as to whether or not to engage an agent to carry out negotiations on one's behalf.[1] This decision is often a vexing one. This chapter looks closely at negotiations through agents, focusing particular attention on the potential benefits and costs of various ways that agents can be used.

---

[1]We could have chosen to treat this topic, as in Chapter Nine, as a case of "adding" parties to negotiations.

When Does an Agent Further a Principal's Interests? In his "principle of similarity," Stephen Ross suggested a criterion for the ideal agent: a principal should want an agent to act in any situation exactly as would the principal.[2] A perfect agent is thus an extension, a surrogate, or a clone of the principal. Beyond identical action in a setting in which the principal could not or chose not to place herself, there are numerous reasons why a principal might choose to employ an agent. A principal might believe that an agent is simply "better" at bargaining. The agent may be thought to be more familiar with the subject at hand: a tax lawyer might be the right choice for a complex tax deal or a real estate agent for a building negotiation. In each of these cases, the agent might also be more familiar with the norms and expectations that govern such interactions. The agent may also know the opposing parties (or their agents), though this need not be beneficial.

Though the principal may want an agent who satisfies this "similarity" criterion, an agent with *different* incentives or interests from those of the principal may sometimes be preferable. For example, suppose that an insurance company lawyer is bargaining on behalf of his client, a defendant in a personal-injury suit. Compared to the client, the lawyer may be more convincingly able to reject a high settlement demand lest his reputation as a firm bargainer be diminished for a whole stream of unrelated future cases. A client may hire a longtime Washington lawyer precisely because the lawyer has important relationships and a number of favors owed to him by the parties with whom the client wants to strike some sort of deal.

One of the most common reasons to engage a bargaining agent is that the agent's authority may be limited with respect to making certain concessions or types of agreements. In this way, the agent may be able to resist proposals that the principal would find harder to turn down. One of the most common pleas of U.S. diplomats is "don't tie the hands of the negotiators." Yet it may be precisely because their hands *are* tied that they can resist otherwise barely acceptable proposals and, perhaps, do better. As we have elaborated in Chapter Six, the ability to restrict oneself can be a great source of bargaining strength. Agents can provide a helpful device for this purpose. Of course, the mechanism for limiting an agent's actions need not be a lack of delegated authority; if the agent is paid on a contingent basis,

---

[2]See Ross (1973,1974). For a useful discussion from an economic viewpoint of the agency relationship in organizations see Pratt and Zeckhauser (1985).

with a sharp increase in her percentage share at some level of settlement, her aspiration level may be visibly and convincingly increased.

By remaining unavailable and incommunicado and dealing through an agent, a principal may be able to commit to a position more effectively than if he were available to the other side. Of course, such a stance risks the other side's making a prior commitment. It may also engender a spiteful, if irrational, response. And should an agent make a commitment that turns out to be ill-advised, the principal may choose to dismiss the agent as a handy means of escaping the inauspiciously frozen position. For example, the lawyer for a plaintiff in a large personal injury case made a "rock bottom" final offer to the defendant, which was definitively refused. Rather than being stuck going to court, the principal was able to fire his counsel and replace him with another that "committed" to a "bedrock bottom" offer (that was accepted and was preferable to court).

If an agent is able to secure an agreement from the other side, this fact in itself may convey valuable information to the principal who can infer that the other side's reservation price is some distance from the agreement point. The principal may then find some pretext to increase his settlement demands. Just such actions are common—albeit often as a product of different forces—when a U.S. ambassador brings back a signed treaty for Senate ratification. Frequently, the Senate then sends the diplomat back to negotiate for advantageous changes. Since the other countries have revealed that the signed document was worth at least something to them over their alternatives, there is presumably some room left for changes before an unacceptable point is reached. Of course, foreign experience with such "salami tactics" may prompt them to hold out for more on the first round in the expectation that subsequent concessions will be demanded of them. (This technique can also occur in negotiations without agents. For example, when Dom Mintoff, the Prime Minister of Malta, was negotiating with Britain for an increase in rental payments for NATO use of his island's naval facilities, he became somewhat infamous for the "yes, but" technique. Each time the British thought they had a deal at a new, higher rent, Mintoff would add a new demand. That the British had been willing to settle at the previously set level told Mintoff that, to them, there was still something more to be extracted. Though this hardly endeared him to the British, it did result in a quadrupling of the rent.)[3]

---

[3]Wriggens (1976).

Not only is it common for an agent to be used as a means for finding out valuable information about the other side, the agent may be kept in the dark about, or forbidden to reveal, crucial information about his principal. Thus the principal's real reservation price or relative issue valuation may be concealed—sometimes a distinct advantage in seeking to claim value.

We have observed that interests in being seen as "nice" in the immediate relationship may exert a pull during a face-to-face encounter. Sometimes this is desirable, but in other instances, a negotiator may decide that such responses could be detrimental to more important interests. The use of an agent less prone to such reactions may avoid this "problem." A classic, if unsavory, example is in the use of collection agencies to obtain payment from unfortunate debtors whose pleas might sway the actual creditors in a personal interaction. In like manner, a person with tendencies to become belligerent, insulting, or enraged during a negotiation may want to hire a cooler agent. Similarly, if there has been a long history of bad relations and conflict between the principals to a negotiation, the use of agents may be a good means of "shearing" these undesirable attributes from the dealings. For example, two constantly warring siblings faced with a negotiation over a large inheritance may have their lawyers work things out. Finally, a sports star may use an agent during contract talks to be extremely tough on money issues. If an agreement results, the star will be able to join the team unburdened by direct residue from the brutal distributive bargain over salary. This may facilitate a better relationship with the team's management.

When Does an Agent Work Against a Principal's Interests? Ironically, just as the differences between a principal and her agent may be used to advantage, the asymmetries often result in undesirable agent actions. One of the most common pitfalls in protracted negotiations is for the agents to become more committed to the *fact* of an agreement than to its contents. Though the sunk costs of long bargaining and the relationships built up with the other sides ("going native") may be irrelevant to the principal, they may lead the engaged agent to seek "something" to show for the labor.

The desire to ensure that an agreement is reached may even lead the agent to withhold information that, if known to the principal, might impede a deal. Months of delicate negotiations over the British Steel Corporation's purchase of a huge "direct reduction" iron pelletizing plant were coming up against a deadline imposed by Korf, the West German construction firm that was selling it. Since British Steel's negotiating agent thought that this deadline would spur his company to a final deal-closing concession, he *never conveyed* Korf's last minute offer to extend the deadline. Though the sale went through, it was possibly on worse terms for British Steel than otherwise might have been available.

It need not be a bad thing for an agent to understand and even to identify with the interests of the other side. Take the case, discussed in Chapter Three, of the Washington lawyer who represented a group of states in a negotiation with the federal government for an out-of-court settlement of a long-standing dispute over billions of dollars of expended funds. The lawyer actually performed a role somewhat between a mediator and a double agent. When dealing with the feds, he was a strong advocate for the state's point of view. When he dealt with his own group of state clients, however, he forcefully presented federal concerns and interests. As a conduit for understanding and a strong prod to each side for a settlement, the lawyer served as a catalyst for a $543 million settlement that had eluded the parties for years and with which they and the Congress were pleased. Especially where the different parties to a negotiation have complex internal dealings and relationships, this mediator-double agent role for a bargaining agent is quite common. In fact, middle managers often find themselves in an analogous situation when dealing back and forth with superiors and subordinates. (We examine this role in depth in Chapter Seventeen.)

It is extremely common, however, for an agent's incentives to run counter to the principal's interests. Suppose that a lawyer is paid on an hourly basis until a trial and at a higher rate for each day in court. What will be her incentives to reach an early out-of-court settlement? Consider a merger negotiation in which the investment bankers are paid on an hourly basis if there is no deal but a percentage of the sale price if a deal results. Such arrangements are likely to result in more frequent but less advantageous mergers than if the bankers' incentives were lined up more perfectly with those of their principals.

Or contemplate the incentives of a lawyer paid on a contingency basis for an out-of-court settlement negotiation. Though it might seem that the incentives are identical to those of his client—each profits more from a higher settlement—there may still be divergencies. Say that the lawyer is considerably more prone to take risks than the client. Hoping for a better settlement, the lawyer might strongly, if tacitly, discourage an offer that the principal would be delighted to accept. Or say that the lawyer has a strong interest in building a reputation as a winner of high settlements. Though the client may not in the least care about counsel's subsequent reputation, the lawyer may take actions to enhance it that risk the present client's interests. An international consultant who used to represent numerous developing countries in their mineral contract negotiations sought a reputation of winning extremely favorable terms for his clients. Though the deals that he concluded were exceptionally lucrative, his tough tactics resulted in enough impasses (where agreements on somewhat more modest terms seemed possible) that other countries became somewhat leery of engaging him. Of course, that did not salvage the lost time for his earlier clients whose negotiations came to naught.

Suppose that an agent does not or cannot know his principal's real bottom line or reservation price. This could be the case for an ambassador who must submit any treaty to the Senate for approval, a union bargaining agent whose deal comes up for rank-and-file vote, or a corporate official who negotiates a contract and gives it to his board of directors. Since agents in such situations inherently cannot know whether or not certain agreements will be approved, they must make probabilistic judgments. In many instances, the higher the uncertainty about what their principal bodies will approve and the higher the agent's own risk aversion, the higher will be their own bottom lines in the negotiation. Though such behavior may result in more favorable settlements some of the time, in other cases the agent who holds out for more than the principal body might accept is risking an impasse where agreements on lesser terms might be desirable.[4] A body of psychological experimentation suggests that, when representing constituent bodies, bargainers tend to behave less flexibly than they would otherwise.[5]

The reverse situation may come about as well. The owner of an apartment building in which a fire occurred started negotiating with her insurance company for a settlement. After one negotiating session, she felt that a professional fire adjuster might do better and engaged one on a contingency basis. Though a settlement was quickly reached and accepted, it did not seem to be on very advantageous terms. Investigation after the fact revealed that there was a very small number of such fire adjusters and that they all dealt on a continuing basis with representatives of insurance companies. Rather

[4]See Lax and Sebenius (1983).
[5]See, e.g., Bacharach and Lawler (1981).

than press for the best deal for each client, these men nurtured an ongoing relationship with the insurors. An agent without such an interest may well have been preferable for the apartment owner.

Agency and Ratification   Though the foregoing discussion largely considered the promise and peril of using an agent from the principal's viewpoint, it is worth looking through the eyes of an agent. Then the negotiation changes since the principal must ratify the results. As discussed above, such a requirement may be a source of strength in enabling certain demands or suggestions to be resisted more easily. Of course, such a situation risks the other side's concluding that the agent is without enough authority and seeking to deal directly with the principal.

For the same reasons that an agent may prove advantageous to a principal, a negotiator may wish to "create" the real or apparent requirement of ratification; that is, he may wish to have or feign a principal. Notice that the requirement of approval or ratification automatically places one in the position of agent. In some cases, the "principal" may be someone brought along to the negotiating sessions. The venerable "good guy–bad guy" routine, wherein one member of a negotiating team is conciliatory while the other is hard and demanding, sets up a dynamic of ratification at the negotiating table itself. (The good guy may seek to create joint value with the other side while the bad guy may look after the more one-sided claiming.) And a negotiator may pretend to have more limited authority than in fact is the case in order to elicit information from the other side while pleading inability to reciprocate.

Thus, the agency relationship is ubiquitous in bargaining situations. Agents may be used because they are thought to be more skilled or familiar with the subject matter. They may have or be given different incentives that enable them to resist demands, make commitments, or escape them more effectively than their principals. They may be used to flush out valuable information about the other side while concealing or simply not knowing analogous information about their principals. They may bring desirable incentives, interests, or attributes to the bargaining or they may prevent undesirable qualities of their principals from asserting themselves in face-to-face sessions.

Yet the advantages of these differences between principals and agents may also entail risks. Agents, acting in accord with their own interests, may consciously or unconsciously subvert the interests of their principals. When considering "adding" a party to the negotiations in the form of an agent, a principal should scrutinize the agent's real interests, incentives, attitude toward risk, and outside relationships. A divergence may spell trouble. And, of course, when one is negotiating as a principal, the option of "creating" the requirement of ratification by some entity is equivalent to becoming an agent, with all the associated potential and perils.

*   *   *

We have found the agency relationship important in explicit, acknowledged negotiations with parties outside the organization. Likewise, we have seen its role in mandate and direct production settings. It will scarcely be surprising that it pervades the problems of indirect management as well, a subject to which we now turn.

CHAPTER SIXTEEN

Negotiating in Networks: Indirect Management

TEXTBOOKS URGE that authority be carefully matched to responsibility, that control and accountability dovetail. In this chapter we examine the increasingly common situation where this match does not hold and often cannot hold, where managers bear responsibility for production that is carried out through organizations or units that they do not directly "control."[1] In such cases of "indirect management," the importance of the manager-as-negotiator dramatically increases.

We have characterized indirect management situations as those in which authority and resources are diffused among many people while accountability is relatively concentrated. Product managers, those who must rely on the efforts of autonomous departments or others who have some independence—inside the firm or out—as well as many public sector managers constantly face this challenge. With the rise of complexity and interdependence, with increasing professionalization, with heavier emphasis on the role of information, with new

---

[1]Many have carefully described this state of affairs and offered analytic generalizations about it. See footnote 11 in Chapter One for references to authors who have discussed this management situation in various public and private settings.

organizational forms, and with the continuing decline in the automatic acceptance of formal authority, indirect managerial skills promise to be ever more necessary.

In this chapter, we discuss the extent and nature of indirect management and suggest two complementary approaches to it. First, one can try to restructure the situation itself, to bring authority and accountability more into alignment, thus making the problem less "indirect." Sometimes, however, individual managers have no way to do this. Still, it is often possible for a manager to alter elements of the mandate, renegotiating purposes, authority, resources, and expectations. A second broad approach is for the manager to make the most of a given indirect management situation, and simply produce results more effectively within its constraints.

Extent and Nature of Indirect Management

Earlier, we discussed a federal official who was responsible for increasing the fire safety of nursing homes in Massachusetts. A state agency has jurisdiction over the fire inspections he is seeking. To get these inspections carried out, his actions must reach across organizational and jurisdictional lines.

The traditional direct managerial tools and systems are inaccessible to him. He has little or nothing to do with the state agencies; their budgeting processes; or rewards, punishments, and other aspects of their employees' career paths. In short, if he seeks their "agreement" to carry out these inspections, his ability to manipulate their alternatives to such agreements is extremely limited. But the federal official's political and organizational superiors hold him accountable for achieving this result. Should there be a disaster in such a federally funded nursing home, he would be held responsible by members of the legislature, the victims, the general public, elements of the media, and, quite conceivably, the courts.

This situation—where authority and resources for given tasks are shared, but accountability seems to be concentrated—characterizes indirect management situations. In other words, the federal official's degree of direct "control" is less than his degree of direct "accountability." We now examine the extent and nature of indirect management before discussing two general approaches to it.[2]

---

[2]In the last sentence, quotation marks enclosed the term "control." The concept has problems even in the most traditional, hierarchical organization. As we have

The most stark instances of indirect management occur when production must be carried out by organizations across jurisdictional lines.[3] In the Aid to Families with Dependent Children program, members of Congress hold the Department of Health and Human Services strictly accountable for the so-called error rate (of overpayments and welfare disbursements to "ineligible" persons). Yet state and local welfare departments determine eligibility and actually dispense the money. The operation of their management systems ultimately determines the error rate.[4] Environmental officials responsible for reducing pollution must "produce" the reduction through the efforts of private firms. Similar situations can be found with respect to a variety of health, education, welfare, and other programs.[5]

Production that takes place across organizational boundaries is equally common. When an organization decides not to "make" something but rather to "buy" it, the managerial systems involved in the "seller's" production are often out of the buyer's reach. This lack of control is unimportant when the object being procured is easy to specify and the contract is simple to enforce. But for procured "products" like research, services such as consulting or accounting, "rehabilitation" of ill or disturbed persons, or complex weapons systems, even specifying performance requirements—let alone the designs—can be difficult. The inaccessibility of management systems to the procuring entity can become a problem, especially when the buyer is completely accountable for the result. A similar situation holds for all sorts of regulation (for example, with respect to air safety, occupational health, or drug safety) in which a public agency has responsibility for the result, but the production of those "goods" is carried out by other organizations.

Hale Champion's experience points to an explosion of indirect managerial situations. When he was Budget Director of the Califor-

---

noted, the view that authority relations and management control systems "control" or "determine" organizational outputs with certainty is quite misleading given extensive discretion, conflicting interests of the parties throughout the organization, difficulties of monitoring and enforcement, and a host of other influential factors (expertise, access to information, powerful external allies, and the like). We highlight this point to put the reader on notice that, though we now draw an apparently sharp distinction between direct and indirect management in terms of control, the demarcation ultimately blurs. We return to this point later.

[3]That is, across legally defined boundaries, such as federal versus state versus municipal agencies.

[4]See Brodkin (1983).

[5]See Elmore (1978), Ingram (1977), or Elmore and Williams (1976).

nia state government in the 1960s, for example, he administered a $6 billion budget and 145,000 state employees. This contrasts starkly with his stint as Undersecretary of the federal Department of Health, Education and Welfare (HEW) in the 1970s. There, the number of federal employees was also 145,000, but some $200 billion were being spent. Often, these employees were not directly producing anything, but instead were supervising others, dealing intergovernmentally, and contracting with private firms and providers.

Within HEW itself, a "New Deal" program such as Social Security, a classic, directly managed agency, had some 80,000 federal employees. It was a paper culture, systems oriented, and directly responsible for its output. By contrast, a "Great Society" program, such as the Health Care Financing Administration (HCFA) also picked up about 80,000 paychecks. Only 4000 of them, however, were directly issued as part of the federal payroll. While Social Security might be characterized as a kind of marine corps, HCFA could be likened to a street gang in terms of the complexity of its "indirect" management.

Indeed, as Frederick Mosher points out in a carefully argued study, "in decades gone by, most of what the federal government was responsible for and expended money for it did by itself through its own personnel and facilities. Consequently, much of the doctrine and lore of federal management, like that of private enterprise, was based on the premises that its efficiency rested on the effective supervision and direction of its own operations." Mosher surveys the very dramatic changes in federal operations, and concludes that only about 5 percent to 7 percent of the federal budget is now allotted to domestic activity that the federal government performs itself. The challenge of this sea change in public management is immense since most of these activities "fall beyond the limits of the traditional controls, budget, and personnel, that we have inherited from our forebears."[6]

Similar situations occur when a manager is responsible for producing something but depends on peers or parallel units. For example, product managers or "integrators" in private firms must shepherd their projects through many organizational units and coax agreement and coordination from them, but without the line authority that is traditionally associated with production responsibility.

Or, recall the case of the Bob Furz who "sold" a new South American strategy to world headquarters in London. With the go-

[6]Mosher (1980).

ahead, he became accountable for the results. London granted him nominal control over the various other South American country operations in that each country manager had to report to him. Though he was given authority over their pricing and manufacturing policies, he did not gain the right to make decisions with respect to compensation, hiring and firing of personnel, country organizational structures, or within-country budget processes. His problem is identical to the more stark, public situations.

As organizations have taken novel forms, becoming "flatter," involving matrix concepts, and the like, the ease of applying traditional notions of accountability has declined. Paul Lawrence and Jay Lorsch noted that the rapid rate of market and technological change has placed accompanying strains and stresses on existing organizational forms and has prompted increasing concern with the difficulty of reconciling the need for specialization with the need for integration of effort. They go on to describe the need for functions and even departments of "integration."[7] As these trends intensify, we can expect a blurring of traditional notions of control, thus requiring much more indirect management within organizations.[8]

IMPLICATIONS FOR INDIRECT MANAGERS

What does a situation of shared authority and resources but concentrated accountability mean for managers? At a minimum, it calls for tools beyond those of traditional administration. Formal author-

[7]See Lawrence and Lorsch (1967a,b).

[8]We do not equate indirect management with all situations in which a manager is responsible for performance that depends on some exogenous, uncontrollable uncertainty. What is critical is that the manager is accountable but shares authority and resources necessary for production. A number of cases make the difference clear. Sometimes, the organizational *outputs* produced, such as fire-safety inspections or deployment of police officers, differ from the social or economic *outcomes* of interest (fire and public safety). Similarly, a firm may have a production line efficiently going and may complete an advertising campaign as planned. The outcomes of interest (actual purchases by consumers and generation of revenue), however, inherently lie beyond the direct control of the managers. Similarly, profit or cost centers (wherein groups of managers are held responsible for revenues or costs) may involve some controllable costs, but other costs depend on exogenous events such as crops, interest rates, consumer spending patterns, or the weather. To the extent that managers in these sorts of situations are held accountable for the ultimate outcomes, as opposed to their organizational outputs, a very much larger class of management seems to have "indirect" qualities.

In some of these cases, the approaches we develop are more or less applicable. However, if extension of traditional management systems and/or organizational

ity will be insufficient, commands will go unheeded, management systems will be inaccessible, and organizational culture will not flow across boundaries. Instead, the manager must create and modify networks of linked decisions and agreements. But this carries several implications.

Managers depend on "outsiders" for results. Consequently, managerial jobs are thus defined more by the required network of agreements than by organizational boundaries. In fact, this observation renders less interesting the old conundrum of just where the organization "stops." An indirect manager who stops where her organization does cannot do her job.

Sometimes, the required networks of linked agreements and decisions are not fully "inside" any set of organizations. In these cases, the network's porosity and visibility will open them to many of the pressures that are often associated with legislatures. Interest groups, regional organizations, legislators, as well as other local, state, and private entities may seek to intrude on indirect managerial processes that would have been invisible had they been carried out "inside" organizations. Moreover, the obvious discretion associated with indirect managerial activities invites review by courts and administrative law judges.

WHEN OLD EXPECTATIONS ACCOMPANY INDIRECT MANAGERIAL JOBS

When old notions of accountability are superimposed on newer structures of shared authority and resources, the involved managers will almost certainly bear an increased risk of failing to meet expectations.[9]

The "mismatch" of authority and responsibility does have some advantages. All organizations face uncertain events and risks. Some

---

boundaries could not conceivably have affected the outcomes for which the managers are held responsible, we would not generally find it useful to consider such situations as indirect management. Similarly, a number of public policies such as loan guarantees or tax expenditures clearly are intended to produce results by decentralized means. Although the organizational systems of the entities that are supposed to respond to such policies lie far beyond the "control" of public managers, accountability for the results should fall more directly on the policy design itself rather than on the relatively passive managers. Though these situations are significant, we will not discuss them in the context of indirect management.

[9]Some of their actions will deserve scrutiny on procedural and technical grounds. But, increasingly, in relatively diffuse indirect dealings in the public sector,

are natural, others involve the actions of different organizations, the public, consumers, and the like. Some of these uncertainties and risks can be controlled or affected by managers. For example, a determined marketing campaign may result in much greater sales; a publicity campaign might result in more members of the public being immunized against particular diseases.

Yet it is very difficult, especially from "above" or "outside," to determine how much of the result can be attributed to managerial action and how much is beyond its control. If responsibility for particular outcomes is fixed on certain managers, a sense of unfairness and frequent disappointment may occur.[10] Nonetheless, in such situations the controllable risks are more likely to be controlled. Inability to distinguish what is controllable from what is not and the need to motivate action may conspire to fix responsibility on specific managers when a more "objective" analysis might suggest that this is unrealistic.

In the public sector, however, popular images of and belief in control and certainty are widespread and essential to political promising. Similarly virile claims of being fully "in control" and "completely responsible" for the bottom line are prevalent and useful in the private sector. Thus, managers will likely continue to find themselves sharing authority and resources while remaining highly accountable.

Unfortunately, expectations based on assumptions of total control will be disappointed where the reality of the situation is one of indirect management. We can expect weaker results from these "indirect" sitautions. Managers' frustration and disillusionment with such situations can exacerbate the problem. General disillusionment based on unrealistic expectations about government performance can ultimately affect governability.

Approaches to Indirect Management

Apart from yearning for the old hierarchy, we see two broad approaches to the challenge of indirect management.

---

managers will effectively make choices among conflicting values. That is, they will act in political rather than purely technical capacities. Yet, legal and political accountability will frequently be on far narrower grounds. Thus, many managerial choices will involve more personal and career risks. Or, risk aversion and obviously "inadequate" authority and resources will be the excuses when very little gets done.

[10]As well as inefficient risk bearing.

SEEKING A BETTER MATCH
OF AUTHORITY AND ACCOUNTABILITY

The first response is to change the situation itself, to seek a better match of authority and responsibility. This may be done by renegotiating purposes, realigning expectations and accountability and/or increasing authority and resources. This is an appealing course, but it is often impossible for individual managers who increasingly find themselves in such situations. Negotiating for more authority and resources is a familiar response, yet indirect managers often focus efforts on their accountability.

An important question to ask is precisely to whom one is accountable. To the extent that organizational or political superiors are accessible, it may be possible to work out accountability more carefully for that which is controllable. Sometimes, effective accountability is to a more "distant" body, say one's constituents. One may spread the risk of nonperformance by making sure that others share the key decisions. To change unrealistic expectations, one may bring advisory committees and members of affected groups into the decision-making process.

This is common in politics. Consider a city government that has formed a partnership with private firms and others for urban development. The city may help the developers obtain grants and give them certain services, zoning variances, tax breaks, and the like in return for going ahead with the project. The city government may be politically accountable for the success of the project itself, associated employment, increases in amenities, and so on. Of course, the government must rely on the developers for much of this. The city can approach this accountability-control mismatch with strenuous efforts to make the partnership work better; it may also try to publicly unload a great deal of responsibility on the developers so that they will be blamed for any failures.

Similarly, in procurement contracts, defense department officials are held responsible for results produced by organizations beyond their control. Defense officials often seek to shift blame and culpability for overly expensive, nonperforming military hardware onto the shoulders of private contractors. They leak horror stories about padded contracts, incredibly expensive spare parts, general incompetence, and venality among defense contractors.

A manager may attempt to shift blame (and hence accountability) to other "intransigent" parts of the organization that failed to cooperate. ("The engineering folks kept insisting on much stricter specifications than we felt we needed and the production people insisted on long runs when we need flexibility." Or, "The old-timers in sales just don't know how to sell this sort of product.")[11]

MAKING THE MOST OF AN
INDIRECT MANAGEMENT SITUATION

Beyond trying to wriggle out of the situation, managers may simply seek to be more effective. Instead of wishing for more control and ineffectually applying traditional tools, they must acknowledge that they face networks of linked agreements and that effective action requires extensive negotiation. To give up the illusion of control is not to give up the game.

We now present a basic approach to indirect management. Like direct production, the place to start is with a careful specification of desired results, followed by a delineation of the "production function" or required network of linked agreements. Then it is possible to determine the most promising bases for influencing needed decisions and agreements.

Desired Results—The Central Interest in Indirect Management Negotiations A first question to ask is about the nature of the "product," or desired results. The answer can be straightforward where design and/or performance characteristics can be fully specified. However, if one is seeking a particular kind of research or an advanced technological development, a contract or formal agreement may be exceedingly difficult to write. Sometimes, one must distinguish between "process" objectives and "substantive" objectives (e.g., meeting a safety standard, whatever it is, versus actually making a product safer).

The capacity to specify the product will drive many subsequent management problems. Where characteristics can be well specified, management by means of formal agreement or contract is a possibility; where characteristics of the desired product elude such description, other approaches are needed. For example, specification of the

[11]When the uncertainty is uncontrollable and the mandate-givers cannot be convinced of this fact, some managers have been known to blame the incompetence of a subordinate, who is eventually fired.

inputs to the production process (e.g., so many hours of design time, so much material, so many intermediate tests, and so on), reliance on a continuing relationship among the parties with the understood possibility of frequent adjustments, or the substitution of professional judgment for specification may be the best choices.

The Required Networks of Linked Agreements[12]   After a careful attempt to specify the "product," a second key step involves specifying the network of linked agreements most likely to yield it. Two related sets of questions facilitate this analysis. First, who is needed to carry out each part of the specified "production" process? To what must each agree, and what sort of decisions must be made? Second, to whose action or inaction is the desired result likely to be vulnerable? In effect, the desired product will come about through a network of linked agreements and decisions among the critical parties. Often, it is most efficient to begin with the desired result and carefully "map backward" through the necessary chain of actors and events, taking note of alternate paths and contingencies, until one reaches the original manager.[13]

Obtaining Desired Agreements and Influencing Decisions   The next step begins with a creative inventory. Having looked at the product, the network, the parties whose involvement is needed at each stage, and to whom the results may be vulnerable, it is time to analyze the bases for potential agreement and decisions.[14] The analysis proceeds along familiar lines: interests, alternatives to agreement or favorable decision, potential agreements, creating and claiming, and changes in the game.

INTERESTS.   A first set of questions involves the manager's and others' interests in the issues as they may be presented. Prime managerial interests, of course, derive from the desired outputs. Often there are shared interests in substantive outcomes, in good working relationships, in respect for professional standards common to the participants, even across jurisdictional or organizational lines. Interests typically conflict over resource and accountability questions. Then come the questions of relative values and tradeoffs.

[12]This might be thought of as the production function.

[13]See Elmore (1979) and Sebenius (1982).

[14]We highlight decisions as well as agreements since the amount of interaction between the manager and the involved parties may vary from intense (negotiation) to rather little (decision influence). Similar factors operate in each case, however.

And since interests are perceived subjectively, what role will information play? Is information needed to create shared perceptions of the issue and its importance? How and by whom will it originate and be diffused? How credible will it be? Is there to be an appeal to supposed expertise? If so, how do the experts' messages relate to the experience of those in the linked network of necessary agreements? Where do they usually get their information, and to whom do they defer on matters of such judgment?

In some cases, interests derive from an indirectly managed program itself. For example, a long-standing grant program may heighten or make monetary interests salient. More subtle aspects of program design may also evoke interests. For example, information on performance is often collected, sometimes with a view to improvement, sometimes looking toward enforcement.

In theory, measurements may be a means to an end; in practice, performance measures may become virtual ends in themselves. For example, an important aspect of welfare delivery, which is federally funded but largely carried out by states, may be avoiding payments to ineligible persons. Ineligibility may be far easier to measure than how well individual circumstances are taken into account or even the extent to which genuinely eligible persons are assisted. Nevertheless, as the information that can be most easily collected, ineligibility data may cause error reduction to become a primary interest of managers, who may focus almost exclusively on it to the detriment of other possibly worthy program interests.[15] In general, if a measure is intended both for monitoring and some kind of enforcement, it is unlikely to be neutral in its effects and probably will induce a set of interests.[16]

ALTERNATIVES TO AGREEMENT. To decide to go along or "agree" to a proposed measure, an actor in the productive network must see going along as better, from his or her point of view, than not so doing. This focuses central attention on the parties' alternatives to a favorable decision or agreement. Often, of course, a perfectly sensible alternative is simply to ignore proposed joint actions and continue with the status quo.

Managers' lack of measures to affect alternatives to desired decisions or agreements perhaps constitutes the most salient distinction between direct and indirect management. In the direct case, man-

[15]Brodkin (1983).

[16]Lipsky (1980). The sometimes undesirable side-effects of improperly specified performance measures are prevalent in private and public sector organizations.

agers typically enjoy a relatively greater ability to affect career prospects, rewards, punishments, and realizations of interests across a broad set of linked issues and people.

A common way to effect a favorable decision or desired agreement is to make the other party's alternative to such an action considerably worse. Thus, enforcement tools such as fines, adverse publicity, legal sanctions, threats not to renew contracts or to find a new supplier or to make the product in house, court suits, contract termination, funding cutoffs, and the like are candidates for the indirect manager. Yet bad publicity and a shutdown threat, for example, by the federal government against state nursing homes that do not meet fire regulations, can engender a powerful counter response: "old people will be thrown onto the streets by this highhanded federal action." Forcible actions to change the other side's alternatives to an indirect manager's preferred policy notoriously have this character of "sticks with handles at both ends." Each side can use them to beat the other into submission or at least to a standoff.

In situations like this, the credibility of threatened sanctions may be at issue, as may the legitimacy of imposing them. Sanctions sometimes go against the very shared goals, professional assumptions, orientations, and other factors that the manager seeks to cultivate and must depend on for results. Clumsy reliance on real or threatened sanctions can damage one's capacities for cooperative action elsewhere. Sanctions may also hurt one's primary objectives. In the above example, closing nursing homes for lack of fire safety may deprive elderly people of housing when there is a shortage of such facilities that pass muster. In the same way, withholding educational funds can harm the very children that the funded program itself was supposed to help. In fact, the magnitude and character of threatened sanctions often erodes their credibility.

If, on careful consideration, sanctions still appear desirable, it may be possible to break them up and to threaten milder, more credible (perhaps less effective) measures. Some managers publicly proclaim their enforcement intentions to increase the apparent or feared likelihood of actual measures. Though it may be obvious that a certain manager's real incentives are *not* to impose sanctions, that same manager may be able to interpose someone whose incentives in fact are to enforce them. (To the extent, of course, that onerous sanctions become likely, end runs around this intermediate agent are the predictable consequences.)

It may also be quite possible to create a kind of "double agent" between one and another level of government. For example, a person who has worked in state government may be hired at the federal level to help with state relations. Such a person may, in effect, serve as a mediator and trusted advocate for the cause of each side.

Apart from this kind of measure, managers may try to arrange for some other body to "force" them to impose sanctions, thereby hoping to escape the attributions of implied bad motives or bad faith. For example, in negotiations between the Department of Health, Education and Welfare and several states over reducing the incidence of welfare error, the federal negotiators could truthfully, if a little disingenuously, point to an increasingly restive Congress that was likely to take blunt and unwanted action on the problem if a federal-state accord did not come about. In fact, federal officials highlighted impending congressional action, while at the same time quietly prodding it along. The feds hoped that this emphasis would have the character of a warning or notice rather than a threat.

Still, the distinction between warning and threat about one or the other side's alternatives to negotiated agreement can easily become blurred. The ability to change the other side's alternatives in order to induce agreement is often a blunt and generally impotent instrument in indirect managerial situations. As one observer noted after studying a number of such programs, "When it becomes necessary to rely mainly on hierarchical control, regulation, and compliance to get the job done, the game is essentially lost."[17]

AGREEMENTS.   If one strategy to induce favorable decisions or agreements is an attempt to make the alternative to such agreement worse, a complementary strategy is inducement, that is, to make agreement more valuable. Such a positive strategy may rely on shared interests or differences that may be dovetailed into more jointly beneficial arrangements.

Take shared interests first. An obvious first possibility is an appeal to shared goals; that is, all parties care a great deal about the same objective whether it be the provision of a particular human service, the improvement of public health, or the success of a complex joint venture. Second, shared financial incentives tend to line up behavior in the same direction. For example, in certain welfare programs costs are shared between the federal government and the states. Everyone involved may also have a common political interest

[17]Elmore (1979:27–28).

in enhancing the legitimacy of the welfare system. Similarly, if different parties come to perceive a class of actions or decisions as "legitimate," there may be a strong pull toward acting in accord with them.

Often norms and professional standards cut across organizational boundaries. Public health, a social work ethic, or a professional orientation shared by economists, accountants, physicians, lawyers, or others may provide powerful coordinating and motivating mechanisms. Along with norms, professional standards, economic and political incentives, and notions of legitimacy may go what might be termed proper conceptions of one's role. If an ethos can be induced or enhanced that moves different parties to "do something" by virtue of their roles or in deference to others, or in service of a larger conception, such actions may be made more likely.

Shared interests offer potentially powerful inducements to the indirect manager. Many actions can strengthen these interests, make them more salient, and thus improve the chances of favorable decisions and agreements.

Of course, differences in values, resources, and capabilities among the different parties may lead to more valuable arrangements for all sides. Suppose that a federal agency has dollars, personnel, the ability to waive or alter a regulation, or the capacity to mobilize support among other agencies and even within the state legislature. All of these may be useful carrots to induce action or agreement.

Sometimes inducements may be more subtle than a trade of say, money, personnel, and technical assistance from the feds in return for a state coastal zone management plan or upgraded crime fighting units. Take the case of fire safety inspections considered above. State inspectors were understandably reluctant to certify certain buildings that were generally considered to be fire safe but that did not meet the artificially rigid standards of the applicable national fire codes. One inducement that federal managers could offer was a willingness to share that risk—to grant waivers and thus allow safety certification. Here, a difference between the federal and state officials' ability and willingness to bear risk led to a desired result. And elsewhere, differences in valuations, resources, and capabilities may be creatively combined into arrangements for joint gain.

Indirect managerial agreements sometimes take the form of contractual provisions. This is especially true for procurement of standardized goods or services. In other cases, agreements are simply informal statements of what each party will do or give. Sometimes, managers must simply rely more on professional judgment and ongoing relationships. In general, the ability to specify the product and to gauge the degree of certainty about conditions over time affects the form of any agreement. When the amount of explicit negotiating interaction is less and the manager primarily seeks to influence decisions, a favorable choice can often be interpreted as "agreement" with the manager's desired action.

One class of strategies intended to result in favorable decisions or agreements relies on making the alternatives to such actions worse, but such "forcing" actions are notoriously weak in indirect management situations. Instead, ferreting out, strengthening, and emphasizing shared interests, along with dovetailing differences in valuation, resources, and capability, can make desired action or agreement more valuable to the parties and hence more likely to come about. In most indirect management situations, strategies to "induce" and "enable" agreement offer far more promise than "forcing" tactics. Tactics that emphasize an ethos of joint value creation and that seek to downplay claiming are especially apt for these cases.

CHANGING THE GAME.   As with any negotiation, tactics for indirect managerial situations include moves to change the issues, parties, evoked interests, alternatives, and so on. We focus on two types of "reconfiguration" that are common to indirect management situations. The first involves a change in the parties, sometimes brought about by federal granting programs that are intended to build up state capabilites to perform desired functions.

As state capacity increases, as a network of beneficiaries of the federal program expands, and as the recipient grows in local political prominence, a subtle but important shift may occur in federal–state bargaining. No longer is it merely the "feds versus the state," but now there is an increasingly powerful ally of the federal agency within the state government. A private sector analogue might be "lending" personnel to another department or unit to ensure a favorable voice in the "other" camp. To be sure, the state entity will have interests other than those of its federal sponsors, but unlike the situation beforehand, an important ally has been created and strengthened with respect to the original federal purposes. Thus, grants can act as an inducement, as a means of capacity building, but also as the means of altering the interests and parties in a federal–state negotiation.[18]

---

[18]As Ingram (1977) noted, however, grants and technical assistance can set the stage for and tip the scales in favor of desired actions, but by no means can they insure it unless other factors at the state level are favorably disposed.

Indirect managers may also seek to change the existing organizational structure and systems to be more suited to indirect tasks. When Caspar Weinberger was the Secretary of HEW, he tried to move ("devolve") both accountability and authority to the regional offices of HEW. This action encountered problems, since the regional offices were organized according to *programs*. Virtually direct links connected those in the field to their national counterparts. Moreover, congressional committees were organized according to programs. Thus, regional directors were often effectively cut out of the picture. The actual devolution of authority and accountability was never very successful, rendering the indirect managerial role of regional officials very weak.

Under HEW Secretary Joseph Califano, the regional organization of the same department seemed to correspond better to indirect managerial tasks. Rather than try to devolve authority and accountability to the regions, Califano appointed a Deputy Undersecretary for Intergovernmental Relations in Washington. Officials in the field served as regional "ambassadors" who could go among the various regional programs and convey concerns directly to a fairly high level of HEW (the Deputy Undersecretary). At this level, cross trades and program modifications could be made relatively easily. This regional organization was driven much more directly by information than by nominal lines of authority, and, as such, seemed more appropriate to a world where indirect management was the norm.

In some cases, an agency may move from predominantly direct managerial responsibilities to indirect ones. For example, the Massachusetts Department of Youth Services itself had long provided services directly to juvenile delinquents. When a strong movement toward "deinstitutionalization" came, the internal agency organization needed substantial modification to contract more effectively for services from outside providers. The functions of contract negotiating, monitoring, evaluating, and correcting began to be far more important than direct provision of services. A new organizational structure appropriate to the indirect task had to be designed to implement the evolving network of private provider agreements.

Relationship to Direct Management

We have defined indirect management situations as those in which authority and resources are shared and accountability for any output or product is concentrated. Such situations are especially stark where production takes place across jurisdictional and organizational lines. Yet even in the most traditional direct management situations, actual control may fall far short of accountability.[19] When that is the case, the distinction between direct and indirect management blurs and may disappear entirely.

An Example of Indirect Management: Swine Flu Immunizations

Early in 1976, ominous signs began to appear of a possible major epidemic or "pandemic" of what looked like "swine influenza." This was particularly fearsome, since in 1918 an apparent swine flu pandemic had struck down some half a million Americans including a disproportionately large number of young parents and soldiers. Much uncertainty about the proper interpretation of the scientific evidence and many conflicting opinions about the appropriate government response to this health threat followed the early signs of a possible pandemic.

In any case, though, in a dazzling display of bureaucratic entrepreneurship, the Assistant Secretary of Health, Theodore Cooper, and Dr. David Sencer, the Director of the Centers for Disease Control (CDC), convinced then-President Gerald Ford to endorse a program to immunize "every man, woman, and child in the United States," as Ford put it publicly, against swine flu. The program was scheduled to start in the summer of 1976, before flu season began. In short, Cooper and Sencer obtained a mandate—the authority and resources to carry out the program they had advocated.

Myriad questions attend this decision: Should the program have been undertaken at all? Should it have been designed differently, or have had built-in triggers, program reviews, and stopping points? Ultimately, the swine flu program foundered. Insurers refused to provide insurance for vaccinations; Congress not only had to pay for the vaccine, but also had to pass special liability-assuming legislation; timetables slipped; and distribution of the vaccine fell far short of the President's goal, a situation fortunately relieved by the persistent *failure* of the disease to make an appearance. Vaccinations, however,

---

[19]We have in mind situations in which a manager depends on peers or others in his apparently hierarchical organization for production or in which he depends on his subordinates but has concentrated accountability.

caused occasional bad side effects and some three hundred deaths which were intensively publicized. In shambles, the program was suspended. It is now widely recalled as a public health fiasco, and its story has been admirably and insightfully told in Richard Neustadt and Harvey Fineberg's book, *The Epidemic That Never Was*.[20]

Despite the possibly ill-conceived nature of the original decision and the ultimate fate of the program, this situation provides a useful vehicle to analyze a particular indirect managerial problem in some detail. In retrospect, it is fairly obvious that this situation was not amenable to the techniques of direct management. Neither managers' orders nor their equivalent here, "doctors' orders," proved very potent.

Consider the situation as of March 1976, when with mandate in hand, Cooper and Sencer faced the problem of accomplishing universal swine flu immunizations by early the next fall. Had Cooper and his associates carefully brainstormed, or "mapped backward" from what ultimately needed to be done, their list would have included the following: people had to be convinced to go to health centers; injections had to be provided; plans and explanations for private physicians as well as state and local health bodies had to be in place; air guns and syringes had to be distributed along with the vaccine. Consent forms had to be printed and distributed. Monitoring and statistical reporting systems had to be installed. The vaccine itself had to be ordered, then produced in bulk, bottled, and insured. It also had to be paid for with funds appropriated for the purpose. These had to be legislated by Congress after being requested by Ford.

This "backward" recitation of requisite actions carries an immediate implication of the people and organizations who needed to agree to perform these tasks. The public had to be convinced to go and connect with syringes and air guns; the media had to convey much of the necessary information. Private and public physicians had to be convinced of the crisis and instructed about what to do. State and local health bodies had to formulate plans and coordinate them with the national Department of Health, Education and Welfare. Pharmaceutical companies needed to make the vaccine; in turn, they had to be insured by private insurers or, as it turned out, by the federal government. HEW was responsible for procuring the vaccine, for completing field trials and other tests, and for coordinating the entire effort. Congress needed to appropriate the money and, later,

[20]Fineberg and Neustadt (1982).

to deal with liability questions when the insurers balked. All of these early steps needed to be cleared through channels in the Ford administration. (See Figure 16.1 for a schematic of the network of decisions and agreements required for this program to succeed.)

Cooper, of course, "directly controlled" only a small fraction of this long chain of actors needed to implement his policies. Yet many held him and CDC head Sencer accountable for the program's ultimate perceived failure; Cooper, for example, was not reappointed by the next administration. Moreover, their superiors, such as HEW Secretary David Matthews and President Ford, arguably paid a political price for this program's apparent ineptitude and taint.

Congress, the media, and ultimately, the electorate, exacted this price and rarely drew fine distinctions about authority, resources, and the ideal or actual span of control. Instead, those "at the top" failed with respect to a set of expectations they themselves had had a large hand in generating. Of course, this example—of shared authority and resources, combined with tight political accountability—defines the situation as one of indirect management. Though Cooper and Sencer did not have access to the traditional tools of public administration (personnel systems, budget systems, information systems, ability to alter organizational structure, and so forth), many techniques nevertheless existed that could have enhanced the chances for success.

Though the above discussion focuses on Cooper's problem of managing the swine flu program itself, Cooper had a variety of larger interests at stake. "Failure" would mean not only that his personal career was likely to suffer, but the Centers for Disease Control and other units formally subordinate to him would almost certainly lose substantial credibility. Future immunization programs would take place under a shadow and innovative preventive health initiatives would face much higher hurdles than before. Cooper and Sencer, understandably, focused on the immediate substantive issues and managed for the short-term, worst case—a major epidemic—which, it turned out, was regarded by many as unlikely. The more likely outcomes seemed outside their field of vision, as did some of the other interests that rode on the performance of the swine flu program.

A look at the organization of that small part of the network under Cooper's direct control shows a traditional organization on strict programmatic lines. After all, the Department of Health, Education and Welfare and the Centers for Disease Control had always carried out immunization programs along such lines. No matter that this

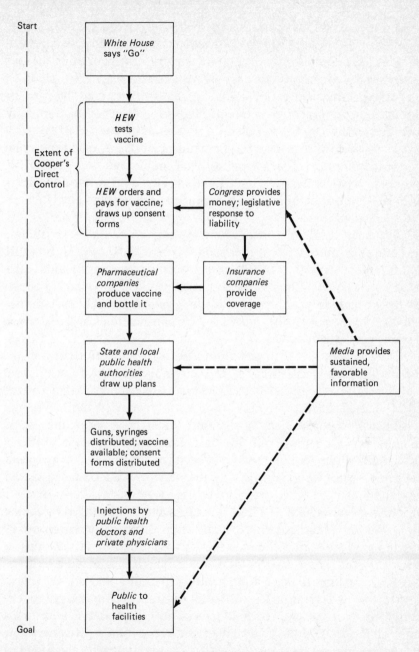

FIGURE 16.1: **"Mapping Backwards" to Find Cooper's "Production Function"**

To map backwards, start with "Public."

program envisioned vaccinating twice as many people as had ever before been run through such a program and in half the time. Information requests and orders were transmitted through a structured many-leveled hierarchy. In other words, nominal program channels were the conduits for information. It frequently took a long time for a crucial piece of information (e.g., that insurers were reluctant to insure the vaccine at all) to reach those who desperately needed it for managerial purposes. Yet program managers needed, on a timely and continuing basis, a vast amount of legal, public relations, scientific, production, logistical, and coordination related information. Timely information is crucial for direct managers; for indirect ones in a crisis, it is still more so.

The need for such information argues strongly for establishing a structure for this project rather than relying on the existing program management structure. In former HEW Undersecretary Hale Champion's words, the "hierarchy should be squashed" where there is short time and much uncertainty. The organization and its responses should be driven by information, not by nominal lines of authority in routine program channels.

Having diagnosed the situation as one of indirect management, having noted the central roles of uncertainty and information, and having tentatively prescribed a project-management system for the direct managerial aspects, it is now time to turn to the indirect managerial task. The problem at the time could be easily stated: How could Cooper get those outside HEW to do what he wanted? What means existed to get them to agree to act in accord with his program, especially since he would be accountable for what they did or did not do?

The relevant chain of actors and tasks can be identified by asking two questions: One, who needs to do what for the program to work? And two, to what and whom are the desired program results vulnerable? As noted above, the chain of actors stretches back from the public, to the media, to state and local health bodies and private physicians, through pharmaceutical and insurance companies, to the Congress, to the Centers for Disease Control, to HEW, and to the rest of the administration. The discussion that follows considers how a manager can get these required actors to go along with the program idea. In the jargon of negotiation, how can one get the nearby actors to "agree," and how can one favorably influence the decisions of those farther down the line? The next sections very briefly ask these questions of the major involved actors.

The General Public To go along, members of the general public had to be convinced that the shots would be safe, available, and effective. Further, they had to perceive their alternatives to a decision to go along with the program as painful and dangerous. A combination of HEW educational efforts, the advice of public health bodies and private physicians, and, primarily, mass media impressions would spread perceptions of the program's safety and views about the dangers of not going along (the "alternative" to agreement with the program).

Advocates of immunization had to base their appeal on scientific credibility and the legacy of previous successful immunization programs, such as that for polio. Through a televised image of Gerald Ford receiving a swine flu shot, presidential authority would be invoked. In other times this may have been potent, but as a campaigner that year in tight presidential primary and election races, Gerald Ford needed to "borrow" authority. In fact, to persuade the public, it may have been necessary to have a more vivid image: swine flu actually sighted in the southern hemisphere (where the flu seasons alternate with those in the northern hemisphere), bodies, a genuine crisis atmosphere. All of these elements, however, point to the key role of the media in the "production" of public immunization.

The Media The last section suggested the need for sustained favorable reporting about the program. The swine flu program clearly had any number of easily foreseeable public relations vulnerabilities. First, in advance of an actual epidemic, members of the media could simply ignore the program or attack it on any number of grounds. If the vaunted "consensus" of top scientists in favor of the program were to unravel, it would look contrived (in fact, there were prominent defectors from the consensus). Ford's announcement of the swine flu decision the day after his North Carolina primary loss to Ronald Reagan did not help the program's image.

Moreover, in any sustained national immunization drive, one could readily predict that "temporally coincident deaths" would occur. Just as confidently, one could predict their sensational coverage. Similarly, any hitherto unknown side effects were almost sure to be revealed by the unprecedented surveillance system put in place for the vaccinations. Finally, once the federal government had assumed all the liability risks of producing the vaccine, the question of "profiteering" by vaccine makers could be expected.

Cooper and his associates might have taken any number of steps to counter such vulnerabilities: simple recognition of the media's importance and less confidence in the doctors' infallible and persuasive authority would have been a vital first step. Rather than appoint an inexperienced doctor as the informal press liaison, the program managers might have tapped a great deal of in-house media expertise at HEW. When three deaths occurred in a Pennsylvania clinic, local officials there conveyed a great deal of confusion and intimated that it must have been a batch of "bad vaccine." Some early planning by HEW officials could have alerted local public health people everywhere to this statistically foreseeable possibility and helped the Centers for Disease Control to change the "bad vaccine" image that ultimately and unnecessarily resulted. Recognizing the crucial role of the media as part of the entire immunization program—for which Cooper and Sencer were held accountable—it is hardly too much to suggest that some media-wise input should have been sought early on and emphasized thereafter by indirect program managers.

State and Local Health Bodies and Private Physicians These groups represented the implementation capability of the program. Though Cooper had little "direct authority" over them, a number of factors might have enhanced the chances of their agreement with his vision. If they had shared Cooper and Sencer's perceptions of the problem and concurred in the scientific judgment, strong professional norms and shared purposes of protecting public health should have guaranteed their participation.

Conversely, if upon revealing all evidence and analysis that the Centers for Disease Control had, these groups remained unenthusiastic, then who else would have been likely to go along? Yet in some early dealings with key state and local public health bodies, there was a great deal of dissent about the nature of the threat and the possible response. Physicians and public health professionals in these meetings pointed to any number of difficulties in mounting a universal program. They pointed to the opportunity cost of swine flu in terms of other programs. They seriously questioned the scientific merit of the program. These questioning voices should at least have given some pause to Sencer and Cooper. Information should have flowed in *two* directions here. An unjustifiable certainty and arrogance with respect to "the proper response"—which they "knew"—ended up costing the two dearly.

The Congress If the job had been done well with state and local physicians and the media, keeping the program separate from "politics'' should have gone a long way toward maintaining congressional support. It then would have become a fairly simple matter to keep the appropriate congressional committees informed and designate someone or some unit to be the official source of ongoing information. Many congressional complaints had their origin in the apparent lack of someone at HEW that was ''in charge.''

The Pharmaceutical Companies It should have been fairly straightforward to manage this relationship contractually. HEW had a long-term relationship with these companies and could expect relatively easy bargaining with them over this program given the many immunization programs with which they would deal jointly.

The Insurance Companies The insurance companies were an essential ingredient in the production of the vaccine. Moreover, a ''will not insure'' decision would have appeared to convey to the public fatal misgivings about the safety of the program. A simple prescription was appropriate to this twofold vulnerability. Given the program's central reliance on insurance companies, HEW officials should have probed their motives and procedures and sought to understand them better. Instead, they did not deal or negotiate with them directly, but only through the vaccine manufacturers. In dealing only with the manufacturers, HEW program managers incurred substantial unnecessary risks.

* * *

In review, once the program was adopted, Cooper and Sencer needed to manage with respect to *two* sets of interests. The first was the substantive product they sought; that is, they wanted a certain number of needles in a certain number of arms. The second interest concerned the long-term credibility of their institution.

Further, backward mapping would have revealed the long chain of actors that composed the ''production function.'' This chain displayed the classic symptoms of an indirect management situation: shared authority and resources but concentrated accountability for program results. The many scientific and managerial uncertainties suggested the key role of information and communication, and implied that the direct organizational effort should have been organized more along project lines than by existing programs. These direct managerial decisions would have complemented the larger, indirect task of getting people to agree or decide to go along with their plan.

The answers to two questions would have offered indispensable insight: Who was needed for success, and to whom and what was the program vulnerable? A minimum prescription would have been to focus attention on and try to understand entities that turn up in answer to these questions. The harder managerial task was influencing them to go along with the program. Standard tools of administration did not appear to offer much help. Instead, the methods of bargaining and persuasion should have been used: legitimacy, credibility, norms, information to create shared perceptions, reliance on shared goals and the like. Perceptions of program value and safety, versus the undesirability of the alternatives, were key.

Cooper's task was to synchronize direct and indirect managerial techniques. He should have managed more for the long-term, likely outcome (a mild epidemic or none at all, many future CDC public health missions) rather than for the one that was short-term and feared (acting as if the pandemic were certain). An acute consciousness of the indirect managerial aspects of the program might have prevented considerable grief. And that is the case in almost all indirect management situations.

*　*　*

This chapter's discussion completes our examination of the basic components of any manager's job: shaping a mandate and producing, both directly and indirectly. In tandem with this investigation, we have explored two aspects of negotiation beyond the basic framework, namely, sustaining agreements and agency negotiations, that are especially relevant to management.

In so doing, we have dealt with increasingly elaborate negotiating structures, from Part I's basic analysis, to the relative simplicity of negotiating through agents, to the complexities of the process in hierarchies and in networks. It is now time to analyze a final negotiation topic that finds constant application in each of these structures and provides an analytic bridge between the basic parts of a manager's job, parts that so far we have discussed in isolation from each other. Chapter Seventeen looks at the questions of linked negotiations, the "manager in the middle," and more generally, the "negotiator in the middle."

The Manager Is Always in the Middle:

Linked Bargains, Internal-External Negotiations, Mediation, and the Essence of Strategy

FORMER SECRETARY OF LABOR John Dunlop once remarked that any bargain really involves three separate transactions: one across the table and one on each side of it. Making a deal with the "other" side is normally only part of the process; often the interplay within one's "own" side is as difficult or even more so. After months of trying to hammer out a common U.S. government position for the Strategic Arms Reduction Talks, a Navy man was reputed to have said of the other American players, "After this process, the Russians have dropped to number five on our enemies list!"

Straightforward dealings like collective bargaining or industrial procurement often place the manager in the familiar "middle" between the "internal" and "external" negotiations, that is, the linked bargains in and outside the organization. This chapter will take a closer look at how each of these two negotiations can affect the other.

A moment's thought, however, suggests that this same structure characterizes much of a manager's job as well. Inside hierarchies and within networks, the issues are linked, requiring negotiations that are at once "upwards and downwards," or "side to side." Recall Chris Hubbard, who negotiated with his boss while mediating among his divisions.

Managers negotiate with subordinates over issues of direct concern to their superiors. And managers deal with superiors over questions that have occupied their dealings with subordinates. More generally, we have seen how a manager negotiates for a mandate; in this sense, she is an agent. Yet she also negotiates for production on behalf of that mandate; thus, her role is also that of a principal delegating to an agent.

This chapter elaborates the observation that the manager is almost always in the middle. Whether the form is a conventional "internal" negotiation linked to an "external" one, a dealing "up" that must coordinate with a dealing "down," entities "side to side" that must be mediated from "between," or a mandate that must cohere with actions to produce, these situations have important elements in common.

The negotiator in the middle hopes to create value by finding agreements that are better for all than no agreement, and to claim that value through an advantageously designed outcome. But to do so means striking two or more linked agreements. Not only must the negotiator in the middle strive for *individually desirable outcomes* that leave *no joint gains on the table*, but the agreements struck should be *consistent* with each other: the agreement she reaches with party A must be compatible with the agreements she reaches with party B. Sometimes, as she bargains with A and B, she finds outcomes in the bargaining set with A that are also acceptable to B. At other times, to reach consistent agreements, she must change the game with A or change the game with B, or both. She may do this by shaping the others' perceptions of the bargaining sets, by altering the issues considered, or by carefully sequencing the bargaining interactions. This process is the subject of this chapter, which investigates the tactics and dynamics of linked bargains.

Bob Furz in the Middle

Throughout this book we have referred to various aspects of the situation faced by Bob Furz, head of the large Brazilian subsidiary of the firm we call "Empire," a British multinational. Like Empire's other South American subsidiaries, Furz's unit manufactured and installed ventilating and air-conditioning equipment for the medium and large buildings that were springing up on that continent before and during the oil boom. At the price of some repetition, we now pull together the various strands of Furz's experience. This gives a much fuller picture of the problems facing managers in the middle and some of the negotiating responses that are possible.

Two years ago, Furz proposed to Empire's board that all South American operations be centralized. Especially given the threat of American and Japanese encroachment, Furz also urged a move away from their previous strategy of high-quality, customized production and installation on a country by country basis. Instead, he pressed for mass, standardized production. In particular, he argued that they should design and make a small number of relatively standardized models that could be lightly modified for each country's market. Instead of maintaining virtually complete manufacturing operations in each country, Furz sought to rationalize the process, with each country specializing in a few key components under a new regional management organization. By cutting price, they could boost volume, achieve greater scale economies, and further cut costs—enabling yet more price cuts, and so on. In turn, this would put pressure on some of Empire's weaker competitors, who could well be forced to fold or sell out to Empire, still further upping volume and continuing the process. As the different pieces of the strategy fell into place, Furz expected a dramatic increase in market share and then profits.

It was a compelling vision to Furz—though there was always the question as to why none of his competitors had seen the light. (About a decade ago, a smaller firm had failed trying an analogous approach.) Dealing with Empire's CEO and chairman on this matter and then with many of its board members had proved arduous. Along the way, Furz had made enemies at London headquarters, especially among those whose strong direct links with their functional counterparts in the many South American subsidiaries would be severed by his proposed reorganization.

The board ultimately agreed with Furz's strategic concept but gave him only a part of what he wanted. Though he was made nominal head of the new South American organization, he was granted limited authority over hiring and firing, pricing, and manufacturing policy. Many of the formerly autonomous country managers deeply resented his new status; the sales force seemed to prefer the old customer relationships and the higher-quality image; and the company's engineers liked their prerogatives of individual design. After eighteen months, losses had begun to mount and the strategy was significantly behind schedule. Furz had taken some steps toward implementing his new strategy, yet he needed better cooperation from key South American players. At the same time, he had to protect his vulnerable mandate from London.

At the early stages of the new strategy, each South American group's alternative to "agreeing" to act in accord with Furz's new strategic vision was simply to ignore it or to make end runs around him to the British headquarters. Furz was well aware that tossing off orders right and left would bear little fruit. London had simply not given him the tools to force compliance.

At the outset of his new venture, Furz's only real option was to try to tempt each critical South American group into "agreement" with him by holding out the lure of joint gain from the new strategy. He began by exercising his formal authority over pricing policy, making deep cuts for products sold by some of the less glamorous elements of his sales force in geographic locations he judged to be fairly price sensitive. At first these sales people balked, preferring the accustomed comfortable "quality" image and slow pace, but the strong customer response quickly energized them. Soon they acted more aggressively and the other sales people began to envy the excitement of higher volume. Though Furz had planned to hold off further price cuts until new production efficiencies warranted them, the pressure from the rest of the sales force prevailed. He agreed to further cuts.

Furz found ways to tempt other key players as well as into the coalition behind his strategy. Prior to his reorganization, the various country managers had enjoyed considerable status but without great substantive influence; the tight links between their subordinates and their London counterparts had effectively cut the country managers out on that score. Initially, they saw Furz's actions as further undercutting their status. Yet Furz saw them as important potential backers. Thus, instead of insisting at the outset on a very small number of models to be used by all countries—his ultimate strategy—he suggested that individual country models be developed, under the supervision of the individual country managers. This effectively enfranchised them, gained Furz some useful allies, and went at least part of the way toward standardizing the present jumble of custom models.

The engineers and designers presented similar problems: they liked high quality, custom production. Yet with the rest of the staff enthusiastic about the changes, Furz could tempt the technical people with significant technical challenges: to design and engineer models for each country leading toward the task of a more universal design. In this way, Furz got them on board too. And he was able to centralize production of some critical sub-assemblies in three new regional facilities.

It was one thing to get the sales force, the country managers, the designers and the engineers to begin to act in accord with his vision. Yet the compromises he had had to make to overcome their reluctance—premature price cuts, only partially rationalized designs, too much emphasis on country rather than regional organization—began to take their toll. Soon, competitors—alarmed at their rapid loss of share—began to match Empire's prices, losses began to mount, and complaints were heard in London and in the field from old customers. The perception spread that even if Empire raised prices again, its competitors would not follow suit until they had at the very least won back their markets and taught Furz a lesson. Something akin to panic began to sweep through the operation.

But Furz's strategy was designed in such a way that, once embarked on, it could not be easily abandoned. The price war with competitors had already been declared and destruction of the old organization, production lines, and other ways of doing business was well advanced. In short, though the lure of *joint gains* had induced initial cooperation, the South Americans' *alternative* to continued agreement, once the strategy was underway, was a very much worse situation than had earlier prevailed. This kept the entire group on board and worked against the incentives and opportunities to resist, not to go along, or to defect.

Though London had originally agreed to Furz's strategy, appropriate milestones had not been negotiated. By long habit, London expected the steady high margins and few cash demands associated with the lower-volume approach. The initial losses, mounting debts, and quality complaints, which Furz had thought likely to accompany the new course, clashed with London's expectation and was read there as a disaster in the making. Bob Furz had carefully negotiated the new strategy by painting an attractive picture of the end result. Yet, the lack of agreed interim milestones compatible with the unfamiliar elements of his new approach doomed him to a debilitating battle with London over "staying the course"; his job was constantly at stake.

London was in the same predicament as the members of the various South American operations; their alternative to continued "agreement" with Furz's strategy was an attempted return to the *status quo ante*. Yet, the old organization was no longer intact, a vindictive price war was on, and competitors were desperate to regain lost market share. Thus, as distasteful as it seemed, the situation as it had evolved virtually forced London to stick with the new strategy; Furz had secured this agreement as well.

Of course, whether London had to stick with Furz was another issue altogether. Effectively reducing a superior's freedom of action without his or her knowledge or consent runs contrary to unspoken assumptions about what constitutes acceptable conduct by a subordinate. Furz ran considerable personal risks by his strategic maneuvering.

Ironically, though he spent enormous energies trying to placate a hostile and skeptical-seeming London and keep them on board with his plan, his real interests and those of the CEO and board were virtually parallel. Instead of building and reinforcing these natural links along the way, and shaping expectations to be consistent with interim losses and a changed image, Furz had to attend to this task when it was the most difficult. Yet the combination of genuine joint gains if the strategy worked and a vastly worse alternative to agreement—jettisoning his plan in mid-stream—together with nearly superhuman efforts at coalition building on his part, kept London on board. Furz was able to buy precious time.

Luckily for him, the strategy finally caught fire. Though his competitors had matched his lower prices, they had not put in place the means to lower their costs. In that department, Empire had almost a two-year lead. Deep pockets could not over time match a significant cost advantage. Furz then began to make enormous profits and soon took over many of his former competitors and added their volume to his base, further solidifying his position. London was ecstatic and Furz's new problem became an embarrassment of riches. (Within a year, he had been made the Executive VP for *all* Empire's overseas operations, and later became Empire's first non-British President.)

A look back at Furz shows a manager in virtually nonstop negotiations. He offered the lure of higher profits to his superiors and the Empire board but he needed authority and resources from them; hence interdependence, laced with some conflict over the terms of his new mission. Not only did Furz negotiate "upward" but also "downward" and, to some extent, "sideways" with elements of the various country organizations (their managers, sales forces, designers, and engineers) that were not fully under his control. Each of these parties had to reckon with him but had distinct interests, beliefs about the best approach, and capacities to help or obstruct. As he proceeded, therefore, Furz constantly had to initiate, nurture, and secure two evolving networks of agreements, an "external" one with London over goals and resources linked to an "internal" one with the South Americans over actually producing results. At a minimum, these two networks of agreements should be consistent; ideally, in a potent strategy, they should strongly reinforce each other.

Just as Bob Furz was in the middle of the London and South American organizations, other managers find themselves in linked bargains, in trying to coordinate "internal" with "external" dealings, and in mediating between different entities. The rest of this chapter investigates the characteristic dynamics of such dealings much more closely.

Tactics and Dynamics

The tactics and dynamics associated with linked bargains appear in a broad class of similar situations, including that of the manager in the middle of mandate and production negotiations, the agent representing a principal or organization in negotiations with an external body, or an interested mediator. Rather than continually referring to this wide range of situations, we will cast much of the discussion from the point of view of someone who negotiates both "externally" and "internally."

Let us be more precise about our perspective in this chapter. Consider a very simple case in which a senior boss (call her "A") "internally" works out the appropriate specifications and price of a new computer system with a middle manager (call him "B"). In turn, B negotiates "externally" with a vendor ("C") over the actual purchase of the system. In this chapter, we would look at this interaction from B's vantage. Similarly, we might consider the problem of another "B", mediating between his peers, A and C. In a more complicated setting, A and C might be complex coalitions with B acting as the intermediary whose role we would highlight; recall our focus on Bob Furz as a "B" negotiating "internally" with the South Americans (as "A") and "externally" with London (as "C"). Likewise, we might examine a lawyer (B) negotiating as an agent for her principal (A) with another side (C) composed of yet another lawyer who had *her* own principal. It is easy to spin out further complications of this structure, but even in more complex cases, we mainly look at the situation through the eyes of a "B" faced with internal and external dealings.

Our intent is not to work systematically through the full range of such situations, but instead to examine some of their characteristic dynamics. We begin with a few observations on primarily internal negotiations, namely building favorable coalitions (as Furz did in South America), blocking adverse ones, and reaching agreement on an internal bottom line for use in external negotiations. But, the external negotiation can often be manipulated favorably to affect the internal one and vice versa. The interplay between the two gives rise to a rich variety of tactical choices. We will look at each class of actions in turn.

DEALING WITH INTERNAL PARTIES

"Internal" dealings taken by themselves represent special cases of negotiations we analyzed in the first part of this book. Yet certain aspects of building and blocking internal coalitions, as well as developing "common" internal positions, deserve more discussion.

Dealing Internally: Building Coalitions

A negotiator can build a coalition of support for desired positions among those on his "side." Bob Furz did this with his moves toward the sales force, country managers, and engineers. Or a negotiator may simply design and press for a proposal that serves the interests of a large enough internal group. For example, in labor negotiations with the National Football League, Ed Garvey, head of the National Football League Players Association, advanced a proposal that provided substantial salary increases for the veteran players in "nonglamorous" positions, who made up the bulk of the union. He did not seek very high salaries—obtained in other sports—for the relatively few and highly visible star players. The design of this proposal, though surprising to some who focused on "star" salaries, ensured that the majority of the union supported Garvey and strengthened his hand with the owners.

Dealing Internally: Blocking Adverse Coalitions

The negotiator may likewise try to prevent unhelpful coalitions from forming within his side. He may do this by preventing potential opponents from meeting without him. He may "buy off" potential adversaries by structuring his proposals to their relative advantage. He may link issues in this negotiation to others on which he may be able to help adversaries or may make side payments, as U.S. Presidents sometimes are alleged to do when they tacitly concede new weapons systems to members of the Joint Chiefs of Staff in return for their support on treaty negotiations. Sometimes, the manager in the middle can change the incentives of opponents to align better with his preferences; in discussing the budgeting system negotiations (Chapter Eight), we suggested that Chris Hubbard alter compensation and promotion standards to induce fuller cooperation from his recalcitrant department heads.

Dealing Internally: Developing A Common Position or Bottom Line

Quite frequently, the effort to arrive at an explicit common position or to develop a common reservation price creates animosity among the internal parties and induces them to misrepresent what is minimally acceptable. When the internal parties' interests on various issues are not in direct conflict, consensus is sometimes reached only on an overall "minimally acceptable" agreement that gives each party sufficiently favorable terms on "its" issues but results in a proposed package that is completely unacceptable to the external party. As we mentioned earlier, this sort of collective wish list may result when internal negotiations are delegated to lower levels of the organization and only contested issues rise to higher levels. In such cases, internal agreement on a bottom line for external purposes can be costly to the negotiator, who may have to work very hard to "undo" the internal agreement as its unacceptability to the outside parties becomes manifest. Of course, negotiations with the external party may sometimes be used to nudge (or occasionally, shove) the internal process in this kind of situation, as we now discuss.

USING EXTERNAL NEGOTIATIONS TO AFFECT THE INTERNAL NEGOTIATIONS

Once we begin to allow the internal and external processes to affect each other, the dynamics can become much richer. To illustrate, we shall consider how the manager in the middle can affect the outcome of internal dealings by four related tactics.

External Effects on Internal Negotiations: Controlling Information

The negotiator often serves as the internal parties' source of information about the external process. By controlling that information, the "in-between" manager can influence the outcome of internal deliberations. The garden variety version of this tactic occurs when Ms. Middle manager wants something done, and urges Mr. Bottom to do it, since Mr. Top (to whom Mr. Bottom has scant access) allegedly demands it.

In another example, the managers of a firm nearing bankruptcy were involved in linked negotiations with their unions and creditors in what we might call internal and external dealings, respectively. In a classic ploy, the managers misrepresented their creditors' minimal conditions and used this outside pressure to wring painful wage concessions from the union.

Negotiators in the middle sometimes use their control over contact with the external party to "create" deadlines that are designed to force action from recalcitrant internal bodies. Recall the head of project engineering for a state-owned steel company who was negotiating with a large outside engineering firm for the purchase of direct reduction units for his firm. In his "internal" negotiations, he was having trouble getting agreement on whether one or two large direct reduction units were needed from a supplier. To force this process— and influence it toward agreement on his preferred solution of two units—he treated the expiration date of the other firm's bid internally as if it were absolutely binding. At one point, he even concealed from others in his company the supplier's offer to extend the deadline. Similarly, in New York, Robert Moses often arranged federal financing for a public works project he favored, but only informed city agencies of the financing just before crucial deadlines. Other city officials frequently chose to forego the time needed to review, modify, or reject projects rather than risk being held responsible for losing considerable funding.

In a closely related tactic, a negotiator can act as if the results of the external negotiation are fixed and use this to pressure internal parties for concessions. For example, when ESSELTE merged with DYMO, managers at ESSELTE-DYMO were asked to press formerly decentralized country and product organizations to install uniform information and control systems to report back to headquarters. One manager in the middle reported that, "It was a rough job; we were left in-between, and when problems arose, we had to go back and explain again to the subsidiaries or beg for flexibility from the top." In essence, he *only* attempted to renegotiate with headquarters when he felt stymied by the country organizations. Chris Hubbard similarly took the order to implement a zero-based budgeting system as a given and negotiated with subordinates on that basis—even though initially he might have argued for a modified version that would have been easier for his subordinates to accept.

In an example discussed in Chapter Three, an attorney represented several states negotiating with HEW over the resolution of a lawsuit. This attorney did not advise his clients to try to undo HEW's commitment to a certain monetary settlement and to push for more. Instead, he treated this total as fixed in his dealings among the states, and used it to try to work out a realistic allocation among them.

In all these cases, the negotiator in the middle can use his apparently superior access to the external process to shape internal parties' perceptions of what in fact is feasible. At a minimum, this may facilitate consistent agreements; often, however, it allows the negotiator in the middle to claim value in his internal bargain.

External Effects on Internal Negotiations: Shaping the Agenda

The ability to define issues and shape the agenda for external negotiations can also be used to affect internal bargaining. In the talks with the Soviet Union over controlling intermediate range nuclear weapons, for example, Defense Department official Richard Perle cultivated support for his "zero-option" proposal among members of the Joint Chiefs of Staff. In return, he agreed with the Chiefs to exclude any consideration of aircraft from the U.S. proposal—an issue on which the Chiefs were adamant, but which might have been advantageous to raise in dealing with the Soviets. Later, the State Department suggested a different arms control proposal for internal consideration that began to attract the Chiefs' support. Perle then argued that to open up the variety of issues raised by the State Department's proposal would also require internally reopening the question of whether aircraft would be excluded from the arms control package. Rather than risk what they saw as the possibility of a great loss externally, following an internal re-opening, the Joint Chiefs threw their support behind Perle's internal zero-option proposal. In short, Perle's ability to shape the set of issues to be raised in the external negotiation was used to gain internal agreements he deemed favorable.[1]

[1]See Talbott (1984:66–68).

External Effects on Internal Negotiations:
Changing One's Mandate

Finally, a manager in the middle may negotiate for a grant of authority in one negotiation that will aid him in another. Bob Furz gained authority in his dealings with London headquarters over the product line, pricing decisions, and organizational structure; it was precisely this formal authority that gave him the means to bring members of the country organizations on board.

When Caspar Weinberger was newly appointed director of the Federal Trade Commission (FTC), he employed an interesting twist on this approach. The FTC staff contained a number of incompetent people who were retained because of their relationships with senators on the committee that appropriated the FTC's budget. These senators privately assured Weinberger that his budget requests would breeze through Congress as long as their favorite employees were untouched. Weinberger cleverly refused to protect these employees and the angered committee chairman drastically cut the FTC budget. Weinberger then used the cut as the pretext for firing the incompetent employees. Pressure from the ascendent consumer movement the following year restored the FTC budget, but after the cadre of incompetents had been pared from the public payroll.

Using the external process both to shape the agenda and to alter one's mandate allows the negotiator in the middle to claim value internally by changing the game. In one instance given above, the game was changed by the threat to add aircraft as an issue in the external dealings. Further, as the mandate examples show, external dealings can give the manager new issues and added capacity to shape the alternatives to agreement of internal parties.

USING THE INTERNAL NEGOTIATIONS
TO AFFECT THE EXTERNAL NEGOTIATION

Many of these effects of external dealings on internal ones—controlling information, acting as if others' positions are fixed, shaping expectations, manipulating demands and deadlines, altering agendas, changing mandates, and so on—have close parallels in how internal dealings affect external ones. Let us consider a few variants.

Internal Effects on External Negotiations: Controlling Information

As a conduit of information, the negotiator can shape the expectations of external parties and influence the agenda. Relying on superior access to his board, the CEO negotiating the sale of his firm persuaded the buyer that the board would not approve an offer below $49 per share—when in fact, the board would have accepted $45. To take another example, a vice president negotiating a joint venture successfully argued for specific clauses protecting her firm against certain uses of proprietary information that might be supplied to the joint venture. Without these clauses, she argued, the whole agreement would not be approved because her firm's general counsel, whose judgment "carried a lot of weight on the executive committee," firmly opposed any joint venture lacking suitable protection on this score.

Internal Effects on External Negotiations: Internal "Collusion"

A negotiator might even "collude" with internal parties in order to alter external expectations. To convince certain countries to drop their insistence on attaching onerous conditions to seabed mining, Elliot Richardson, as U.S. Ambassador to the Law of the Sea negotiations, urged key members of the Senate and House to go forward with legislation. The threatened bill would lead to a mini-treaty of industrialized nations that would allow mining under more favorable terms. This smaller arrangement was intended to act as Richardson's alternative to an onerous deal with other nations in the larger international negotiations. But, as we will see below, stimulating internal parties to make such a commitment for external tactical purposes may not be an easily reversible process in case concessions are needed.

THE INTERACTION OF INTERNAL AND EXTERNAL NEGOTIATIONS

Thus far we have looked mainly at interactions that have tended to be "one-way"; that is, where internal dealings affected the external ones, or vice versa. More interesting than the one-way influences are the two-way interactions. We consider several approaches the manager in the middle might take to handle both negotiations. Essentially these involve a choice of *what* information to convey to each about the other, *when* to convey it, and whether to treat the two "sides" separately, together, or sequentially—and, if so, in what sequence.

The aim of these tactics is to facilitate reaching *consistent* internal and external agreements on the terms most preferred by the negotiator in the middle. In other words, *creating value* by reaching linked agreements while *claiming* it by influencing where the accord comes out.

Dealing Internally and Externally: Separating the Parties

Frequently, a negotiator may wish to keep internal and external parties separated. Separating the parties can leave some useful ambiguity about what different parties have accepted. Often, this is done when consistent internal and external agreements cannot be made simultaneously, at least for a while. For example, when Henry Kissinger acted as mediator during the Middle East talks, he did not always obtain consistent agreements from all parties. Instead, by keeping the agreements ambiguous, he hoped to coax the parties toward consistency over time. Bob Furz's agreements with London headquarters were inconsistent with those he initially had to strike with his country managers. He hoped to bring the agreements into alignment over time, by renegotiating each when circumstances presented themselves. To do so, he felt that he needed to keep headquarters separate from the former country organizations.

Often, a negotiator separates principals because he perceives that a natural adverse coalition of the principals might form to his detriment. A broker or dealmaker who brings buyer and seller together risks their making an agreement without her. Here, the intermediary merely claims some of the value created by the others' agreement. Or to return to an earlier example, the president of a financial consulting firm saw a potentially disastrous (for him) coalition forming between his aggressive protégé and the firm's other partners who, he feared, might succumb to his protégé's persuasion. To block the coalition, the president fired him.

While such drastic "separations" are infrequent, managers in the middle and other negotiators often go a long way to create and protect control over information by keeping principals separate. Lawyers with hourly or contingent fees might have an interest in not allowing principals to meet without them, which may "risk" settling the case, obviating the costly fees for litigating.[2]

Often, the primary asset of the negotiator in the middle is his control over information about the principals or his relationships with some of them. This can be primarily self-serving, to claim value, as in the above examples, or it may create value for all of the parties. For example, a mediator might be helpful precisely because he can learn information from the parties separately that enables him to suggest agreements that neither party alone could envision or propose. Destructive interpersonal dynamics between internal and external parties can also prevent agreements; this is another reason for the one in the middle to keep the parties separated.

Dealing Internally and Externally: Keeping the Elements of Adverse Coalitions Separate

In some cases, a powerful confluence of interest exists between subsets of the internal and external parties. From the standpoint of the negotiator in the middle, an agreement between those elements—in other words, the formation of a natural coalition—might be very disadvantageous.

When a natural coalition exists between one or more of the internal and external parties, external opponents can sometimes lure these parties away from supporting the internal group. Sometimes a negotiator can defuse these adverse coalitions by placing on the negotiating team potential "defectors" from his "side." This may cause the "defectors" to see more clearly their responsibilities to others on their "side." For example, "star" football players had a natural link with National Football League management that pushed for a modest free agency system. Such a system greatly rewarded a few stars at the expense of many more less-publicized veterans. The union's offering the stars some concessions and making a point of having them explicitly represented on the negotiating team were two ways to prevent them from undermining the union leadership.

To take a more extreme example, consider the negotiations between Chrysler and the British government over the sale of the money-losing and inefficient Chrysler-UK operations. Given Chrysler-UK's debt at the time and its likely future losses, liquidating the

---

[2]One rationale for "mini-trials" is that they promote precisely this outcome. See Marks, Johnson, and Szanton (1984).

UK operations would have been costly; thus Chrysler should have been willing to pay any lesser amount to avoid these costs.[3] The British government in power at the time was relatively fragile. Its existence depended on the support of Scottish labor. Chrysler's Scottish workers feared unemployment. Indeed, given the costs of unemployment and welfare as well as other political considerations, this Labor government should have been willing to pay a great deal to keep the Chrysler operations going. Hence the bargaining range between the company and the government was quite large.

Tony Benn, the British government negotiator, pushed for a fairly low price. Chrysler, reacting to Benn's offer and mounting losses, threatened to liquidate its plants one by one, starting with a Scottish plant in a key electoral district. Intense union pressure from this district on key cabinet ministers forced Benn's hand, and he ended up paying Chrysler's handsome price for the inefficient operations.

Ironically, there was a natural coalition between these workers and the British government behind a low purchase price. The money saved by a low purchase price could have been used to the workers' benefit—for retraining, for investing in more modern equipment, and so forth. Further, a low price could have implied lower costs for the subsequent operation, thus making employment there more stable.

Yet because the workers and their union leaders were not a part of the deliberations, they did not see how Benn's tough tactics (a very low offer) could in fact further their interests. Their pressure on the key ministers played right into the company's hands. If Benn had brought union leaders into the negotiations, created a plan that shared the benefits of a low purchase price with the workers, and persuaded them to build support for their common interests in a low price, British taxpayers might have paid considerably less. So Chrysler—in the "middle" between union and government—managed to prevent this adverse coalition from forming by its strategically chosen plant closings before Benn had taken any steps to forge the alliance.

In short, there are several possible effects of separating the parties—from preventing adverse coalitions, to making inconsistent interim agreements that, with luck, can be brought into alignment over time.

---

[3]Therefore, their reservation value in the sale of the operations should have been negative.

Dealing Internally and Externally: Bringing the Parties Together

Now let us consider some reasons why the negotiator in the middle might want to take the opposite tack, that is, to bring the internal and external parties together.

Dealing Internally and Externally: Bringing the Parties Together to Highlight Real Interests

Obviously, bringing separated internal and external groups together can sometimes facilitate agreement. Where intermediaries have been handling negotiations, direct and full communication between the parties may have been impaired. Often intermediaries do not completely understand the sides' interests and are unaware of the full range of such interests that may be ingredients for a more comprehensive and valuable agreement. Further, suppose that lawyer B is negotiating "externally" with lawyer C over a settlement between their respective clients. Lawyer B may suspect lawyer C of having his own agenda that is hindering agreement.[4] If so, B's strategy may be to get the clients in a face-to-face negotiation, in effect to "subtract" the issues on lawyer C's suspected agenda from the bargain. Naturally B may be mistaken, and, in any case, lawyer C will likely oppose B's efforts.

Dealing Internally and Externally: Bringing Parties Together to Deflate Unrealistic Perceptions

When principals have unrealistic, partisan perceptions of what the other will accept, a negotiator in the middle may choose to bring the principals together to "teach" them about each other and perhaps to co-opt them. A dose of reality can sometimes be provided by placing the unrealistic party on the negotiating team. An interview with an experienced union negotiator provides a good example:

"I'll tell you about one instance, just to show you: I went through a real tough negotiation—how we made it, I don't know. So finally, we brought back a package I didn't hesitate to recommend. Sure, we gave up a lot of our demands—but we made some real gains, too—that's bargaining, and I was satisfied. So some guys with more mouth than brains—nobody's kidding me, they were put up to it—raised the roof

[4]For a set of possible such reasons, recall from Chapter Fifteen the set of reasons *not* to use agents.

about the things we conceded, and got the membership so stirred up that in spite of my recommendations the package was rejected.

"Do you think I folded? Not me. I just asked the membership to put the two super dupers on the committee, so they could try their luck."

He chuckled: "Yup, I just leaned back and let them go under the gun for a change. Hah! It was something to watch. When management sailed into them at the next session, they found out: Speeches in union hall are one thing; being on the firing line is something else. They had it! And from then on I had no more trouble from that bunch—not since then."

I asked him, "Did the rejection of your recommendation by the membership damage your effectiveness with the management?"

"Not a bit—not after the way I handled it. In fact, I came through with the membership and management."[5]

Not only can this tactic "teach" realism to unrealistic constituents, it can also educate external parties about the realities of one's own side. Of course, either side can be tacitly "coached" by the middleman to convey a particular impression to the newly brought-in party. The simplest, classic version of this gambit is for a carefully primed "bad guy" to be brought in to underscore the relative reasonableness of the negotiator as well as the tight limits ostensibly placed on his freedom. Such tactics can powerfully influence perceptions of the bargaining range.

Internal and External Negotiations: Dealing Sequentially

The choice of how to negotiate internally and externally is hardly limited to deciding whether the parties should be separated or joined. Generally, various sequences are possible.

DEALING SEQUENTIALLY: NAIVE SHUTTLING. One often-followed approach involves simply shuttling between the parties until agreement is reached. For example, the managers in ESSELTE-DYMO first accepted top management's assertion of the need to implement information and control systems. They then went to the formerly autonomous country and product organizations and sought cooperation. Even after their best efforts, some organizations would not comply. The managers returned to headquarters, bargained for flexibility, and then continued the process.

[5]Peters (1955:189).

Their choice to pursue this sequence seems natural enough, but it was hardly their only choice. For example, they might have approached new top management at the outset, arguing that those in the field would never accept their blunt proposal, and sought some flexibility—thus increasing the chances of "prevailing" in their first round with the country organizations. Or, they might have sought to bring all parties together, perhaps in a sequence of meetings. The point is that there are many options, each with different strategic consequences.

The choice of whom to approach first may be critical: the outcome can be dramatically affected if the first one approached is primed to make a commitment to a particular position or set of issues, or merely to anchor perceptions of the bargaining set. Sophisticated negotiator-mediators in the middle anticipate and make use of the dynamic effect of each bargaining session with one party on the bargaining with the other.

When the person in the middle does not realize that a negotiation is taking place or fails to recognize the existence of conflicting interests, shuttling between the parties without any well-thought-through strategy is a likely behavior pattern: "I'll just go to Ralph and then Jane to figure out how to solve the problem." Lack of advance planning can lead to undesirable outcomes for the naive negotiator in the middle.

In the next few sections, we consider some common sequences of internal and external dealings. Generally, the goals of the tactical choices are to facilitate agreements—but on favorable terms, that is, to create and claim value. Let us turn first to a sequence primarily intended to create value.

DEALING SEQUENTIALLY: SEPARATE, THEN JOINT MEETINGS TO FACILITATE AGREEMENT.   Sometimes a negotiator keeps internal and external groups apart at the beginning and later brings them together. For example, a mediator may separate the parties to gather information in order to devise and propose creative deals and to shape expectations of the parties about what is mutually acceptable. With this preparation and an agreement in sight, she may bring the parties together so that they themselves can realize it.

DEALING SEQUENTIALLY: MAKING COMMITMENTS IN ORDER TO CLAIM VALUE.   Frequently, a negotiator in the middle engineers the sequence of dealings to make a commitment to a favorable position in the final outcome. For example, under the threat of the bank calling an overdue loan, Martin was trying to sell his company to venture capitalists on terms detrimental to his partner Bart. To do this, Martin prevented contact between Bart and the venture capital firm until he had coaxed a "final" offer from the firm that he felt Bart would barely accept. Then, he scheduled a meeting at which the firm presented its fait accompli to Bart. In effect, Martin used the process to fashion a commitment to a point in the bargaining range that was favorable to him, and left Bart little time to generate other alternatives. An earlier three-way discussion might have led to terms relatively less favorable to Martin.

Moreover, the threat of actions by the external party can solidify an internal coalition, which, in turn, can serve as a commitment in dealing with the external party. For example, in renegotiating British military base rights on the island of Malta, the British threatened to withdraw altogether from the base rather than pay high rentals. Prime Minister Dom Mintoff used this British threat to arouse the passions of radical Maltese.[6] Once his constituents were thus energized, Mintoff could credibly argue that he could not to agree to a low settlement; his hands were tied and *only* a high settlement was possible. (Mintoff prevailed.)

Earlier we discussed Elliot Richardson's use of Third World intransigence in the Law of the Sea negotiations to stimulate a congressional commitment to internationally preempt treaty negotiations unless terms more favorable to the United States were forthcoming. That initiative gathered momentum and eventually passed the Congress *despite* the administration's objections that following through on the threat would scuttle, not prod, the international negotiations.

Other such tactics run a similar risk: that the activated internal party will in fact not relent and instead will insist on a settlement unacceptable to the external party; that is, that the commitment will in fact stick—but at a point outside the bargaining set.

A similar structure can generate even more complex dynamics. For example, in U.S.–Soviet talks over intermediate range nuclear weapons, consider an incident springing from initial U.S. pressure on West German Chancellor Helmut Kohl to support a "zero option." As time passed with no progress in the talks,

> Kohl himself held to an unequivocal endorsement . . . mainly because he knew it to be Reagan administration policy and he did not want to appear to be wavering. He would have been glad, however, had the U.S.

[6]See Wriggens (1976).

. . . adopted a more flexible approach. . . . But in Washington, [Kohl's] support for the zero proposal was used to justify the Administration's own adherence to it.[7]

Whether this was genuine confusion or cynicism, this example illustrates the potential reverberations of tactics ostensibly directed at one layer of many-layered internal-external dealings. But the intended effect was very clear: to reinforce Soviet perceptions of a firm Western commitment to the "zero option."

WHY DOES THE NEGOTIATOR IN THE MIDDLE HAVE THIS TACTICAL LEEWAY?

Across these various tactics, the negotiator in the middle often plays a role similar to that of a "double agent," providing one side with (often self-serving) information about the other and vice versa. Knowing that the person in the middle may act in such a way, therefore, why do the other parties give credence to what he says? Why don't the others simply go around him? Often, they do. But sometimes the accepted structure of the situation leaves them little choice but to deal with the "middleman." For example, a manager frequently controls crucial information because norms and penalties minimize communication between his superiors and subordinates. Further, because the intermediary has repeated dealings with the involved parties, he may be seen to have incentives to act fairly and honestly; he may already have such a reputation. And, his repeated dealings may have given him expertise in addition to well-developed relationships and some degree of trust. Others might defer and share information with him merely because he has access to and is well regarded by "senior," influential people. The manager in the middle may choose to enhance and protect such sources of his credibility in order to minimize the possibility of undesired end runs.

Conclusion

We started our discussion above with a look at internal negotiations: building coalitions of support, preventing adverse ones from forming, and avoiding some of the pitfalls of trying to thrash out a com-

[7]Talbott (1984:171).

mon position. Then we widened our focus to include ways that negotiators in the middle can use the external to affect the internal: by
controlling information, taking external results as fixed, shaping the
agenda, and otherwise advantageously changing the perceived internal game. The in-between negotiator can use internal dealings to affect external ones in almost identical ways (e.g., controlling information about "minimum" internal requirements in order to make a
commitment externally). From there, we examined common tactics
and dynamics in "two-way" interactions—where internal and external dealings affect each other. Here the negotiator in the middle can
choose to keep the two processes separate, join them, or approach
them sequentially. There are many possible effects associated with
each of these choices (e.g., to prevent an adverse coalition from
forming, to make a commitment, to subtract an issue that prevents
an otherwise valuable agreement, etc.) but all can be understood as
ways for the negotiator to create and claim value—the setting is
merely more complex than in earlier chapters.

For convenience, we illustrated these points from the vantage of a
negotiator in the middle of "internal" and "external" dealings. Yet
our examples show that the same tactics and dynamics recur across a
wide variety of linked bargains from "mediating" between divisions,
to superior and subordinate relations, and to the concept we have
called "strategy." We have characterized the strategic task as bringing into being a favorable set of consistent agreements that create
value for the parties. It is a simple idea, yet it unifies much of our discussion of the manager as negotiator. It is the tie between otherwise
disconnected managerial tasks involving mandates and production.
Its usual tactics and dynamics are the same as those we have examined in terms of "internal" and "external" negotiations.

This strategic task is exemplified by Bob Furz's efforts to bring
his South American and London dealings into alignment with each
other and with his overall vision of what the firm could become.
Over time, he successfully managed the evolution of these networks
of linked agreements into an arrangement that created great value for
all involved.

Furz was a manager in the middle of linked bargains, the structure that has occupied our attention throughout this chapter. If there
is one central theme across this variegated set of points and examples,
to us it would be the crucial role of information. The manager in the
middle often has special access to a range of information about the
parties, their interests, aspirations, expectations, positions, and, es-

pecially, their potential commitments. With this access comes the possibility of complex tactics to influence others' perceptions of these factors. Sometimes the tactics are potent; often, the complexity of the situation causes them to backfire.

Access to information and the potential to control it certainly facilitate moves to claim value in linked dealings. Yet from this special negotiating vantage, the manager also has a unique view of what might create genuine value for all. In Bob Furz, we find much of the potential of the manager as negotiator: to distill a compelling vision from the vast array of possibilities, to imagine the network of agreements needed to support that vision, and to engage others in negotiating and renegotiating that vision into reality.

*   *   *

Negotiation is a process of potentially opportunistic interaction by which two or more people, with some apparent conflict, seek to do better by jointly decided action than they could otherwise. In Part I of this book, we developed a special logic for this widespread activity. Its basic elements, explored in separate chapters, can be evoked by simple phrases: interests make up the raw material and measure of negotiation; alternatives to agreement set its lower limits; agreements embody its potential. Within this fixed game, the parties act to create and claim value; yet, the elements of the game may themselves evolve or be intentionally changed. This structure gives rise to the Negotiator's Dilemma: competitive moves to claim value tend to drive out cooperative ones to create it; inferior agreements, impasses, and conflicts result. To do better, negotiators must manage the inherent tension between creating and claiming value.

Part II extended this basic logic in the context of management and organizations. A few directions were especially relevant: the means of making agreements more secure, the effects of agents and ratification, and the dynamics of linked bargains. More generally, in the webs of agreements that make up organizations, managers must deal with superiors, subordinates, and others outside the chain of command. Beyond specific transactions with "outside" parties, managers negotiate about goals, authority, accountability, resources, and production. They do so directly in hierarchies and indirectly in networks.

We have only covered some of the more prominent features of the territory; the twists and turns of multiparty bargaining, the effects of culture and style, the roles of misperception and "irrationality," are

but a few of the less charted areas whose exploration will complement the basic structure we have sketched. Yet, perhaps more important than further topics are the most basic points. Interdependence
and conflict permeate life in and out of organizations. To act as if
this is not so invites missteps and disillusionment. Yet, recognizing
conflict as legitimate and dependence as inevitable need not imply
anarchy. Instead, it should spur the search to make negotiated agreements better for all than the alternatives.

References

AGUILAR, FRANCIS J. Harvard Business School Case 9–380–038. Boston: Intercollegiate Case Clearing House, 1979.

ALLISON, GRAHAM. *Essence of Decision: Explaining the Cuban Missile Crisis.* Boston: Little, Brown, 1971.

_____. "Public and Private Management: Are They Fundamentally Alike in All Unimportant Respects?" J.F. Kennedy School of Government Discussion Paper Series, 84D, Harvard University, 1979.

ANDREWS, KENNETH. *The Concept of Corporate Strategy.* Homewood, Ill.: Dow-Jones, Irwin, 1971.

ARGYRIS, CHRIS. *Integrating the Individual & the Organization.* New York: Wiley, 1964.

ARROW, K. J., and R. C. LIND. "Uncertainty and the Evaluation of Public Investment." *American Economic Review* (1970), 60:364–378.

ASANTE, SAMUEL K. B. "Restructuring Transnational Mineral Agreements." *American Journal of International Law* (1979), 73:335–371.

AUMANN, ROBERT J. "Agreeing to Disagree." *Annals of Statistics* (1976), 4:1236–1239.

AXELROD, ROBERT. "Conflict of Interest: An Axiomatic Approach." *Journal of Conflict Resolution* (1967), 11: 87–99.

_____. *Conflict of Interest: A Theory of Divergent Goals with Applications to Politics*. Chicago: Markham, 1970.

_____. "Effective Choice in the Prisoner's Dilemma." *Journal of Conflict Resolution* (1980a), 24: 3–25.

_____. "More Effective Choice in the Prisoner's Dilemma." *Journal of Conflict Resolution* (1980b), 24: 379–403.

_____. *The Evolution of Cooperation*. New York: Basic Books, 1984.

BACHARACH, S. B., and EDWARD J. LAWLER. *Power and Politics in Organizations*. San Francisco: Jossey-Bass, 1980.

_____, and _____. *Bargaining: Power, Tactics, and Outcomes*. San Francisco: Jossey-Bass, 1981.

BACHRACH, PETER, and MORTON S. BARATZ. "Two Faces of Power." *American Political Science Review* (1962), 56:947–952.

BACOW, LAWRENCE and MICHAEL WHEELER. *Environmental Dispute Resolution*. New York: Plenum Press, 1984.

BARCLAY, SCOTT, and CAMERON PETERSON. "Multi-Attribute Models for Negotiations." *Technical Report 76–1*. McLean, Va.: Decisions and Designs, Inc., 1976.

BARDACH, EUGENE. *The Implementation Game: What Happens After a Bill Becomes a Law*. Cambridge, Mass.: MIT Press, 1977.

BASS, BERNARD M. *Leadership and Performance Beyond Expectations*. New York: Free Press, 1985.

BAZERMAN, MAX H. "Negotiator Judgment." *American Behavioral Scientist* (1983), 27: 211–228.

_____, and R. J. LEWICKI. *Negotiating in Organizations*. Beverly Hills, Calif.: Sage, 1983.

_____, and M. A. NEALE. "Heuristics in Negotiation: Limitations to Dispute Resolution Effectiveness." In M. H. Bazerman and R. J. Lewicki (eds.), *Negotiating in Organizations*. Beverly Hills, Calif.: Sage, 1983.

BECKHARD, R. *Organization Development*. Reading, Mass.: Addison-Wesley, 1969.

BECKMAN, N. *Negotiations*. Lexington, Mass.: Lexington Books, 1977.

BELL, D. E. "Regret in Decision Making." *Operations Research* (1982), 30:961–981.

BENNETT, D. C., and K. E. SHARPE. "Agenda Setting and Bargaining Power: The Mexican State Versus Transnational Automobile Corporations." *World Politics* (1979), 32:57–89.

BLAU, P. M. *Exchange and Power in Social Life*. New York: Wiley, 1964.

BOK, SISSELA. *Lying: Moral Choice in Public and Private Life*. New York: Vintage Books, 1978.

BOURGEOIS, L. J., III, and D. R. BRODWIN. "Strategy Implementation: Five

Approaches to an Elusive Phenomenon." Stanford Graduate School of Business Research Paper Series No. 646, 1982.

BOWER, JOSEPH L. *Managing the Resource Allocation Process.* Homewood, Ill.: Irwin, 1972.

BRODKIN, EVELYN Z. "The Error of Their Ways." Doctoral dissertation, MIT, 1983.

_____, and MICHAEL LIPSKY. "Entitlement Programs at the Local Level: Quality Control in AFDC as an Administrative Strategy." Paper delivered at the 1981 Annual Meetng of the American Political Science Association.

BROWN, REX, and CAMERON PETERSON. "An Analysis of Alternative Middle Eastern Oil Agreements." Technical Report. McLean, Va.: Decisions and Designs, Inc., 1975.

CALLIÈRES, FRANÇOIS DE. *On the Manner of Negotiating with Princes*, trans. A. F. Whyte. Boston: Houghton Mifflin, 1919; originally published, Paris: Michael Brunet, 1716.

CHAMBERLAIN, N. W. *Collective Bargaining.* New York: McGraw-Hill, 1951.

CHANDLER, ALFRED D., JR. *Strategy and Structure: Chapters in the History of the American Industrial Enterprise.* Cambridge, Mass.: MIT Press, 1962.

CHATTERJEE, KALYAN. "Incentive Compatibility in Bargaining Under Uncertainty." *Quarterly Journal of Economics* (1982), 82:717-726.

_____, and WILLIAM SAMUELSON. "Bargaining Under Incomplete Information." *Operations Research* (1983), 31:835-851.

COHEN, H. *You Can Negotiate Anything.* Secaucus, N.J.: Lyle Stuart, 1980.

CONDLIN, ROBERT J. "Cases on Both Sides: Patterns of Argument in Legal Dispute-Negotiation." *The Maryland Law Review* (1985) 44,1:65-136.

CRAMTON, PETER C. "Bargaining with Incomplete Information: An Infinite Horizon-Model with Continuous Uncertainty." Stanford Graduate School of Business Research Paper No. 680, 1983.

_____. "Bargaining with Incomplete Information: A Two-Period Model with Continuous Uncertainty." *Review of Economic Studies* (1984a), 51:579-593.

_____. "The Role of Time and Information in Bargaining." Stanford Graduate School of Business Research Paper No. 729, 1984b.

_____. "Sequential Bargaining Mechanisms." In Alvin Roth (ed.), *Game Theoretic Models of Bargaining.* Cambridge: Cambridge University Press, 1985, pp. 149-179.

CRAWFORD, VINCENT P. "A Theory of Disagreement in Bargaining." *Econometrica* (1982), 50:607-637.

_____. "Compulsory Arbitration, Arbitral Risk and Negotiated Settlements: A Case Study in Bargaining Under Imperfect Information." *Review of Economic Studies* (1982), 49:69–82.

_____. "Dynamic Bargaining: Long-Term Relationships Governed by Short-Term Contracts." University of California at San Diego Research Paper No. 83-13, 1983.

CROZIER, M. *The Bureaucratic Phenomenon*. Chicago: University of Chicago Press, 1964.

CROZIER, MICHEL, and ERHARD FRIEDBERG. *Actors and Systems: The Politics of Collective Action*. Chicago: University of Chicago Press, 1980.

CYERT, R., and J. MARCH. *A Behavioral Theory of the Firm*. Englewood Cliffs, N.J.: Prentice-Hall, 1963.

DAHL, ROBERT A. "The Concept of Power." *Behavioral Science* (1957), 2:201–215.

_____, and CHARLES E. LINDBLOM. *Politics, Economics, and Welfare*. New York: Harper Torchbooks, 1963.

DERTHICK, MARTHA. *The Influence of Federal Grants*. Cambridge, Mass.: Harvard University Press, 1970.

_____. *Uncontrollable Spending for Social Services Grants*. Washington, DC: The Brookings Institution, 1975.

DEUTSCH, MORTON. *The Resolution of Conflict: Constructive and Destructive Processes*. New Haven: Yale University Press, 1977.

_____, and R. M. KRAUS. "Studies of Interpersonal Bargaining." *Journal of Conflict Resolution* (1962), 6:52–76.

DIAMOND, P., and J. STIGLITZ. "Increases in Risk and in Risk Aversion." *Journal of Economic Theory* (1974), 8:337–360.

DONALDSON, G., and J. W. LORSCH. *Decision Making at the Top*. New York: Basic Books, 1984.

DRUCKER, PETER F. "What is Business Ethics?" *The Public Interest* (1981), 63:18–36.

DUNLOP, J. T. *Wage Determination Under Trade Unions*. New York: Augustus M. Kelley, 1980.

_____. *Dispute Resolution: Negotiation and Consensus Building*. Dover, Mass.: Auburn House, 1984.

ECCLES, ROBERT G. *The Transfer Pricing Problem: A Theory for Practice*. Lexington, Mass.: Lexington Books, 1985.

ELMORE, RICHARD F. "Organizational Models of Social Program Implementation." *Public Policy* (1978), 26: 185–228.

_____. "Complexity and Control: What Legislators and Administrators Can Do About Implementation." *University of Washington Public Policy Report*, Seattle: Institute of Governmental Research (1979), No. 11.

_____. "Backward Mapping: Implementation Research and Policy Decisions." *Political Science Quarterly* (1979–1980), 94:601–616.

_____, and Walter Williams (eds). *Social Program Implementation*. New York: Academic Press, 1976.

EMERSON, R. M. "Power-Dependence Relations." *American Sociological Review* (1961), 27:31–40.

ETZIONI, A. *A Comparative Analysis of Complex Organizations*. Rev. ed. New York: Free Press, 1975.

FABER, MIKE, and ROLAND BROWN. "Changing the Rules of the Game: Political Risk, Instability and Fairplay in Mineral Concession Contracts." *Third World Quarterly* (1980). 2:100–120.

FAYERWEATHER, JOHN, and ASHOOK KAPOOR. *Strategy and Negotiation for the International Corporation*. Cambridge, Mass.: Ballinger, 1976.

FINEBERG, H., and R. NEUSTADT. *The Epidemic That Never Was*. New York: Vintage Books, Random House, 1982.

FISHER, GLEN. *International Negotiation: A Cross-Cultural Perspective*. New York: Intercultural Press, 1980.

FISHER, ROGER. "Fractionating Conflict." In Roger Fisher (ed.), *International Conflict and Behavioral Science: The Craigville Papers*. New York: Basic Books, 1964, pp. 91–109.

_____. "What About Negotiation as a Specialty?" *American Bar Association Journal* (1983), 69:1221–1224.

_____, and WILLIAM URY. *Getting to Yes: Negotiating Agreement Without Giving In*. Boston: Houghton Mifflin, 1981.

FLEISHMAN, E. A., E. F. HARRIS, and H. E. BURTT. *Leadership and Supervision in Industry*. Columbus, Ohio: Bureau of Educational Research, Ohio State University, 1955.

FRENCH, J. R. P. JR., and B. H. RAVEN. "The Bases of Social Power." In D. Cartwright, (ed.), *Studies in Social Power*. Ann Arbor: University of Michigan Press, 1959.

FREUND, JAMES C. *The Anatomy of a Merger: Strategies and Techniques for Negotiating Corporate Acquisitions*. New York: Law Journal Press, 1975.

FRUHAN, WILLIAM. *Financial Strategy: Studies in the Creation, Transfer, and Destruction of Shareholder Value*. Homewood, Ill.: Irwin, 1979.

FUDENBERG, DREW, and JEAN TIROLE. "Sequential Bargaining with Incomplete Information." *Review of Economic Studies* (1983), 50:221–247.

GEANAKOPLOS, JOHN, and HERAKLIS POLEMARCHAKIS. "We Can't Disagree Forever." *Journal of Economic Theory* (1982), 26:192–200.

GOLDBERG, S. B., E. D. GREEN, and F. E. A. SANDER. *Dispute Resolution*. Boston: Little, Brown, 1985.

GREENHALGH, L., and S. A. NESLIN. "Conjoint Analysis of Negotiator Preferences." *Journal of Conflict Resolution* (1981), 25:301–327.

GROVES, T., and J. LEDYARD. "Optimal Allocation of Public Goods: A Solution to the 'Free Rider' Problem." *Econometrica* (1977), 45:783–809.

GULLIVER, P. H. *Disputes and Negotiations: A Cross Cultural Perspective.* New York: Academic Press, 1979.

HAAS, ERNST B. "Why Collaborate? Issue Linkage and International Regimes." *World Politics* (1980), 32:357–405.

HALL, EDWARD. *The Silent Language.* New York: Doubleday, 1959.

———. "The Silent Language in Overseas Business." *Harvard Business Review* (1960), May–June.

HARGROVE, ERWIN. *The Missing Link: The Study of Implementation of Social Policy.* Washington, D.C.: Urban Institute, 1975.

HARSANYI, JOHN C. "Games of Incomplete Information Played by Bayesian Players," Parts I–III. *Management Science* (1967–1968), 14:159–182, 320–324, 486–502.

———. *Rational Behavior and Bargaining Equilibrium in Games and Social Situations.* Cambridge: Cambridge University Press, 1977.

HIRSHLEIFER, JACK. "On the Theory of Optimal Investment Decision." Reprinted in S. Meyers (ed.), *Modern Developments in Financial Management.* Hinsdale, Ill.: Dryden Press, 1976, pp. 282–305.

HOFSTADTER, DOUGLAS. "Metamagical Themas: Computer Tournaments of the Prisoner's Dilemma Suggest How Cooperation Evolves." *Scientific American.* May 1983, pp. 16–26.

HOLMES, J. G., W. F. THROOP, and L. H. STRICKLAND. "The Effect of Prenegotiation Expectations on the Distributive Bargaining Process." *Journal of Experimental Social Psychology* (1971), 7:582–599.

HOSPERS, JOHN. *Human Conduct.* Harcourt Brace & World, 1961.

HUNTINGTON, SAMUEL. *The Common Defense.* New York: Columbia University Press, 1961.

IKLÉ, FRED CHARLES. *International Encyclopedia of the Social Sciences*, s.v. "Negotiation."

———. *How Nations Negotiate.* New York: Harper & Row, 1964.

INGRAM, HELEN. "Policy Implementation Through Bargaining: The Case of Federal Grants-in-Aid." *Public Policy* (1977), 25:501–526.

KAHNEMAN, DANIEL, and AMOS TVERSKY. "Subjective Probability: A Judgment of Representativeness." *Cognitive Psychology* (1972), 3:430–454.

———, and ———. "Judgment Under Uncertainty: Heuristics and Biases." *Science* (1974), 185:1124-1131.

———, and ———. "Prospect Theory: An Analysis of Decisions Under Risk." *Econometrica* (1979), 47:263–291.

_____, PAUL SLOVIC, and AMOS TVERSKY (eds.). *Judgment Under Uncertainty: Heuristics and Biases.* Cambridge University Press, 1982.

KAUFMAN, HERBERT. "The Next Step in Case Studies." *Public Administration Review* (1958), 18: 52–59.

KEENEY, R., and H. RAIFFA. *Decisions with Multiple Objectives.* New York: Wiley, 1976.

KEOHANE, ROBERT O., and JOSEPH S. NYE. *Power and Interdependence: World Politics in Transition.* Boston: Little, Brown, 1977.

KISSINGER, H. A. *The Necessity of Choice.* New York: Harper and Row, 1961.

KOCHAN, THOMAS A. *Collective Bargaining & Industrial Relations.* Homewood, Ill.: Irwin, 1980.

_____, and MAX H. BAZERMAN. "Macro Determinants of the Future of the Study of Negotiations in Organizations." In Roy J. Lewicki, Blair H. Sheppard and M. H. Bazerman (eds.), *Research in Negotiation in Organizations.* Vol 1. Greenwich, Conn.: JAI Press, 1986.

_____, and A. VERMA. "Negotiations in Organizations: Blending Industrial Relations and Organizational Behavior Approaches." In Bazerman, M. H. and R. J. Lewicki (eds.), *Negotiations in Organizations.* Beverly Hills, Calif.: Sage, 1983.

KOTTER, JOHN. *Power and Influence.* New York: Free Press, 1985.

KREPS, D. "Corporate Culture and Economic Theory." Mimeographed. Palo Alto, Calif.: Stanford University, 1984.

LANDAU, M., and R. STOUT, JR. "To Manage is Not to Control: Or the Folly of Type II Errors," *Public Administration Review* (1979), 39: 148–156.

LAWRENCE, PAUL R., and JAY R. LORSCH. "A New Management Job: The Integrator." *Harvard Business Review* (1967a), 45,6:142–151.

_____, and _____. *Organization and Environment: Managing Differentiation and Integration.* Cambridge, Mass.: Harvard University Press, 1967b.

LAX, DAVID A. "Optimal Search In Negotiation Analysis." *Journal of Conflict Resolution* (1985), 29,3:456–472.

_____, and JAMES K. SEBENIUS. "Insecure Contracts and Resource Development." *Public Policy* (1981), 29:417–436.

_____, and _____. "Negotiating Through an Agent." Harvard Business School Working Paper 83-37, 1983.

_____, and _____. "The Power of Alternatives and the Limits to Negotiation." *Negotiation Journal* (1985), 1:163–179.

LELAND, HAYNE E. "Optimal Risk Sharing and the Leasing of Natural Resources, with Application to Oil and Gas Leasing on the OCS." *Quarterly Journal of Economics* (1978), 92:414–437.

LEWICKI, ROY J., and JOSEPH A. LITTERER. *Negotiation*. Homewood, Ill.: Irwin, 1985.

LIEBERT, R. M., W. P., SMITH, J. H. HILL, and M. KIEFFER. "The Effects of Information and Magnitude of Initial Offer on Interpersonal Negotiation." *Journal of Experimental Social Psychology* (1968), 4:431–441.

LIKERT, R. *New Patterns of Management*. New York: McGraw-Hill, 1961.

_____. *The Human Organization*. New York: McGraw-Hill, 1967.

LINDBLOM, CHARLES E. *The Intelligence of Democracy*. New York: Free Press, 1965.

_____. *Politics and Markets*. New York: Basic Books, 1977.

LINTNER, JOHN. "The Market Price of Risk, Size of Market, and Investor's Risk Aversion." *Review of Economics and Statistics* (1970), 52:87–99.

LIPSKY, MICHAEL. "Standing the Study of Public Policy Implementation on Its Head." In Burnham and Weinberg (eds.), *American Politics and Public Policy*. Cambridge, Mass.: MIT Press, 1978.

_____. *Street-Level Bureaucracy*. New York: Russell Sage, 1980.

LUCE, R. D. and H. RAIFFA. *Games and Decisions*. New York: Wiley, 1957.

MACMILLAN, I. C. *Strategy Formulation: Political Concepts*. Saint Paul, Minn.: West, 1978.

MALOUF, MICHAEL W. K., and ALVIN E. ROTH. "Disagreement in Bargaining: An Experimental Approach." *Journal of Conflict Resolution* (1981), 25:329–348.

MARCH, JAMES G., and HERBERT A. SIMON. *Organizations*. New York: Wiley, 1958.

MARKS, JONATHAN B., EARL JOHNSON, JR., and PETER L. SZANTON. *Dispute Resolution in America: Processes in Evolution*. Washington, D.C.: National Institute for Dispute Resolution, 1984.

MAYO, ELTON. *The Human Problems of an Industrial Civilization*. New York, Macmillan, 1933.

MCALLISTER, LEIGH, MAX BAZERMAN, and PETER FADER. "Power and Goal Setting in Channel Negotiations." *Journal of Marketing Research* (forthcoming).

MCGREGOR, DOUGLAS. *The Human Side of Enterprise*. New York: McGraw-Hill, 1960.

MILGROM, PAUL. "An Axiomatic Characterization of Common Knowledge." *Econometrica* (1981), 49:219–222.

_____, AND NANCY STOKEY. "Information, Trade, and Common Knowledge." *Journal of Economic Theory* (1982), 26:17–27.

MINTZBERG, HENRY. *The Nature of Managerial Work*. New York: Harper & Row, 1973.

Moore, Mark H. "Notes on the Design of a Curriculum in Public Management." Harvard University, 1982.

Mosher, Frederick C. "The Changing Responsibilities and Tactics of the Federal Government." *Public Administration Review* (1980), 40:541–548.

Myerson, R. "Incentive Compatibility and the Bargaining Problem," *Econometrica* (1979), 47:61–74.

_____. "Analysis of Two Bargaining Problems with Incomplete Information." In Alvin Roth (ed.), *Game Theoretic Models of Bargaining*. Cambridge: Cambridge University Press, 1985.

Nader, Laura, and Harry F. Todd (eds.). *The Disputing Process: Law in Ten Societies*. New York: Columbia University Press, 1978.

Neale, M. A., and M. H. Bazerman. "The Effect of Perspective Taking Ability on the Negotiation Process Under Different Forms of Arbitration." *Industrial and Labor Relations Review* (1983a), 36:378–388.

_____, and_____. "Systematic Deviations from Rationality in Negotiation Behavior: The Framing of Conflict and Negotiator Overconfidence." MIT Working Paper, 1983b.

Neustadt, R. E. *Presidential Power*. 4th ed. New York: Wiley, 1980.

Nicolson, Harold. *The Evolution of Diplomatic Method*. London: Constable, 1954.

Nyhart, J. D., et al. *A Cost Model of Deep Ocean Mining and Associated Regulatory Issues*. Cambridge, Mass.: MIT Sea Grant Report MITSG 78-4, 1978.

Olson, Mancur, Jr. *The Logic of Collective Action*. Cambridge, Mass.: Harvard University Press, 1965.

_____, and Richard Zeckhauser. "An Economic Theory of Alliances." *Review of Economics and Statistics* (August 1966), 48:266–279.

Ouchi, W. *Theory Z*. Reading, Mass.: Addison-Wesley, 1981.

Oye, Kenneth A. "The Domain of Choice: International Constraints and Carter Administration Foreign Policy." In Kenneth A. Oye, Donald Rothchild, and Robert J. Lieber (eds.), *Eagle Entangled: U.S. Foreign Policy in a Complex World*. New York: Longman, 1979.

Pecquet, Antoine. *Discours sur l'art de négocier*. Paris: Nyon Fils, 1737.

Pen, J. "A General Theory of Bargaining." *The American Economic Review* (1952), 42:24–42.

Perry, M. "Who Has the Last Word?: A Bargaining Model with Incomplete Information." Unpublished, Princeton University, 1982.

Peters, Edward. *Strategy and Tactics in Labor Negotiations*. New London, Conn.: National Foremen's Institute, 1955.

PETERS, THOMAS. "Symbols, Patterns, and Settings: An Optimistic Case for Getting Things Done." *Organizational Dynamics* (1978), 7: 3–23.

PETTIGREW, A. *The Politics of Organizational Decision-Making.* London: Tavistock, 1973.

PFEFFER, JEFFREY. *Power in Organizations.* Marshfield, Mass.: Pitman, 1981.

PORTER, MICHAEL E. *Competitive Strategy: Techniques for Analyzing Industries and Competitors.* New York: Free Press, 1980.

———. *Competitive Advantage: Creating and Sustaining Superior Performance.* New York: Free Press, 1985.

PORTER, ROGER. *Presidential Decision-Making.* Cambridge: Cambridge University Press, 1980.

PRATT, JOHN W., and RICHARD J. ZECKHAUSER (eds.), *Principals and Agents: The Structure of Business.* Boston: Harvard Business School, 1985.

PRESSMAN, JEFFREY L., and AARON B. WILDAVSKY. *Implementation.* Berkeley: University of California Press, 1973.

PRUITT, DEAN G. *Negotiation Behavior.* New York: Academic Press, 1981.

———. "Strategic Choice in Negotiation." American Behavioral Scientist, (1983a), 27,2:167–194.

———. "Integrative Agreements: Nature and Antecedents." In M. H. Bazerman and R. J. Lewicki (eds.), *Negotiating in Organizations.* Beverly Hills, Calif.: Sage, 1983b.

———. "Achieving Integrative Agreements." In M. H. Bazerman and R. J. Lewicki (eds.), *Negotiation in Organization.* Beverly Hills, Calif.: Sage, 1983c.

———, and STEVEN A. LEWIS. "The Psychology of Integrative Bargaining." In Daniel Druckman (ed.), *Negotiations: Social Psychological Perspectives,* Beverly Hills, Calif.: Sage, 1977.

RAIFFA, HOWARD. *Decision Analysis: Introductory Lectures on Choices under Uncertainty.* Reading, Mass.: Addison-Wesley, 1968.

———. *The Art and Science of Negotiation.* Cambridge, Mass.: Harvard University Press, Belknap Press, 1982.

———. "Post-Settlement Settlements." *Negotiation Journal* (1985), 1:9–12.

RANKIN, DEBORAH. "Personal Finance: The New Economics of Custody Suits." *The New York Times,* April 6, 1986, Section 3, p. 11.

RAPOPORT, A., and A. M. CHAMMAH. *Prisoner's Dilemma.* Ann Arbor: University of Michigan Press, 1965.

RASKIN, A. H. "The Newspaper Strike: A Step-by-Step Account." In I. W.

Zartman (ed.), *The 50% Solution*. Garden City, N.Y.: Anchor, 1976, pp. 452–480.

RAVEN, B. H. "A Comparative Analysis of Power and Power Preference." In J. H. Tedeschi (ed.), *Perspectives on Social Power*. Hawthorne, N.Y.: Aldine, 1974.

RAWLS, JOHN. *A Theory of Justice*. Cambridge, Mass.: Harvard University Press, Belknap Press, 1971.

REIN, MARTIN, and FRANCINE RABINOVITZ. "Implementation: A Theoretical Perspective." In Burnham and Weinberg (eds.), *American Politics and Public Policy*. Cambridge, Mass.: MIT Press, 1978, pp. 307–335.

ROGERS, C. *Client-Centered Therapy, Current Practice, Implications, and Theory*. Boston: Houghton Mifflin, 1951.

ROSS, STEPHEN A. "Equilibrium and Agency." *American Economic Review* (1979), 69:308–312.

———. "On the Economic Theory of Agency: The Principal's Problem." *American Economic Review* (1973), 53:134–139.

———. "On the Economic Theory of Agency and the Principle of Similarity." In M. Balch, D. McFadden, and S. Wu (eds.), *Essays on Economic Behavior under Uncertainty*. Amsterdam: North-Holland, 1974.

ROTH, ALVIN. *Axiomatic Models of Bargaining*. Berlin: Springer, 1979.

ROTHSCHILD, MICHAEL, and J. E. STIGLITZ. "Increasing Risk, I: A Definition." *Journal of Economic Theory* (1970), 2:225–243.

ROTHSTEIN, ROBERT L. *Global Bargaining: UNCTAD and the Quest for a New International Economic Order*. Princeton, N.J.: Princeton University Press, 1979.

RUBIN, JEFFREY, and BERT BROWN. *The Social Psychology of Bargaining and Negotiation*. New York: Academic Press, 1975.

RUBINSTEIN, ARIEL. "A Bargaining Model with Incomplete Information." Unpublished, Department of Economics, Hebrew University, Jerusalem, 1983.

SABATIER, P., and D. MAZMANIAN. "The Implementation of Public Policy." *Policy Studies Journal* (1980), 8:538–560.

SALOMON, LESTER M. "Rethinking Implementation." Paper delivered at the American Political Science Association Meetings, Washington, D.C., 1980.

SALTER, MALCOLM. "Negotiating Corporate Strategy in Politically Salient Industries." Harvard Business School Working Paper 84-07, 1984.

SAMUELSON, WILLIAM. "First Offer Bargains." *Management Science* (1980), 26:155–164.

SATHE, VIJAY. *Culture and Related Corporate Realities*. Homewood, Ill.: Irwin, 1985.

SAWYER, JACK, and HAROLD GUETZKOW. "Bargaining and Negotiations in International Relations." In Herbert C. Kelman (ed.), *International Behavior: A Social-Psychological Analysis*. New York: Holt, Rinehart & Winston, 1965, pp. 466–520.

SCHEIN, E. H. *Process Consultation*. Reading, Mass.: Addison-Wesley, 1969.

———. *Organizational Culture and Leadership*. San Francisco: Jossey-Bass, 1985.

SCHELLING, THOMAS C. *The Strategy of Conflict*. Cambridge, Mass.: Harvard University Press, 1960.

———. *Arms and Influence*. New Haven: Yale University Press, 1966.

SEBENIUS, JAMES K. "The Computer as Mediator: Law of the Sea and Beyond." *Journal of Policy Analysis and Management* (1981), 1:77–95.

———. "Rough Notes on Indirect Management." Mimeographed. Harvard University, Kennedy School of Government 1982.

———. *Negotiating the Law of the Sea*. Cambridge, Mass.: Harvard University Press, 1984.

———, and MATI L. PAL. "Emerging Trends in Mineral Agreements: Risk, Reward, and Participation in Deep Seabed Mining. *Columbia Journal of World Business* (1980), 15:75–83.

———, and PETER STAN. "Risk Spreading Properties of Common Tax and Contract Instruments." *Bell Journal of Economics* (1982), 13:555–560.

———, J. D. NYHART, and DOUGLAS MCLEOD. "Revenue Sharing from Deep Ocean Mining." Review Draft No. 2, Sloan School of Management and Department of Ocean Engineering, Massachusetts Institute of Technology, August 1979.

SIEGEL, S., and L. FOURAKER. *Bargaining and Group Decision-Making*. New York: McGraw-Hill, 1960.

SMITH, D. and L. WELLS. *Negotiating Third World Mineral Agreements*. Cambridge, Mass.: Ballinger, 1975.

SNYDER, RICHARD C., H. W. BUCK, and BURTON SAPIN. "Decision-Making as an Approach to the Study of International Politics." In Snyder et al. (eds.), *Foreign Policy Decision-Making: An Approach to the Study of International Politics*. New York: Free Press of Glencoe, 1962.

STEIN, ARTHUR. "The Politics of Linkage." *World Politics* (1980), 32:62–81.

STRAUS, D. B. "Kissinger and the Management of Complexity: An Attempt That Failed." In J. Z. Rubin (ed.), *Dynamics of Third Party Mediation*. New York: Praeger, 1981, pp. 253–270.

STRAUSS, ANSELM L. *Negotiations: Varieties, Contexts, Processes, and Social Order*. San Francisco: Jossey-Bass, 1978.

STRAUSS, A., L. SCHATZMAN, R. BUCHER, D. ERLICH, and M. SABSHIN. "The Hospital and its Negotiated Order." In E. Friedson (ed.), *The Hospital in Modern Society*. New York: Free Press, 1963.

TALBOTT, STROBE. *Deadly Gambits*. New York: Vintage Books, 1984.

TEDESCHI, J. T., R. B. SCHLENKER, and T. V. BONOMA. *Conflict, Power, and Games: The Experimental Study of Interpersonal Relations*. Chicago, Ill.: Aldine, 1973.

TOLLISON, ROBERT D., and THOMAS A. WILLETT. "Institutional Mechanisms for Dealing with International Externalities: A Public Choice Perspective." In Ryan C. Amacher and Richard J. Sweeney, (eds.), *Law of the Sea: U.S. Interests and Alternatives*. Washington, D.C.: American Enterprise Institute for Public Policy Research, 1976. pp. 77–101.

_____, and _____. "An Economic Theory of Mutually Advantageous Issue Linkages in International Negotiations." *International Organization* (1979), 33:425–449.

TVERSKY, AMOS, and DANIEL KAHNEMANN. "The Framing of Decisions and the Rationality of Choice." *Science* (1981), 211:453–458.

ULVILA, JACOB W., and WARNER M. SNIDER. "Negotiation of Tanker Standards: An Application of Multi-attribute Value Theory." *Operations Research* (1980), 28:81–95.

VAN METER, DONALD S., and CARL E. VAN HORN. "The Policy Implementation Process: A Conceptual Framework." *Administration & Society* (1975), 6:445–487.

VICKREY, W. "Counter Speculation, Auctions, and Competitive Sealed Tenders," *Journal of Finance* (1961), 16:8–37.

WALLACE, WILLIAM. "Issue Linkages among Atlantic Governments." *International Affairs* (1976), 52:163–179.

WALTON, RICHARD E. *Interpersonal Peacemaking: Confrontation and Third Party Consultation*. Reading, Mass.: Addison-Wesley, 1969.

_____, and ROBERT B. MCKERSIE. "Bargaining Dilemmas in Mixed-Motive Decision Making." *Behavioral Science* (1966), 11:370–384.

_____, and _____. *A Behavioral Theory of Labor Negotiations*. New York: McGraw-Hill, 1965.

WEINBERG, MARTHA. *Managing the State*. Cambridge, Mass.: MIT Press, 1977.

WENK, EDWARD C. *The Politics of the Ocean*. Seattle: University of Washington Press, 1972.

WILDAVSKY, AARON. *The Politics of the Budget Process*. Boston: Little, Brown, 1984.

WILLIAMS, G. R. *Legal Negotiation and Settlement*. St. Paul, Minn.: West, 1983.

WILSON, ROBERT. "The Theory of Syndicates." *Econometrica* (1968), 36:119–132.

_____. "Reputation in Games and Markets." In Alvin E. Roth (ed.), *Game Theoretic Models of Bargaining*. Cambridge: Cambridge University Press, 1985.

WRIGGENS, W. "Up for Auction: Malta Bargains with Great Britain, 1971." In I. William Zartman (ed.), *The 50% Solution*, New York: Anchor-Doubleday, 1976.

WRONG, D. H. "Some Problems in Defining Social Power." *American Journal of Sociology* (1968), 73: 673–681.

ZARTMAN, I. W. "The Political Analysis of Negotiations," *World Politics* (1974), 26:385–399.

_____. "Negotiations: Theory and Reality." *Journal of International Affairs* (1975), 29:69–77.

_____. *The 50% Solution*. Garden City, N.Y.: Anchor-Doubleday, 1976.

_____, ed. *The Negotiation Process: Theories and Applications*. Beverly Hills, Calif.: Sage, 1978.

_____, and MAUREEN BERMAN. *The Practical Negotiator*. New Haven, Conn.: Yale University Press, 1982.

Index